PERSONA GRANADA

By the same author

SON OF ADAM
TO REASON WHY

★

MOZART'S PIANO CONCERTOS
THE GOOD OPERA GUIDE

PERSONA GRANADA

*Some memories of Sidney Bernstein and
the early days of Independent Television*

DENIS FORMAN

ANDRE DEUTSCH

First published in 1997 by
André Deutsch Limited
A subsidiary of VCI plc
106 Great Russell Street
London WC1B 3LJ

A catalogue record for this title is available
from the British Library

ISBN 0 233 98987 0

Typeset by Derek Doyle & Associates
Mold, Flintshire.
Printed in Finland by WSOY

The two most important people in television are the producer, and by 'producer' I mean, of course, all the creative people who combine to make television, and the viewer. So far as possible they should be left alone to communicate with each other. The viewer should receive the producer's work untouched by human hand, not massaged by politicians, not manipulated by bureaucrats, nor again groped by the censorious fingers of those whose trade is outrage. This is not to say that all producers are perfect. Some of the most imperfect people I have ever known were producers. But they are the best thing we have got, and the whole apparatus of state and industry should be designed to give the producer freedom and support. In any country in the world, if you look at the status and morale of the producer you will see it reflected in the nature of that country's television. If the producer is treated like a hack you will get hack television; if like an apparatchik, propaganda; if like a free and creative human being you may get some good programmes, and certainly some trouble as well.

Denis Forman, the Richard Dimbleby Lecture, 1987

THE BERNSTEIN FAMILY

Alexander Bernstein (c. 1860–1922)

Selim	Sidney	Cecil	six brothers and sisters
1895–1916	1899–1993	1903–1981	

Alex
1936–

GRANADA TELEVISION 1954–1987

Founder Members	Sidney Bernstein	Chairman
	Cecil Bernstein	Deputy Chairman
	Joe Warton	Group Finance Director
	Victor Peers	General Manager
	Reg Hammans	Chief Engineer
	Denis Forman	
Executives	Julian Amyes★	Drama Director and Labour Relations
	Bill Dickson★	Finance Director
	Peter Eckersley	Writer, Drama Producer
	Derek Granger	Producer
	Barrie Heads★	Producer, Current affairs; Managing Director, Granada International
	David Plowright★	Producer, *World in Action*, Programme Controller; Managing Director, Chairman
	Mike Scott★	Performer, Producer, Programme Controller
	Joyce Wooller★	Central Planning, Programme Personnel

★ company directors

THE INDEPENDENT TELEVISION AUTHORITY

(later the Independent Broadcasting Authority)

Chairmen

Sir Kenneth Clark	1954–1957
Sir Ivone Kirkpatrick	1957–1962
Lord Hill	1963–1967
Lord Aylestone	1967–1975
Lady Plowden	1975–1980

Directors General

Sir Robert Fraser (previously Director General, Central Office of Information)	1954–1970
Sir Brian Young	1970–1982

Deputy Director General

Bernard Sendall (previously Deputy Director General, Central Office of Information)	1955–1977

PERSONA GRANADA

PREFACE

It is said that most people can remember precisely what they were doing on the day that Kennedy was assassinated. Until recently I was confident that I was one of this number. I was in the central control room, the nerve centre of any television station, of Granada Television, Manchester, when a phone call came through from CBS News in New York telling us the President had been shot. I passed on the news to the studio where a local programme was on air, and called ITN in London, who refused to broadcast anything until their man in New York had verified it. I protested that it would be quite proper simply to announce that CBS was broadcasting the story to the American nation, but in vain. The local programme was interrupted and an announcement went out immediately. So it was that Granada brought the news of Kennedy's death to viewers in the North of England some thirty minutes before it was broadcast to the rest of the nation.

Imagine my surprise when David Plowright, in a recent issue of *Broadcast* magazine, indicated that he had played a principal role in getting the Kennedy story on air ahead of the field. It was an even greater surprise when Barrie Heads wrote to *Broadcast* saying that it was he, not David, who had done it. Neither of them mentioned me at all.

On searching the Granada archive I was able to find an account of what happened in the newsroom that night. Joan Riley, the News Editor's secretary, had written:

> It was a quiet night, nobody else in the office apart from the News Editor, Terry Dobson, and myself, and I was sitting at the desk waiting for work when at 6.35 the phone rang – it was a direct line, not the switchboard. Terry answered. I could see from his face that it was a big story. Then he said, 'I'll ring back,' and put down that line

and picked up the internal to get on to Barrie Heads, who was in the director's box in the *Scene* studio. All at once he had Barrie on the line saying, 'I'll check back with the Press Association', and was dialling out again on the other line. 'Can you confirm?' Terry said to the Press Association, and they said, 'Yes.'

The television was on in the office and I sat there and watched as, within seconds, Barrie was on the studio phone relaying the news to Mike Scott, who was presenting *Scene* that night, and Mike Scott told the people.

Barrie, thoroughly vindicated, has since told me he believed that neither David nor I was there at all. But this is going too far.

So it is that memory can make heroes of us all, for as time goes on we come to believe that it is our version of the past that is true and those who recollect things differently are lying in their teeth.

In this memoir I have striven to avoid such heroic fallacies and have been greatly assisted by having access to two histories of Granada Television – the Crow history and the Chanan history. Both were commissioned for Granada by myself with Sidney Bernstein's approval. Duncan Crow was a journalist on *The Economist* when I first met him at the Central Office of Information in 1947. During my time at the British Film Institute he wrote the report for Political and Economic Planning (PEP) mentioned in this memoir, and he joined Granada as a researcher shortly after we went on the air. His history is a straightforward narrative of the early days and continues up to 1969. When Sidney read the manuscript he called me in to see him. What did I think of Crow's work? I thought it was a full, fair and accurate account. He thought it was not worthy of Granada. He was against publication. This was a shock. I went away and read it again and the light began to dawn. It gave Sidney full credit for Granada's success, but it gave others credit too. Hitherto Sidney had been seen as the onlie begetter of all Granada's achievements. He had, of course, assembled a splendid supporting team, but they were behind-the-scenes workers and the public and the press had no need to know about them. But from Crow's account it became clear that Sidney had had little to do with quite a number of Granada's major successes. Every copy of the history was called in as a matter of security, Sidney keeping just one copy under lock and key. Unknown to him I kept another.

Nothing daunted, I invited Noel Chanan – a man of many parts, producer, writer and director of a wonderful film about the Oxford philosophers – to compile a replacement for the Crow history. Chanan adopted the novel style of using only personal interviews and press clippings to tell the story. The interviews are pure gold to any would-be Granada historian, in that they reflect vividly the spirit and style of the early Granada days. When the first volume (1955–63) was completed it was submitted for Sidney's approval. Once again he found it unworthy, this time, as it seemed to me, not because too much credit went to others but because there was not quite enough for him. Once again the order went round to return all copies and once again, officially, only one copy was retained.

The third work of reference from which I have quoted extensively is the excellent four-volume history, *Independent Television in Britain*, covering the year 1958–80, the first two volumes (1958–68) written by Bernard Sendall in his best civil servant prose, prim but perspicacious, and volumes three and four (1968–80) written by Jeremy Potter in a more pungent and personal style. This work was commissioned jointly by the Independent Broadcasting Authority and the ITV companies for whom I acted as editorial adviser. In the pages that follow I refer to it as the Official History.

I also make reference from time to time to Caroline Moorehead's invaluable book *Sidney Bernstein, a Biography*, and I would like to make it clear that when I challenge the accuracy of a passage in her book this does not imply any lapse on her part. It simply reflects the fact that Sidney's recollection of past events as recounted to her were frequently subject to the heroic fallacy mentioned above.

I am conscious that many of my old Granada colleagues will be disappointed to find that this memoir does not treat the history of early television days in a more balanced manner. By concentrating on the relationship between myself and Sidney I have had to omit whole chunks of the Granada story and leave unmentioned the names of a dozen and more men and women whose efforts were absolutely central to Granada's success. At one time I considered appending a Who's Who of the people whose names are *not* included rather than one of those who are, thereby achieving some sort of balance between those mentioned and those who, often quite arbitrarily, are not.

Amongst the letters and memoranda reproduced here some are quoted in full, some in extracts complete in themselves, and some are abridged. In this last case I have shunned the practice of indicating gaps by a string of little dots, since as a reader I find this tedious and unsightly. In condensing a passage the syntax frequently has to be adjusted and this I have done without inhibition so long as the alterations do not affect the sense. I have corrected literals in the original memos, and occasionally mistakes in grammar where they are clearly unintentional but not when they reflect a degree of illiteracy in the author. Needless to say, I have taken pains to ensure that my own memos are error-free.

I am grateful to Peter Heinze and Josephine Weston for their unstinting efforts in carrying out the research for this book. Josephine in particular has been of enormous assistance owing to her encyclopaedic knowledge of Sidney's personal archive.

I would also like to acknowledge the help I have had in checking facts with old Granada hands too numerous to mention, but in particular Barrie Heads, Raymond Fitzwalter, Desmond James and Joyce Wooller.

I would also like to thank my assistant of twenty-three years, Beryl Milnes, for her part in typing, in collating research material, and for the substantial contribution her own memory has made to this memoir.

I have to thank Granada and the Bernstein family for allowing me free access to the company archives and also to Sidney Bernstein's personal archive, a monster collection of some 12,000 files extending over seventy years of his working life. Granada has allowed me complete freedom in writing this memoir. It is not, of course, an official history in any sense, nor is it a commissioned work, nor is it approved nor 'authorised', nor yet subject to any check or supervision. Where it falls down the failure is mine.

Finally, I would like to record my gratitude to Alex Bernstein, who as Chairman of Granada Group encouraged me to embark on this enterprise and rejected all offers of any form of reference back. It is my dearest wish that when he reads this memoir he will not regard this decision as unwise.

CHAPTER ONE

In the autumn of 1945 I and my friend Fred Majdalany were comfortably housed in an officers' club in South Audley Street, London. It was a general rule that no officer should spend more than three consecutive nights in the club, but at the time my story starts we had been in residence for some eight weeks. This was due to the goodwill of the two women (we called them ladies then) who ran the establishment, handsome, true-blue, middle-aged persons, of a kind to be found at all the Allied centres of war dispensing tea and good cheer to officers and men (officers preferred), usually in green battle-dress. Our two, who would have been equally at home in the hunting field or in a box at Ascot, had been manoeuvred by Maj and myself into making us their pets, and so long as we occasionally disappeared for a tactical weekend with friends we could have stayed on for ever.

The food, like all post-war food, was horrible, but Maj, who was inordinately greedy, had worked up our breakfasts from the standard ration of one egg fried or boiled to two eggs, bacon, mushrooms, tomatoes, black pudding and fried potatoes. It was not appropriate, of course, to settle down to this in front of the rank-and-file one-egg officers, so we had resorted to a large bathroom on the ground floor, where we installed a card table. The coffee pot stood at the bottom of the bath surrounded by scalding water, the breadstuffs (Maj had made contact with a nearby Hungarian baker) on top of the lavatory lid, and we two eased ourselves in on two stools to attack the steaming centrepiece. We thus avoided having to eat spam and blancmange at lunch, and in the evening we had a jolly supper with our hostesses in their private apartments – phoney caviare on toast, a casserole made from sausages with nuts and dried apricots, or some variation of the famous but utterly revolting Woolton pie. We shared a spacious attic bedroom, with our own telephone and loo, and all in all – after six years of army quartering, ranging from bed-boards in requisitioned hotels to slit trenches – we were very nicely placed to conduct our main business: finding a job.

My own aim was to become a film director. Maj had ambitions to be a film critic. His plan was simple and methodical. Every day of the week he went to see a film. Every night he wrote a column. Every morning he posted his copy to a newspaper – *The Times* on Monday, the *Daily Telegraph* on Tuesday, and so on throughout the week. Sometimes his work was acknowledged, more often not. I would go to the cinema with him and we usually had to pay unless one of Maj's contacts in show business (he had worked in C.B. Cochran's publicity department before the war) managed to sneak us into a trade preview.

It was one of these occasions that we had to wait a long time for the film to start. The delay was caused, we were told, by the non-arrival of an important exhibitor. 'Bloody tycoons', said Maj. 'Forty people waiting for a guy who is probably having it off with his secretary.' Just then a tall erect figure, his overcoat draped over his shoulders, appeared in the doorway. He made an entrance like an actor, pausing for a couple of beats on the threshold, and then strode powerfully to the back row, where bowing acolytes ushered him to his seat. Immediately the lights went down. 'One of the Bernstein brothers,' said a man sitting next to me. 'Sidney Bernstein, the boss of Granada.' After the film, even as the lights were going up and the common people were groping under their seats for their mufflers, the same figure stalked out majestically, again at speed. 'So that was the bastard who kept us waiting,' said Maj. 'Name of Sidney Bernstein,' I said. 'Never heard of him,' said Maj. So back to South Audley Street, where Maj sat down at his war-weary typewriter, a refreshing glass of Guinness in his hand, and immediately started to type out his notice.

Maj's book, *The Monastery* – a brilliant description of the battle of Cassino – had just been published to good notices, and he made full play of this in his covering notes to editors. His Lebanese father had come over to run a business in Birmingham and sent his son to a minor public school. Although his English accent and phraseology were perfect, Maj still looked foreign, especially about the eyes, which had a shadow of dusky purple around them. It was for this reason, and because of his roly-poly shape and thick pebble-glasses, that he avoided meeting any potential employer if he possibly could. 'Anglo-Saxon editors think that I must be Jewish,' he said, 'and Jewish editors know I'm not. So it's better if I just send them my stuff.'

During the Italian campaign Maj's battalion and mine had been in the same division (the 78th), and in the dog days before the battle of Cassino we happened to meet on a fraternal visit between messes. We found we were both carrying the same book – *A Narrow Street* by Elliot Paul – and were reading it with equal amusement, and since Paul's humour was something of an acquired taste this created an immediate bond. From then on, as the rain pounded down day after day and prevented Bradman from batting – the somewhat transparent coded message for the battle to begin – we met frequently. Some time after Bradman had finally reached the crease and I had lost a leg in the battle of Monastery Hill, Maj came to solace me in hospital with caviare in huge quantities, a gift from an officer in the Polish brigade who was then running what Maj thought to be a very high-class brothel. Once sufficiently recovered I was recruited to an Officer Cadet Training Unit, along with Maj, by my old commanding officer in Italy, Paul Bryan, whom we thought (almost certainly rightly) to be quite the best, bravest and most experienced battalion commander in the British Army. It was after this congenial group was disbanded that Maj and I drifted to London.

We were both still in uniform waiting to be demobilised, and whereas for Maj it was only a matter of time, for me there was the possibility of the War Office requiring me to write a manual on infantry training before I was let off the hook. This did not lessen my anxiety to secure a job. I realised, of course, that the act of directing a film from a chair with my name stencilled on the back was some way off, but was ready to start as the traditional tea-boy as soon as might be. I soon learned the first Catch 22 of film life, which was that unless you had a union ticket you couldn't get a job and unless you had a job you couldn't get a union ticket.

One day at breakfast Maj tossed me a letter. It was from the editor of the *Daily Mail*. The *Mail*'s film critic, it said, was going to be absent for some weeks: would Maj care to fill in for him? Maj tried to look inscrutable. 'Well, I suppose it's worth a try,' he said. 'Oh come on, Maj,' I said, 'it's the break you've been waiting for. Once they see your stuff the poor guy will never be allowed to write again. He'll be put on to the obituaries.' Maj's defences crumbled, he broke into a broad smile and began a sort of elephant dance around the bathroom in which I joined, both swinging towels and whooping and yodelling until one of the ladies tapped on the door to see if we were all right. She was familiar with this sort of thing happening in the small hours but it was not common at nine o'clock in the morning. When she heard the news she went for a bottle of champagne and joined in the celebrations. My forecast was right. Fred Majdalany was to write the weekly film column in the *Daily Mail* for the next sixteen years.

Spurred on to intensify my own campaign, I decided to write a film script on the subject closest to my experience – how a disabled person adjusts to a changed life. I went to Roehampton and to St Dunstans, filled notebooks with data collected from patients and doctors, sent the finished script to a number of documentary producers, and got no replies. This was not surprising, for the script was terrible. But one letter, one precious letter, from Edgar Anstey offered me an interview. Edgar had been one of the founding members of the Grierson family of documentarians and was now one of the movement's notables and a partner with Arthur Elton and Stuart Legg at Film Centre, a sort of general consultancy on all matters documentary and the centre of the documentary world at that time.

'This is an interesting script,' said Edgar as he turned over the pages of the ghastly thing. 'It makes the dilemma of the disabled vivid and moving. There are, of course, some things that could be done better', and he outlined some of the grosser errors of taste and judgement. I took at once to this kindly man, with his frank, intelligent face whose main feature was a large sandy moustache. I explained I was not necessarily a documentarian. I wanted a job in films, any job – teaboy, janitor, mail-room clerk. Somehow I must get in. He looked at my colonel's crown doubtfully. 'Tea-boy?' he said.

'Yes,' I replied. 'Anything.'

'I'll see what I can do,' said Edgar, and that very night he phoned me at the club. There was possibly something going in the MGM publicity department. It was very menial, but perhaps . . .

Next morning I reported to MGM's offices off Shaftesbury Avenue and was seen by Mr Margolis, who was lugubrious and picked his teeth.

'References?' he asked.

'From the army,' I said.

'That's no good,' he said. 'What diseases you had?' I told him. 'You healthy now?' he asked. 'Nothing infectious?' I told him no. 'Do those things bother you?' he asked, pointing at my crutches. 'You got to get about the office.' I assured him I was mobile on my crutches. Mr Margolis said that, subject to a doctor's certificate that I had no diseases, I could start on Monday. 'You work for Judy,' he said, 'but I must tell you the prospects here are not great.'

Judy was a huge American blonde with a chest like a pouter pigeon. She called me 'laddie' and instructed me in my duties, which were those of an office boy. At twelve noon we were told to assemble in Mr Margolis' office. He looked even more lugubrious. 'I have

just had notice from head office,' said Mr Margolis, 'that this department is to be terminated today. You can clear up your desks and leave
at five o'clock tonight. There will be two days' pay for everyone at the
cashier's office. Except for Farmer [me].' My first job in films had
lasted just eight hours, unpaid.

I went back to the patient Edgar Anstey at Film Centre. 'There
might be something at the MOI,' he said. 'That is the Ministry of
Information, Films Division. They generally like to take graduates.
What sort of degree did you get at Cambridge?'

'Failed Classics part 1,' I said. 'Aegrotat in agriculture part 2.'

'I see,' he said, and his sandy moustache twitched a little sadly.

'Brendan Bracken, the Minister,' I said, 'is crazy about rugby football and public schools, and knew my uncle who was Captain of
Scotland and headmaster of Loretto. But I wouldn't want to get a job
because Lloyd George knew my father.'

'I wouldn't be over-scrupulous if I were you,' said Edgar. So, a traitor to my principles, I wrote to Brendan Bracken. By return of post
I had a note over the clear bold signature of Bernard Sendall – one
which I was to see a thousand times over the next four decades:
would I call on the Minister at ten o'clock next Tuesday?

Come Tuesday I was in the Minister's outer office by 9.45 reading
the *Financial Times* (of which there were half a dozen copies and none
of any other daily) when a minor whirlwind swept by. It was the same
tall figure of the film preview. He slipped off his overcoat, which he
was again wearing cloak-style, and asked if he might telephone.
'Certainly, Colonel Bernstein,' said a terrified junior clerk. The call
was almost finished before the words were uttered, and Colonel
Bernstein stood for a moment in his full sartorial glory – plain,
exquisitely cut navy-blue suit, white shirt, grey-flecked Ascot tie,
brogued elastic-sided black shoes shining like a guardsman's bayonet
scabbard, and an initialled white handkerchief just showing from his
breast pocket. Above this there was a handsome face with a broken
Roman nose and a carefully styled coiffure. The general impression
was un-English in its perfection – the sort of thing one saw only in
the pages of *The Tailor and Cutter* or in the advertisements going up
the escalator in Austin Reed. He waited only for seconds before the
door opened and he was ushered in to the presence to jovial Hello
Sidneys, Hello Brendans. He reappeared five minutes later and
streaked through the outer office like a navy-blue kingfisher.

When my turn came, a clean-shaven face with a blue-black sub-tinge
owing to a pallid skin and an exceptionally strong beard poked round

the door. It was Bernard Sendall. 'Colonel Forman?' the face asked, and I rose, marvelling at the fact that war, the great leveller, had given an equal title to the mighty tycoon who had just left and the supplicant for a job who was just going in. Brendan Bracken was once described as the only man with real hair who looked as if he were wearing a wig, but today it was not only his hair that was terrible. He sat there like a man with a hangover who had slept all night in his suit and failed to find time to shave.

'You Forman?' he asked. I acknowledged that I was.

'Loretto?' he said.

'Yes,' I replied.

'First Fifteen?' he asked, and when I nodded, 'How many years?'

'Three,' I said.

'Rugger at Cambridge?' he said.

'I gave it up for athletics,' I said. I could see he was cast down.

'Blue?' he asked.

'Yes,' I said (a white lie – I got two half-blues but I could see we were dealing with matters that could be decisive to my career in films).

'Your Uncle Sconnie was a great full back,' he said. 'Great Captain of Scotland. Great Headmaster. Great man. What you want to do?'

'I want to get into films,' I said.

He turned to the lurking Sendall. 'Bernard, get me Alex,' he said. The dark-faced Bernard went to the phone and lo and behold in a trice Alex Korda was on the line.

'Alex, I've got a poor fellow here who had his leg shot off in the war, and wants to get into films. Will you give him a job?' The Minister paused. 'Comes from a good stable. Knew his family. Cambridge blue,' said he. Another pause. 'That's very good of you, Alex,' said the Minister. 'I'm much obliged.' He turned to me. 'Alex will give you a job,' he said and stood up for the valedictory handshake.

I got an appointment with Alex within ten days. Not bad, I thought. On the due date I turned up. A smiling Mayfair secretary offered me tea and biscuits. Alex was very busy but there might be a chance before lunch. Two o'clock came and no summons. I went to another plainer but still well-born lady and said, 'Any hope this afternoon?' She didn't know, we must await her Mayfair colleague's return from lunch. The Mayfair lady returned at four o'clock weighed down by parcels from Debenhams. She would slip in and see what she could do. She slipped out, still smiling, to say that Alex was in a meeting that would go on until evening and then he was at a première. Would I come back tomorrow? . . . Sure enough, I came tomorrow, and the next day, and the day after that, and for another four days. Then I had a couple of days' furlough because Alex was in Paris. When the vigil started again I began to lose hope, but one wet Wednesday morning the Mayfair smiler came up to me positively grinning. Alex would like me to join him at dinner that night, 8.15 at Claridge's.

Later that day, as I made my way to Claridge's, I wondered if there would be anyone else or whether it could be just *à deux*. At Claridge's I was directed by the concierge to a private room. Alas, there were several people there already drinking rum hoolas (a drink I had never heard of before and have never encountered since). They were all talking, mostly in Hungarian, about Alex's latest production. There was a table laid for twelve. At 9.15 there was a phone call and one of Alex's henchmen said Alex had been delayed, we were not to wait dinner. The henchman did the placement, putting me at the foot of the table between a make-up girl and a Hungarian accountant with halitosis. I asked the make-up girl why she was there. She said she had met Alex only once – and thought he wanted a second sighting to decide whether or not he really fancied her. I asked the Hungarian what he did. 'Tax,' he said. 'Tax, tax, tax. Hungarian tax. French tax, American tax, not UK tax. I am not Alex's London taxi man,' he said, 'I am his abroad taxi man,' and laughed uproariously, sending puffs of poison gas across the table.

At 10.15 Alex swept in, and gave a general greeting and a charming speech of apology. He had broken a tooth and his dentist had taken an unconscionable time to get to his flat. He sat down and talked intensely with one or other of two starlets who were placed on either side of him. At eleven o'clock, with a few elegant farewell words to the party in general, he exited with one of the two starlets and the party broke up.

I wrote to Brendan Bracken saying that Alex apparently had no job for me, so was there perhaps a vacancy in the Films Division of his Ministry which had made the great wartime documentaries which I so admired? This time there was no reply and life settled down to a routine of seeing films with Maj in the mornings and writing scripts hopefully for documentary films in the afternoon. The weeks passed quickly, as they do when each day has a regular pattern, until I became convinced that nothing was going to happen unless I made some fresh move. I was wondering what that should be when one morning there were three letters lying beside the bacon and eggs in the bathroom. The first was from the Director of Military Training, saying that he required me to write a new training manual on

Methods of Instruction for the Infantry. The second was from
Bernard Sendall, saying that subject to this and that the Ministry of
Information would offer me a position as Production Controlling
Officer in the Films Division at a salary of £500 per annum; and the
third was from a different part of the DMT's empire which clearly
knew nothing about the first letter. The writer, a general, said he
would like to discuss with me the possibility of an important and
interesting assignment abroad. By the end of the day I had accepted
three jobs. For three months I would write the instruction manual; I
would go to India late in February 1946 to assist in the handing over
of the Indian Military Academy (the Sandhurst of India) from the
British to the Indian army; I would join the Ministry of Information
Films Division not later than the end of June.

A valuable member of Paul Bryan's officer training team had been
Sergeant Major Davey, a sort of Jeeves in khaki, who produced visual
aids of great style and clarity, typed, bought and sold motorcycle
parts, and cooked excellent crêpes suzettes on the office gas ring. I
told the War Office I could not contemplate either assignment (the
manual or India) unless I was supported by the services of Sergeant
Major Davey, and this request was granted.

Davey and I set to work on the manual with zest. We were assigned
a room in a gloomy requisitioned building off Kensington Mall,
furnished with two trestle tables, a filing cabinet, two chairs, and four
fire extinguishers. The light bulbs were naked and shone relentlessly
on the graffiti on the wall (my favourite: 'My Mother made me a
homosexual' in sprawling characters, and beneath, in a neat, rather
prissy script, 'If I send her the wool will she make me one too?').

We started work at 8 a.m. and went on until 7 p.m. in the evening.
I wrote. Sergeant Davey typed, drew, and cooked crêpes suzettes,
occasionally throwing in a fried egg for variety. There was only one
distraction. Our one window looked out into a dungeon-like area
and each morning at eleven o'clock a young woman was to be seen
in silhouette against the blind of the room opposite. The light inside
her bathroom was strong, outside it was dim, and we could watch her
every movement as she disrobed, folded her night things and stepped
into the shower. After a short interval she reappeared and dried
herself very thoroughly before dressing. It took a little time after this
shadow-play for us to settle into the mood for infantry instruction,
but the pressure was on and soon we were once again toiling with
flanking movements and supporting fire.

The manual was handed in to the Director of Military Training on time and we set off for Delhi in a Sunderland flying boat. The journey, broken at Cairo, Basra and Karachi, was made memorable mainly by the presence of Edwina Mountbatten, who moved regally amongst the motley crew of red-tabbed staff officers, talkative generals and saturnine air vice-marshals. She sat in the midst of a bevy of WRNS reading papers, shouting orders and dictating personal letters at the top of her lungs – on the lines of 'Darling Bertie, How sweet of you to remind Dot about Boohoo's birthday', and so on. She chummed up with one of the more senior generals (they would wait for each other when they went to the loo) but the rest of us she treated like dirt, so we were not sorry when she met her Waterloo in the airport at Basra. This occurred as she was negotiating the steps down from our plane and another came by with a mighty whirr and sent her skirt up over her head. The main interest here was less the sight of the vice-regal thighs than the fact that her elegant silk stockings were kept secure not, as one would have expected, with elegant lace suspenders but with a curious makeshift device of what looked like the laces from a pair of brown tennis shoes.

We travelled from Delhi to the Military College at Dehra Dun in fifteen-hundredweight trucks protected by wire netting to keep off the stones and the missiles that were directed against us ('Indian grief at the prospect of British withdrawal', wrote the *Daily Express* that same week, 'is coloured by fears for the future once the friendly shield of the Raj is withdrawn . . .')

At Dehra Dun Academy I spent a happy time with my own bungalow, seven servants, a swimming pool, two horses and the fascinating job of trying to inculcate the training methods needed for modern warfare into the officer instructors who had themselves been trained for a repeat of World War I by the greatest blimps of all – old Indian Army hands.

'So you are proceeding down this track when the enemy opens fire and your leading scout lies down and refuses to go any further. What would you do? Amarjit Singh?'

'Shoot him, sir.'

'Anil Bastri?'

'Shoot him, sir, in front of the platoon, as an example.'

'Ashok Advani?'

'Shoot him, sir, discreetly and post the knowledge subsequently on a notice board.'

'But suppose all twenty-five men in the platoon refuse to go forward. Are you going to shoot them all? Then you wouldn't have any soldiers left.'

Attempting to change the attitudes the British had pummelled into the Indian Army for over a hundred years was a daunting task. When I visited the Academy some forty-five years later and saw the wonderful display of power and polish, I wondered whether we had made any impression at all. But we did what we were asked to do. When I arrived there were only one or two dark faces in the mess. But when I left there were only three or four white ones, including those of Brigadier Balltrop the Commandant, Captain Wilson the Adjutant, and myself.

The return journey was uneventful, except that the York bumped its undercarriage on leaving Malta and made a forced landing eight hours later in North Africa on soft sand when it split neatly into two halves, leaving its passengers only slightly hurt but facing several feet of sand. When we got out we were forced to spend forty-eight hours in hospital 'to get over the shock'. I was not aware of any shock and at the time found the delay intolerable.

A week later I walked into a small but handsome room in the head-quarters block of London University. There were two deal tables pushed together in the centre, with a chair on each side. In one of the chairs sat a cheerful curly-haired young man.

'Hello,' he said, 'I'm Mackie.'

'I'm Forman,' I replied. 'How long have you been here?'

'About ten minutes,' he said.

'What are we supposed to do?' I asked.

'We wait for some civil servant Johnny to come and tell us,' said Philip Mackie.

We waited for two hours. (We had plenty to talk about, since Philip's path during the Italian campaign had missed mine by only a couple of miles and one day. He had been a prisoner of war in north Italy, had escaped and walked through the British line in the Abruzzi town of Cassoli where I was in command of a battalion.) Suddenly a tall woman came into the room, saying as she walked, 'Hello, I'm Helen de Mouilpied, the Chief Production Officer and your boss.' I saw at once that here was the most beautiful and intelligent woman I had ever met. She told us what we had to do. We were the middle-men between the government department who wanted a film made and the documentary film company who made it. She allocated Low Sugar Content Jam Making (Min of Food) to me and Winter Milk Production (Min of Ag) to Philip. We asked if we could swap because Philip liked his jam very sweet and I had read agriculture at Cambridge. She agreed reluctantly – but sternly, because she could

16

see that Major Mackie and Colonel Forman were going to be a handful. So life in the newly named Central Office of Information (COI) began. They had lost their minister but won the war and were ready to set about winning the peace for the newly elected Labour government.

None of us had the slightest doubt that this was possible. Unemployment was a thing of the past. Keynes had solved our economic problems once and for all. Beveridge had laid out a blueprint for health and social security from the cradle to the grave. The coal mines were no longer to be plundered by capitalists but given over to be properly run by the miners themselves. New towns would be built, there would be housing for all. Education would be liberalised and the school-leaving age raised. There would be twenty new universities. All class distinctions would disappear. And it was our job to assist the government to explain to the citizens how this brave, brave new world would be brought about.

In those days a temporary civil servant was not much respected by the professionals – especially not by the Finance Department, which saw him as a wild unpredictable creature who might commit HMG to all manner of irregular expenditure (as had indeed been the case with John Betjeman who, finding his office a little drab, ordered a white carpet and four Hepplewhite chairs from Heals: two years later Betjeman carpet memos were still flowing into a bulky file, and I doubt if the matter is settled yet). We were an enthusiastic and energetic bunch, and the old civil service fail-safe mode of progressing step-by-step did not suit us. Even a two-line memo had to be attached to its own file weighing up to three pounds and taken by a messenger summoned from the bowels of the building to a colleague who might be in the next room.

Philip and I soon twigged that the documentary film companies were taking the Central Office of Information for a ride. Commissions for films were awarded not by competition but by selection, and once a company had secured a contract for, say, a £3,000 film, it immediately went ahead and spent twice that sum. There was nothing a distraught Finance Department could do about it except cancel the film (nugatory expenditure) or pay up (operational overspend). Within the service nugatory expenditure was the more disgraceful, and the documentary companies knew this. Philip and I remonstrated with Helen over a particularly blatant overspend incurred by one Tim Boxer. Helen fixed us with a steely gaze and said, 'Tim Boxer may not be a good businessman but he gave us wonderful service during the war and we must always remember

17

that.' We had the good taste to refrain from pointing out that Tim Boxer had not spent time in an Italian POW camp nor lost a leg in the battle of Cassino. But things got so bad that we made a *démarche* about the biggest overspender in the business, one Paul Rotha, whose company Films of Fact went broke when, after years of condoning his extravagances, the COI refused to underwrite his debts or pay for some of the more outrageous items in his overspend. A couple of films went down the pan, but the effect undoubtedly encouraged the other companies to be more cautious.

The films we made were mainly humdrum. How to grow more food. How best to make the most of the food ration. How industry was shifting from tanks to cars. How new coal-cutting machinery lightened the miners' job. The documentary movement of the 1930s had been fathered by John Grierson, the son of a Stirling schoolmaster, who jumped to prominence as head of the film propaganda units of the Empire Marketing Board and the GPO. His reputation depended as much upon his powerfully persuasive writing and rhetoric in promoting the documentary ideas as upon the films themselves, for seen in retrospect only two (*Song of Ceylon* and *Night Mail*) seem to be of more than archaeological interest. Nevertheless Grierson gathered behind his banner a band of film-makers who regarded him as a father figure and political leader. Once the war broke out documentarians did make a number of films valuable to the war effort, such as *Desert Victory, Fires Were Started, Western Approaches, Listen to Britain, Words for Battle*, whilst their guru and leader reigned over them from afar, as the Canadian Film Commissioner. After the war the documentary makers seemed to lose their sense of purpose. The grand vision of socialism sweeping all before it was taboo because it was political, and Herbert Morrison had been quick to see that a politicised COI would be of greater value to the Tories (if they got back to power) than to Labour. So most of the films were pedestrian.

Many of the leading characters in this new world were to play a part in my later life. Within the Central Office of Information, Bob Fraser and Bernard Sendall were the Director General and Deputy DG respectively, and little did I know that they were to be translated to another sphere and become my masters for wellnigh two decades. Bob was an Australian journalist who had been a *Daily Herald* leader writer. He was offered a Labour seat before the election of 1945 but the odds seemed so heavily against his winning it that he opted to stay on as Head of the Publications Division at the COI. Come the election and the Labour candidate for the said constituency won the seat easily. As a consolation prize Bob became Director General of the COI. In those days he was jolly, supportive and a great fan of Helen. His main claim on our attention lay in his liaison with Barbara Fell, an attractive blue-stocking lady who was head of the COI photographic division. She became involved in the Nunn May spy affair, was tried and sent to prison. Office sentiment was on her side and it was generally felt that Bob should have come out of the closet and spoken up for her publicly, which he did not. In later years Bob's devotion to his wife, who was gradually losing her sight, was a matter of public amazement and wonder, and whenever people mentioned this touching relationship it always conjured up for me, perversely, the memory of Barbara Fell in her lonely cell in Holloway.

Bernard Sendall was a different article, an Englishman to the roots of the blue-black beard that lay beneath his swarthy cheeks, a loyalist to his masters and to their cause whatever it or they might be, and in general dedicated to sustaining the traditional values of old England. He had worked in Churchill's private office and had become his devoted fan. Bernard had the true civil servant's ability to adjust his political beliefs, his conscience and even his emotions to support those of his master, and for more than a quarter of a century he was to be Bob Fraser's chief staff officer, alter ego and ringside second. He was adept at drafting and could make a U-turn in policy appear to be an absolutely logical consequence of unchanged circumstances. He could imply a threat in a way that appeared innocent and open. He could hint at a deal in a matter so ambivalent that a subsequent withdrawal could be carried off in a perfectly gentlemanly manner. He was in fact a past master at the craft of government by paper, a latter-day Francis Bacon, and despite the depth of his guile and his deeply discreet nature a very nice chap and a devotee of English county cricket.

I sometimes gave Bernard a hard time. Many of the film-makers who worked for the COI were fellow travellers or communist sympathisers – not surprisingly, since Russia had been our ally and the decisive factor in winning the war in Europe. As a result they would often throw into their films morsels of left-wing propaganda which had nothing whatever to do with the topic in hand. For instance, a film on the history of domestic architecture paused when it reached a servants' bedroom in a great town house to deliver a homily on the wretched way in which the aristocracy had treated the lower classes. The Crown Film Unit, the COI's own in-house production arm, was one of the worst offenders. One day I tackled John Taylor, the head of Crown, about this practice and got the reply that any sensible person could see that it was only a matter of time before true socialism spread across the world: everyone had hoped that the war would unify Europe as a group of socialist states, but alas it now looked as if there were going to be continuing divisions in Europe and that the great confrontation between Europe and America was going to be delayed. This I took to be the current version of the doctrine according to John Grierson. John Taylor had been a working-class boy whose sister had married Grierson. Grierson had paid for his university education and trained him as a cameraman. From that John, who was one of the most able and likeable men in the documentary movement, went on to become a director, then a producer, and finally was appointed to the top job in documentary films as head of Crown.

All my colleagues – save one or two who were so far left as to see nothing amiss – were becoming increasingly exasperated by having to weed out gratuitous chunks of propaganda from all manner of films, even those about sewage, rickets and the control of vermin. So I asked Bernard to sit in on a debate between John Taylor and myself in order to clear the air. This encounter took place in a pub off Baker Street. John, generally monosyllabic, waxed eloquent in developing the thesis that all the films we were making were the consequence of Labour's victory at the polls; that to try to distinguish between a socialist programme and the driving force of the ideology behind it was bureaucratic hypocrisy, and who was complaining anyway? In reply I plugged away rather boringly with the line that there was a distinction between left-wing propaganda and government policy as sanctioned by Parliament, and it was our job to hold the line between the two. The argument raged for over an hour. Bernard said little, sucking an unlit pipe and gazing into his beer. He was extremely uncomfortable. At the end of the debate he uttered a few sentences which were mildly in my favour and then went off no doubt to write an inscrutable *aide-mémoire*. Twenty years later, in a heated discussion over *World in Action* when Bob Fraser accused me of being a communist sympathiser (of which more later), I sought to remind Bernard of the Baker Street discussion, but alas it had faded from his memory.

In those early days at the COI the shadow of Grierson still lay over the documentary world. He had reached his zenith as Film Commissioner in Canada, where he gained the ear of Prime Minister Mackenzie King and exercised his influence by remote control over his alumni who were now making films for the war effort in the UK, in Australia and in the armed services all over the world, after which he was brought low by his involvement in the Canadian spy trials, which – although nothing positive was found against him – left a cloud of suspicion over his name. Nevertheless he secured a job under Julian Huxley in the newly formed UNESCO. Now there were rumours of a second coming – he was going to make a glorious return to take over our Films Division and restore British documentary to the status it had enjoyed in the great days of the past.

He did come, but expectations had been pitched too high. In discussion and debate he was still irresistible. Both his office and his nearby flat became places of public entertainment. What might start as a business meeting grew into an assembly of persons who dropped in or were summoned to give their views on the topic in hand, and in no time the original purpose of the debate would disappear far over the hill as the discussion surged back and forth over the role of the government, who should select the nation's teachers, new methods of growing strawberries, the rival claims of Eistenstein and Griffith to be the founder of the motion picture industry, and much else. To listen to Grierson in full flood addressing a roomful of young people, whisky in one hand, the other beating the air to make his points, was a memorable experience. His wit, his speed of response and his flights of fantasy were all a delight, and his line of hype for any projected film or publication was unbeatable. When it came to the reality of business affairs the debates were just as enjoyable, but alas all action stopped there. Time after time we would leave his office with no decision, and when deadlines came and were passed and we took action ourselves he would be uncertain if we had done right. Often he tried, too late, to reverse decisions; even more often when you thought you had at last got him to agree to some course of action, the phone would ring and you would hear the dreaded words, 'I have been thinking over what you said about the coal film . . .' The heart sank: we were back to square one. Gradually disillusion spread through the division: the second coming had turned out to be a flop.

Meanwhile Grierson devoted a large part of his energies to arguing that the civil service should pay for his attendance at football matches. Recreation, he held, was an essential part of a creative person's life and it was the duty of the employer to provide the means for the employee to enjoy it. The permanent civil servants had no difficulty in deciding that the case was outrageous, but they did have a problem in that they could find no way of stopping Grierson from writing about it.

One day there was a meeting of the top people in the Films Division to discuss a problem we had with the 'Monthly Release', a one-reeler distributed each month to all cinemas in the UK, which, under some deal done by Herbert Morrison, they were meant to show for at least one week. The films were stunningly boring, so most exhibitors gave them only a token showing and some did not show them at all. I suggested that we should enlist the help of an influential exhibitor such as Sidney Bernstein. The response was electric. 'Sidney Bernstein,' snorted Helen. 'He's an absolute menace. We spent half the war fighting to stop him interfering with MOI productions.' 'He would stop at nothing,' said another. 'Pinch a negative for the American cinemas without so much as a by-your-leave, and return it cut to ribbons.' 'No,' said Grierson. 'Sidney is too much the great dictator to bother with a thing like this!'

The heat generated by the name Bernstein astonished me, so after the meeting I made enquiries. It was true that, as film adviser to the MOI, Sidney had played fast and loose with Civil Service rules in supplying film propaganda to the American public. In this he had been brilliantly successful, many people believing that his prompt delivery of *London Can Take It* (introduced by the gravelly-voiced Quentin Reynolds) had been critically important in swinging American public opinion in favour of entering the war. But in achieving this success he had trodden on many toes in the UK and had run into a major confrontation with Grierson. As the Canadian Film Commissioner, Grierson had taken it upon himself to re-edit the MOI films in such a way as to make it seem, as far as it could be done, that Canada was winning the war, assisted by a somewhat clapped-out old mother country. Sidney got wind of Grierson's tampering and challenged his right to interfere. After a diplomatic wrangle Sidney won, and Grierson was put firmly in his place. One result was that the name of Sidney Bernstein had become anathema to all loyal members of the Grierson group; another was that Sidney had developed an intense dislike of all documentarians, especially Grierson himself, whom he regarded, not altogether unfairly, as a windbag who had never made any worthwhile films.

This blight affected even the distinguished baronet Arthur Elton, a brilliant scholar and producer of scientific films, and Stuart Legg, a top-class film editor and print journalist, both of whom in normal circumstances Sidney would have been quick to describe as 'just my cup of tea'. He made exceptions only of Basil Wright, whose gentle talents had produced *Song of Ceylon*, and of Humphrey Jennings, who had produced three of the acknowledged masterpieces of the war years – *Listen to Britain, Words for Battle* and the feature-length *Fires Were Started*. When these films were shown more than a decade later to Italian film-makers, who were in self-congratulatory mood because they believed that Rossellini's *Rome, Open City* and De Sica's *Bicycle Thieves* had laid the foundations for the new school of neo-realism, they were dumbfounded. 'Jennings discovered *verismo* ten years before we did,' they said, more in admiration than in envy, and it was true.

The other documentarian of the war years who reached some eminence was Harry Watt, whose talent was coarser-grained but effective and lay in directing action adventure films – *North Sea, Target for Tonight*, and later *The Overlanders* – and who was to play an extra-ordinary role both in Sidney Bernstein's private life and in the early days of Granada Television. We at the COI also had much traffic with the fashionable writers of the day. E.M. Forster wrote the commentary for Humphrey Jennings's *Diary for Timothy*, John Betjeman was always on hand, and Montague Slater (who had written the libretto for *Peter Grimes*) sat in his office near the roof composing an epic poem. He found it undignified to scuffle the papers into a top drawer every time a colleague came in, so (it was alleged) he gave each canto a production number, opened a file for each one and could be heard requesting the Registry to send up 'P144 Angels of Death Surround My Bed'. Meanwhile a huge mountain of routine files teetered in his in-basket. He was said to reach the bottom of the pile only once a year, during a bank holiday.

Our years with the COI made important contributions to the private lives of both Philip Mackie and myself. He saw a pretty secretary through the opposite window in the well of the building, wrote her a love poem and married her, and shortly after that I married Helen, thereby falling heir to her job as Chief Production Officer. She went to Crown as a hands-on producer, a job we all secretly coveted. The Mackies and the Formans set up house together in Highgate. This gave Philip and me plenty of time to work on COI reviews – he writing the lyrics and I the numbers. In one of them we had an item which listed the names of the documentarians who had made it to the top, which included the lines:

> There's John Taylor, Donald Taylor
> Donald Alex, Alex Shaw
> Who've made it through the wire because
> They're Grierson's brothers-in-law.

The next morning Grierson sent for us. 'Excellent show,' he said. 'There was just one thing wrong.'

'What was that?' we asked innocently.

'I have never been accused of nepotism in my life. It was a disgraceful, damaging allegation and I want it formally withdrawn.'

By this time neither Philip nor I had any fear of Grierson. 'You must be mad, John,' we said. 'It's a joke and quite untrue. Only one of them was your brother-in-law.'

Grierson stormed up and down the room. Nothing would calm him. At last Philip said, 'Look, John, in Canada they accused you of being a communist spy and a traitor. If you could live that down, I don't think this one is going to bother you too much.' This had the desired effect.

A few days later Grierson sent for me again. 'I'm going to put you in for the BFI,' he said.

'BFI?' I asked. 'What's that?'

'British Film Institute,' said Grierson. 'At the moment it's a dim little number messing about with schoolroom films. Herbert Morrison wants to make it something worthwhile and has put in Cecil King of the *Mirror* to sort it out. You could do it. It could be important.' I had a feeling I was being sent to the salt mines.

'King is expecting a call from you,' said Grierson. Although irritated by the proprietorial way in which Grierson pushed his employees and alumni about the film-job chessboard, I picked up the phone and made an appointment to see Cecil King.

I found the Film Institute to be not only dim but sleazy. The outgoing Director, Oliver Bell, was also the Chairman of the Magistrates Association, and although reputed to be the scourge of petty criminals he was certainly pretty lenient with himself. He and other senior staff, including the Secretary (who was said to have appeared in jackboots and a Nazi armband until the outbreak of war made this unwise), spent a great deal of the day in Soho drinking clubs and seemed to regard bogus expense claims as a simple and perfectly acceptable way of augmenting their incomes. The rest of the staff were rarely to be seen at their desks but were 'viewing films' or 'visiting schools'. By the time I arrived in 1949 as the new Director Cecil King had bundled out most of the top management and it was up to me to recruit new staff and to change the culture of those that remained, an operation they bitterly resented.

One of the first things to do was to give the Institute credibility amongst what were then called '*New Statesman* readers' and particularly amongst those who believed that film was, or could be, an art form – and here I was lucky. There was only one serious British film journal in those days, *Sequence*, edited by four Oxford ex-undergraduates – Gavin Lambert, Lindsay Anderson, Penelope Houston and Peter Ericsson. I had met the first two of this quartet one day when Grierson summoned me to his office to discuss with them ways and means of keeping the magazine alive. No solution was found. From that discussion the idea was born that *Sequence* should be allowed to sink and the editorial group should take over the Institute's official journal, *Sight and Sound*, instead. At first they shied away from this proposal with terror, for they were accustomed to complete editorial freedom – indeed they rightly felt they couldn't contemplate any editorial job without it – and they were convinced that at the Institute some big brother would be breathing down their necks. But after many hours of discussion in the Casa Bianca (a Soho restaurant where you could eat your fill for two shillings and sixpence and sit all day over one cup of coffee), and after many assurances, three of the four agreed to give it a try. Peter Ericsson we lost to the Foreign Office, but Gavin became editor of *Sight and Sound*, and Lindsay and Penelope agreed to work with him.

The first few editions of *Sight and Sound* under its new management created a sensation. There was little serious film criticism in Britain in those days, for people regarded film as something to keep the lower orders amused – much as they thought of television ten years later. Perceptive reviews in the newspapers came from two stalwart women, Dilys Powell and C.A. Lejeune (later to be joined by Richard Winnington and Philip Hope Wallace), but their values tended to be E.M. Forsterian: an American film had to be liberal and preferably funny before it got good marks (*Mr Deeds Goes to Town*), continental films were preferred (Clair, Renoir, Rossellini) and the Ealing comedies were the tops. Now here was *Sight and Sound*, the mouthpiece of a government institution, saying that the Western was the great classical form of the cinema, that John Ford was the greatest director of them all, that the American musical was high art (especially when directed by Vincente Minnelli), and that British films were boring and parochial.

It was over this last item that we nearly came to grief. *Sight and Sound* published a review of an Ealing film called *The Blue Lamp*, a very thorough demolition job written by its editor, Gavin Lambert, under a pseudonym. Jack Warner as your friendly neighbourhood copper was held up to ridicule, the simple Huggetry of the other characters was derided without mercy, and the whole film was declared to be a reflection of the smug suburban self-satisfaction of the British cinema. Nearly every other reviewer had hailed *The Blue Lamp* as yet another Ealing triumph.

At ten o'clock on the day of publication the phone rang. It was Michael Balcon, the great and good man of British films, head of Ealing Studios and a governor of the British Film Institute. 'Have you read this disgraceful piece in *Sight and Sound*?' he asked.

'Yes, I have,' I said, 'and . . .'

'Outrageous, despicable,' he barked.

'Mick,' I said, 'Mick . . .'

'Highly damaging. Probably actionable' (he was barely coherent). 'Withdraw the issue.'

'Impossible,' I said.

'Then issue an immediate apology. Call an emergency Governors' meeting today or tomorrow latest.'

'Mick,' I said again, 'Mick, please . . .' But he had rung off.

I called Cecil King, our Chairman, who was wryly amused. 'Give him twenty-four hours to cool off,' he said.

'But if he insists on this emergency meeting?'

'Tell him that only the Chairman can call an emergency meeting,' said Cecil. 'I am leaving for Lagos in four hours and after that my movements are uncertain.'

There was no emergency meeting. But at the next regular meeting Mick deployed his case with vigour. He had the majority of the board on his side but the day was saved by a stratagem. From the chair Cecil proposed that an editorial committee (including two governors) should be set up to curb the excesses of our headstrong editor. The members would be nominated by him after he had had a chance to discuss the composition of the committee with the Director. This proposal was accepted, but only because Mick assumed he would be a member of the committee, probably its chairman. In the event Dilys Powell and Basil Wright were the nominees, plus of course myself and Gavin Lambert. At our first meeting we decided that the remit of the committee was to widen the editorial conspectus of *Sight and Sound* by discussing any topic under the sun save one – the copy for the next edition. After a few agreeable lunches together in Soho the committee fell into disuse. Thus was the editorial freedom of *Sight and Sound* preserved.

The second priority for the Institute was to get possession of a cinema. We made the case that the BFI without a cinema was like the National Gallery with no pictures on show, and here again we were lucky. The Telekinema had been built for the 1951 Festival of Britain, mainly to show off the technical wonders that were shortly to surprise and delight cinemagoers, such as 3D pictures, ambient sound and bouts of live on-screen television (none of these came about).

Although small, out of the way and rather ugly, the Telekinema was better than nothing, and we mounted a vigorous campaign to stop it from being pulled down. Our opponents were the London County Council and the Treasury, our allies Herbert Morrison and the *News Chronicle* (Gerald Barry, its editor, had been chairman of the Festival of Britain committee, a jolly bunch of enthusiasts which included Huw Wheldon, Hugh Casson, Ralph Tubbs, Paul Wright and myself). We won the day, getting the Telekinema for a year, which was extended from year to year until it was pulled down in 1954.

The Telekinema transformed the Institute overnight. We introduced a new class of membership at five shillings per head, and put on the screen the classics of the cinema (many of which had never been seen in London before) and a ravishing series of contemporary films arranged and presented by the *Sight and Sound* team and including, naturally, John Ford and Vincente Minnelli seasons.

Membership of the Institute rose from something like 2,000 to 26,000. The newly joined members flocked to the theatre which was often booked out, and this gave rise to another problem. The news got around in the film trade, whose leading figures had been persuaded in the cause of art to allow us to show the films free, that the Telekinema now under the name of the National Film Theatre was making money. There were cries of 'unfair competition' 'exploitation' and 'we've been conned'. Walter Fuller, the general secretary of the Cinematograph Exhibitors Association, took the matter up with me personally. His office was in the same building, several storeys above the BFI. Frequently he would pop down to deliver vague threats and make intimidatory noises. He had green teeth and whilst he talked he kept flashing sinister underworld smiles at me. His whole manner was unnerving and he would usually make his exit, still flashing, and tapping his nose on one side, saying, 'I'm sure you know what's good for you, old boy.'

Amongst the several members of the cinema trade who attended the formal negotiating meetings there was one man who never spoke much but when he did was heard with respect. He usually supported our interests, but so diplomatically as to make it appear he was only trying to be fair. This was Cecil Bernstein, unmistakably Sidney's brother, but more compact and less overwhelming in appearance. He too was impeccably dressed with the same Bernstein white shirt and shining shoes, but his suits were of a more modest cut and clerical grey, not blue. He walked with a limp and favoured a black walking stick of a kind known as the Dowager. I sought Cecil out and asked him if he would chair a standing committee, the National Film

Theatre Committee, which would act as a referee to smooth out the little difficulties that constantly cropped up between the film trade and the Institute. He said he would think about it. Subsequently I came to know that the phrase 'think about it' from either brother meant that they wanted time to consult the other. In this case it must be pretty certain that Sidney would not have been in favour ('ridiculous distraction'), but Cecil could be dogged and after a few days he rang back to say that he would do it, and that was the end of our problems with the film trade.

Cecil was the ideal chairman. True, he had a speech impediment when under pressure and sometimes the meeting would sit in dumb sympathy for what seemed like a full minute whilst he struggled to extract some recalcitrant syllable. This affliction disappeared when chatting in a relaxed atmosphere, and in later years, when I was alone with Cecil and he suddenly went into a verbal paroxysm, I knew that something sombre was coming from round the corner – a suggested budget cut or the admission of some rare defeat at the hands of Lew Grade. One other weakness of his was a tendency, when it seemed impossible to get agreement on some tricky point, to move on to the next item without resolving the last. Sometimes this stratagem was successful but more often one of the more stubborn members of the committee would say, 'But are we going to raise prices or not?' and the debate would go back to square one. But these minor drawbacks were outweighed by his enormous ability as a diplomat, umpire and fixer.

So the National Film Theatre went from strength to strength, thanks to a free supply of films from the trade, to the enthusiastic but shrewd programme policy of the *Sight and Sound* team, and to the showmanship of Frank Hazel, the manager. Frank, recruited from the Rank circuit, threw himself into this new and often mysterious world of art films with enormous energy and skill, making only the occasional howler, as when he printed up the title of Buñuel's *L'age d'or* on the NFT posters as 'Large Door'.

Behind the scenes Cecil King gave steadfast support to all these moves. He was one of two men I came to know well who felt that they had played a major role – perhaps *the* major role – in winning the war on the home front and in returning the Labour Party to power. The other, J.B. Priestley, whose epilogues were radio's greatest domestic propaganda success of the war, expected recognition in the form of the chairmanship of the Arts Council. Cecil King, whose *Daily Mirror* had sustained the voice of populist socialism during the wartime coalition, expected a peerage and then an appointment as –

at least – a Secretary of State in an important government department. Both were bitterly disappointed. Priestley was offered no job, only a peerage which he refused, and Cecil King was offered the Film Institute which, surprisingly, he accepted. His decision was no doubt influenced by the recently published Radcliffe Report, which recommended that the Institute's terms of reference be extended beyond the use of films in education and that it should become something more like an Arts Council for film. However that may be, Herbert Morrison, then Lord President of the Council, persuaded King to take it on and he – realising, no doubt, that this was the only direct relationship with the Government on offer – swallowed his pride and settled for a five-year term as its chairman.

My relationship with Cecil King was a happy one. He took a detailed interest in all the Institute's affairs, and we would visit and inspect together every one of its several premises, from the film vaults standing like a cluster of pill boxes in a field at Aston Clinton in Buckinghamshire (for safety reasons there had to be an open space between each vault holding nitrate films) to the ramshackle collections of attics and cheap offices that housed the Institute's other departments in Soho. Each Tuesday morning at 11 a.m. I would visit Geraldine House and be ushered into Cecil's office on an upper floor. Apart from a huge desk, this was furnished more as a country house drawing room than as the command post of a great Fleet Street newspaper. A coal fire burned brightly in an elegant Georgian grate, which was serviced from time to time by a footman in striped pants, black jacket and white gloves. This functionary operated the fire irons with great precision whilst making a hissing noise through his teeth like a groom brushing down a horse. Ther was a choice of a dry natural sherry or an Amontillado. There were Bath Oliver biscuits and a caraway seed cake, which I never saw cut but was which was no doubt fresh each day.

Cecil sat in a high-backed leather armchair on one aside of the fire and I sat in its (slightly smaller) fellow on the other. I would go through my agenda first and he would respond, and then we would have a brief discussion of the political scene. On one occasion he had a criticism. He said he had seen a scruffy door at Aston Clinton on a visit some months ago and had asked that it be repainted. On our visit last week he noticed this had not been done.

'Sorry,' I said, 'I'll make a note of it.'

'Ring up Aston Clinton now and tell them to do it,' Cecil responded. He pressed a bell attached to the side of his chair and the black jacket appeared silently.

'Telephone,' said Cecil. The black jacket produced a small table and a telephone on a long lead and placed it between us. I looked at Cecil and Cecil looked at me: it was a critical moment. Eventually I picked up the phone and asked for the number.

'Could I speak to Goddard Brown?' I asked.

'Goddard speaking,' came the reply.

'Ah,' I said, 'When Mr Brown returns would you tell him that Mr Forman called and will call again later today.'

'But it's me speaking now,' poor Goddard began – but I put the phone down before he could say more. Cecil looked at me intently.

'The Curator was not in his office?' he asked. Clearly he had over-heard Goddard's voice, which was unmistakable.

'I will speak to him when I get back to Shaftesbury Avenue,' I said, and gazed back at him innocently. We passed on to other matters. And that was the only hiccup in what became a friendship as well as a good working relationship between Chairman and Director. I liked Cecil. I found him quick, witty and loyal, although I knew it might have been different if he had been paying my salary, for he was reputed to be a holy terror as a boss. As it was, we had a mutual regard which is reflected in his autobiography, of which someone said that throughout its considerable length he spoke well of only two persons, himself and Denis Forman.

One day, when chatting with the other Cecil (Bernstein), I told him that as a newcomer to cinema lore I was stunned by the power of the early Russian classics and like any enthusiastic novice I was writing a piece on Pudovkin and Eistenstein. Could I perhaps have a word with his brother Sidney who, as one of the organisers of the famous Film Society in the 1920s, had first shown *Battleship Potemkin* in London and who had become a friend of Eisenstein? Of course, said Cecil (he didn't even need to 'think about it'.) I rang Sidney's office and received a courteous but formal response. Mr Bernstein would see me at 11 a.m. on Friday next week. I made my entry to 36 Golden Square (a threshold I was destined to cross many thousands of times) punctually and was ushered to the lift by a modestly grey-suited janitor. At the lift door I was met by a neatly dressed secretary with a faintly military air who seated me in an alcove between a striking bust of Sidney Bernstein (by Frank Dobson) and a photo-graph of Cecil Bernstein. On the opposite wall was a photograph of Sidney Bernstein. Well anyway, I thought, I've come to the right place.

Almost at once the door was opened for me and Sidney rose from his chair, exquisite in fresh laundered linen and perfectly pressed navy-blue serge. He grasped my hand. 'Mr Forman, my brother tells me your Institute is taking over where my Film Society left off.'

'Well,' I said, 'we are doing our best but we have the disadvantage that most of the directors who used to come and talk about the early films are dead.'

'Including my old friend Sergei Eisenstein.'

'Just so.'

'He was an extraordinary man, a genius and also a bit of a horror,' said Sidney and for an hour we talked about him, his methods of film-making, his obsessive interest in painting, his passion for porno-graphic drawings, his freedom to do whatever he wanted within the Soviet regime, his huge energy, his ambivalent relationship with his cameraman Tisse and his producer Alexandrov, and with his leading Western groupie and biographer Marie Seton, and above all about the Mexican fiasco which resulted in thousands of feet of uncut rushes being left on the cutting room floor for others to butcher as they wished.

I was enchanted. Sidney's enthusiasm, his sense of fun, his charm and the way he offered instant friendship were something special. I walked back to the Institute exulting in the meeting. I wanted to meet him again, soon.

I did not have to wait long. A week to the day after our first meeting I received an invitation to lunch at the Café Royal with Sidney and 'some of my Film Society friends'. The first was Ivor Montagu, the unlikely son of Lord Swaythling, the banker – bespectacled, unkempt, bubbling with enthusiasm, a great amateur of film and a dedicated communist. The second was Iris Barry, recently curator of the film archive at the Museum of Modern Art in New York, a film critic of distinction and a figure in café society in New York, London and Paris. The third was Herbert Marshall, a sluggish conversationalist but a true Party member and one who had worked with Eisenstein in Moscow. The lunch passed in a flash with strong competition by all but the lugubrious Marshall to hold the floor. It was, of course, the first time I had encountered Sidney in his café society mode. He spoke in a rather high voice and delivered his lines as if they had been written for him by a good playwright. In this way he could quickly get the ear and he was seldom interrupted. At the same time he kept a firm hold on the general drift of the conversation and could unobtrusively sustain, deflect or terminate the discussion of any topic at will.

The Film Society lunch led to many further encounters. I would ask Sidney round to the Institute to meet some visiting dignitary such as Erich von Stroheim or René Clair; he would ring me and suggest we should drop round to a preview of a forthcoming film. We had lunches and dinners with mutual friends. We went to the Edinburgh Festival together. We would drive down to a film studio to see a film being shot on the floor. These were luxurious trips. In cold weather the chauffeur embarrassingly tucked a travelling rug around my knees. We would pull into some quiet lay-by and Sidney would produce a packet of smoked salmon sandwiches and half a bottle of white wine ('Studio food is always abominable'). Frequently we would stop at a cinema. If it was a Granada, Sidney would carry out one of his surprise inspections, prizing open ashtrays, flushing lavatories and inspecting the usherettes' fingernails whilst the manager stood two paces behind him, the old hands taking the bombardment of quick-fire questions with robust good humour, the younger men rigid with terror. If it was not a Granada, Sidney would buy two tickets in the back row and we would sit watching the film for about ten minutes. 'Disgraceful projection,' Sidney would say as we left. 'Forty people at six o'clock on a wet Thursday for *The Cruel Sea*. About four and a half fillings a week.'

'Would you buy it at the right price?' I would ask.

'No,' he would reply. 'No underground station within two miles, only one bus route and shops under the back of the auditorium which means two flights of steep stairs straight up from the street.'

But it wasn't only cinemas that attracted Sidney's attention. A 'For Sale' sign on any major property would cause him to turn his head and sometimes to turn back. On these occasions I would remain in the car as he paced the pavement, often disappearing into some entrance only to emerge a few minutes later making notes on a travelling pad. Very few of these properties can have been of any serious interest to Granada in those days, for it was not until the 1960s that we began to build a substantial property portfolio, but both brothers enjoyed property-spotting for its own sake just as train-spotters enjoy spotting trains.

I was often to see Sidney entering the office and, as he took his coat off, ringing Cecil to ask, 'Seen the factory property at the back of Battersea Park?' To which Cecil might reply, 'No good, Sidney, there's a compulsory purchase order on the access land.' I was always mystified as to what they would want these properties *for*. But no matter how often our journeys were interrupted, we always got to the studios in the end and Sidney was given a royal welcome, greeting and being greeted by an amazing number of people as we moved through dingy offices and draughty corridors towards the floor. The jolliest visit I remember was to Shepperton when Frank Launder and Sidney Gilliat were making *Green for Danger.* As I recall it, we saw an hour's shooting and then adjourned to a nearby restaurant (where Launder and Gilliat had taken an interest in the appointment of the chef) for an hilarious lunch which ended at about 5 p.m. On the way back I said, 'How will the film do?' 'Money back and a little over,' he said, and although I never checked I am sure he was right.

From time to time I would try to enlist Sidney's support for one or another of the Institute's ventures. In September 1953 I tried to enlist his help in a scheme to promote art films put forward by Orson Welles. He was sceptical about such a grand plan, although he did prove willing to join in a group formed under the aegis of PEP (Political and Economic Planning) to produce a plan for the future of the British Film Industry. A number of like-minded film-makers, economists and exhibitors met fortnightly in the evenings, and over sandwiches and wine discussed the great problem of the day – indeed the problem that has always been and still is with us: how to ensure a viable and durable film industry. Our secretary was Duncan Crow, a freelance who wrote mainly for *The Economist* and who was later to become the author of the vetoed Crow history of Granada mentioned on page 4. The report, when published by the Film Institute, was well received and may have done something to accelerate the formation of the Eady plan, under which a levy on the box office was used to subsidize film production. (The plan worked well for some years but declined and eventually died as a result of exhibitors falling on hard times and from lack of government interest.) Sidney was an assiduous member of the group, never missing a meeting and always ready to mobilise Granada's resources to provide data. There was, however, a noticeable rivalry between himself and Mick Balcon, the group's two leading figures, which often ended with Sidney stating his point emphatically and then sitting silently as Mick rambled on in a contrary vein until he ran out of steam.

By now Sidney and I had established an easy rapport and were of one mind on most matters, but we did not always agree. I remember when I made some reference to the nauseating sentimentality of Noël Coward's *In Which We Serve* and dismissed his plays as precious and outmoded. Sidney turned on me in anger and delivered a stern lecture on the folly of denigrating true talent when it was temporarily out of fashion. I did not know at the time that when Sidney had built the Phoenix Theatre, his opening play, put on in partnership with Noël Coward, was *Private Lives*. He, in turn, could see little merit in the early Ealing films ('schoolboy films' he called them), perhaps because of their association with Mick Balcon with whom there had been some serious rift since their happy association working in wartime propaganda. Although I warily quizzed both individuals about the origin of this mutual antipathy, neither of them was willing to enlighten me.

One of the topics Sidney and I often discussed was television. When television restarted in January 1946 the BBC was generally perceived to be the natural proprietor of all broadcasting. The War Office ran the army, the Admiralty ruled the waves and the BBC the airwaves. Radio had emerged from the war covered in battle honours and was credited, along with Monty and Churchill, as one of the reasons why we won it. Television, which could be seen only by a few thousand people in London, was regarded as radio's little brother, which might grow but would never challenge the mighty power and influence of radio. It would be an entertaining side-show for people who could afford it, and not much more. In June 1949 a committee under Lord Beveridge met to consider the future of broadcasting. After sixty-two meetings and a great deal of high-minded debate they reached the conclusion that all broadcasting should remain under the aegis of the BBC. But there was one dissenting voice. Selwyn Lloyd, already an influential figure in the Conservative Party, filed a minority report which made the case for ending the BBC monopoly.

Even before the Beveridge report was published there had been a television crisis at the BBC. Norman Collins, author of the enormously successful novel *London Belongs to Me*, had been Controller of Television for some three years. He believed – in a phrase that came to be worked to death over the decade – that television was the medium of the future. George Barnes, Director of the Spoken Word (a title gloriously redolent of Reith's BBC) and Head of the Third Programme, was put in over the head of Collins as Director of Television. He believed that radio was the medium of the past, the present and the future and that minority interests such as television should be kept firmly in their place. Collins resigned immediately. On the day of his resignation – 13 October, my birthday – I had a call from him inviting me to a party at the Savoy that very night. The guests were people of his persuasion from the BBC, Tory MPs and the press in full force. Norman made a forceful speech in which he vented his anger at the BBC for their lack of vision. Next day *The Times* printed a more moderate version of this speech. This was the beginning of the campaign for independent television. Its eventual success was due more to Norman than to anyone else.

At the time of his resignation Norman was a governor of the Film Institute and I had therefore got to know him well. I found him a likeable and energetic person who looked more like the head of a successful advertising agency than of a department of the still sedate BBC. He was naturally anxious that the Film Institute should support his cause and he directed the full force of his personality, which was considerable, at myself and the editorial group on *Sight and Sound*. Unfortunately he laboured under a heavy load of personal vanity which made him a *persona* not wholly *grata* with us, and perhaps explained why, despite his great abilities, he never became a figure of any real importance in ITV. At Norman's famous Savoy party he handed me a copy of his letter of resignation as a governor of the Film Institute, which he had sent to Cecil King. Within a week George Barnes was appointed in his place.

Unlike Norman, George Barnes was lofty, academic and cultured, a true Third Programme man, and one who could quote Lucretius or T.S. Eliot at the drop of a hat. He too had a good opinion of himself but of a more acceptable establishment kind. His relationship with me was that of a college tutor with a promising but immature under-graduate. His deities were our anglicised versions of Christ, Homer and Reith, and of the three I guess it was Reith's influence that predominated.

With two such figures frequently at my ear I was well briefed on both sides of the television controversy. My own inclination at that time was to agree with Norman that television should have its own separate corporate life and its own source of funds (for television *was* the medium of the future, no doubt about it) but that – and here I supported George – it should remain in the public domain. I remem-ber sketching out a scenario which envisaged a British Radio Corporation and a British Television Corporation with equal status, a proposition that pleased neither Norman nor George. But as the debate thundered on in Westminster and Fleet Street, and as we passed the milestones of the White Paper (May 1952) which recom-mended the introduction of commercial television and the passage of the Television Bill (March 1954), I had no difficulty in deciding that if independent television came about (and by now it looked a virtual certainty) I wanted to be a part of it. I had been at the Film Institute for five years and I had done what I could do.

One day I was chatting with a number of media folk, including my old mentor Jack Beddington – lately of the Ministry of Information Films Division and now returned to his mother ship, the advertising agency Coleman Prentice and Varley – and he said, 'You'll apply to be

DG of the new authority of course? Or will you stay where you are until you get your K?'

'My K?' I asked.

'Knighthood,' he said (I could see everyone present was amused that I did not know about Ks).

'Never thought about either a K or being DG,' I said.

'Oh, come on,' said Jack. 'Don't play Simple Simon. You should apply.'

But I was a Simple Simon in that I was only interested in a job that would allow me to direct and produce programmes. When Bob Fraser was appointed DG of the Independent Television Authority and Bernard Sendall was announced as his deputy (the old firm from my time at the Central Office of Information), I went to see Bob and told him I had been approached by several putative programme contractors (including Norman Collins) and by independents who wanted to set up production companies. Bob advised independent production – 'the contractors will have an awful lot on their hands, Denis. They will be hungry for programmes' (he was proved to be quite wrong). He also endorsed the view that television was the medium of the future.

Jack Beddington asked me to lunch to meet John Metcalfe and Edward Montagu (Lord Beaulieu), who were directors of a lively media company called Voice and Vision. They wanted to set up a film production company. Would I like to be the Managing Director? I trusted Jack and liked the other two, but in my Scottish way was slightly scared by their racy talk and dashing business methods. The 64,000 dollar question was: what kind of programmes? How many? What budget? Features and documentaries, they said. Also commercials. The portfolio would be very much up to me. I would have almost complete freedom and all the financial backing I needed. Television was the medium of the future. I thought about it for a week and then, mainly because Jack was known to have stood for all that was good in the documentary film world, I accepted subject to meeting the board, who were being appointed by Varley, no doubt assisted by the shades of Coleman and Prentice, who had left the scene some long time ago. I informed the Film Institute, where Cecil King had been succeeded as Chairman by S.C. Roberts, the Master of my old college (Pembroke, Cambridge) and secretary to the Syndics of the University Press. He immediately set about recruiting my successor.

When I was summoned to meet the board I sat outside the door for half an hour. Occasionally I heard raised voices. They were discussing the important matter of remuneration for non-executive directors. When I went in I was faced with eight grey-faced, grey-suited men, all of whose names I have mercifully forgotten.

'You come to us with a great reputation, Mr Forman,' said the chairman. 'You got a blue at Cambridge and were wounded at Cassino. Royal West Kents, wasn't it? In the same brigade as the Buffs. Did you come across my old friend Bungie Hooper?'

'No,' I said, 'I don't think I met Bungie Hooper.'

'Have much trouble with your leg?' asked another. 'Having a bath and that?'

'Not much trouble now,' I said.

'We believe you could make a great success of this company,' said a third. 'We hear you did well at the National Film Institution.'

'British Film Institute,' I said.

And so on. Jack Beddington's face, which had greeted me with a warm smile, got longer and longer. I asked them about the programme policy. 'Gibbs and Cadburys are coming in for sure,' said one. 'We had a really good chat with the tobacco companies,' said another. I realised they were thinking only of commercials. 'What about features and documentaries?' I asked. There was a pause. 'Well, of course we would not rule out anything that was profitable,' said a tall very grey man who had placed his wrist-watch on the table in front of him and was clearly counting the minutes until he could get back to his desk. Finally the chairman drew a deep breath. 'Mr Forman, we are prepared to offer you £3,000 a year with expenses, generous but not too uppity – West End premises and a 5 per cent stake in the company.' 'Of course, if you do well we will recognise it,' said another. 'Bonuses, increased holding, that sort of thing.' 'All possible,' said a third.

After leaving the room I went into Jack's office and waited until he entered, looking uncommonly shifty. 'Jack,' I said, 'how could you do this to me? I couldn't work for those men.' Jack fiddled furiously with an indiarubber band and a pencil. 'I know, I know,' he said. 'I knew the game was up after the first five minutes. And the way they offered you a *pourboire* for good work as if you were a gardener or a gamekeeper . . .' His voice trailed off.

I rang John Metcalfe and Edward Montagu and said I was sorry. I asked S.C. Roberts if I could stay on at the Film Institute a little longer, and he was flustered because he had already 'put out feelers' and had an advertisement for my successor in print. I was mystified as to how I could have put myself in such a silly position and marvelled not so much at my treatment by the board as at Jack's poor judgement and my own folly.

A week after this débâcle I heard casually that Granada had applied for and been awarded a television franchise by the new Broadcasting Authority. I went round to Golden Square. It was Christmas Eve, 1954. Sidney was not available, so I was ushered in to see Cecil.

'Cecil,' I said, 'if you and Sidney are going into television I would like to go in with you.'

'Just give me a minute,' said Cecil, and he disappeared through the communicating door to Sidney's office. He was back in more than one minute but certainly less than five. 'D–D–Denis,' he said, 'S–S–Sidney wants to know when you can start.' As I went down in the lift I wondered why I hadn't thought of this simple solution much earlier. Sidney and Cecil were my kind of people and television was, after all, the medium of the future. And there is a postscript. For many years I believed Cecil had broken into a meeting in Sidney's office to put the question. This was not so. Sidney was in New York getting married to his new bride, Sandra Malone. Cecil had got his positive response by telephone.

It is interesting to compare the above account with Sidney's recollection of the same events. He dictated this to a researcher on the Chanan history (see pages 4–5) some twenty-five years later:

> When I read one day while abroad that Denis Forman was joining an advertising agency, I telephoned Cecil and said that it was ridiculous that we should allow a man with so much talent to join any other organisation. Eventually Denis came to see me and I told him he had made a mistake. He didn't really want to work for the agency and in addition they had misled him on practically every point regarding his responsibilities. He was relieved that somebody he could trust wanted him. He joined Granada in 1955 and we have worked together ever since. He has made a great contribution.

Of such stuff are myths made.

CHAPTER 2

My first appointment at Granada was as chairman of the furniture committee, perhaps because Sidney liked the style of the fittings in the Film Institute. I visited warehouses and second-hand furniture shops along with hard-bitten buyers for Granada Theatres, who were astonished by my spendthrift ways. I was prone to buy a well-designed desk for £5 when an ugly but perfectly serviceable article could be had for three. 'He'll never let that one through,' my mentor would say, and, sure enough, I found that my order for an item that was even 10 per cent above the rock-bottom price was always mysteriously cancelled. Sidney never spoke to me about this and I never spoke to him because I did not care to refer to such a menial activity in his company.

The next job I got was to prepare a Granada stand for a radio exhibition in Manchester. My assistants were two young women who had been employed at the lowest rate as casual labour. Neither knew anything about radio, television or exhibitions. I called on the services of a designer I knew, who cooked up a charming rooftop scene featuring an H-shaped ITV antenna (an object which was unknown at the time) with chimneys with real smoke and a couple of stuffed cats. It was my idea that the cats should be indulging in sexual activity since this was certain to attract interest, especially in the press, but I found that this notion so profoundly shocked the two young women that they would resign rather than be associated with a display of such depravity. I also produced a four-page throwaway with sparky copy, striking illustrations and even more striking claims about the Granada TV service to come.

Sidney had been away until the eve of the exhibition and on his return he called me to his office. He was sitting behind his desk studying the throwaway. He looked broody. 'Denis,' he said, 'I am very worried about this brochure,' (he pronounced it 'brosher').

'Bro*shure*,' I said.

'Brosher,' he repeated.

'What worries you, Sidney?' I asked.

'This is not Granada,' he said, pointing at the company name.

'In what sense?' I asked.

'The typography is not Granada,' said Sidney.

'It's upper-case Rockwell stymie,' I said, 'which is surely the standard Granada typeface.'

'The "G" is not right,' said Sidney. 'The "G" is not thick enough. We always thicken the "G" in Granada. Look at this.' He pulled out some notepaper to make the comparison. I could see little difference. Sidney laid the paper down and brooded silently for a minute or two. Then he rang for his secretary, the redoubtable Miss Haselwood. 'Miss Haselwood,' he said, 'look at the word Granada in this brochure.'

She gazed at if for a moment and said, 'There seems to be something wrong with the "G".'

'Thank you, Miss Haselwood,' said Sidney, and after she had left he turned to me and said, 'You see?' There was a pause. 'I'm afraid the brochure cannot go out, Denis,' said Sidney.

I was amazed. 'What? Not go out? No one will notice the thickness of the "G", Sidney.'

'It's not right. It's not Granada,' said Sidney.

'But there are 2,000 copies waiting to be picked up at the printers now,' I said. 'We couldn't possibly re-set and print again by tomorrow.'

'Too bad,' said Sidney. He looked at me stonily. I got up slowly and left the room.

This was a new Sidney, quite different from the amiable companion of our studio jaunts and the elegant figure who held court in the Café Royal. What had happened? Slowly it dawned on me that I was now an employee. I had to learn that in Granada people did what Sidney wanted. If Sidney wanted perfection, perfection he must have. I was being broken in like a young colt. Hitherto I had been allowed to run free as his companion in all sorts of treats and adventures off the estate. Now I had to learn to respond to the bridle. If I trained on I would become a good Granada man. If I didn't . . . I cannot deny a degree of personal pique. At the Film Institute I had presided over a sizeable publications department which was renowned for its elegant layout and typography. James Shand, the leading typographer of the day, was my friend and adviser. I had discussed the evolution of Times Roman with the great Stanley Morison. And now I was being treated like a schoolboy who had made a howler in Latin prose and whose brochure was being cancelled as a form of imposition.

Also there was that Miss Haselwood bit. Could that have been a put-up job? Although I hardly knew Miss Haselwood at the time, it was already clear that she was not that sort of woman. Sidney had required her to find something wrong with the word Granada and she had obliged with the correct solution. I sat alone in my very small office for some time, thinking.

For a large part of my first six months with Granada I was in a sort of limbo. My colleagues were working away in their own cells. Sidney and Cecil worked separately, Cecil now almost wholly responsible for Granada Theatres but still answerable to Sidney for a low attendance at Plumstead on a bank holiday Monday or the cost of the new uniforms for doormen. Sidney was the centre of an electrical storm of activity, shaking and moving in every quarter in the campaign to get Granada on the air efficiently, with the maximum of publicity and at the minimum cost, organising with the unions a quota for imported material, setting up the news company (curiously enough, it was called the 'newsreel' company within Granada in the early years – shades of Gaumont British and Pathé), looking for a site for the studios in the North, deciding on the colour of the paint for the Granada Television vans, considering the claims of several rival brands of linoleum, and constantly telephoning his friends in the USA for advice.

Joe Warton, the finance man, who had grown up with the company since he joined as office boy at the age of fifteen, seldom spoke with anyone except Sidney and Cecil, and then only when required. He sat figuring in a fog of cigar smoke in a singularly unaesthetic front office, under the shadow of a large Jewish woman with horn-rimmed glasses like headlamps, who was his typist, his filing system, his remembrancer and his statistical department. Joe's methodology appeared to be Dickensian. He used blue foolscap paper, ruled with the several lines required by accountants, and a Swan fountain pen. He would cover sheet after sheet of the blue paper with figures of a generous size. Subtotals he would underline once, significant totals twice, and the final outcome of perhaps twenty pages of figuring would be triumphantly underscored six or seven times. Joe and his secretary supplied Sidney and Cecil with financial guidance, and with the full range of accountancy and company secretarial services which in other television companies were provided by a department of upwards of a dozen people using calculators and primitive but expensive computers. Joe had a special relationship with Sidney and Cecil, and no major decision was ever taken without his consent. To others he was gruff until mellowed by his six o'clock whisky, which was of the deep amber hue of strong ungrocered Indian tea. He then became quite jolly and would address one as 'old lad'.

In the week before joining Granada, when I raised the practical matter of a salary, Cecil had told me to go and see Joe to settle things. I went to see Joe armed with a ten-page draft contract drawn up by the Film Institute's lawyers. It was after 6 p.m. and Joe greeted me (without rising from his seat) with 'Hello, old lad. I gather Sidney wants us to settle things.' I handed Joe the draft, and after reading the first page he looked up at me and said, 'Do you really want this thing? The salary is 3,000 pound.' (Joe had a way of saying the word 'pound' – he never used the plural – in a reverent fashion, rather as a clergyman modulates his voices when he refers to 'Our Lord'). I reflected. No, I didn't want this thing. I was in with these people for better for worse, so in for a penny, in for a pound, or rather 3,000 pound. It was a little more than I was getting at the Film Institute. 'OK, Joe,' I said, '3,000 pound and forget the other thing.' So it was that from that day until the day I retired – which fell on precisely the same date forty years later – I never had a contract, letter of agreement or document of any kind defining my relationship with Granada.

The fourth member of the Granada cabinet in early 1955 was Victor Peers. Victor was some twenty years older than I, and had been a fighter pilot in World War I and subsequently a studio manager for Gaumont British. In 1947 Sidney sought him out to help him set up Transatlantic Pictures in Los Angeles, where he was going into partnership with Alfred Hitchcock. Victor, perhaps foolishly, flew out and started work before he had settled things with Joe: his summons had been urgent and he was dazzled by Sidney's charm. After a few weeks, although staying in a very modest hotel, he had run out of money and was obliged to inform Sidney that he could not pay his bills. Sidney was astonished and outraged. Why had things not been settled? Victor should go and settle things with Hitch immediately. Hitch saw Victor and said it was no concern of his and he must settle things with Sidney. Victor, now almost speechless with embarrassment, telephoned Sidney, who was back in London and who was once again amazed that Hitch had failed to settle things. He would get his friend Jack Warner to giver Victor an immediate advance and sort things out with Hitch when he got back to California. Victor, a nervous and apprehensive man, found himself signing a personal IOU to Jack Warner for several thousand dollars. But his faith in Sidney was rewarded because things *were* eventually settled with Transatlantic, and Victor stayed on as a much valued member of the

Transatlantic team until in 1951 Hitch and Sidney decided to go their separate ways.

Victor then returned to London to help install CinemaScope in the Granada theatres. When I arrived, he was Sidney's shadow on the managerial side of the television enterprise, always busy and always carrying a huge bundle of files under his arm. In fact he carried too many, for often when called upon in a meeting to produce some factual data he would whip through file after file in a desperate search until, as his audience began to run out of patience, he would become unsighted by panic and throw in the sponge. These failures of discovery were of little significance to others, but they upset him terribly. He had a mind meticulous for detail and was eager to codify and guide all company behaviour by edict, much as is done in the Catholic church of which he was a keen member. After we were on the air, his greatest desire was to perfect his magnum opus, a manual laying down procedures for every aspect of the television operation. In a new business that was evolving new ways of doing things every day, this – as I never wearied of telling him – was a hopeless task, for the amendments published each month were almost as bulky as the entire original document and were usually out of date before they hit the user's desk. In the early days he treated me as if I were a new boy at a school whose hallowed traditions he, as a prefect of some seniority, could explain to me. When describing one of the real or imagined hazards of life within Granada – such as the danger of wearing a wrist-watch in Sidney's presence – he would preface his lecture with the words 'When you have eaten below the salt at the Bernsteins' table for as long as I have.' This embarrassed me. I was not going to eat below the salt for any Bernstein. If there was any salt going I would expect it to be amongst us, and Sidney or Cecil to offer it to me just as I would to them. Conversely, my attitude of equality with the Bernsteins embarrassed Victor. He felt it quite wrong for a new boy to be more equal with the Bernsteins than one of their trusted senior advisers such as himself.

Reg Hammans, our Chief Engineer, was the fifth and last member of the Granada Television staff *in situ* when I arrived. He had been a big wheel at the BBC, Head of Television Planning and Installation, but had been frustrated by their hidebound philosophy and mean allocation of resources, and also, I guessed, by the lack of promotion prospects, for the Army List was as nothing compared to the meticulous scrutiny of the scale of seniority in the upper echelons of BBC Engineering, where dead men's shoes, or rather retiring men's shoes, were a matter of obsessive interest. Reg was a top-class engineer who tackled the job of setting up a television station in the grand manner. 'About a £4 million pound job,' he said casually in a conversation with Sidney, luckily after he had been appointed. This figure rocked Sidney to his foundations. He never felt quite the same towards Reg again, and awaited each of his monthly reports with extreme apprehension. Actually Reg's figures turned out to be about right, but it took some four years to build a fully-armed studio complex, and the initial outlay (1955–6) was less than three-quarters of a million. But Reg enjoyed an advantage over the rest of us in that Sidney's knowledge stopped short on the frontiers of electronic engineering, and whereas in other fields such as building, design, production and management Sidney would have been in there scrutinising every detail, he left Reg pretty well to his own devices. 'The trouble with Sidney is that he doesn't know a cathode ray tube from a corkscrew,' Reg would say. To which I would reply, 'That's not trouble, Reg, that's your salvation.'

Whilst every one of my four colleagues was busy doing his own thing, I had no specific role apart from the furniture committee, and no one seemed to bother about me. There was a weekly 'television lunch' in the Café Royal, but no regular formal meetings, and although one might be called up to Sidney's office at any time to sit in on a discussion about foreign quota, performing rights or the design for the Granada symbol, for most of the time I was in limbo. The first meaningful role I found for myself was that of recruiting officer. I don't think anyone told me to do this, but it became the custom to pass job applications to me. Engineers went to Reg for their first interview. I gave them a second and took them on, or not. As time went on, all programme and production staff and most others came direct to me. In all this I was totally unsupervised and had no guidelines. It was one of those strange things that could happen in the embryonic Granada of 1955. Sidney and Cecil must have known what I was doing and must have thought, 'Somebody's got to do it and he doesn't seem to be making more mistakes than anyone else would.' In the late summer of 1955 there was an attempt prompted by Victor to formalise procedure, but it came to little and for over a year I continued to be the chief doorkeeper, with the job of letting in only the best people from the long queue of hopefuls who wanted to work in 'the medium of the future'.

I had, of course, picked up, mainly from Sidney, a company philosophy about the sort of people we wanted to take on. 'Open-minded', 'ready to learn', 'bright young men' (opportunities were not all that equal in the Bernstein scheme of things) were the phrases one heard. This led to a policy of shunning the BBC – the most obvious source of recruitment – and seeking out people with related experience – post office engineers, theatre directors, plus a sprinkling of experienced professionals from the USA and Canada. Our fear of letting in BBC attitudes and practices was very great. We did not want to be a hierarchy or a bureaucracy, we wanted to break the dominance of the engineering men, we wanted to befriend the viewer, not patronise him, we wanted to be different. In the later stages of recruitment I was joined by Harry Watt, then a famous director of documentary films who had fallen out with Grierson and become friendly with Sidney by helping him in some mysterious way over the matter of his divorce from his first wife, Zoë. Each morning Harry and I would face a pile of job application letters, 95 per cent of which were instant rejections. Our main source of production recruitment was through the grapevine. Every now and then we would strike pure gold as when, on Mick Balcon's recommendation, I approached the construction staff at Ealing Studios and carried off the four top people, led by George Spellor, who were, over the next fifteen years, to run the most cost-effective and ingenious construction department in television.

There was another cell of recruits who were to become central figures in Granada. Kenny McCready was a lighting supervisor with a small outfit called the Rank Electronic Unit. I took a great shine to him, signed him up on the spot and asked if any of his colleagues might be interested. This led to the engagement early in 1956 of Mike Scott, later to become Programme Controller, and one of the best-known on-screen faces in television; Mike Wooller, soon to lead many of Granada's major documentary ventures; and his wife Joyce, whose judgement in selecting and appointing creative talent was fundamental to Granada's success and who became a director of the company in 1980.

Salaries were not high. The bottom rate we offered was £7 a week, the average £10, and £15 was the top. Anything above that level – £750 a year – had to go to the board. But very few offers reached these giddy heights.

Early in this limbo year I found myself in another role, that of unofficial go-between, between Granada and the Independent Broadcasting Authority. Although I was not privy to Granada's plans, Sidney or Cecil would often say to me, 'When next you see your friends from the Authority you might ask them about the transmitter programme', or what they thought about a quota, or the number of hours of broadcasting or whatever. As it happened, I did often see

Bob Fraser in the Savile Club (he had proposed me as a member in 1946), which was within walking distance of the Authority's first premises in Woods Mews off Park Lane. Although it seemed that almost everyone in London wanted to speak to him, Bob did not hold court at the Savile as did club lions such as Compton Mackenzie or Stephen Potter, who every night would sit in the centre of a group of star-struck fans. He would slip in for a quiet drink in the darker recesses of the card room, where he could conduct a business conversation with two or three companions. I also lunched occasionally with Bernard Sendall in inexpensive restaurants, and both he and Bob treated me as an old friend, although they were certainly aware of my potential as a double agent. Indeed Bob would sometimes speak so freely as to alarm himself and would hastily say, 'Denis, that information is for you and not for the companies.' By 'the companies' he meant Sidney to whom, of course, I reported everything when necessary with the caveat of confidentiality. Alas, I was of less service to Bob and Bernard when they quizzed me about how things were going with 'the companies', because since Sidney and Cecil played their cards very close to their chests I simply did not know, although I often pretended I did.

I had no preconceived ideas of my own about the future shape of ITV, being wholly at sea on these uncharted waters, but I listened wide-eared to Bob's and Bernard's account of their journey through the early mists of uncertainty and shared with them some of the excitement of seeing a new broadcasting system take shape.

Bob Fraser is today regarded as the architect of a public service-cum-commercial broadcasting system, which turned out to be practical, durable and a shining example to the world of the right balance between private enterprise and public control. There is truth in this, but it is not the whole truth, for he and his Authority made three major misjudgements at the very start.

First, they believed that the initial allocation of a single licence to each region was only a preliminary move towards a time of abundance, which was just around the corner, when there would be enough wavebands available to have several competing contractors in each territory. In their first annual report, when they said that 'No problem exercised the Authority more than the need to secure competition', it was clear that this applied only to phase 1, and that they confidently assumed that competition would come about automatically as ITV licences proliferated. But this never happened: one licence in each region was to be the rule – indefinitely. They could

hardly be blamed for short-sightedness, since a belief in the prolifer-
ation of wavelengths was the received wisdom of the day and they
were probably given firm assurances from the Government that
multiplicity was a virtual certainty, just as in the late 1980s Granada
was given solemn (but in the event not binding) assurances that there
would be no satellite broadcaster to compete with British Sky
Broadcasting only months before Rupert Murdoch jumped out of
his part of the sky with a cheaper and more effective alternative.

The second and major miscalculation arose partly from the first.
Fraser sought a system during this (as he thought) interim stage
which would cause the companies to compete with each other in
programme sales. In his official history of Independent Television,
Bernard Sendall reports a memorandum from Fraser to Sir Kenneth
Clark, the first Chairman of the Authority, in September 1954 saying:

> I want a network connection technically capable of giving
> an unlimited introduction of programmes from any one
> region into either of the others. I want London to be in
> full competition with the Midlands in selling programmes
> to Northern, Midlands with Northern in selling to
> London, Northern with London selling to the Midlands.
> Each will be eager to sell, each eager to buy. This will be
> competition with a vengeance, and with all its fruits. The
> network must be optional or it is not competition but
> cartel or market-sharing.

What came about was, of course, not competition but the cartel
which was, over the next quarter of a century, to cause more friction,
and do more damage to the image of ITV, than anything else. But
more of this later.

The third error was to imagine that the companies would be eager
to farm out a major part of their production to subcontractors. Fraser
clearly believed this when he advised me to join Voice and Vision. In
the memo he continues:

> I would like to see the Authority insist that each producer
> company should secure a proportion of its own original
> programmes from sub-contractors. I do not see why this
> should not be fixed as a percentage, either. This would give
> competition at another level. Sub-contractors would be in
> competition with one another and the main contractors
> would be competing with one another for the best

programmes of the sub-contractors. (If the network were compulsory, there would be only one buyer for sub-contractors to approach.)

This proposal was far-sighted, but he didn't follow it up; and although independent producers were quiescent for many years, their eventual rebellion during the 80s succeeded in gaining a statutory quota for independent production of 25 per cent not only for ITV but for the BBC as well. If Fraser had had the courage of his convictions this sea change in the structure of British broadcasting would have taken place some thirty-five years before it did.

Both Bob Fraser and Bernard Sendall were intensely inquisitive about Sidney, whom they regarded as something of a mystery man. With Cecil they felt quite at home. His friendly manner and his form of apparently open diplomacy was just the kind of relationship they liked, but Sidney treated them with great formality and could freeze them in their shoes with a show of hauteur if he felt they were presuming too much on Granada's goodwill. Because he kept them at a distance they harboured the totally unfounded suspicion that he might not be wholehearted in his loyalty to ITV. This was partly because of his known association with the Labour Party (who opposed it) and partly because of things he had said long before Independent Television became a practical proposition. I told them that the idea that Sidney was constructing in Granada some sort of wooden horse to assist the Labour Party to transform ITV into a second BBC was nonsense. In fact Sidney's (Granada's) changing attitudes over the years were clearly shown through a number of published statements. But a general election was imminent, and if one were to go entirely by Sidney's public statements there were, I suppose, reasonable grounds for some unease.

When Granada applied for its franchise in the North, much play was made with the fact that they, with infinite foresight, had been the first in the field to apply for a television licence in 1948, long before anyone else had even thought about the possibility of Independent Television. Like most Granada mythology this claim was both true and untrue. It is true in that a letter went to the Postmaster-General in September 1948 applying for a 'licence to erect a television station [sic]', but it is untrue in that the purpose of this station was only to 'transmit films to our various Granada theatres' from a central control room. This would have eliminated the cost of prints and projectors. Granada, no doubt to avoid the charge of monopoly, said they 'would be prepared to provide facilities to other theatres' and would consider

48

'the possibility of the retransmission of some of the BBC programmes', but it seems clear that the letter was the result of a Bernstein brainwave about cutting costs in running their cinema chain. As time passed, the letter was credited with the idea of showing West End plays on the last night of their runs, and great sporting events; and as it faded further and further into the past, it came to be quoted as a request to broadcast a general television service.

If we disregard the 1948 letter, and some desultory correspondence with the Postmaster-General which followed it, the first real statement of Granada's views came in 1950 when they submitted a somewhat prissy paper to the Beveridge Committee, which concluded:

> the right of access to the domestic sound and television receivers of millions of people carries with it such great propaganda power that it cannot be entrusted to any persons or bodies other than a public corporation or a number of public corporations.

This is hard-line Reithian stuff, but when in 1953 the Government published its intentions in a Memorandum on Television Policy, Sidney was told by friends in Westminster that legislation to allow commercial television was now certain. He then went on the record – saying, in a phrase illustrating a delightfully flexible approach towards history, 'It seemed prudent to update our application for a licence, to keep it alive.'

But by the time the Independent Television Authority (ITA) invited applications for television licences in July 1954, Sidney's ambivalence had given way to certainty. Again, he had to explain (in a not altogether convincing fashion) why Granada had changed its mind:

> When the Bill received the Royal Assent we'd still not fully made up our minds whether or not to proceed. Rumours began to fly about who was applying for licences, and rather late in the day we said to ourselves – why should we let all the big boys have it, we're just as capable as they are? Things were happening pretty quickly, and we realised that if we didn't commit ourselves others would soon be granted the available contracts. It seemed to me that though my ideas on the development of television hadn't come about, it was going to benefit nobody if we left the field free to others, most of whom – perhaps all

of whom – were less qualified than ourselves, than
Granada, to undertake the operation of a television
company.

So it was by this route that Granada came to support the principle of
Independent Television, and it was not for me to be in any way critical since I had followed the same process of conversion in private
that Sidney had had to defend in public. By the time I joined there
was not the slightest doubt that everyone on the top deck of Granada
was wholly committed, and if the Labour Party had approached
Sidney about the possibility of transforming ITV into a non-commer-
cial public service (which I don't believe they did), they would have
received short shrift. Indeed Sidney had made his position clear soon
after the application for a franchise in a letter to Herbert Morrison,
then shadow Home Secretary,

> I think you should know that my company have applied
> to the Postmaster-General for a licence to operate a
> Commercial Television Station. This does not indicate any
> change of feelings about commercial or sponsored televi-
> sion; I still think the country would be better off without
> it. However, if there is to be commercial television in this
> country, we think we should be in, and this may very well
> be useful one day.

Morrison's reply was brief: 'Like you I hope no one gets the chance.'

As time went by, Sidney began to find me useful in another area,
namely public relations. Although he personally controlled every
facet of Granada's public image, he liked to gather a group of 'bright
young men' to bounce ideas around and to discover how they reacted
to his more venturesome notions. Granada was going to be a northern company and it had to be proved that the North held all that was
best in Britain, whether it be Yorkshire grit, the *Manchester Guardian*,
Morecambe Bay shrimps, the Brontës or Blackburn Rovers, and
conversely that London and the South-East were inhabited by a mass
of displaced persons who had no regional identity and were rather
weak in character, whose region was important only because it
contained the monarchy and the seat of government. We dreamt up
the notion of a screen caption reiterating 'From the North Granada
Presents' before every programme; we worked on an up-to-date
version of Cobbet's concept of London as the Great Wen, a cesspool

of sin, corruption and idleness; we started a campaign to move a significant member of the royal family to Harrogate; and Sidney began to promote the idea of 'Granadaland'. At first I opposed this as pretending too much. But Sidney was right and I was wrong, for it caught on almost at once, although Sidney's dream of having the Granadaland frontiers marked by mock customs posts on every road never came about. I came up with the concept that Sidney had selected the northern franchise as a result of co-ordinating the maps of rainfall and population in Britain, and this was to be heavily used over the years.

For a few weeks Sidney went mad on eyes, pinching from CBS the idea of the pre-launch advertising campaign: 'Keep your eye [picture, not word] on Granada'. He wanted to add a subtitle to the company name: 'Granada – the Northern Eye'. This we managed to scotch, but he stubbornly insisted on calling the Outside Broadcasting Units, including their fleet of accompanying vehicles, 'Travelling Eyes'. This was a flop, for no one ever called them that and the many hours spent discussing their livery (was the blue too grey? Should the letters be two inches taller? Half an inch wider? Was the insignia at the right height for the following motorist?) were wasted. All this was within the PR tradition of Granada Theatres, namely that Granada was the brightest, most alert, most friendly and easily the most enterprising show-business company in the world, and cultured with it. This style was so ingrained that when I made a suggestion that did not please, Sidney would say, 'That is not the way we do it in Granada', meaning Granada Theatres, to which I would reply, 'But this *is* Granada, Sidney, Granada Television.'

I soon learnt two things for certain: that Sidney had a talent amounting to genius for public relations, and that a part of that genius was to ensure that every bit of credit for Granada's success reflected on him personally. This he did whilst at the same time appearing to be the most modest and unselfish of colleagues – insisting, for instance, in the early years of television that unlike Lew Grade or Val Parnell, whose names appeared on the screen in huge letters before any important show, his own name never appeared at all. This was done, he said, so that all credit should go to 'the creative people'. At the same time he took pains to ensure that no other names appeared except those of comparatively little-known directors. For many years producers were not given a credit at all, and so it came about that Sidney was seen as the onlie true begetter of Granada's programmes. I for one was quite content to see him credited with shows in which he had taken no part (or which he had even opposed) on the grounds that, in the wider scheme of things, to have him perceived as the benevolent patriarch of all Granada's output, indeed of everything that made up Granada, was a positive plus.

Early in 1955 the great transmitter crisis broke. The newly appointed Independent Television Authority had been assured by the Postmaster-General that ITV would be allotted transmitters on the masts already being used by the BBC. Unfortunately these assurances were not treated with the scepticism they deserved, for the BBC, bitterly opposed to ITV and in those days dominated by engineers, was quickly able to shoot down this plan as impracticable and probably unsafe. Although undoubtedly false, these objections were easy to sustain given the decision-makers' total ignorance of technical matters and the British engineering tradition of recommending not only belt and braces but an extra two pairs of trousers as well.

The Authority's engineers panicked. The ITV signal had to be on air before the impending general election or there might be no signal at all. All manner of makeshift devices were considered in order to get quick coverage of the three main ITV areas. Granada was told that since their region could no longer be served by the single BBC transmitter at Holme Moss there would now have to be two transmitters, one for Lancashire on Winter Hill and another for Yorkshire at some point in the mid-Pennines. So far so good, but then the dreadful news broke that although the Lancashire mast could be up by May 1956 the Yorkshire transmitter would not be ready until several months later. So Granada would have to go on air at half-cock.

Sidney was outraged. Delegations went between Golden Square and Woods Mews, and there was an exchange of letters which became ever firmer in tone, leading to the following:

> Instead of starting commercial transmissions with an audience potential of 12 millions, we are now being asked to go into business with a potential of 6 millions.
> We cannot escape the impression that we are being asked to pay a very high price indeed to hasten the inauguration of ITA service elsewhere. The economic base of all our planning has been continuously chipped away.

When it seemed that Granada's objections were to be overruled there were consultations with Granada's friends in the USA and Canada, meetings and discussions went on all day, and Reg Hammans got no sleep. Slowly Sidney's sense of outrage turned to anger and he began a process I was to witness many times in later years. Lawyers were called in. Opinions were taken. A case was prepared, and then Granada had to face the big question: to issue a writ or not to issue a writ. Soon I was to become a principal in this process, but at that stage I was not yet a member of the inner cabinet, so I can only surmise that events took their customary course. Sidney would call in Cecil and Joe Warton to hear the lawyers' appraisal of the Granada claim. He would then extract from the lawyers an opinion that there was 'a better than fifty-fifty chance' of winning. Cecil and Joe would say little until the lawyers left, when they would subject Sidney to an agonising period of silent disapproval, after which chance remarks would start to be dropped. The lawyer had worn a poorly cut suit and had talked with a cigarette in his mouth. He had admitted that the damages might be small. When asked point-blank whether he advised an action, he had been evasive. Kenneth Clark disliked becoming involved in legislation and might take it personally. Fraser and Sendall were clever people. At no time during this apparently desultory conversation would the main issue be addressed directly: was it sensible, for the sake of some notional amount in damages, to alienate our masters in the ITA upon whose goodwill we were going to be dependent for many years to come?

In the end no action was taken, but the fact that Sidney had contemplated a writ was known to the Authority and affected relations with Granada right up to the time that Bob Fraser retired in 1970. Whilst the deliberations with lawyers were going on, I got a message from Sidney through Victor Peers that it would be unwise for me to see my friends from Woods Mews. For some years after this I lost the easy familiarity with them of the early days, Cecil and Victor were treated by them with more formality, and Sidney himself became an even more remote figure, sometimes sulking in his tent and refusing to answer letters and, when he did deign to do so, addressing the Authority's officers with such frosty formality as to keep them in a constant state of fear.

It was Sidney who found our site in Manchester. By the time I joined Granada the search had already been going on for some months, but now there was urgency and Victor Peers, Reg Hammans and I were despatched to explore the three preferred options of Leeds, Liverpool and Manchester. After several days of travelling in buses and trudging the streets, Reg found something in Leeds and Victor a promising site near the docks in Salford. The two places I found in Manchester – a shopping arcade near Victoria Station and a large factory close by the racecourse – were instantly dismissed as too expensive. Victor's site was subjected to search and a price negotiated, and it was finally visited by Sidney, who within seconds told Victor it was no good. On the way back to the station they passed a site in Water Street surrounding an old Manchester Ship Canal basin. There was a 'Sold' notice on a board outside the entrance. Sidney went in and, again within seconds, told Victor, 'This is our site.'

'But it's already sold,' said Victor.

'Find out who's bought it,' said Sidney. Victor found out. It was reserved for the City Council. Sidney immediately began to bargain with the Town Clerk, Philip Dingle, who not only agreed to let Granada have the site but became one of Granada's greatest supporters in the years ahead. The four-acre site was bought for £82,000.

It was during this period, when both time and money were short, that I was first to see Sidney acting in the role of architect. On his extensive desk in Golden Square would be spread innumerable plans, one below the next, with an overspill lying on the surrounding floor; behind one shoulder would stand Ralph Tubbs, our site architect, sometimes enthusiastic, sometimes disconsolate; behind the other, Reg Hammans, guarding the engineering interest with the eye of a raptor ever ready for a strike. Sidney himself would talk and draw simultaneously. 'Suppose we took four and a half inches off the width of the corridor [long straight stroke from the blue pencil] and put in a joist by the outside wall [now the red pencil makes a change in structural work], we would be able to get two doors comfortably into the partition wall [single door annihilated by a stroke of the blue pencil and two new doors sketched in]', and so on. A small posse of observers, who had become accustomed to reading plans upside-down, would stand on the other side of the desk and would occasionally be asked for information about the width of a camera pedestal or the minimum acceptable size for a conference room. Whilst the frenzy was on no telephone calls came through, no visitors were admitted and no tea was served.

Anyone who witnessed Sidney at work in one of these sessions had to acknowledge his practical genius as an architect. Indeed there was evidence of his handiwork on display in every one of Granada's new buildings, and he had one outstanding triumph when he set his mind to converting the range of boiler rooms and cellars under the Golden Square offices into some productive use. He worked alone for several months in the face of universal scepticism and eventually produced an entirely new suite of rooms consisting of a preview theatre, commodious male and female lavatories, a roomy kitchen and two dining rooms which, when the folding partition doors were thrown open, would house a press reception for upwards of seventy people. It was a little miracle.

Overall he had few failures and some spectacular successes. One of his successes was during the construction of the first motorway service area at Toddington, when he queried the architect's assumption that the first floor must have fourteen feet of headroom. 'Why so high?' asked Sidney. 'Because,' said the architect, 'lorries have to be able to drive through the centre of the building and their height is increasing every year.' Sidney immediately sent a man out on the motorway, who came back with a report that the standard height for all bridges was twelve feet. Collapse of the architect. There was, however, a price to pay for the privilege of having an architectural genius as chairman. Sidney was a perfectionist who believed that it was never too late to modify or improve. Plans would come to him for final approval, perhaps a week or two before building was due to start. He would immediately spot half a dozen design flaws and call a meeting such as the one described above. This time there was no enthusiasm from his team, only a dogged defence of the status quo. 'Sidney,' some beleaguered executive would say, 'if you want us to open on the due date that lift shaft will have to stay where it is.' But Sidney would have none of it and the lift shaft would be moved from one end of the building to the other, well within the allotted time, for the infuriating thing was that he was nearly always proved right. An anonymous contributor to the Crow history had this to say about this aspect of Sidney's character:

> In the opinion of someone who worked with him for many years this last–moment–decision–taking of Bernstein's is not so much a well-drilled business method, though it has the effect of such, as a quality in his charac-ter which makes him question anything he sees or hears or experiences. It began to find expression in the early days of Granada when the theatres were being built, when he was refusing to accept finality until he had satisfied himself that everything possible had been done towards achieving the idea even though those around him were telling him that it was 'too late' and then being able to show that not only was it not too late but that what had been done was that much better because he had held back, because he had questioned, because he had compared. Always questioning the limiting factor – in this way of course is progress made.

Irritating (if not stronger) as are his shattering criticisms he is in fact one of those who epitomise the principle of dynamism, who drag mankind along by refusing to allow the inertial acceptance of a static society.

I once debated the nature of Sidney's architectural talent with Solly Zuckerman, at that time the Government scientific adviser, and we agreed that Sidney was no conceptual architect. He would have to call in Lutyens or Komisarjevsky to supply the great design. But when it came to the layout and interior fittings of a kitchen, a cinema or a lavatory there was no one to touch him. He was, in fact, a jobbing architect of genius.

At the turn of the year 1955–6 progress on the programme side was not impressive. Harry Watt had been with us for nearly a year and had helped me with the recruitment of programme staff. Apart from that he had little to show. He had pursued the idea of a crime series featuring Duncan Webb, a well-known and commercially minded crime journalist, who seemed to pay out information to Soho's underworld in exchange for ever-increasing financial inducements, as a belly dancer reveals more flesh only if the ante is upped. He was also initially keen on a series called 'Where Are They Now?' which tracked the forgotten heroes of yesteryear (such as Jackie Coogan, Lindbergh, Jack Hobbs) into the obscurity of their private and usually penurious lives in retirement. This he gave up because he found all ex-heroes to be excruciatingly boring people. But Harry was an active man who had to be doing something. So he set out on another ploy which looked more like coming off: the notion of an afternoon chat show to be chaired by an actor, John Sharp, in whose personality Harry saw enormous screen potential. Day after day I would find these two at work in a small office in Golden Square. 'Work' took the form of Harry coaching John in the art of making gazpacho for the benefit of the television audience. Like many documentary directors Harry was better at dealing with things than people. 'Do that bit about slicing the cucumber again, John,' he would say, holding his hands out to frame the shot as all extrovert directors loved to do. 'Try holding the knife in the other hand.' So poor John would plough on through his gazpacho-making with Harry darting from side to side shouting 'Camera 3! Camera 1! Camera 3 again!' One day he burst into my office. 'It's no good,' he said. 'I give up. He's getting worse, not better.' Here he proved to be wrong, for later in the year John Sharp did have a successful afternoon show, *Sharp at Four*; but, alas,

Harry had nothing to do with it. So he dived back into Soho and *Webb of Crime*.

The most professional member of the programme team was Eddie Pola, a song -and-dance man who had once been a tap-dance champion (billed as Twinkletoes). He had actually worked in television and radio, mainly in California, and produced quite a successful series named *Twisted Tunes*. Eddie was a cheery fellow with a fertile mind which dreamt up innumerable formats for light entertainment shows. But he was easily discouraged, and if either Sidney or Cecil showed the slightest coolness towards one of his projects he would drop it at once. This perhaps was understandable, but he would also scrap an idea on the strength of a brief discussion with the steward on the Manchester Pullman or the janitor at Golden Square.

In the summer of 1955 Bob Heller, an American, was encouraged by Sidney and Joe Warton to head the programme side of Granada. From the first he was something of a mystery man, his main qualifications for the job being a recommendation from the dean of American television journalism, Ed Murrow, and the fact that he had fallen foul of the Un-American Activities Committee. He was reported to have had television experience in Mexico, but when pressed to expand on this he tended to be vague. He had been in charge of network relations with CBS, he said, and there were also frequent references to some responsibility for sport. As soon as he arrived he sent a memo to Sidney, dividing his empire between Eddie Pola (light entertainment), Harry Watt (sport, documentaries, drama and Outside Broadcasts – known as OBs), and myself (discussion programmes, public affairs, etc.). He saw his function as 'sitting on top of the total programme operation and being available for advice and consultation'.

This sounds a passive role, and so it turned out to be. Bob withdrew from the hurly-burly of programme-making and sat in lonely isolation on the top floor of Golden Square. His only practical activity appeared to be the production of a puppet called Jolly Good, which was to be the lead character in a forthcoming programme – 'The Jolly Good Show'. On the rare occasions when I went to see Bob to report progress or to seek advice, the conversation would end in a chat about Jolly Good. 'Whenever I feel depressed I get Jolly Good out of his box and set him up on my desk,' Bob would say, opening the lid of a coffin-like case that lay at his feet and displaying the ghastly features of an almost life-size puppet of a schoolboy, smirking with the insufferable self-satisfaction of Archie Andrews and all the puppet tribe. When I shuddered and turned away to raise the matter of all the non-puppet programmes which were not being made, Bob would look at me with an air of weary wisdom and say that television programmes could only be made when television was up and running. 'The programmes will be there,' he would say, with the air of a Harvard professor talking to a freshman, 'when the programmes are needed. There is a natural empathetic relationship between the dynamism of an oncoming event and motivational response.'

So the year rolled on, and by the early spring of 1956 we had recruited some twenty hopefuls, who went through a directors' training course in London and then were shipped to Manchester where another training operation was in progress under a quiet but immensely effective American, David Lowe. This had to be confined to the use of the OB units since the studio was not yet ready. But still there were very few programmes. Eddie and Cecil had cooked up one situation comedy, *My Wife's Sister*, and a couple of quiz shows; Harry was struggling full-time with his *Webb of Crime*; I had a unit working on a weekly show from the London Zoo; there was a current affairs show, *Youth is Asking*, and several ideas for regional programmes; and Sidney was entirely immersed in planning the programme for the opening night, for which he had ambitious ideas. From time to time both Victor Peers and I had alerted Sidney to the fact that there was no programme portfolio worked out and very few programmes on the stocks, but he was impatient of any distraction from his absorption in the first night.

Towards the end of March I could see we were cruising steadily towards disaster and made one final attempt to galvanise Bob into action. He was busy working on 'a marketing exercise' for Jolly Good cereals and Jolly Good soft drinks, and as I said my piece the frightful creature sat grinning at us. Bob listened attentively to what I had to say and agreed that there were very few programmes. Having said that, he looked listlessly out of the window. It was clear that he had some sort of mental blockage. I went straight to Sidney's office and said we were going on the air in six weeks' time and although the first night would no doubt be a brilliant success, we had no programmes to fill the remaining 200 days of the first year. We had in fact only five weekly programmes for networking, whereas the other contractors had a dozen or more. We had no firm plans for regional programmes at all. The programme journals were already asking for details. Sidney panicked. He called together Cecil, Eddie Pola, Harry Watt, David Lowe and myself (Bob Heller was ill). We ran through all proposals and projects and possibilities, but finished up with no more than the original five network programmes. There was no time to get any more ready. Then Therese Denny, a young Australian researcher, David Lowe and I were told to organise an afternoon and evening series of OB shows and studio chat shows.

One result of this meeting was that Bob Heller surfaced and sent out two memos, one to me relieving himself of network responsibilities and coolly stating that 'I am informing the Secretary of the Networking Committee that I have asked you to represent Granada at all meetings on this Committee'; and one to all programme staff:

> 1. It will be necessary for me to continue to devote most of my time to negotiations on the method and policy of networking and of Granada's acquisition of British and imported films.
> 2. In order to expedite the development of Granada programmes before our opening day, I am assigning to other persons certain day to day responsibilities.
> 3. In London, all Programme Department Heads and all producers developing new programmes should report direct to Denis Forman. All approval of budgets and programme expenditure will come from Denis Forman. All programme assignments will be his responsibility. He will fix Granada's programmes schedule and will inform all departments.
> 4. Producers once assigned and working on programme developments in Manchester will report to David Lowe for guidance and decisions.
> 5. I will continue to be available to all TV Department Heads on all matters of general policy.

So it seemed I had suddenly become Programme Controller or something like it. Neither Sidney nor Cecil said anything to me about this unexpected elevation, nor, so far as I know, was there any confrontation with Bob Heller, who continued to sit aloft brooding over the coffin of Jolly Good. Everyone carried on much as before. David Lowe and I hired researchers and set up a dozen or so daytime OBs and some studio chat shows. But to my great sorrow, David – who was on loan – had to return to CBS, leaving with me a parting missive:

> What can I say? I shall miss you, I'd rather not think of how things would have been without you. As the one steadying influence you were a life-saver and when the day comes you will be head of this good organisation, please

remember you heard it first from me.

Many thanks for your help and faith and perseverance.

Eddie Pola got his act together and started rehearsing *My Wildest Dream*, an ad lib show featuring the leading comics of the day, and a couple of quiz shows. Cecil took over the situation comedy *My Wife's Sister* – by far the biggest production of the week – and Harry Webb got deeper and deeper into his *Webb of Crime*, so deep in fact that one night when I was working late in Golden Square the telephone went and he asked me in a hoarse whisper if I could raise £200 in cash and get it round right away to an address in Soho – 'otherwise,' he said darkly, 'they won't let me out.'

Meanwhile Sidney expended an immense number of man-hours and almost infinite pains on the Opening Night, due on 3 May. The first programme, *Meet the People*, was to be a grand parade of all those who had helped Granada to set up shop in Manchester, from Kenneth Clark, Chairman of the ITA, and the Mayor of Manchester down to the brickies and chippies who had built the studio. The master of ceremonies was to be, God knows why, Quentin Reynolds, an American war correspondent who had served time in London during the blitz and was an old buddy of Sidney's. The evening was to end with a tribute to the BBC, an idea Sidney and I had nurtured because of our genuine admiration for all they had done for broadcasting, and perhaps, because it was the sort of generous and at the same time slightly cheeky gesture that would go down well with the press. The tension engendered within the company by the preparation of these two events was almost unbearable. Victor Peers sent round a note two days before D-Day saying that only the people directly concerned with the Opening Night programmes would be allowed access to the studio. He attached a list of names, and mine was not on it. This hurt me deeply. Although not concerned with the Opening Night, I was concerned with everything else and for two days had to hold meetings in the bar of our local pub, the Balking Donkey, instead of in the tiny conference room in the TV Centre.

But my angst was avenged by a stroke of providence. On the afternoon of D-Day, Quentin Reynolds turned up at the studios for the final run-through hopelessly drunk. He had found it hard to hold his lines and the whole event was just too much for him. He was hustled off for a cold shower and black coffee. Sidney, white-faced and monosyllabic, called me into the studio for a consultation in the desperate hope that with my Cambridge background I would know more about drunkenness than he did. I remember opposing the idea

of a stomach pump and advocating an understudy to walk behind
Quent, steer him on the approved course, and if necessary articulate
his lines.

In the event, all went tolerably well. Victor Peers read the opening
announcement in a dry, nervous voice, and although Quent lurched
a little he played his part well enough for most viewers to see nothing amiss. Then came a Val Parnell variety show from London;
another tribute, this time to Lancashire; and some boxing from
Liverpool, with only one short blackout. The *Tribute to the BBC* film
made an unimpeded passage through telecine – and so to bed. The
press was good.

Looking back today at the opening night, cataclysmic as it was in
its time, one is struck by a sense of wonder at the vanity of human
affairs. There is the unhappy memory of the highly inappropriate
Quent lurching unsurely down the line of workers by hand and by
brain, vilely mispronouncing their North Country names; and in the
BBC film we see a diminished Sidney Bernstein perched on a desk
mouthing in a high falsetto (the sound quality was dreadful) some
truly appalling lines written, I fear, by myself for an earlier press
release. ('The North is a closely knit, indigenous, industrial society; a
homogeneous, cultural group, with a record for music, theatre, literature and newspapers not found elsewhere'). It is a shameful misrep-
resentation of this great and wonderful man. I also recall with a shudder a bizarre little announcement which was read out before the
opening programme and by which Sidney hoped to mollify his
Labour Party critics, who accused ITV of encouraging people to
spend money they could not afford:

> Wise spending eventually saves money. And savings can
> help deal with our country's economic problems. So
> before we shop let us say to ourselves, 'Is it essential. Can
> we save?' Save not only for a rainy day but also to make
> sure that tomorrow will be sunny.

It is hard now to see how this tiny event, amounting to some fifty
minutes of airtime in all, should have dominated the lives of so many
people for so long.

After close-down there were, undemocratically, two parties at the
Midland Hotel, one for the workers and one for the toffs, and it was
not long after the celebrations began that Quent was assisted to his
bedroom for a long and peaceful sleep.

CHAPTER THREE

I woke up the morning after the opening night and peered into the future. It looked grim. The schedule for the day (Friday 4 May 1956) was as follows:

5.00 LASSIE
A good, tried friend in a new series for television.
CLOSE-DOWN UNTIL 7.00

7.00 LATEST NEWS

7.05 THE TRAVELLING EYE
Granada visits one of the traffic trouble spots of the North – Barton Bridge.

7.30 TAKE YOUR PICK
Starring Michael Miles who asks the questions and awards the forfeits.

8.00 DRAGNET
The show that changed American television. A new kind of reporting. Actual cases from Los Angeles police files. Jack Webb as Sgt Joe Friday.

8.30 JACK HYLTON presents THE TONY HANCOCK SHOW

9.00 JACK SOLOMON'S SCRAPBOOK
Britain's famous promoter reminisces about the fight game, turns the pages of his Scrapbook and recaptures from historic films highlights from some of the exciting fights of the century.

9.30 NORTHERN SPECIAL

10.00 WEATHER
Regional forecast

10.01 WEBB OF CRIME
Ace crime writer, Duncan Webb of *The People*, reports on criminals and the social problems behind crime. Produced by Harry Watt

10.30   ALAN MOOREHEAD
        journalist, war reporter, historian and author of the
        recently published *Gallipoli*, reassesses the most
        controversial campaign of our times.

10.45   Independent Television News. Final Edition.

11.00   GOODNIGHT

Of the four Granada-produced programmes the 'Northern Special' slot had yet to be filled. Alan Moorehead's reassessment of Gallipoli took the form of the author reading one chapter. A studio discussion show, 'Pub Forum', was not ready (and when it did take the air in the next week was so diabolical that it lasted only two days). There was also a note from Harry Watt on my desk, sent on by Sidney, making it clear that we would be lucky if we squeezed more than one more half-hour out of *Webb of Crime*.

So that was the end of Webb (and of Harry Watt too, who drifted back to feature films). As the days wore on, things got no better. In the Barton Bridge show the presenter stood resolutely on the bridge in the pouring rain for twenty-five minutes, assuring us that 'any moment now' the bridge would open to permit the passage of a great sea-going vessel, which it never did.

The Barton Bridge fiasco was not unique. A visit to a gypsy camp introduced by the bright young assistant editor of the *Manchester Evening News*, one Harold Evans, later to become the editor of the *Sunday Times*, was marred by the disappearance of all the gypsies just as the programme began, leaving the wretched commentator to chat for a full hour with the gypsy 'expert' whose expertise was exhausted within the first ten minutes. Then there was the coverage of sand-yacht racing at Southport, when the timing of the tides had been poorly researched and the sand-racers were confined to an ever-shrinking area of sand until there was nothing to be seen but a jumble of masts, wheels and angry racers in an area about the size of a tennis court. Perhaps the lowest point ever reached by a television commentator occurred in a programme on Liverpool docks, in which, after the programme had actually begun, the union representatives refused to take part, leaving the commentator to quiz a sea captain, the only speaking human being available, about his ship, his last voyage, and his family, and then in absolute desperation to ask, 'Say, Captain, is that a blue jersey you are wearing?'

Nevertheless it was upon Outside Broadcasts that our schedule depended. Under our contract with the Authority we had to fill 15 per cent of our time on the air with local programmes, and nothing like this amount could come from the studio. So every afternoon for an hour or so there had to be a visit to a dog show, a glass factory or an exhibition of cheese-making. Today these OBs would seem grotesquely primitive, and even then they were exceedingly boring, but they caused a stir because the BBC did nothing of this kind and the experience of showing the North to the North in a workaday manner was something new and astonishing.

It was a hand-to-mouth business, and every day in the canteen I would sit surrounded by teams about to keep their appointment with destiny at some horticultural show or brass band contest. Not content with squeezing every moment we could from daytime OBs, we started on a series of evening shows as well – *While the City Sleeps* – and soon found that OBs at night were even more prone to disaster than by day. We arranged to start a fire in a street of abandoned houses to show how expeditiously the Manchester Fire Brigade would put it out. Unfortunately the fire was cued too soon and by the time the gallant firemen arrived it had burnt out, leaving the director with the problem of keeping the cameras focused on the firemen without showing the Granada riggers all around them desperately pouring petrol on the embers in an attempt to revive the flames. This sort of tampering with reality aroused the anger of some purists in our midst.

A show which was set up to cover the casualty department of a 'busy city hospital' yielded only one client in half an hour – a man who had cut his thumb with a penknife. A suggestion that it might have been wise to have a few plants in reserve – a battered wife, perhaps, or a violent drunk – was met with a blast of moral outrage which taught me that the methods of Rossellini and De Sica, who often used skilful subterfuge to create the realism for which they were famous, was not for the young lions of Granada. Soon the city was allowed to sleep in peace without the intrusion of any OB units or cameras.

But the OB units did score one mighty success. None of the top Granada people were football fans, but after Manchester City had won the FA cup we sensed, or were told (rather late in the day), that their return to Manchester and their parade around the city with the cup in an open-topped bus was going to be a huge local event. On the morning of their return we decided to cover it. At noon the OBs were called from their planned locations. Permission was obtained from the police, camera positions were selected and that evening Granada triumphantly transmitted full coverage of the slowly peram-bulating buses, the victorious footballers and the cheering crowds. It was a knockout and one of the local papers claimed that nothing so thrilling had been seen on television since the coronation in 1953. Granada's speed into action became the talk of the television profession: the BBC's record of quick reaction had been smashed to smithereens, and morale soared. From now on the OBs were always on the alert for a quick reaction call, and this was soon to come with an air crash at Ringway, which again broke records.

Sidney was not involved on this battlefront, save once, and then disastrously. On the night before a flower show in Liverpool, Dave Burton, the OB Technical Supervisor, dropped in to the studio manager's office where a group of us, including Sidney, were having a drink. He wanted to change the plan for the OB because there were two separate sites some 500 yards apart and he thought the cable run was too long for a single OB scanner and that we should use two. I told him that to pull out the second scanner would disrupt the OB schedule for the week, so we would have to risk it with one. We agreed on a revised plan for the cable runs and Dave returned to the site. Sidney listened to this discussion with interest. The riggers worked through the night in teeming rain and by noon next day there was nothing but bad news: water had got into the cable joints on the long run, only one camera was working, the show was due to start in two hours. At this point Sidney arrived on the scene. He quizzed one of the crew, who forecast doom and disaster. Sidney jumped to the conclusion that Dave Burton was not carrying out the agreed plan properly. He summoned Dave and asked him to explain why things had gone wrong. Dave said he had warned Mr Forman of the risk and was doing his best. 'Mr Burton,' said Sidney, 'I will accept no excuses. You are suspended from duty. Hand over to your deputy and return to base.' A witness of this scene later reported: 'The two men glared at each other, one a millionaire who had not the faintest understanding of the technical set-up, the other a professional engineer who knew that he and his crew were doing everything he could to get the show on the air. He lost.' Granada was not yet unionised but the crew rallied round Dave and said they would stop work if he gave the word. He said, 'No, carry on', and left the scene. Somehow the show did get on the air.

The next morning none of us were quite sure what 'suspended' meant. Was Dave to be paid? Was he to be punished? How did he become unsuspended? Victor Peers and I must have sorted things out, but the events of that night certainly speeded up the unionisation of Granada and became a part of union folklore. On their side they formed an impression of Sidney as a domineering autocrat with (in a phrase frequently on their lips) a 'whim of iron', and on his side the episode sowed the seeds of lasting resentment against the engineering members of the ACT (the technicians' union).

As the summer wore on it struck me that instead of sending out each OB scanner surrounded, like a great mother-ship, by half a dozen tender vehicles and with Simon towers placed at intervals to bring the signal home by line of sight (the whole flotilla manned by some twenty or thirty souls) it would be simpler to dismount the equipment in one of the scanners into one of the sheds on site and thereby create a rough-and-ready second studio, bringing programmes to the site rather than taking the OB units to the programmes. We also had the ingenious idea of putting a sheet of plate glass in front of a sort of cave which lay under the control room of our one little real studio, which meant that immediately our evening show was over we could run the cameras up the glass and cover a discussion between three local worthies who sat in the brightly lit airless cavern behind it. Thus was born the nightly programme *Let's Listen*, adding twenty minutes a day to our local tally.

Behind the flurry of getting a television service on the air lay the shadow of a financial crisis. As early as March 1956 Bob Fraser had said that the two companies operating – Associated Rediffusion and Associated Television – had already lost £600,000 and £700,000 respectively. (This was shown to be an underestimate when Associated Rediffusion published its first year losses as £3 million.) The wave of optimism on which the new service had been launched had given way to gloom. We consoled ourselves by reasoning that Associated Rediffusion was a notably spendthrift outfit (Granada had gone on the air with a staff of 345; Rediffusion with over a thousand); that the advertisers who were holding out against the rates set by the contractors must sooner or later capitulate; that once the four contractors worked out a system of networking programmes cost would fall, and so on.

Some thirty years later when, as Deputy Chairman of Granada Group, I was dealing every day with three-year and even five-year rolling financial forecasts, with biennial budget reviews, and with carefully prepared business plans for any new venture, I looked back with disbelief at the way the old Granada had entered into television. Although not privy in those days to the financial secrets known only to Sidney, Cecil and Joe Warton, I did know that Victor Peers had prepared an estimate of the cost of running the television service which had proved to be so wildly inaccurate that it became an embarrassment ever to mention it. I knew neither Victor's figures nor the actual cost, but Joe once let it drop that 'Peers led us to believe television would cost about a third of what it did'. The Crow history puts Granada's outgoings in the summer of 1956 as £20,000 a week, or approximately £1 million a year. Presumably Victor's figure had been some £300,000.

The sales side was better organised and the figures more accessible. In the autumn of 1955 Alex Anson had joined us from Quaker Oats as head of sales. A rough, tough, buccaneering salesman who went for every penny he could get, he supported the figure which Stuart McLean of Associated Rediffusion had plucked out of the air, setting the value of advertising airtime in London at £2,000 per minute of peak time. The advertisers howled with outrage. The companies stood firm. Alex set his rate card in January at about 25 per cent of Rediffusion's rates, the Northern Region viewership being about half of London's, and Lancashire without Yorkshire being only about half of that. There was no rush to fill the order book. The first night was nearly fully booked and we took £14,215. Subsequent nights dropped below 10 per cent of capacity. Granada was losing money at a speed that was frightening.

One can only speculate how three such wary businessmen as Sidney, Cecil and Joe could go into so great an adventure with so little calculation, and the answer lies, I believe, in the way they approached decisions. They did not waste time in seeking to measure and define what was imponderable. In this instance they would have noted the excitement within the Conservative Party and the City at the prospect of ITV ('They always know where the salmon are running', Sidney would say). They would have taken the view of a large number of people in show business, in the City and in politics, and analysed very carefully the pros and cons put forward by each one. And above all they would have been swayed by the success of commercial television in America. The opinions of the great generals of American television, William Paley and David Sarnoff, as well as those of Hitchcock and Jack Warner, would have been canvassed, and all would have been positive. They knew ITV could put on better entertainment than the BBC, that Granada could manage a ship more tightly than anyone else. Television had proved itself to be the best of all advertising media. The only question was when the advertisers would come in. And the best advice they got indicated that they would come in right away.

But they did not come in, and by June 1956 Granada was running out of cash. They had pledged the theatres to raise the capital for television. They had this debt to service as well as the haemorrhaging from television itself. Kemsley had pulled out of television long ago, Associated Newspapers more recently, there was a whiff of possible bankruptcy in the air: vultures, like Cecil King, were gathering round. Great efforts were made to conceal the cash crisis from the workers. Even greater efforts were made to cut costs, but since the direct costs of our shows were already minimal (*Sports Outlook*, £30 for fifteen minutes; *Let's Listen*, £20 for twenty minutes) there was not much scope here. During these weeks I saw little of Sidney, Cecil and Joe since they were in London and I was in Manchester. I was asked to stand by to visit certain leading advertisers with Sidney or Alex to ask them to support us now in exchange for some (mainly notional) future favours, and some of them did. Then one week in July the wages were paid late. (This was subsequently denied by Sidney, but the evidence is overwhelming.) When it happened a second time, we began to fear the worst.

Indeed, it seemed almost too good to be true when suddenly one day we learned the news that in a single bound Granada was free. Our cash problems were solved. Sidney had done a brilliant deal with Rediffusion. They would supply Granada with all of their programmes free of charge. In exchange they would take Granada's programmes and show them in London. No one (including myself) had any knowledge of the real terms of the deal, which were to remain a mystery until 1972 when Peter Black published his book *The Mirror in the Corner*. He wrote:

> The agreement had been signed by Sidney Bernstein and Spencer Wills on July 26, 1956. It ran to just over two sheets of foolscap papers. It provided that Associated Rediffusion and Granada would show each other's programmes. Granada would continue to make the 15 per cent of the programmes it was required to originate under its contract. Rediffusion undertook to produce or procure for Granada the remaining 85 per cent, not including the contribution supplied by ITN, and to reimburse the whole of Granada's operating costs. The situation was therefore that risks of Granada's television operation had been taken over by Wills' company. In consideration Granada undertook to pay to Associated Rediffusion the whole of its net annual advertising revenue, less an agreed proportion. The proportion of surplus Granada kept was calculated on a

sliding scale: 10 per cent of the first million pounds, 12 per cent of the next three million and 15 per cent in excess of four million.

The total sum taken by A–R within the four years was £8,044,238.

This deal was done without any consultation with the Independent Television Authority, who reacted to it with shock and anger because it seemed that a hole had been shot right through the clause in the licence which forbade collaboration between companies. But as clever lawyers talked, and finance officers did their sums, tempers cooled and the Authority, as was to happen so often in years to come, finally accepted the deal as an economic imperative and quietly endorsed the new relationship. But from now on any notion of competition between two of the four major companies was clearly farcical.

At the time, within Granada, there was a complete security clamp-down. At any mention of the deal Sidney, Cecil and Joe would look out of the window and change the subject. After the first burst of euphoria, when the rest of us spoke about it we would lower our voices as if speaking about cancer or VD. Even thirty years later, when all the facts were known, Sidney was still ashamed of the Rediffusion deal. Although he put a bold front on it – 'Granada has secured a London shop window, a thing we wanted from the start' – his sense of shame was both personal and corporate (Sidney often found it hard to distinguish between the two). Perhaps it was because he felt that independent, brave little Granada, when it was forced against the wire and its arm was twisted, had given way to one of the big boys. He also knew in his heart that the terms were ignominious. If ITV succeeded at all Rediffusion would take almost all of any profit. And for this there was no quid pro quo except the guarantee of a Granada window in London, which would surely have opened up anyway as Granada's programmes got better. But mainly he was mortified to stand by and see Rediffusion make such huge profits at Granada's expense. He had sold the mineral rights in his patch for a pittance to another operator who had struck oil and struck it rich. He could only watch helplessly and calculate what profit might, could, or – as he felt – should have been his. This was not a situation Sidney Bernstein could endure with equanimity.

So it was that when the days of prosperity arrived I was sent to test the temperature of the water at Rediffusion. It was chilly. A deal was a deal; all right, things had turned out better than expected for

Rediffusion, but this was the luck of the draw and no reason for read-justment. Granada's profits continued to be siphoned off, Rediffusion waxed fatter and fatter, and Sidney, Cecil and Joe lost more and more sleep. Eventually a more formal meeting at Golden Square was set up at which I was not present, but I happened to be passing the door when I heard raised voices and saw a furious John Spencer Wills, the Chairman of Rediffusion and its parent company British Electronic Traction, stride into the lift, scarlet with anger, leaving his aides to follow more decorously and wait for the next one. From then on relations between the two boards were frosty.

Meanwhile another, more personal, crisis was working itself out. Bob Heller had still not joined forces with the programme-makers in Manchester but remained aloof in his London eyrie. On his occasional visits to the North he spent most of his time in the Midland Hotel with his wife and son, only occasionally venturing out into the converted tobacco warehouse that served us as offices. I was curious to know whether Jolly Good made this trip with him, but never found out, since he left his London office locked and Jolly Good's coffin could have lain concealed amongst the very considerable pile of his baggage at the Midland. He spent most of the day brooding on network matters, but did issue the weekly transmission schedules and would occasionally discuss with me the future shape of Granada's programmes, being happier dealing with great concepts in the mists of the future than with problems such as filling two empty slots next Tuesday.

As the summer wore on he began to fall out with his network colleagues. On 13 June he wrote to Bill Ward of Associated Television:

> Dear Bill,
> I would appreciate it very much if you will send me at the earliest possible moment Minutes of the Afternoon Networking Committee Meeting which took place yesterday.
>
> It has been reported to me this morning by Granada's representative at that meeting that my personal contributions to the solution of network problems have been highly amateur. According to our representative this was the considered opinion both of Associated Rediffusion and Associated Television.
>
> I deeply regret that twenty years of active life in

network broadcasting and television have not brought me to the state of professional perfection which you gentlemen possess. Were it not for the fact that I am under contractual obligations to Granada I should be prepared to immediately withdraw myself from the field of Commercial Television so that you can proceed to pioneer this new industry with all the enlightenment and intelligence you have thus far displayed.

I had hoped to attend meetings with you on various subjects today and tomorrow in London. With the sincere desire not to complicate and confuse your discussions I have decided not to be present.

With warmest personal Regards,

Sincerely,
Robert P. Heller

cc Mr Sidney Bernstein, Captain Brownrigg, Mr Lew Grade.

He also began to resent any interference from Sidney or Cecil in his domain, as shown by this exchange of notes in July 1956.

From Sidney:
Could you please let me have the best play recommended to you by Narizzano [Silvio Narizzano, the senior drama director].

Bob's reply:
No. Have let drama go for a month. Will have to catch up. Ask SN yourself if you wish.

Once I found him in his gloomy office in the tobacco warehouse in an attitude of grief. 'What's the matter, Bob?' I asked. He raised his head from his hands and, looking at me like a whipped spaniel, he said, 'It's the brothers, Denis, it's the brothers.' I tiptoed away to the noisy turmoil of the floor below.

Nothing was ever said about Bob Heller's mental absenteeism. If I raised the subject with Sidney or Cecil they would look down at the carpet and quickly talk about something else. Victor would only cluck his tongue and shake his head. Then early in August Bob sent me a surprising memo:

Will you please make a list of all programmes, individually by days, which will require more than ordinary attention during your holidays in the last two weeks of August?

I myself will be leaving from the first day of September without any positive date of return. Between now and then I will continue to dictate notes about areas that will have to be covered. I hope to get them into your hands before you leave.

This was followed a week later by another memo, copied to Cecil and Victor but not to Sidney:

Re: Programmes Generally
I promised you that, before I left on holiday, I would try to leave you detailed notes about some of the tasks that may be added to your present burdens while I am gone.

I feel that I should add the information that my holiday is likely to be a very long one, and it is very much within the realm of possibility that, when I return from it, I shall only spend a few weeks in London and Manchester clearing my files before I enter other completely unconnected activities in the field of entertainment.

A list of notes on the forward schedules followed. I went to see Cecil. 'Bob seems to be leaving,' I said. 'I suppose it's OK if I go ahead and do the things listed in his memo.' Cecil nodded. A final memo was sent to me by Bob on 22 August 1956, whilst I was away on holiday:

Re: Weekly Schedules
Before I leave this week I will have issued weekly programme schedules up to, and including, week 41.

You will note that, in many instances, the schedules have had to carry TBA [To be announced] instead of the actual names of the programmes.

In the case of film, Cecil Bernstein will have the required information.

In the case of other live programmes, I assume the Chairman will have made the appropriate decisions.

And so the waters closed over the head of Bob Heller. His exit was casual and unremarked. Because he did so little there was no formal reallocation of duties. Everyone seemed to pretend he had never existed: it was like the old music hall song: 'Oh no we never mention her/Her name is seldom heard.' And yet Bob was a likeable and highly intelligent man who in years to come went on to mastermind

Associated Television's documentary output for Lew Grade. It was not so much his vanishing act that gave me cause for thought as Sidney and Cecil's absolute refusal to acknowledge that it was happening. We shall never know what became of Jolly Good, but the likelihood must be that he remained in his coffin for ever, because he certainly never appeared on the screen.

As the autumn went on desperate efforts were made to strengthen our national presence. In the North the local programmes had settled down into a reasonably professional run of studio chat shows kept on the boil by two informal and friendly television presenters – John Sharp, the survivor from the gazpacho débâcle, and Elaine Grand, an experienced broadcaster from Canada. Their show now graduated to the network, where we also had *Zoo Time* with Desmond Morris, educating his famous chimp Congo (whose paintings were shortly to sell in New York for thousands of dollars), a situation comedy and a couple of quiz shows.

When I joined Granada I brought with me a list of programme ideas, most of which fell by the wayside, but there was one which read 'a weekly review of the press: different voices for different papers'. When I mentioned this notion to Sidney he jumped at it like a trout after a mayfly. 'Good idea,' he said, 'like Liebling's column "Our Wayward Press" in the *New Yorker*.' 'Well, not exactly like that,' I said, doubtfully, 'because Liebling's column lists contradictory accounts of the same event, which is not exactly what I had envisaged. More to show how the editorial view affects new reporting. Comment is free, facts are sacred is baloney. C.P. Scott played around with facts, probably unconsciously, just like any other editor.'

But Sidney was already ringing for copies of that morning's papers, which reported the attendance at a meeting in Hyde Park variously as 10,000, 5,000 and a few hundred, and this wrangle was to last a lifetime. I never liked or wanted Lieblingisms, except perhaps as a throwaway at the end of the show, while he believed they should be the main ingredient. As time went on, assisted by producers, I got my way, but to the end of his life, when the origins of *What the Papers Say* were mentioned, Sidney – unless I was present – would claim authorship, and indeed Caroline Moorehead's biography records:

> Towards the end of 1956 Sidney decided to start a short, critical programme about the content of British newspapers – highly characteristic of him, given his ambivalence

about the press – based on A.J. Liebling's column in the *New Yorker* called 'Our wayward Press'. Once again it was to America he was looking.

Wherever he was looking, I had my eyes firmly fixed on Fleet Street.

We decided to invite the editors of the three leading weeklies to do the show: Brian Inglis, on the threshold of his long and happy reign at the *Spectator*; Kingsley Martin of the *New Statesman*, the guru of the literary left and a man more listened to than most within the Labour Party; and Geoffrey Crowther of the much respected *Economist*. The first two accepted, Crowther refused and we had to cast about to find a replacement from the right. Eventually we settled on John Connell, a columnist on the *Daily Sketch*. Early in November, in the week before the first show, Brian Inglis came to me and said there was no big news story running. What did I think he should cover? He need not have worried. Twenty-four hours before transmission British troops had landed at Alexandria and the Russians simultaneously invaded Hungary.

Brian's first script (he was paid twenty-five guineas for writing and performing it) was something of a masterpiece, conveying the sense of being present at the scene of momentous events and at the same time finding angles in the way the news was reported. The show was produced in the most primitive fashion. We were allocated Studio 4, the shed with the dismantled OB gear, two cameras, a teleprompt and a Peto Scott machine. One camera kept a fixed shot on Brian (there were no zooms in those days); the teleprompt machine, the latest marvel of technology, stood beside it on a thing like a music stand; the second camera shared the captions with the Peto Scott machine – that is to say, to allow for quick movement from caption to caption the director cut between the camera and the Peto Scott machine. This was perhaps the most Heath Robinson contraption ever to be seen in a television studio, consisting of a long canvas belt which passed underneath a fixed industrial camera. Captions were printed up and pasted on to the belt, which was cranked from one roller to another at a speed to meet the requirements of the script, by the producer – myself. Many years later when a journalist asked me what was the most frightening moment of my life, I replied, 'Cranking the Peto Scott machine', which left him a little lost.

The second week's show fell to Kingsley Martin. As the date approached he got more and more exercised. There were innumerable meetings in the *New Statesman* offices to discuss content and for Kingsley to read passages to me in order to ensure a tip-top performance. After perhaps a dozen drafts a script was ready. On the day of the performance I got a warning from the researcher in the Midland Hotel. 'Kingsley is sweating up a bit in the paddock.' And soon after, another: 'Kingsley wants to see you at once.' I went up to his room, tapped at the door. A distant voice bade me come to the bathroom. Kingsley was lying full-length in a hot bath, his eyes tightly closed. 'I don't think I can do it, Denis,' he said. 'I can't remember it. I've never been an actor, you see.'

'But I told you, Kingsley,' I said, 'You will have the whole script set out on a teleprompt.'

'I can't trust the teleprompt,' said Kingsley. 'There are certain distances at which I am sightless. This may be one of them.'

'We also have the scripts on idiot boards,' I said, 'and if the teleprompt doesn't work you can use them.'

'Will the man hold them still?' asked Kingsley. 'If there is any movement I find I can't focus.' He was clearly in a state of considerable alarm and looked like death. I went out and got him a large scotch. 'Kingsley,' I said, 'your bath must be getting cold by now. Put your clothes on, come down to the studio and we'll show you how easy it is.'

I went back to the Television Centre and sent the very pretty production assistant to bring Kingsley down to the studio. I went down to the floor and sought out the redoubtable Sister Ross, a veteran of the battlefields of World War I. I told her we had an elderly man performing in Studio 4 who looked a bit groggy and we had better have a doctor present in case he needed attention. By now Kingsley had arrived and started to rehearse. At first he rattled off his script like a machine-gun, but soon the studio therapy (and an especially long session in make-up) began to relax him and he had settled down into a sort of anticipatory coma when Sister Ross marched in, a doctor at her heels and shouted, 'Where's the old man who needs a doctor?' Kingsley perked up at once and looked around eagerly to see who might need a doctor. 'Who is the doctor for, Denis,' he asked. 'Never mind, Kingsley,' I said. 'It's time to stand by.' The show was bad but not quite disastrous, and we persevered.

His second show passed off slightly better and, finding that Kingsley paid little attention to what you said to him but absorbed every word if it were written down, I sent him a note explaining that the less he worried the more relaxed – and therefore the better – he would be. But it did not really do much good, and it was no surprise when, after the third programme, he decided that television performing interfered too much with his editorial duties and retired gracefully to Great Turnstile Street.

Another hazard lay in the path of the new show. Bob Fraser reluctantly decided that it was not in accordance with the Television Act to have three political points of the compass. Every show must be politically balanced *within itself.* As an ex-journalist he sympathised with our dilemma. 'But Denis,' he said, 'the rules are too clear for me to bilk.' But were they? An intense period of lobbying followed. We had already got rid of the Toddlers' Truce (a close-down period to allow the very young to retire to bed) and of the forty-eight-hour rule, which decreed that no topic to be discussed in the House of Commons could be mentioned on television during the preceding two days. Now we had to get rid of this, in our opinion, ridiculous ruling. After several weeks of wrangling, during which the show never came off the air, Bob Fraser conceded. The precious right to 'balance within a series' had been won.

And so was launched the longest-running show in the history of British television – and almost certainly of world television – which, as I now write forty years on, still runs, albeit through a window provided by the BBC instead of ITV. And this perhaps is the time to look back over its 2,000 or so editions and salute the memory of the Great Cham of *What the Papers Say*, Brian Inglis, who pioneered and masterminded the early programmes; the indefatigable director of over 1,000 editions, Peter Mullings; and the succession of learner-producers who later became mighty men of television – Jeremy Isaacs, Tim Hewat, Derek Granger, David Plowright, Barrie Heads and more.

At a stroke the programme gave television the weapon it needed to help keep a mainly hostile press at bay. As the years rolled on it became feared and respected in Fleet Street, the *What the Papers Say* annual awards gaining a status as high as or higher than any of the internal accolades. But mainly it has given the brightest journalists of the day a chance to monitor the fourth estate under the guise of reviewing the weekly news. Its stock in trade has been its fearless assault on editors and proprietors alike, conducted with an air of debonair impudence.

Another show, with a career shorter than that of *What the Papers Say* but more hectic, was *Under Fire*. Bob Heller had been pressing me to devise a North versus South show that could be networked with Rediffusion. At the end of July 1956 I sent him a note, from which the following is an extract:

> I suggest a programme based upon an attitude towards
> politicians which is prevalent through the whole of Britain
> at the moment, which can be summed up in the words of

a performer on *Let's Listen* – 'the Conservatives are bad and if anything Labour is slightly worse. At the next election I would like the freedom to vote against both of the major political parties.' This disillusionment is a respectable form of Poujadism.

I would like to give the most vocal critics of politicians a chance to harass them in public – and, 'in order to conserve the status of our political institutions', the politicians a chance to answer back. The show is, in essence, the Country *v* Westminster and Whitehall.

Robin Day accepted the role (later to be filled by Bill Grundy) of anchor man and intermediary between the VIPs in London and the Manchester mob and it turned out to be a bit of inspired casting. Week after week angry Northerners bombarded startled Government ministers and company chairmen with blunt questions about the service they were supplying to the forgotten people of Yorkshire and Lancashire. But soon the grievances of Granadaland were exhausted and the programme's catchment area spread over all of Britain outside the South-East corner – the people of a Welsh village who were about to be moved out to make room for a new reservoir, aircraft workers on the Isle of Wight threatened with unemployment, crofters in Uist who objected to the imposition of a rocket range, and many other groups, all seething – and soon the show became Whitehall *v* the rest. On one occasion we advertised a special edition featuring a bitter intra-union dispute between Hugh Scanlon (Manchester) and Jack Jones (London) as 'The Contest of the Year'!

The programme lived up to its billing in terms of animosity, but it was a fight neither side could win by argument and as the lights went down in the studio it became physical. Robin Day and myself found ourselves on the floor trying to quell violence between the supporters of the two factions. This was the only time in television I found my experience as a one-time amateur heavyweight to be useful.

One of the hazards of this quick-fire show was the possibility of an embarrassing or wholly irrelevant question coming from the floor. After a particularly rowdy programme on blood sports a distinguished-looking elderly woman sidled up to the producer and explained that she had a very important question to ask but had failed to catch the chairman's eye. Would the producer help her to put the question to the Minister personally? Of course he would, said the producer, and what was the question? 'I wanted to ask him,' said the lady, 'why there are so few lavatories at lay-bys.'

It is hard today to comprehend the extent of the shock suffered by those of the ruling classes who watched this uncouth and unruly programme, which they perceived as a socialist ploy against the Conservative government then in power. In June 1958, the Tory Central Office whipped up a campaign against Granada based mainly on complaints about *Under Fire*, which culminated in a meeting between Lord Hailsham, then party chairman, and Sidney at Golden Square. Hailsham concluded his speech for the prosecution by accusing Granada of deliberately selecting obscure and incompetent MPs to represent the Tory cause. Sidney, who took enormous pains to be well-briefed for such an occasion, was able to tell him that every MP who had appeared in the programme had been sent to us by the Conservative Central Office. In confrontations of this kind the programme-makers had complete confidence in Sidney. There was never a fear that he would compromise or trim: indeed sometimes I was a little afraid that he might give an MP or an interfering officer of the Authority too hard a time or be so adamant with a Minister as to generate even more establishment hostility to Granada. We had plenty already.

From the time of going on air there had been talk of making plays. We had one director, Silvio Narizzano, who had worked in television drama in Canada, and who had been enticed to join Granada on the understanding he would be our senior drama director. As it turned out we made no drama for the first six months, and since he was our only experienced director he had to turn his hand to more humdrum shows, and had also spent much of his time training the bunch of tyros we had recruited mainly from the theatre and pushed through a hastily organised directors' course in London. Silvio stuck it out until he got Sidney to agree in October 1956 to put on an undistinguished little play about a crooked footballer with the rather dreadful title of *Shooting Star*. Shortly after that our play reader, Ernest Borneman, sent round a memo:

> On Thursday 24 May I saw John Osborne's new play *Look Back in Anger* at the Royal Court Theatre, Sloane Square.
>
> Let me say straight away before I report on plot and acting that I think this is the most powerful play by an English author that I have seen in the last six years.
>
> Some of the play is so atrocious as to be almost unbearable. At the same time it is written with astonishing skill. Osborne's dialogue is brilliant as it veers between the

idiomatic and the epigrammatic. In its present form the play is unthinkable for television for the language is completely frank, abounding in four-letter words, and the situations are such as to make most advertisers shudder!

We all went to the Royal Court. We were all bowled over. This was just the sort of play Granada should put on. But there could be no question of doing it, or indeed of doing any play, until the cash crisis was over. In October, Sidney made the first move. We wanted a national audience for *Look Back*. Would Cecil check the reaction of John McMillan, the programme chief of Rediffusion? Cecil told him the play was unusual, very special, very powerful. Knowing the mood of Rediffusion in those days, I can only think that McMillan must have reacted by telling Cecil that Granada must be mad. What wiles Cecil used and what bargaining counter he had to forfeit to persuade McMillan I do not know, but within a week he had done it. Lew Grade was not so tough a proposition, for he had not heard of the play and I have reason to believe that Cecil told him it was a rather unusual love story.

Then the news broke that the BBC were going to televise an excerpt. We were daunted but unshaken. Sidney asked a number of cinema managers to watch the extract and to report. They were unanimous:

> The masses do not generally like this type of theme.
>
> The bad language was unnecessary. Not a play for the majority.
>
> Sordid and unedifying, with the 'bloodys' and 'bastards' it would shake a lot of family viewers.
>
> If this writer could turn his talents to a really commercial play instead of 'plays with a message' I am sure he could be successful.

I remember reading these dismal little notes with mounting fury and looking back with retrospective anger at the way this kind of exhibitor mentally had smothered the talents of the younger generation of British film-makers. I felt like ringing Lindsay Anderson and Karel Reisz and telling them that the jig was up and they should set up shop in Paris right away. They could never lick the suburbanity of the British exhibitor.

Meanwhile we had to get the show on the air. Silvio had never worked with British actors. Tony Richardson, who had put the play on the stage, had never worked in a television studio. Our Studio 2 in Manchester was thought to be too small (though looking back today, I cannot for the life of me see why Jimmy Porter's modest little flat could not have been fitted into an area which was shortly to have enough room for the aeronautical adventures of Biggles). In the end we borrowed a larger studio from ABC in Didsbury. Silvio directed the cameras, Tony directed the actors and I sat behind doing, as it turned out, nothing.

The rehearsals went well, the crew was enthusiastic, but a deep sense of apprehension built up outside the studio. Alex Anson, the Sales Director, called me and said he was anticipating disaster. Calls were coming in from other sales directors – could we, even at this late stage, cut out half an hour? Ernest Borneman, who had edited the script (very little) to make it acceptable on television, was suddenly seized with panic and rushed into the control room with a sheet full of deletions. 'I have decided,' he said in his strong German accent, 'we go too far. Damns and sods I leave in. Lavatory pieces I leave in. I take out six bloodys and four bastards.' I led him quietly to the rear and over a cup of tea explained that the actors now had their parts fixed in their minds and it was not possible to change them. His hand was shaking so much that he crushed his paper teacup and spilled tea all over his trousers. He was suffering the censors' nightmare that the whole nation was going to ring up in disgust and fury and write to *The Times*.

Before transmission I made a quaint little speech to camera:

> My name is Denis Forman and I am speaking for Granada.
> *Look Back in Anger* is a play for adults and we at Granada feel that parents should know this so that you can send the children to bed. We're giving you this warning not because it is a sensational play, but it deals with love and hate in language that is very direct.
> If you are over forty-five, I think I should tell you that some critics think it is not very suitable for you either.

The transmission passed off. Although there were 700 shots scripted for the ninety minutes' run of the play, there was only one lens change in vision. The actors were full of steam and the sets looked appropriately dowdy. As soon as the show was over I knew from the telephone calls we were all right. The next morning the press coverage was enormous and we gloated over it:

Bouquet – a big one – to Sidney Bernstein for his courage and initiative. This angry bitter scary play . . . was perfect for TV.

It arrested the attention from the moment it opened. Rough language, brutish humour, poured in a torrent from the TV screen into millions of homes.

Not all were favourable: 'I look back in anger when I recall how that horrid child Jimmy Porter spoiled my evening. I don't blame the cast. I blame Granada. Surely they read the script.' But the greater triumph was that there was not one single complaint over the bad language and the ratings were 62 per cent, more than double the level predicted by the sales departments. *Look Back in Anger* was Granada's first major victory over the caution, the conventionality, the cowardice of those custodians of the business interests of the media. It proved that at least in this case we knew what the public wanted and they did not. It proved that in those days when the IBA sucked its teeth over every expletive more vivid than 'damn' our viewers would accept, in its proper context, language as she was really spoken.

In that first year Sidney was everywhere. He watched every Granada programme, often slipping out of a theatre early or disappearing from an evening meeting in order to do so. After each programme he sent notes. They were usually addressed to me but sometimes to the director as well. After an evening with two or three Granada programmes the notes fell next day in Manchester like a snowstorm. Their critical range was wide and no detail was too small to escape his notice:

Opening title Thursday had Granada in non stymie type stop. Please instruct design department this must never happen again. [This one a telegram.]

We should not allow commentators to mention people in the newspaper world – living or dead – like Lord Northcliffe, who the public would not know.

The word 'Manchester' on the speakers stand was not fully visible.

I noticed Robin Day didn't close the show properly. Is this part of the new plan? [*Under Fire*]

There were three 'good nights' again last night in the final speech by our announcer.

We should not have a palm on the set [*Youth is Asking*]

Too many pictures on the walls.

The last tablecloth was a 'check' one. Bad for viewers. Nothing should be done to take the viewer's eye off the main character.

Unhappily for him, but perhaps luckily for us, he could not see the local programmes that went out in the North, for it was here that some trial and a great deal of error took place. I had the duty of reporting to Sidney and Cecil each week on the local output and there can be no doubt my notes tended to look on the bright side:

Watched *Guest in the House*. In spite of efficient production and gallant effort by Petula Clarke, I didn't find much in the hour to ennoble the human spirit.

Local News has now run all week and has shown that Heads can provide really first-class copy and at least one of the three Newscasters could be good. Geoffrey Cox [then the Editor at ITN] wants to sign him up if we don't want him.

Under Fire a bit quiet but good reasoned discussion of the Death Penalty. Silverman and Angus Maude.

Youth Wants to Know. Several variations from the previous night. Have found a suitable Chairman at last – Hubert Gregg, Pat Kirkwood's husband. Owing to last-minute change in format shooting was untidy. Next week – Lord Tweedsmuir for Emigration and Bob Boothby against it.

Sometimes they were more frank:

Comment not good. Robin Day introduced Randolph Churchill, Kingsley Martin and Ralph McArthey. Robin Day's introduction and Granada credit card cut off in the South. Churchill sober, but completely out of hand – Kingsley crucified and poor Ralph McArthey in a state of terror. Several production points wrong. This particularly annoying since Tom Driberg had given up whole column to this show in the *Statesman* of the same day. Most people thought it a lively 10 minutes, but it wasn't good enough. Dinner after the show an uneasy feast. Kingsley choking with emotion.

The memory of that dinner is only too clear. The discussion got round to the subject of mental illness, on which we were preparing a show called *Insanity or Illness* in which Kingsley Martin was going to advocate the humanitarian view to which he was deeply committed. Randolph Churchill could not understand why there should be any debate over the matter – 'Either a fella's mad or he's not mad,' he said, striking the table with heavy blows. Kingsley did indeed choke, went white, lost his appetite and finally left the table as Randolph ranted on, accusing half the inmates of mental asylums of being scroungers on the state and more of the same kind.

It was mainly Sidney's scrutiny of programmes that led to a conflict between us which was gradually to become more acute. Sidney was a perfectionist and he expected every man to do his duty perfectly. When he saw a miscast artist, a lens change in vision, a missed caption, he immediately reached the conclusion that the director was incompetent and should go. Of the sixteen or so directors appointed in the first year at one time or another Sidney wanted to fire all but two. The procedure was always the same. He would call me to his office. 'Did you see *Make Up Your Mind* last night?' he would ask.

'Yes, I did,' I would reply.

'Disgraceful,' Sidney would say. I had learnt that at this stage it was best to keep quiet.

'The compère had no idea what he was doing. Asked the wrong questions. That silly little gal held the prize up to the wrong camera. Badly shot. I couldn't read the caption with the result on it. Disgraceful.'

'Sidney . . .' I would say, but it was probably still too soon and he would run on for another minute or two until he reached the question we were both waiting for.

'Who was the director?' (He knew who the director was and I knew who the director was, but now I had to speak his name as if he were being formally charged in court.)

'Herbert Wise,' I said.

'Ah, Mr Weitz,' Sidney would say. (It was an early sign of displeasure when Sidney moved from a person's Christian name to his surname, and his hostility became certain when he began to mispronounce the surname. The final stage came when he was unable to recollect the name at all.)

'Mr Wise,' I said.

'Was it Mr Zeiss who directed *What the Papers Say* last week?' Sidney would ask.

'Yes,' I would say, 'Mr *Wise*.'

'That was disgraceful too.'

Then a pause. 'Denis, I think we should let Mr Witz go.' (When it came to a firing, Sidney always spoke as if the person at risk was an unwilling prisoner of Granada. In vain I would say, 'But Sidney he doesn't *want* to go. He is happy here. Granada is his life, he loves it.' Sidney would persist in the fiction that we were somehow doing a person a kindness in letting him go to some unspecified happy land where he would be freed from the pain and grief of Granada's high standards.)

'Sidney,' I would say, 'I think you should know that on the day of the show the regular compère, David Jacobs, phoned in to say he was sick and couldn't make it. Jim Johnstone, who you saw doing it, had only two hours' rehearsal. Max Witts, the regular floor manager, was called down to London by you to attend a conference about the new studio. Herbie Wise went on the air with a compère and a floor manager who had never done the show before. I thought he got through it magnificently.'

There was seldom any argument. Sidney had sounded me out. We both knew that I would win round one. At worst I would defend every director on the grounds that he was still 'in training' and it was too early to judge. But sometimes I knew in my heart that a director would not make it and Sidney was quick to pick off a victim when I wavered.

Perfectionism was the reason for his disillusion. The famous — sometimes quite irrational — whim of iron was another. Once he had taken a stand it was next to impossible to persuade him to change his mind. A well-documented example of this was the early firing (or resignation) of Therese Denny, a senior researcher and one of Sidney's most trusted lieutenants. She had, after due consultation (though not alas with Sidney), booked Trevor Huddleston for the opening show of *Youth is Asking*. Sidney, who was always suspicious of people with a reputation for unblemished holiness, did not like Trevor Huddleston. One evening, about ten days before the show, he evidently told her — without reference to anyone else — that Huddleston could not appear. She resigned from the show. The next morning he sent her a note:

Dear Therese,
Mr Warton is not in this morning, so it will not be possible for you to give him your resignation submitted last night.
    As the programme *Youth is Asking* has to be taken over immediately by someone else — I don't quite know who —

I think the sensible thing would be for you to take leave of absence as from today. This will allow freedom of action for your successor, and will probably be less embarrassing.

I don't know what are the legal and moral obligations of your resignation, but I am sure that Mr Warton and Mr Peers can settle them satisfactorily.

Will you please hand all the papers on the show over to Miss Haselwood today.

I am sorry that you have resigned. Thank you very much for all the help you have given us since you arrived.

To which she replied:

Further to our discussion on Friday night, I would like to hand in my formal resignation. I am not resigning because of your refusal to accept Father Huddleston as the first personality in the Youth programme – I accept this as your prerogative – but I am resigning because to me this is a moral issue of some importance.

If I may, I will recap the circumstances that have led to my resignation. Three names were discussed for the Youth Programme with Denis Forman and Harry Watt, whom I accepted as having the authority to approve the List. The names were General Glubb, General Horrocks and Father Huddleston. General Glubb agreed to appear in the programme but was not able to be in Manchester on its opening date. General Horrocks equally was not available; which left Father Huddleston. As his name was accepted and as at the moment he is of far greater news value than either of the other two, a fact to which any of the daily papers of the last few weeks will bear witness, we managed to engage him after a considerable amount of trouble which included telephoning the head of his monastery for permission to appear on Commercial Television and cancelling a meeting at Father Huddleston's old school, to which he had previously committed himself. His final agreement to appear in the programme only came through on Thursday just before I left Manchester, and I reported it to Denis Forman. Mr Forman certainly raised no objection at the time and I must confess that I was delighted that we had been able to achieve such a personality as our first guest.

Then came your refusal to accept him on the programme or to discuss the issue in any sort of reasonable way. As I understand it, your argument is that he has appeared on BBC and Independent TV News; yet General Glubb has appeared on Television on more occasions than Father Huddleston, and General Horrocks has his own programme on the BBC and no objection had been raised to this. Your other point was that he is a man who cannot be 'attacked'. Nor could either General Glubb, General Horrocks or Sir Miles Thomas.

In view of all this, therefore, I have come to the conclusion that one cannot give loyalty when one is not trusted. I deeply regret what seemed a happy and exciting assignment should have ended in this way. I equally regret that it should have ended in the terms of your letter sent to me on Saturday morning.

To this Sidney gave a reply that seems strangely adrift from the real issues:

Dear Therese,
I have your note of 23rd April. Your recollection of our meeting does not tally with mine.

The original programme idea, prepared by Harry Watt with the suggested revision by Bob Heller, has not, and will not, be changed.

You have 'us' wrong in thinking we want anybody attacked – but then a correspondence on this won't be profitable to either of us.

And finally Therese, in a letter which also refers to some earlier meetings:

My dear Sidney,
Thank you for your letter which I received today.

As to 'having you wrong' – I am sorry. Your actual words to me on the telephone on Friday afternoon were: 'He [Father Huddleston] is too fine a man to be attacked.'

You very rightly say 'a correspondence on this won't be profitable to either of us', but I hope you will accept it when I say that very sincerely I wish you every possible success with your venture. And I do hope, Sidney, that one

day in the future – even if it cannot be for some time – we
can meet again 'on neutral ground', with great friendliness
and with both of our senses of humour restored.
Yours *most* sincerely

Clearly Therese was right and Sidney was wrong. He refused, at the
time and after, to discuss the matter with anyone, which may help to
explain the apparently ignoble role played by myself and Harry Watt,
who should both surely have been outside Sidney's door offering our
own resignations when such a spirited lady was being dismissed
because of an engagement we had sanctioned. Nor was this a case
where Sidney disliked the victim. Indeed, until the Huddleston
episode, he and Therese had been good friends.

Amongst those early recruits there was occasionally an individual
whom Sidney regarded as what we came to call a *persona non
Granada*. His reputed antipathy to the wearers of wrist-watches and
suede shoes was a myth, but he disliked sharp dressers and those who
sported flashy ties, especially if they had a matching handkerchief
sprouting out of their breast pocket. He once said he found it hard to
respect any man who wore brown shoes with a blue suit. He was
always aware of the way women dressed. He strongly disapproved of
anything like glamour in the office, where all women, no matter how
pretty, had to dress quietly, with no short skirts and no too-prominent
bosoms and certainly no trousers. Indeed the Bernstein prudishness
spread to the screen, and Sidney would sometimes pull me aside and
suggest that a low neckline should be raised or, when he thought he
could detect the outline of a nipple, that I should tell Wardrobe to see
that a slip was interposed.

Sidney did not care for obesity, and it was hard for him to warm
to a fat man and even harder for him to like fat women. Thus the
heavyweights on the Granada staff had a considerable obstacle to
overcome before they were on equal terms with their thin colleagues.
When the invaluable Joe Warton began to move steadily towards
corpulence, we found that those who used the Golden Square dining
room were on a calorie-reduced diet – no rich soups or sauces, no
potatoes and no bread.

But it was not so much appearance as character that would decide
whether an employee moved in the class of a *persona non Granada*.
Sidney liked speed, vigour, humour and plain speaking in the people
he worked with. He did not like pomposity or verbosity. One of his
most damning judgements was 'He's a bore!' Above all he liked people
who stood up to him. If you gave as good as you got Sidney respected

you. If you were evasive, apologetic or cowed your number was up; for Sidney had a rare instinct for detecting a weakling, and once he had them in his sights he could be merciless. But a show of spirit would disarm him. In the early days we had a researcher named Mary Hewat, the wife of Tim Hewat who had not yet joined us. Mary was a woman of rare quality but in appearance she was large and rangy, with the demeanour of an amiable moose. Sidney took against Mary, I believe mainly because he thought her woolly appearance was matched by a woolly mind. Mary was the researcher on *We Want an Answer* and Sidney kept sending little notes suggesting that more diligent research would lead to more important and more interesting public figures appearing on the show. On one occasion he complained about the appearance of the Bishop of Exeter, whom he did not consider worthy of such an honour. Mary was getting a little tired of Sidney's nagging her and her reply to this last grumble was a model:

To Mr Forman:
Herewith the list of people approached for *Youth is Asking* for August 1st.

Annigoni	In Jersey en route to Italy
R.G. Menzies	Leaving for New York
Jack Benny	Leaving for Paris
Herbert Brownell	Leaving for US
Vincent Massey	Said he shouldn't as Gov Gen of Canada and anyway was on holiday and wanted rest
Archbishop of Liverpool	Not big enough audience. Willing to appear at a better hour
Sir Alexander Fleck	Very firm 'no' to any TV appearance
Sir Jacob Epstein	No television
Evelyn Waugh	No
Viscount Alanbrooke	No
Sir Gerald Templer	Hates being seen. Doesn't mind sound.
Sir John Nott Bower	Unwell. Too much strain.
Graham Greene	No
Archbishop of Canterbury	Away in Aug. Debate in Commons

Earl Alexander	In Canada
Sir John Barbirolli	Tied up till May 1958
Sir Thomas Beecham	In France till next year
Christmas Humphreys	Away in August
Dr Edith Summerskill	Tied up till Sept
Sir Percy Sillitoe	Willing but unable to talk about security
The Aga Khan	Too busy in August
Sir Vincent Tewson	Tied up till Oct
Dame Sybil Thorndyke	Away till next year
Lord Woolton	Tied up till end Sept
Dame Edith Sitwell	Unwilling at present
Kingsley Amis	Unable Aug 1. Undecided otherwise.
Lord Beveridge	Unreachable (since booked)
John Betjeman	Tied up with BBC till mid Sept
Sir William Williams	Tied up till middle or end Sept
A.C.M. Lord Dowding	No. Manchester too far and programme time too short for serious talk.
Sir John Cockcroft	Too busy
Dr Robert Birley	Too busy till Sept
Sir Miles Thomas	On holiday till middle of August
Sir James Bowman	No
Prof Fred Hoyle	Tied up till October
A.J.P. Taylor	Busy till September
Frank Cousins	Too busy
Sir Hugh Casson	Busy

In addition there was a three-line whip in the House of Commons, which ruled out any top-ranking MPs. A telegram sent to Princess Grace of Monaco remains unanswered.

Hence at 10 p.m. Sunday night, the Bishop of Exeter.

Needless to say I lost no time in passing this memo on to Sidney and, lo and behold, Mary became a *persona Granada*.

It would be wrong to leave the impression that Sidney as an employer was an ogre. Intransigent he was, often hasty, sometimes unfair and prone to groundless prejudices. But once a member of the staff had passed through the SLB barrier and become a *persona Granada* he was their friend, ally and supporter against the world, although he would still apply the strictest standards should ever a *persona* – even one who was especially *Granada* – fall out of line. The majority of the staff viewed him with fear, respect and pride. He was in many ways their Monty. He won their battles. He was afraid of no person and no institution. He was witty, he was genuine and he was straight. Nevertheless many of them thought it expedient to keep out of his path as he ranged the Manchester studios.

In the two years since the episode of the exhibition brochure my own relationship with Sidney had changed once again. I was no longer an employee but a colleague. We had regained much of the easy familiarity of our pre-Granada style. We would dream up programmes which would challenge authority in one way or another and relish Cecil and Joe's horrified reactions. We would tease them with outrageous proposals that we never seriously contemplated. We would sit up until the small hours gossiping about the film business and talking endlessly about Granada itself. And when it came to differences of opinion – mainly over the matter of the poor persecuted directors – I knew exactly how far I could go with him and he knew how far he could go with me. There was no longer any question of his being able to fire people or to cancel a programme without my agreement (unless I was out of the country, when on a couple of occasions he did take unilateral action). We were both having the time of our lives, and on the first anniversary of going on the air I sent him a personal note:

> Dear Sidney,
> As I was just saying to Helen, I think this has been the happiest year of my life.
>
> > Yours,
> > Denis

To which Helen added a PS:

> Yes, but not (entirely) of mine.
>
> > Love,
> > Helen

CHAPTER FOUR

During our first year on the air Granada got a reputation as a broadcaster of radical programmes. In those days of placid news coverage and complacent current affairs programmes, *Under Fire* and *What the Papers Say* caused no small stir. In particular, Robin Day's acerbic tone of voice came as something of a shock after years of the soothing cadences of Richard Dimbleby, and Granada's irreverent approach to the leaders of church and state, and especially the Royal Family, contrasted sharply with the BBC's grovelling attitude. Granada soon became identified as the thinking person's television station, especially those thinking persons who read *Tribune* and *New Statesman*.

In June 1957 this was to change. Cecil Bernstein had bought the rights in an American quiz show, *Tic Tac Dough*, adapted it for the British audience and now presented it twice a week as *Criss Cross Quiz*. At the same time he had hijacked the BBC's best comedy producer, Peter Eton, and prepared a weekly comedy show, *The Army Game*, starring Alfie Bass and Bill Fraser. Both programmes instantly went into the top ten ratings and stayed there, *Criss Cross Quiz* going up to three editions a week and *The Army Game* being supported by a writing team led by Barry Took and Marty Feldman which was to serve Granada for many years to come. Granada could make popular programmes too.

Criss Cross Quiz signalled the start of the Granada tradition of making high-rating shows on a shoestring. It cost some £120 (direct) per episode. Over the next ten years Cecil was to mastermind *All Our Yesterdays*, *Cinema* and *University Challenge*, all of them produced on tiny budgets and all taking their place, off and on, in the top ten alongside the mighty *Sunday Night at the London Palladium*.

But Sidney and Cecil also had ambitions for a big-time entertainment show. They remembered the great days of the Stoll variety shows of the 1920s, in which clowns, classical musicians, famous actresses and great ballerinas could all be found on the same bill.

Granada had the site for such a show – the old Chelsea Palace Theatre, which had just been converted into a television studio – but they had neither the experience nor the manpower to put it on. Sidney turned to his American friends and asked the Music Corporation of America, then the most powerful group in the American entertainment business, to produce it. Because of Sidney's astonishing ability to cast a spell over Hollywood tycoons, the top people in MCA (Lew Wasserman, Taft Schreiber and Burl Adams) immediately entered into earnest discussions with the Bernsteins and, with mutual expressions of high regard, undertook to deliver a series of shows starting in September 1957. The title was to be *Chelsea at Nine*, the show of one hour's duration, and the transmission time nine o'clock on Monday evenings.

Alas, the first show was a shambles. In a long and detailed note to Burl Adams, Sidney mercilessly recounted the reasons why: the nominated American producer had withdrawn four weeks before the show, his successor did not agree with his concept and disliked some of the key people he had appointed; the new man had no time to plan the show properly; two days before the show went on there was still no script; the American star, a ventriloquist called Edgar Bergen, flopped. Granada had to make several last-minute bookings to try to save the day, and the second show was no better. Sidney and Cecil decided they had to move in themselves, and for the third and fourth weeks managed to secure the top American comic team of Wayne and Schuster, Charles Laughton, Yehudi Menuhin, Peter Sellers and Petula Clark, and in the succeeding weeks Anton Walbrook, Moira Shearer, Shura Cherkassky, Alan Melville, Marcel Marceau, Segovia, Elsa Lanchester, Mischa Elman, Julius Katchen, Stephane Grappelli and the top American stand-up comic of the day, Alan King. *Chelsea* became airborne. *Chelsea* was a success.

But *Chelsea* was also a man-eater. Sidney and Cecil had little time for anything else. From morning to midnight they were on the phone persuading their many friends in show business to cut loose for three days from whatever dates they might have in their diaries and to appear on *Chelsea*. As a result Granada became a name of ill-omen with agents who several times a week had calls from their artists beginning 'Sidney Bernstein has asked me as a personal favour . . .' The brothers attended rehearsals together. They vetted numbers for the regular song and dance troupe (the Granadiers). They chaired planning meetings and post-mortems. They grappled with problems of production and design. They monitored the selection of members of the live audience, the menus in the canteen, the shift patterns for the cleaning ladies and the nature of the disinfectant to be used in the lavatories. It soon became clear that they had not much time to do anything else.

Victor Peers was the first to grumble that he could never get a brief for his many industry meetings. Then Joe Warton pointed out that it was not appropriate that the two chief executives of the Group should spend the bulk of their time producing one show, however important and however much they enjoyed it. I think it was Joe's allegation of enjoyment (which was true) that stung them into action; at any rate some time before Christmas 1958 I was told I was to take over *Chelsea* in the new year. I asked who would take over the Manchester programmes from me. There was no answer to this. I had to do both.

So began the most hectic six months of my life in television. On Thursday in Manchester, I watched the rehearsal of the Granadiers' production numbers sent up the line from Chelsea. On Friday night I took the night train from Manchester to Euston. On Saturday I caught an early train from Liverpool Street to Stansted, where I spent the day at home. On Saturday evening I went back to London, and called on the visiting artists in their posh hotel suites in the Savoy or the Dorchester, or some meaner abode where the cannier troupers would slum it to cash in on notional expenses. These meetings were wearing because after the opening round of bonhomie the main item on the agenda was cutting. Although each artist had been told precisely what length their act should be (the maximum was ten minutes), he or she always came with the *idée fixe* that they were going to play for at least double the time prescribed and that anything less would be an insult. It was particularly difficult to explain to a prima donna that she could not sing her showpiece aria in its entirety, or to a world-famous pianist that he could not play the whole of the 'Moonlight Sonata', and indeed even the first movement would have to be trimmed back by a few bars. There were some memorable tantrums, but in the course of twenty-six shows only one walk-out.

Late − often very late − on Saturday night I went home. On Sunday morning I was back in Chelsea by 9.30 for the general rehearsal. This finished at about five o'clock and was followed by a planning meeting and rehearsal of individual acts, which could go on until ten or eleven. Then to Stansted and back. On Monday morning there was a band call at nine o'clock off the premises, a first run-through at eleven in the studio (the stagger) a second run at five (the dress), then perhaps some panic rehearsals of individual acts until eight and finally the nervous hour of calm and quiet (the line-up), visiting dressing rooms, sorting out engineering problems, checking and double-checking timings.

Then for the show itself. It was too late to do anything now except to feel relief when an act came off and agony when it flopped. Then round the dressing rooms again – 'you were wonderful!' – chat and cheerio to the band and crew, and once again on to the road to Stansted, with the hope of getting there by 1 a.m. With extreme difficulty, I had extracted a car from Joe and Victor. They thought cars as dangerous as filming in 35mm: if you allowed them to one person there would be no case for refusing others. My car had been grudgingly conceded after a confrontation when I laid out in detail the logistics of my week – but it was for the run of the show only and I was to keep quiet about it. It turned out to be a clapped-out Austin 10, which had clocked up 100,000 miles in the course of being passed down a chain of cinema managers. Three times a week I found myself flogging this decrepit vehicle up the A11 at around midnight and down it at six or seven in the morning. Once I went to sleep and woke up in a hedge, another time the car spun round twice in the middle of the road (I think it did) before continuing placidly in the right direction. But I got three, admittedly short, nights at home and no other car has ever been so precious to me as that one.

On Tuesday morning there was a post-mortem at the Six Bells, the Chelsea pub, followed by a planning meeting. Then to the lunch-time Manchester Pullman (in those days a journey of four hours twenty minutes) and by seven o'clock back into the hurly-burly of Manchester programming.

During the summer of 1957 Sidney had said to me one day, 'Denis, we need help. We all have too much to do.' I agreed, and set about recruiting producers and potential executives with even greater vigour. But this was not what Sidney meant, for Joe Warton, on returning from a trip to Canada, mentioned casually at lunch that he thought Stu Griffiths might be persuaded to come. 'Who is he?' I asked. There was an embarrassed silence and Joe realised he had made a blunder. Then Sidney and Cecil, both speaking at once, said that Stu Griffiths was a very experienced Canadian television executive – he had been a producer and I must meet him. I would like him very much. 'What would he do for us?' I asked. 'Programmes,' said Sidney. 'Programmes generally,' said Cecil. I caught the drift of what was happening and nothing more was said until a week or two later when I urgently needed an answer to a scheduling problem. I could find no one around on the Golden Square sixth floor.

Eventually I put my head into Cecil's office and found both Bernsteins, and Joe and Victor, in close consultation. From the sudden silence I knew they must be talking about me. 'Denis,' cried Sidney, 'just the man we wanted! We are discussing who the Manchester producers should be responsible to when Stu Griffiths arrives.' This was a poser. I didn't know why Stu Griffiths was coming or what he was going to do. 'I suppose the producers who work on his programmes should report to him and the producers working on my programmes should report to me,' I said. Although I don't think this reply solved their problem it was hailed with general relief. Nothing happened for a week or so until a note went around giving particulars of Stu's experience, his date of arrival and a statement that he was going to have a 'general oversight over Granada's programmes and be responsible for programme policy'. It seemed we were going to have another programme controller – but not, I hoped, another Bob Heller. As I was ruminating over this memo, Victor came in and said, 'Sidney has asked me to tell you that Stu Griffiths is to have this office and would you please fix yourself up with an office elsewhere.'

I walked straight across the corridor to Sidney's room. 'Sidney,' I said, 'I don't know who Stu Griffiths is and I don't know what he is going to do. I will work with him and help him in any way I can. But I have been in that office over the road since we started and I am not going to move out now.' I had noticed that at critical moments Sidney was often helped out by some Granada-prone divinity. On this occasion the telephone rang before he could reply. When he put it down he said brightly, 'Did you see *The Army Game* last night? Much better, but we must get new captions.' The matter of moving office was never mentioned again.

Stu Griffiths duly arrived and was installed, with his wife and two children, at the company's expense in a flat in one of the Nash terraces in Regent's Park. I found him to be a friendly eager beaver of a man, but physically unprepossessing, charmless, and crass in his personal relations. There was an early example of this when he got some unfortunate member of the Savile Club to invite the Savile's lions of the day to a 'dinner with Granada' to discuss the future of British broadcasting. Many accepted, thinking that Sidney and I (who were both members) would be there, but many didn't, finding the wording of the invitation distinctly odd. I knew nothing of this affair until Michael Ayrton called me the morning after the dinner and asked, 'Who in God's name is this Canadian clown you and Sidney have hired?' Many old friends had been perplexed at having been invited to listen to a forty-minute prepared speech by a complete stranger comparing the virtues of Canadian broadcasting with the deficiencies of broadcasting in Britain. Later that day I said to Stu, 'I hear you gave a dinner at my club, the Savile, last night.' To which he replied, 'Yes, it is a lovely club, isn't it? We had a really great evening. Quite a lot of the people there said they knew you.'

Alhough I felt slightly betrayed by the way Stu had been smuggled into Granada and appointed to a post apparently over my head, I soon realised that the workaday values of this media man from Toronto were so grossly at odds with Sidney's fastidious tastes that his career as a *persona Granada* could only be brief. So I bided my time.

Meanwhile, although he was given the title of Programme Controller, it proved difficult to find Stu something to do. Cecil did not want him meddling in network affairs. Sidney was in command of all drama. There was no role for him in Manchester, where I continued to operate as before. He therefore busied himself working with the British/Canadian Mafia in London, developing a number of song-and-dance shows. These were so unremittingly awful as to form a serious threat to his honeymoon period with Sidney. Early in 1958 he came up with a show called *Melody Ranch* with Libby Morris, a Canadian comedienne of modest talent, in the lead, singing numbers and cracking jokes in a ten-gallon hat in front of a tacky ranch house. This turned out to be Stu's Waterloo. In the face of continued sharp criticism from Sidney, Stu tried to defend the show on the grounds that it got good ratings. Sidney's reply was curt:

> I don't remember ever questioning that there is an audi-
> ence for Westerns, or even for *Melody Ranch*.
> My criticism of *Melody Ranch* is its lack of style, bad
> taste in design, arrangement, costuming and direction.

The honeymoon was over, and one day Sidney said to me, 'I think it is time we did something about Mr Griffiths.'

'Why not give him *Son of Chelsea*?' I said. We had already agreed that I should give it up. The strain of trying to fill each week with talent good enough to live up to the *Chelsea* ideal had become too great, and the cost was enormous. We decided the series should be run on less ambitious lines, with a lower budget and transmitted at eight, no longer at nine. So Stu took on *Chelsea* and towards the end of the run ceased to be Programme Controller and became Head of Overseas Development, which meant that he was seconded to prepare a bid for a Canadian television franchise in Ottawa in which Granada was to have a substantial shareholding. In the fullness of time the bid was to succeed and Stu disappeared to Canada to become its Chief Executive.

I had been reluctant to give up *Chelsea*. When I took it over from Sidney and Cecil it was a true variety show, one thing after another, some goodish acts, some not so good, some stunning. It had no continuity, no overall character. In order to steer the team towards a distinctive style that would give it its own personality, I wrote an essay (a rare event in Granada) which put forward many of the show-business beliefs and principles that were to become a part of Granada programme philosophy over the years to come. Although the show was generally hailed as a success I was discontented. It would sometimes fall far below the standard of the *Chelsea* ideal and I had failed to recruit a school of writers to deliver what I believed to be an essential item, a weekly, bullet-proof comic sketch. Nearly forty years on, looking again at the bills and the reviews, I can see that I was wrong, as I was to be wrong several times in later years when I gave up on other successful shows because I was dissatisfied that they were not better.

Some memories of *Chelsea* linger on – Daniel Barenboim, dressed in black velvet knickerbockers with white socks and pumps, playing Liszt like a tempestuous cherub; one hundred guardsmen drilling on the stage to a Sousa march and then, as they crept up the stairs after their act to sit in the gallery, fainting by the dozen and having to be brought round with ice cubes slipped down their tunics – and Callas. I had managed to get Covent Garden to release her to do the second act of *Tosca* in the last *Chelsea* of the season and by that time we were able to videotape the show (on the first two Ampex machines to reach Europe). Somehow we had got an edition in hand (I think by taping two in Easter week), and immediately after taping the last show I went on holiday with the family to stay in a farmhouse on the edge of the St David's peninsula in South Wales. From there I wrote to Sidney as follows:

> I saw Callas last night on the most westerly ITV set in Britain. Mr Jones, the farmer, had installed the commercial aerial himself on Sunday. It was a perfect late evening in June, the low sun still catching the bright green islands and white farms. Everything as still as you can imagine. I walked along a cliff path counting down the minutes.
>
> What all this is about is to tell you of the impact Callas made when I returned to that farm kitchen, and I am sure in thousands of other kitchens all over Britain. The rest of

the show (the rest of television) they liked well enough, but immediately Callas appeared it became a great occasion — that rare moment in show business that you catch once in a million. I do not believe there is any film star or actress alive who could have matched her power last night.

In our preoccupation with schedules and ratings we forget that the future of television depends upon moments like these. Silvio did it in *Look Back in Anger*, and last night Callas did it royally. These things must create a loyalty with viewers of greater value than a high rating for *Sunday Night at the Palladium*.

By the autumn of 1958 things had settled into a pattern that was to last for the next four or five years. Sidney could no longer exercise a detailed surveillance across the board; and although his roving eye would light with uncanny accuracy on any programme that was below par, he ceased to send out sheaves of notes three or four times a day, pouncing selectively on carefully chosen targets. All light entertainment he left entirely to Cecil, Stu was running *Chelsea*, and everything else, except plays, he left to me — but not entirely, for we hammered out concepts for new shows together and now he could watch most network shows on tape (a mixed blessing).

Sidney had loved the theatre since he went as a boy with his father to London music halls. A play stood at the top end of 'theatre'. So now in television Sidney kept plays for himself. With the assistance at first of Ernest Borneman and later of Francis Head he read an enormous number of plays. When he had selected one he would talk with our two or three play directors until he was satisfied that one of them was worthy of the subject. Casting and set design were done in partnership with the director, not always harmoniously and with discussion lasting sometimes for four or five hours. The play would go into rehearsal in some Granada-owned hall south of the Thames. When the time was deemed to be right Sidney would slip into the back of the rehearsal room and sit there silently. When the rehearsal came to an end he would applaud. The director would then introduce him to each member of the cast. Sidney would scrupulously avoid any comment, and would merely say something like 'Thank you, Mr Quayle, for your performance. And congratulations on what you did in Stratford last season.' He would then drive back to Golden Square where, half an hour later, the director would join him. I remember Henry Kaplan, one of our Canadian directors, saying to me that the journey to Sidney's office after a rehearsal was the longest ride in

London. Then the debate would start. Once they had overcome their initial terror, directors liked working with Sidney because his advice was always practical: 'He is an inch shorter than the gel – give him lifts and cut her heels down.' He insisted that the author and the text be treated with respect; and he had an innate sense of theatre. He formed a close alliance with our leading drama director, Silvio Narizzano. Once, when watching a play with Stu and myself, he said, 'That boy is a really good director', to which Stu, with his usual tact, replied, 'You only say that because it's your show and he's your direc-tor. You never say that about any of our shows.'

What Sidney sought in a play was a social statement, for Bernard Shaw had been the great playwright of his youth. But he also required a play to be well made and well tried and tested in the theatre before he would venture to put it on. The early plays of his regime were selected mostly because they were available, were pushed at him by the drama directors, and had then passed the Bernstein test of 'something to say' and 'well made'. Sidney found both these qual-ities in contemporary American plays, especially those of Lillian Hellman and Arthur Miller, and in the first eighteen months when he was in sole charge of the play output, out of some thirty produc-tions there were eight from the other side of the Atlantic, including Miller's *Death of a Salesman* and *All My Sons* and Hellman's *Another Part of the Forest*.

But Sidney found that plays, like *Chelsea*, were too time-consum-ing. He wanted help and I told him I knew exactly the right man, Philip Mackie, my old mate from the COI days, now working in films in Paris and writing for the theatre. Philip was the most avid reader of dramatic literature I had ever met. During our lunch breaks at the COI we would take a bus to Farringdon Road and, whilst I sought out books on topography, Philip would look for plays, old plays, new plays, play collections or single plays in floppy actor's editions. His part of the house we shared was full of plays. The baby's cot was supported by Jonson and Goldsmith, and the Americans were under the kitchen sink, Restoration comedy was behind the sofa and the remaining space was littered with modern authors.

Philip was a man of generous size with large blunt features, curly hair and an engaging smile. He had a habit of speaking his real-life lines as if he were an actor playing the part of Philip Mackie, and only escaped appearing affected by playing himself superbly well. He had a ready wit, a roving eye and for ten years now had been my boon companion.

The first meeting between Philip and Sidney, over dinner in the

Midland Hotel in Manchester, was a disaster. Although emphatically warned, Philip, as he was wont, over-indulged in the Granada Mâcon (the cheapest good wine British Rail could provide). He began to tell anecdotes too roguish for Sidney's taste and then to patronise him, asking what experience of actually putting on a play he had had. (None.) I could see he was getting near the point of declamation, and just before he could swing into his favourite speech from *Coriolanus* I broke the party up. Next morning Sidney said to me, 'I think your friend Mr Mackie may be a little too theatrical for Granada.'

But I bided my time because I knew that Sidney, who always recognised quality, would sooner or later see that behind Philip's florid manner there was gold for Granada. The next time I arranged for Philip to meet Sidney in his office and things went better. In the Crow history Philip describes the meeting at length:

> We had one of those charming, and he can be the most charming and courteous man in the world, cups of tea in his office on the fourth floor at Golden Square, and he in effect asked me if I would like to be in charge of the play programme. This partly came about because I had written a very successful play called *The Whole Truth*. He asked me how much I had got for the film rights, and I told him, and he expressed surprise and delight (for it was a noble price), and I discovered afterwards that he had in fact rung around to check on how much I had got for the film rights before he asked me.
>
> The other two great moments in the conversation I remember were that he said he'd been buying some very good plays like Lillian Hellman's *Montserrat*, which she had translated from Emmanuel Robles. 'Yes,' I said, 'a great play. Why have you bought it? The BBC did it only a year ago.' And I saw a look flash into his eyes which said, 'Sack whoever failed to tell me that!' And then within a split second he reverted to his charming courtesy.
>
> The third great moment was that at one stage I asked him out of vulgar curiosity how much he was paying for plays, and he smiled rather winningly and said, 'As little as I possibly can', which I thought was a very good answer, particularly in view of the financial difficulties that ITV had been in.
>
> And the only other thing that I remember over the years from that conversation is that Granada had just done

Saroyan's *My Heart's in the Highlands*, which had got very good ratings. Sidney said, 'Why do you think it got good ratings?' To which I replied rather fumblingly, 'It was a good play, good production.' 'No,' he said, 'press advertising.' And indeed I remember that he had taken a lot of space in the posh Sundays and in the *Statesman* and so on.

Crow takes the story forward:

After the tea and colloquy Mackie was all set to join – until he met Victor Peers who asked him how much money he wanted. 'I named a modest sum and Victor fell backwards out of his chair on to the floor and that was the last I heard from them for quite a time.

Granada was expanding fast and there was too much for the existing top echelon to do. Mackie was re-invited to join, the money ('which was still very modest') was agreed, and in February 1958, 'after a charming correspondence with Sidney', he came to Granada to be in charge of Granada's play programme. He was not, it should be noted, head of the Play Department or the Drama Department. This subtlety was in fact the substance of the 'charming correspondence' and is an important insight into Granada attitudes.

'Dear Sidney,' Mackie had written, 'I understand that you are asking me to be the head of your Drama Department.'

'Dear Philip,' he replied, 'No, I am not asking you to be the head of the Drama Department. I am asking you to be in charge of our play programme.'

These fine distinctions, in Mackie's opinion, were based on Bernstein's 'old theory that you must never give people titles of any kind or they get above themselves – and besides, human beings being different they might be able to do only part of the job, or they might be able to extend it in a new direction, and you follow their capabilities rather than following a set theory of what their job should be – which is not at all a bad idea actually.' Indeed there are many people, including Mackie, who have found that one of the great charms of Granada has always been this flexibility, 'where you can suddenly go and do a documentary or write something or volunteer to do a programme of pop music or do any other damn thing, whereas everywhere else in the world is modelled on the BBC, all very hidebound, and if you are a play producer then that's all you're allowed to do. It's someone else's department if you want to do something else.'

During this time Sidney Bernstein continued to supervise Mackie, 'only too carefully in the early months', for Mackie's taste. He wanted to have a voice in the selection of every play, in the choice of the leading actors for every play, 'and,' Mackie recalled, 'in pretty well everything else about it. He used to make a massively charming appearance at a run-through of every play whenever he could. He would be introduced to the cast, he would watch the run-through and would applaud at the end in a very civil manner and beam around smilingly.' Things went well – except that Mackie, who wanted to go his own way, found his looming presence increasingly irksome and blocking.

'Many magical remarks came out of this period, I suppose the most magical being when Sidney said to me, almost pleadingly, "I'm not trying to steamroller you, Philip. I just want you to agree with me." And there was another moment when there was some new play – I think it was *Promenade* by Peter Nichols – which he did not want to do. He was then very post-Ibsenite and therefore Arthur Millerite in his views on how plays should be constructed, and the subtle structure of *Promenade* was far from this. Also he was very much at this time a believer that plays must say something, the message thing. He has a strong element of propagandist in him and for him as I suppose for Bernard Shaw plays were for propaganda. So I, in a passion of indignation, said to him, "The trouble with you, Sidney, is you only want me to do plays if they've been smash hits in London, New York and Paris, and have been filmed at least three times already." To which he replied, white with hurt and deeply injured, "What do you mean, Philip? I let you do Arthur Miller's *All My Sons*." "Arthur Miller's *All My Sons* was a flop on the stage in London" – which is the most superb non sequitur answer I've ever heard in my life.'

They proceeded 'by splendid disagreement'. There were stresses and strains all the time. Stresses and strains about money. Mackie wanted to do an adaptation of *Wuthering*

Heights. It would have cost £6,000 to produce, a sum which was derisory ten years later but which in 1959 was too extravagant compared with the normal £3,000 or £4,000 for a play. There was also the case of Richard Harris who, having as an unknown actor been paid £50 for the lead in *The Iron Harp*, so impressed Sidney Bernstein by his performance that he sent him a personal cheque for £25 as a bonus. Harris was immediately picked up by film companies. Mackie wanted him back a month or two later for another play. By this time he had got an agent and his fee was £110. 'Sidney nearly went out of his mind – "A hundred and ten? He ought to be paying us. We made him." – and Mackie had the greatest difficulty in getting the new rate agreed. 'If you could get Richard Harris to do a television play for less than ten thousand now you'd be doing very well. What was not quite appreciated was that we had originally cast Richard as the ten-line sentry and then we had promoted him.'

At this stage, and for some time to come, until the growth of the television side and then of the rest of Granada made it impossible to sustain even by someone as continually energetic and enthusiastic as himself, Sidney Bernstein's whole attitude was that he was the producer of everything, in the sense that a stage play had a producer and that Mackie and the others were deputising for him.

'His whole aim was to train us up to do what he would have done had he been there. First of all I had to see him all the time. Then a little less so as productions started coming out and they looked all right. And then it was merely the telephone call every day, and then the telephone call became "Hello, Philip, what can I do to help?" to which my standard answer became, phrased as politely as I could, "Leave me alone." So the telephone call used to start after a time, "Philip, you are noticing how I'm leaving you alone, aren't you?" "Yes, I am. Thank you very much, Sidney, and please carry on that way." '

However, there were still struggles. The besetting problem was to find plays worthy of the public attention. Sometimes the situation became fairly desperate. What with the choosiness of Bernstein, of Mackie, and of the directors there were very few plays in hand. Stockpiling of scripts was avoided, because to buy plays on the off-chance of producing them is both unfair to the author (who has a right to expect his play to be performed when it has been bought) and to the production company itself, which may thereby find itself lumbered with plays it no longer wants to produce but nevertheless feels it ought to for economic reasons if for no other.

The move from live production to tape was also a contributory factor to the problems of reconciling different tastes. 'Whilst we were live I could force a play through because even though Sidney complained that I was holding a pistol at his head – which he did not like – I could point out that we had to put a play out in four weeks' time and this is the only one I've got which is suitable. This pressure which occasionally helped me to get through a play I wanted to put on didn't always work because sometimes his answer would be, "Cancel the slot. We'll put on a film instead", which was his ultimate weapon. No one likes doing such a thing, and indeed I don't know that it ever actually happened, but that was the last ace in his hand if he felt he had to play it.' But with the move to tape Bernstein acquired a stronger weapon because it meant that plays could be stockpiled on tape and Mackie no longer had the argument that it must be one particular play 'or else'.

In due course the strain began to tell, even on the robust Mackie. When he first came he had firmly refused to sign a contract for longer than one year and towards the end of that time he told Granada that 'while it had been a liberal education' working there he was going to leave at the end of that first year. 'In the normal manner they rushed at me and threw pound notes all over me in order to persuade me to stay on for a second year, which I feebly agreed to do. Halfway through the second year it became quite clear that the strain of doing a play a fortnight is enough in itself even if you have total responsibility and total power and I don't think that anyone could or should do it for very long except with very long rest periods in the South of France or the Bahamas. But when you add to the strain the constant struggle it is altogether too much. So halfway through the second year I announced my intention to leave – which, rather splendidly, I managed to carry out. I had one magical moment when, as they always cried in those days, "But who can possibly replace you?" which in effect means "You've got to provide your replacement", I looked around and my eye lit on Derek Granger. Derek had recently come to Granada – highly intelligent, perceptive, ex-drama critic on the *Financial Times*, and at that time the best critic in London, and I thought he would be splendid. So I talked Derek into succeeding me – one of the big con-man jobs of my life – and left Granada, retiring into private life, whence over the next year they kept asking me to come and do things, so then I started doing things on a different and, for me, much better basis.'

The plays of the Bernstein and the Bernstein/Mackie regime gained great acclaim for Granada. Apart from the strong series of American imports and the many powerful one-offs they started a mini-revival of a series of Manchester plays originally produced for Miss Horniman's Gaiety Theatre, which had flourished some fifty years earlier. When I first heard of this project, I thought, 'My God, not all that stodgy old provincial stuff.' But I was wrong: the plays of Harold Brighouse, Stanley Houghton and Allan Monkhouse proved to be alive and well and a tremendous success.

Granada's plays were recognised as being in a class above the rest of ITV – equalling and perhaps surpassing the drama output of the BBC. Except for one thing. A lively and immensely able young television producer – Sydney Newman – had joined ABC Television, Granada's weekend rival in the North, and had started a series called *Sunday Night Theatre* (later *Armchair Theatre*) which featured original plays written for television. Equal acclaim with Granada was given to him, perhaps more, at any rate too much to suit Sidney. He found the Newman plays raw, untidy and sometimes coarse, and he entered into an underground war with ABC in a determined campaign to secure the top credit-rating for Granada.

Meanwhile, in his office in Golden Square, Cecil was discreetly conducting his own affairs. Together with Eddie Pola he worked on innumerable quiz games, mainly filched from America, most of which bit the dust at the stage of dry run; but one of them, *Twenty-One*, fortunately – or rather unfortunately – reached the screen. He presided over *The Army Game*, soon a national institution, and its heirs and successors, which was no easy task. Sometimes on a Monday, when I was in Cecil's office, Peter Eton would burst in. 'It's no good, Cecil,' he would say, kicking a chair-leg viciously, 'we simply haven't got a show this week. Only half a script and that's no good. They're rehearsing it now: tomorrow there will be nothing for that ghastly mob to do.' Cecil would reach for his phone and Barry Took and Marty Feldman would appear. Could they resurrect 'The Colonel's Cat', which was discarded three weeks ago? No? Then could they put in a new version of 'The Mess Kitchen', which always worked, and pad out the first half? Perhaps. After an hour or so the mood changed from one of total despair to inspissated pessimism and the team would return to the rehearsal room and work in corners, gloomily, until a script, which next week would convulse the nation with laughter, was completed. I was soon to learn that all the best people in the comedy trade were manic depressives.

Each Monday morning Cecil would have a telephone chat with Lew Grade. Sometimes he would take these on his own. More often his secretary would summon me, and Cecil would gesture me to take up the spare earpiece and listen in. 'Lew,' Cecil would say, 'if you're asking two thousand more for the Wednesday variety show I tell you I'm not taking it and I'll see the others don't take it either.' 'But Cec,' Lew would reply, 'just listen to the figures. Danny Kaye alone is costing two thousand, the girl singer a thousand, it's ridiculous, I know, but then she thinks she's a star, the vent is asking seven–fifty and that's without the other acts, the chorus and the band' – and he would launch into a whirlwind of arithmetic which soon left me behind and had even Cecil struggling.

'Lew, Lew, Lew,' Cecil would say, 'Lew, Lew, listen, Lew. I'll go another thousand.' There would be dead silence for a minute. 'That's my top, Lew. Any more and I'm not taking it.' Another pause. 'You must be joking, Cec,' Lew would reply. Pause. 'We don't want to start talking about *Coronation Street* at seven o'clock, do we, Cec?' Occasionally at this point Lew, who knew that I was often the dumb auditor of these exchanges, would say, 'Is Denis there? Ask him what he thinks is fair, Cec, just ask him.' Cecil would say to me, 'What do you think, Denis?' – at the same time pushing towards me a piece of paper with £1,500 scribbled on it. 'Here's Denis, Lew,' he would say, and hand me his phone. 'Lew,' I would say, 'I've listened to the pair of you and I think £1,500 would be a fair figure. But maybe Cecil will not go that high.' I would then hand the phone back to Cecil and Lew would say, '£1,500 Cec?' and Cecil would reply, 'Done.' No one had lost face. There was never a written contract between Granada and ATV, not even a confirmation memo. Cecil and Lew had agreed a figure, and that was enough.

The absentee from these telephone conferences was Captain Tom

Brownrigg, RN retired, Chief Executive of Rediffusion. He was a man from another world who could see little distinction between running a television company and commanding a battleship. He feared God, was passionately loyal to the Queen, and believed that the chief role of television was to reflect the values of England's glorious past. But he was a fair man, and once when interviewing a friend of mine for a job he told him, 'I require my staff to produce balanced documentaries of the right.'

Once a fortnight there was a network meeting of the three week-day companies – Rediffusion in London, ATV in the Midlands, and Granada in the North. After Bob Heller had faded from the scene only Tom Brownrigg, Lew and Cecil attended these meetings. But soon Cecil would take me along as note-taker and assistant. The showbusiness style of Cecil and Lew contrasted sharply with the naval demeanour of Tom Brownrigg. He called them Grade and Bernstein (which he mispronounced Bernsteen) when he had to, but preferred to call them by the names of their companies (as a Scottish laird is known by the title of his property). 'If Granada [mispro-nounced to rhyme with Canada] wants to do that and ATV agrees then we [probably the collective we but carrying a whiff of the royal prerogative] will have to consider our position.' These meetings purported to be brisk and businesslike, but educating Tom slowed them down. 'We have decided to move the play from Wednesday to Thursday,' Brownrigg would say. There would be a long silence. 'You can't do that, Tom,' one of the other two would say. 'Thursday's weak on the BBC and we are winning it anyway. To put the play then would make them a gift of Wednesday', and slowly and patiently they would go through the logic of midweek scheduling to help poor military-minded Tom to understand the ways the schedule and view-ing public interacted.

Cecil, as the most trusted of the three, was given the power to buy all the feature films for the network. At the same time, as the most trusted person in the cinema trade, he was charged with the task of preventing the rapacious television contractors from buying up all the new British films before they had earned their money in the cine-mas. Cecil juggled with these two contradictory roles with complete assurance. He raised funds from all sections of the film industry to form FIDO (the Film Industry Defence Organisation), whose purpose was to buy the television rights of British films and to with-hold them from television until they had reaped their proper reward at the box office. Hence the producers benefited, the exhibitors bene-fited and television lost little. At the same time, with the buying power of the network at his back, he set in train a series of strategic purchases in Hollywood and also mopped up large quantities of pre-FIDO British films. As Lew was the master salesman in the network, so was Cecil the master buyer, and over the years his deals saved the network companies millions of pounds, which to some degree compensated them for the realisation, somewhat late in the day, that they had paid Cecil, as requested, on the nail when the deal was done, whereas he had paid the film suppliers only when he had to, which might be months, even years, later, thus ensuring for Granada a tidy income from the interest on the very sizeable credit balance which accumulated in the bank.

Cecil found the work of previewing so many films onerous and he asked me if I could recommend someone to be his assistant. I said I knew just the man, Leslie Halliwell, who was running a cinema in Cambridge. Cecil, who was suspicious of my Film Institute friends, asked if it was an art cinema. Well, yes, I had to admit, you could certainly call it an art cinema, but it was an immensely successful art cinema. Cecil was clearly off Halliwell, and nothing was said for a month or two when, having tried several old hands from the trade Cecil asked me for help once again. This time I managed to persuade him to see Leslie Halliwell. Cecil was impressed to find that aside from art films Leslie knew as much about box-office films as he did. Leslie was given a three months' trial, and soon became Cecil's right-hand man, in due course succeeding him as Network Film Buyer, a job he held with enormous distinction until he retired in 1987. Leslie died only two years later, leaving as his monument his classic work, *The Filmgoer's Companion* and *The Film Guide*.

Meanwhile, two floors down in the Golden Square building, Joe Warton was watching expenditure. With Cecil he had little to worry about, but Sidney, who for most of the time was penny-pinching mean, at times caused him considerable anxiety. Joe thought (correctly) that Sidney's bursts of extravagance were mainly due to his association with me. He saw me as a baneful influence, a dangerous man who could inflame Sidney's imagination to the point where he might break out and spend recklessly in a manner quite unknown in the screwed-down economy of Granada Theatres.

An example of this was that when the money began to flow Sidney thought it would be a good thing for Granada to be seen as a patron of the arts. As so often, it was hard to distinguish between motives which were genuinely noble and disinterested and a shrewdly calculated ploy to enhance the Granada image. Opinions were canvassed on how the money should be spent and I responded readily and expansively. I suggested that in concert with the proper local and national authorities we should set up a museum of the Industrial Revolution in Manchester, celebrating the ancient and monstrous steam engines, the poetry of cast iron, the glamour of the coming of gas and finally the revolutionary power of electricity. If this notion didn't catch on I offered another, to bring alive one of the great Welsh castles, perhaps Harlech, as it was in its heyday. The castle should be bustling with people going about their everyday affairs, the rooms should be furnished, 'the fires should be burning, lavender scattered in the passages, the bakery should be working, the dovecotes populated and the cannons capable of firing ball.' The castle would be brought to life regularly, I suggested, on high days and holidays – and televised. This memo struck fear into Joe Warton's breast. His reaction was brief and to the point:

> I have seen Forman's suggestions regarding 'Contribution to the Arts'.
> The suggestions that we should develop a museum or get involved in refurbishing a castle are wonderful ideas for a wealthy philanthropist to undertake, but we seem to be completely forgetting that the money we are suggesting should be used for such purposes is shareholders' money and not our own.

Of course Joe was right. At that time, and indeed until I began to bear the burden of being a member of the Group Board, the idea that shareholders had any place in our world did not enter my mind. This attitude was best reflected by a Manchester colleague who, when a group of shareholders were being shown over the studios by some striped-pants man from London before a Group Board meeting, was heard to say, 'Who the hell are these people anyway? You would think they owned the place.' We were desperately keen to be efficient, cost-effective and profitable, for the sake of Granada not the shareholders, though I doubt if we could have explained what that meant.

Joe was the company's all-pervading financial deity, the great no-man of Golden Square, who personified the principles of thrift, conservative financial policy and correct business behaviour. As an employer his views were somewhere between those of a Victorian ironmaster and Thomsons of Dundee. He believed in strict office hours, as long as possible, for as little as could be paid, and short holidays – in an ideal world, none. The unionisation of Granada was to cause him deep distress, but in the early days I soon found that proposals for civilised working conditions always came to nothing once they reached Joe. I therefore took the reprehensible course of making agreements with sections of the staff quite independently of the Victor/Joe axis in the certain knowledge that a deal with any one group of employees would slowly but surely spread throughout the company. It was in this mood that I agreed that the dance troupe – the Granadiers, who were long-run contract employees – should have three weeks' holiday a year in place of the miserable one week offered to first-year Granada staff, rising to two weeks in the second. Once again Joe was not pleased. He wrote to Sidney:

> I think you must be advised that I am given to understand that Forman has given the Granadiers permission to take three weeks' holiday.
>
> This does seem crazy to me and quite unjustified and will in my opinion have reactions throughout the permanent staff at Chelsea particularly those whose holidays are limited to two weeks.
>
> I gather that a Minute of the Production Committee provides that they should have three weeks. Why three weeks is beyond me. In any case it would seem that this is another case of an executive acting outside of authority.

To which some unknown hand (not Sidney's) had added: 'EXACTLY!!' – a cry of joy at the discovery that at last someone had caught up with this dangerous tearaway.

Joe continued to watch me suspiciously for many years, until it became clear that Granada was by far the most profitable of the television companies and (for he was a fair man when there was nothing to lose by it) that this was no longer due to Sidney, Cecil or Golden Square, but to the local management, namely myself and my close colleague, the Chief Accountant, Bill Dickson. And indeed in later years in Group matters Joe and I sometimes found ourselves as allies in that we shared a simple horse-sense approach to matters that were made to look complicated. We both disliked hype, and we were both suspicious of the business-school babble which sought to find rules and theories to support concepts that were as old as the hills and, if new, often not supportable. It was only in this later phase that he ceased to call me 'Old Lad' or Forman and adopted the, for him, rare intimacy of my Christian name.

The last member of Granada's founding quartet was not so happily placed. In the run-up to the opening night and during the first stressful months of transmission Sidney had driven Victor hard. He had been Sidney's deputy and factotum, his site manager on a grand scale, and he had been Granada's champion vis-à-vis the Authority and the rest of the industry in matters ranging from labour relations to car mileage allowances. In November 1956 he had a severe heart attack: the doctors gave him a 30 per cent chance of recovery, no more. Sidney was struck with remorse and visited his sickbed almost daily. In notes intended for the Crow history, Victor later wrote:

> After about four weeks I began to look at a newspaper – and during that period the whole of the Suez crisis had taken place. It was over, and it was not any longer a topic of conversation or in newspapers. It was months before I knew it had happened. The other thing was this: the day Sidney came to see me – he came very regularly – and found that I was awake enough to speak he said, 'Victor, our worries are over. Our profits are as big as our losses were!'

For months he convalesced. Then he returned to light duties. Every morning Sidney and I saw him walking the four miles from the house we had rented in Didsbury to the studio. He walked as if his life depended on it, which it probably did. Gradually he started doing things again. In true Granada style he had no title, much less a job specification, so the fact that he did much less went without comment. He was sad, I think, to find he was no longer Sidney's right-hand man, for Sidney now dealt directly with the management people in Manchester who used to look to Victor as their boss. He persevered in his losing battle to establish a Procedure Manual, he continued to sit on the Board and the Programme Committee and to carry out enquiries into specific management items, but alas he was no longer a happy man and a degree of acidity crept into his dealings with others. In his later years even his loyalty to the Bernsteins, and especially to Sidney, who had been his hero and his leader, began to seep away. But never was there a suggestion of demoting him, nor of early retirement. Victor was one of us, he had earned his place, and he kept it until he retired in 1967. How unlike, how very unlike, the management ethos that was to come into fashion in the next two decades. Victor died in 1971.

A cataclysmic event in those early years was the arrival of tape. In the autumn of 1957 I had visited the Ampex factory outside San Francisco and immediately the huge potential of videotape was evident. A technical team followed and the first two trial machines were shipped in to Chelsea. Before they were run in, a further six were ordered for Manchester. At that time we were the only Ampex users in the UK. Then one momentous day an engineer in Chelsea slit a tape diagonally with a razor blade, took out a yard of tape and joined the two ends with Sellotape. It worked. There was a jerk, to be sure but tape editing had arrived.

Now began a mighty battle with the engineers. Reg Hammans had been wholly in favour of importing the machines because tape was a great improvement on the old kinescope, a film made from the electronic monitor, which delivered fuzzy pictures and could not catch fast movement without slurs and smears across the picture. But now he found he was looking into a bottomless pit. He could envisage no greater disaster than that tape editing should be allowed to become a general practice. And indeed in the early days a tape-stop to re-record a mistake was not allowed. Tape existed for the sole purpose of recording live transmission, and that was that. Every producer and every director could see that tape editing could transform our methods of making a show, but the engineers stood firm. Reg himself, writing retrospectively, had this to say:

> We succumbed to this very destructive philosophy of being able to stop the tape whenever we wanted for editing or for re-takes. It's destructive because it results in a perfectionist approach to television and pushes television towards a film approach. Tape had a two-fold effect on television: it destroyed its immediacy, and it put up the cost per minute of production enormously because it took so much longer; everybody knew they could force a re-take, and editing tape is less efficient than editing film in terms of the consumption of equipment-hours and man-hours.

Of course the engineers lost. It was greatly to Sidney's credit that although the machines cost £20,000 each, a large sum in those days, and although he fully realised that production time and costs could double and treble, he took the decision to support tape editing. Perhaps he realised that it was inevitable.

But the engineers' nostalgia for the good old days lingered on. To quote Reg Hammans again:

With a television camera there was more of an element of

Portrait of Sidney as a young dog (1934) in front of Long Barn,
the 'country cottage' he rented from Harold Nicolson.

Bob Fraser (*centre*), Director General of the Central Office of Information, hosts – a little uneasily – a farewell party for a junior executive (*myself, extreme right, hiding a cigarette*), with street entertainers Mick and Mac (1949).

The arduous duties of a Director of the British Film Institute: an exhaustive discussion on neo-realism takes place around a fountain during a seminar in Rome. *Left to right*: Basil Wright, Lady Balcon (Aline), myself.

A further arduous duty: entertaining Orson Welles
at the Edinburgh Film Festival.

The Rochdale by-election. Barrie Heads (*above the front spool on the
camera*), Brian Inglis (*standing at back, tallest, bare-headed*),
interviewer: Elaine Grand.

Slaughter on the avenue, one of Tim Hewat's early
dramatic reconstructions (*Searchlight*, 1959).

There are pictures of that man all
over the place. Who can he be?
(*Barnum*).

The camera of tomorrow in the
hands of the man of the
moment, Tim Hewat.

A Marconi Mark III camera, the workhorse of the early studio years, mounted on a PD3 pedestal, with Lady Burton, in chimney-pot Mark II hat, in conversation with Barrie Heads.

A happy Joe Warton, probably just after preventing someone from spending a sizeable amount of money.

Philip Mackie playing himself in the role of a matinee idol.

Men on the move: Alex, Sidney and myself on the
Manchester–London run.

Men at work. The Programme Committee assembles –
Sidney and I wait for battle to commence.

Orchids and champagne: Sidney and Vivien Leigh,
star of *The Skin of Our Teeth*.

Gin and tonic and posy from the garden: Cecil and Violet Carson,
star of *Coronation Street*.

Getting to know the Russian people:
Sidney (*thinks*): This woman is impossible.
Victoria (*thinks*): These Englishmen are insufferable.

realism to my way of thinking than you can ever get from a film camera – and a television camera with tape is 'emotionally', if you like, just a film camera. I don't know why the realism disappeared. It is psychological or environmental, of this I'm certain. It is not technical.

I thought such regrets were romantic rubbish. As I never ceased to point out to Reg, in the matter of lenses the television camera, as compared with a film camera, was like a Box Brownie.

So Granada Television settled into a pattern that did not change much over the next four or five years: Cecil in London with his gloomy comedians and his phone calls to Lew; Sidney with his plays; myself in Manchester with the rest. There were no more phantom programme controllers, although there was once a faint glimmer. Cecil McGivern, long-time television programme head of the BBC, as decent a man as any in television, was suddenly retired with no handshake and a miserable pension. I suggested to Sidney and Cecil that we should take him on as a consultant. As I spoke I saw a look between the brothers – the Programme Controller look. We engaged Cecil, but his story ended sadly. Although I had been accustomed to see him make serious assaults on a bottle of whisky when we met in Lime Grove of an evening, I had not realised that he set about this activity shortly after breakfast. Cecil died by setting alight his bedclothes with a dropped cigarette. He was the last of the phantom Programme Controllers. It was not that Sidney and Cecil did not trust me, or that they thought I was doing a bad job. The yearning for a real-life programme controller was caused by their lust for experience, one item they held in very high esteem and I did not.

It would be a mistake to give the impression that during these early years Sidney's activity was confined to plays. He dominated the company. Only Joe and Cecil were to some degree exempt. One of his special cares was the administrative management of the Television Centre in Manchester – not the programme management which, unless something caught his eye, he left to me. Each week he would make a tour of a particular area with the General Manager, Simon Kershaw, swinging at his heels, followed by Jack Martin, who ran the production office, then a senior engineer, and at the tail of the procession, notebook at the ready, Mr Pook, ready to dart forward when signalled. Mr Pook had come from Theatres (as the Granada cinemas were called) and remained a foreign body. He was a small ferrety man and was each week responsible for preparing the long list of notes that resulted from the day's work for Sidney to sign. He soon acquired his master's voice and it became hard to tell whether a memo was a Pook for Sidney or an original Sidney:

> SLB to Kershaw
> *Master Clock*
> Would you let me know:
> 1. When this clock went wrong.
> 2. Whether this is faulty manufacture.
> 3. Who is carrying out the repairs.
> 4. When the work will be completed.
> 5. If trouble with this clock is the reason why clocks in various part of TV Centre were inaccurate yesterday and today.

Whoever might have originated a memo it was best for the recipients of such notes not to argue:

> SLB to Gower
> There are some cameras in Studio 3 which have not got the Granada name on. Any reason?

> Gower to SLB
> One of the 'Granada' name-plates on one of the cameras in Studio 3 became uncemented and fell off. This is being refixed. The Engineer concerned with organising this was in all good faith giving priority to such jobs as split network operations, but I have now told him that in view of the publicity angle, we must give priority also to getting these cameras properly labelled.

> SLB to Gower
> I don't find your note of the 15th satisfactory. The word 'priority' can be abused. Exactly how long does it take to stick on a name-plate? Isn't there somebody else, besides the particular engineer you mention, who could have done this job? Must it be an 'engineer'? I would have thought it was a matter you could have done yourself. I would be prepared to do such a job if the necessity arose.
> You might also let me know the date the name-plate came off. Had anybody else in the organisation noticed it was off? I should have thought there would have been somebody in your department who would have seen this

before I did.

But Mr Pook's duties did not stop there. He was an informer. If Sidney required to know who was responsible for the many heinous sins he uncovered, such as putting orange peel into bins reserved for Tampax, Mr Pook would find out. I once fell victim to Pookery myself. When I went for an evening scotch in Simon Kershaw's office, I used to tilt my chair backward and rest my head against the wall. At that time I was using an oleaginous brand of hair oil which stained the wallpaper in a most unsightly way. To put things right, Sidney instructed Mr Pook to insert a patch of new wallpaper. But I did it again, and then once, by pure chance, I saw an exchange of memos on Simon's desk:

> Sidney to Pook: Why has the smear on the wall in Kershaw's office not been made good?

> Pook to Sidney: The wallpaper has been patched twice but the problem recurs. Same person.

So Sidney knew my guilty secret, and from then on I made sure that however frequently Mr Pook changed the wallpaper I would instantly foul it again. Sidney never said a word to me and this must have caused Mr Pook grievous aggravation. All in all, Mr Pook was one of the most feared individuals in the TV Centre.

One of Mr Pook's responsibilities was to ensure there was a Barnum in every office. Sidney believed that an engraving of the great showman facing us on the wall would help us – accountants and all – to remember that we were in show-business and not just office wallahs. This was too much for some of the more rebellious spirits, and Bill Grundy was alleged to throw his Barnum into the waste-paper basket as fast as Mr Pook could put one up. Although he must have known it was risky, Mr Pook bravely wrote a memo to Grundy asking for an explanation for his consumption of six Barnums in one month. Bill surmised, probably rightly, that Mr Pook had sent a blind copy of this memo to SLB, so he replied with an open copy to SLB saying that he thought it his duty to keep his office uncontaminated by the features of a man who was a con-man, a mountebank and a crook. It may have been a coincidence but the supply of Barnums seemed to dry up after that. But it was David Highet who many years later gave Barnum a *coup de grâce* when he was in charge of the newly opened Liverpool office. When Sidney came on a state visit, he looked around and asked, 'Where's your Barnum?' David had no idea what a Barnum was. In his panic he jumped to the conclusion that this must be the word used by sophisticated London folk for a loo. 'It's along the corridor and down the stairs,' he said. Sidney went off to inspect, and when he returned he realised that Barnum's day was done. His own employees were confusing him with the plumbing.

It was the Bernstein style never to commit to paper a word of praise, encouragement or approbation. I once pointed out to Sidney that Arthur Christiansen, when editor of the *Daily Express*, would post a notice for all to see, such as 'A great, great, great newspaper today.' Sidney thought this a form of madness. He expected every show to be great (if not great great great) and if it was not great he would send an acid little note pointing out that it was not. Thus the memos from Sidney scattered over the pages of this memoir tend to give a false impression of his relationship with his colleagues. On paper he was a despot – picky, acid and arbitrarily judgmental. Face to face he was delightful. It is true that even in conversation he never praised, but neither did he find fault unless it were a set-piece wigging, when he could at the least be formidable and, when in a rage, quite terrifying. But for the rest of the time, for nearly all of the time, he was charming, witty, and universally agreeable.

One of the great joys of Manchester life was dinner in the flat above the studios with Sidney at the head of the table. Here would be gathered eight or ten producers and directors. Each person usually had his own agenda and the debate would range from the internal dissensions of the Labour Party to the problems of cutting Dostoevsky down to television size. Sidney would always be in the thick of things and always held his corner, although sometimes with difficulty, particularly when under attack. If the assault became too personal he could draw himself up and issue a formidable rebuke, as when someone, to counter Sidney's boast that he took a salary of only £9,000 a year, once said, 'Oh come on, Sidney, how much dough did you put down on that villa in Italy?'

'That's a private matter,' said Sidney, 'and not for discussion.' But for most of the time he was not even *primus inter pares*: it was gas and gaiters, all round equally. Sometimes we had a guest, and once during some riotous debate Sidney turned to Lawrence Scott of the *Guardian* and said, 'You see, Lawrence, Granada is a democracy.' To which Lawrence replied, 'Yes, Sidney, and when is the next general election?'

During those buoyant early years Sidney had only two setbacks, one more wounding than the other, but both vexing him greatly. The first came in the summer of 1958 with a quiz game, *Twenty-One*, an American import in which the current champion competitor had to answer a series of questions which became increasingly difficult as the weeks went by and ultimately delved into matters of such obscurity that a correct answer left the viewers in stunned amazement. The first big winner was a competitor named Bernard Davies, who knocked out twelve challengers and clocked up the then unheard of prize of £5,560. He was followed by a young woman, Leonora Millington. who reached a similar figure. Both became national heroes, but suspicions were aroused by Miss Millington when, after being knocked out of *Twenty-One*, she appeared on a BBC quiz and was floored by the simplest of questions. Then a previous competitor turned Queen's evidence. He told the Independent Television Authority that he had been given clues about the questions. Another said he had been given 'definite guidance'. The consternation felt by the Authority was as nothing compared to the flurry within Granada, that honourable and socially conscious company which had publicly spurned even mildly dubious practices such as advertising expensive toys for children at Christmas. Sidney flew down to London and set up an immediate internal inquiry with Cecil. The show was taken off the air. The Authority was asked to appoint Sir Lionel Heald, the former Attorney General, to conduct an independent inquiry. Meanwhile Sidney, burning with shame, pointed out that Granada itself had not produced the show: it was subcontracted to an American producer and an American company. Sir Lionel duly inquired and found that there had indeed been skulduggery, but that he could not blame Granada for they had no knowledge of what was going on. This brought great relief to Sidney, but the scar remained and in later years he always referred to this incident as 'the trouble we had with Mr Chester'. (In fact the American producer's name was Kesten.) Years later there was a similar but even greater scandal of the same kind in America which formed the subject of a feature film, *Quiz Show*.

The second unhappy episode of 1958 began in August. A letter, bypassing the Board, went to every Granada shareholder offering to buy shares at fifteen shillings apiece – well below the market price. Nearly all Granada shares were held by the 'Bernstein family and friends', a phrase that became part of the rubric describing the controlling interest which, under the contract with the Authority, could not be sold. A few shares had leaked out to the nephew of a deceased chief accountant and these had been bought by a Mr

Whipp, a professional company busybody who described himself as one who 'looks after the interests of minority shareholders'.

There are two versions of what followed, and here first is the Granada version, substantially as recorded in Caroline Moorehead's biography of Sidney. Sidney wrote to all shareholders advising them not to sell and offering to buy the shares himself if they disregarded his advice. He asked the Stock Exchange to suspend dealings, which they did. Mr Whipp then mounted a takeover campaign by raising an injunction against a resolution to set up a share incentive scheme for the staff, and by mounting an action against the Directors for fraud in that the proposed scheme unduly favoured the directors at the expense of the ordinary shareholders. Sidney wanted to fight the injunction but was restrained by his advisers, and although he felt 'truly humiliated' by his capitulation the injunction was accepted. Everything was put on hold until the AGM on 30 January 1959 (which happened to be Sidney's sixtieth birthday). Before the meeting Jonathan Guinness, of the stout-brewing family, circularised all shareholders suggesting they should request a Board of Trade inquiry. In the Granada version Sidney was persuaded that some of the resolutions passed in the August Extraordianry General Meeting might arguably have been suspect and such were our scruples that we agreed not to proceed: we were prepared not only for right to be done but to be seen to be done, even by the most mean-minded.

At the AGM the resolution for 200,000 Group shares was passed, but a second resolution, more favourable to the directors of the Television company, was withdrawn, Jonathan Guinness's motion was thrown out, and for the rest everyone supported everything unanimously and the Granada world returned to normal 'as befitted an old-established private family-run company of good reputation, despite its infiltration by a Mr Whipp and his associates for his own dishonourable ends.' Sidney took pains to explain that what had shaken him was the possibility of a takeover, the idea that the happy, successful family company, built up by himself and his brother, should be snatched away from him by evil men and subjected to all manner of ill treatment, such as having its assets milked, its economy ruined and the confidence of its staff undermined. 'Just think what the uncertainty must have meant,' he would say, 'to Jack, Jill, Jim (and here he would list all his listeners' best friends). Just think of that.' Actually nobody was in the least perturbed because nobody thought a takeover was even a remote possibility.

The other version of what happened, supported by evidence from minute books of the day, throws a rather different light on the affair.

Special resolutions were put to an Extraordinary General Meeting in September 1958 to issue 200,000 shares in the Granada Group to the directors and staff. There was a second resolution to issue 200,000 shares in the television subsidiary to the directors and staff (Granada Television Network), the distribution to be at the discretion of the Board, which effectively meant that the shares could go to Sidney and Cecil. This would have allowed them to cream off the profits of the Television Network Company by paying themselves a dividend before any money reached the Group. No limits were set. The device of issuing shares in the Network Company entailed a number of changes to the Articles of Association. The EGM was attended by some dozen shareholders, most of them Bernstein friends, and the resolution was passed. It was then that Mr Whipp, an astute company-watcher, used his tiny store of shares gleaned from the family to challenge the second resolution, the allocation of shares in the Network Company. 'It was out of all proportion,' he claimed, 'to the total of the issue available to shareholders.' The issue of 200,000 Group shares to directors and staff (the first resolution) was not questioned. There was no plan for a takeover.

When Mr Whipp launched his attack both Sidney and Cecil were thrown into a state of acute agitation. On the one hand public opinion, shareholder opinion, even the law, might find that they were unduly greedy in staking a claim to what must clearly have been a massive fortune at the expense of the ordinary Group shareholders; on the other hand they wanted the money and were so deeply accustomed to thinking of Granada as their own property that they felt entitled to it. Consultation went on between the central trinity – Sidney, Cecil, Joe – daily, nightly, then hourly. Should they pull back? Should they tough it out? They differed, and their warring instincts were so strong that a resolution became impossible. They called in their closest friends in the company, Victor Peers, Alex Anson and myself. Sidney sat behind his desk, crestfallen, nervous and speaking in a very quiet voice. Cecil sat on his right, grey-faced, his stammer well-nigh insuperable, Joe on his left grasping a full tumbler of his dark amber nectar, the rest of us in a semicircle. Sidney, quite unlike himself, told us that he and Cecil were considering giving up the idea of allocating shares in the Network Company. What did we think? 'That's not Sidney Bernstein talking,' cried Alex Anson. 'Shame on you, Sidney. You must stick with the original plan and tell Whipp and Co. to go to hell.'

'Quite right,' said Joe Warton. 'My view all along, sir.' But Victor and I thought differently. We believed that the good opinion of the world meant more to the Bernsteins, certainly to Sidney, than untold wealth. Sidney and Cecil, worn out by worry, both relapsed into a silent torpor whilst the debate ranged on. Then they asked us to leave. During the night brotherly communion took place, and the next morning they told us they were going to withdraw the Network resolution.

At the AGM in January 1959, well attended and with the press out in force, Sidney read out a nine-page speech. He reminded the shareholders of the Group's history and reputation for honesty, fairness and decent values. Re-investment in the company had always been a first charge on profits; a Gallup poll had just voted Granada an easy first amongst the television contractors. Many of Granada Television's programmes had made a great contribution to the understanding of social problems (three pages unmistakably from my hand), and then on page eight came the news we had all been waiting for. Four months ago on the very morning of the September EGM, said Sidney, he had received a letter from an old and respected business friend, Sir Halford Reddish, Chairman of Rugby Cement, advising against the issue of the Network shares. He was much impressed by this letter. Granada's brokers, Rowe Swann, had supported Sir Halford's view. Thus immediately after the EGM had passed the resolution the board had reconsidered the matter and had decided to withdraw the Network proposal at the AGM. This he now proceeded to do.

In later years Sidney would not, I think, have recognised the true account of the affairs leading up to the withdrawal of the motion, so firmly was the Granada version implanted in his memory. For many years he held at the ready a letter from Jonathan Guinness which he would display triumphantly if ever the Whipp affair cropped up. It was written after the AGM and read:

> Perhaps it is not out of place for me to drop you a personal line to say how much I enjoyed our little exchange of views at the recent meeting of Granada Group.
>
> I was particularly sorry to have been involved in a public misunderstanding with a Company Chairman whose dynamism and acumen I had long admired and whose shares I had recently bought as a long-term investment. I am correspondingly delighted that this misunderstanding should now be cleared up.
>
> You may like to know that one of my main motives for investing in Granada was the clear superiority of their tele-

vision programmes over all others. It must be right to buy the best; and Granada is to TV as Guinness is to stout.

Sidney also formed a view about the motivation of Whipp and Guinness, which he later expressed as follows:

> What was it that these people were after? This was the question which most worried me. I was not so much disturbed by the attacks themselves as by the reasons behind the attempts to discredit us. The attacks were obviously motivated by something beyond the possibility of making a great deal of money. In searching for motive I asked Tim Hewat to investigate the backgrounds of those involved. Guinness, I hadn't previously known, was the stepson of Sir Oswald Mosley; Whipp was a one-time member of Mosley's party. Anti-semitism was not a motive which had occurred to me, and I said to Tim that I found it almost incredible. Tim said, 'I assure you, Sidney, that is what it is all about.'

Perhaps. But there was little need to seek hidden motives. Mr Whipp spotted that the directors of a company were setting out to pull a fast one over their shareholders. He determined to stop them, and he succeeded. It was a fair cop.

CHAPTER FIVE

While each of the founding fathers of Granada settled into his largely self-defined role, the managers of the future were at work in Manchester. First on the scene was Barrie Heads, a journalist from the Northern edition of the *Daily Express*. He worked first on Outside Broadcasts and then as editor of *Northern News*, and soon recruited a fellow journalist from the *Yorkshire Post*, David Plowright, who boasted the byline of Equestrian Correspondent because he rode a horse when covering gymkhanas. He and his sister Joan had won every known prize as young horsepersons, and I will never forget the horror of some of our more tender-hearted colleagues when David demonstrated how they would tie hedgehog skins to the top pole of a jump to touch up their mounts if they did not rise from the ground with sufficient verve. Both he and Barrie could write in the wry economical style of the then *Manchester Guardian* and both were natural leaders, though they retained a determinedly democratic stance from which they could scoff amiably at the follies and vanities of those above them, especially Sidney.

These two were to become the backbone of Granada in the North. Barrie went on to produce every sort of major current affairs programme and then to lead the overseas company. David became the producer and then the minder of *World in Action*; he went on to be Programme Controller and then my successor as Chief Executive and Chairman. They recruited other like-minded Northern journalists – amongst them Bill Grundy, then a practising geologist, who wrote as a freelance; later Michael Parkinson, and Peter Eckersley from the *Guardian*. Collectively, they gave Granada its aggressively Northern outlook. These three, along with Mike Scott, all made their mark on the Northern screen by becoming what was called 'producer performers'; that is, one-man bands who wrote, performed and produced their own shows. Mike Parkinson became the most famous, Bill Grundy – man of many parts, many of them brilliant –

the most notorious, and Peter Eckersley went on to preside over all the latter-day Granada drama as it rose over the horizon with *Country Matters* and reached its zenith with his production of *Hard Times*.

Alongside the hard-core Northerners we recruited an expatriate Lancastrian, Derek Granger; an Australian, Tim Hewat; and a Scotsman, Jeremy Isaacs, who were all to make their mark on British television. Derek was spotted by Sidney in the early days when he was drama critic of the *Sussex Daily News*, but by 1958 we had all come to recognise his work in the *Financial Times* as the best writing on theatre since Ken Tynan. I wrote to Sidney:

> I have this man on my mind. I have seen him three or four times. Mackie has seen him twice. He has been to Manchester and met everyone up here. Stu has seen him and he has a meeting pending with Cecil. He is prepared to fling his cap over the windmill and join us. Everyone likes him, and I suggest he should begin as a writer on current affairs programmes, from which position he might graduate through to be a producer, but not, I think, a director.

Derek never did become a director, but after a time as Head of Plays graduated as a producer through several minor current affairs shows, and one or two unsuccessful comedies, to *Coronation Street* – where he was a huge success – *World in Action* and all manner of current affairs programmes, then *Country Matters*, and finally his *chef d'oeuvre*, *Brideshead Revisited*. He came to be one of the most admired producers in the profession.

Jeremy Isaacs came to us straight from Oxford, where he had been President of the Union. Of him I wrote:

> This is a very bright young man who was sent to us by George Singleton [owner of the Cosmo Cinema in Glasgow, and an old friend]. I will arrange with Jack Martin that he is taken on as an assistant floor manager, although his talent lies more in the field of journalism, where, for his age (about 24), he has had a lot published.

This would seem to be a humble beginning for a man who was to go on to produce the monumental series *The World at War*, and to make his name as the founding father of Channel 4 and General Director of the Royal Opera House; and indeed he never did go to the studio floor but set to work with me as the researcher on *What the Papers Say*, a show of which he was later to produce many editions. His quick wit, well-stocked mind and terrier-like aggression marked him out as someone who would go places, and he soon went on to make his name in Thames Television and the BBC.

Tim Hewat was another matter, for he had to be wooed. His life was journalism, his hero Beaverbrook and his ambition to succeed Arthur Christiansen as the editor of the *Daily Express*. His job at that time was Northern Editor of the *Express*, and after the paper had gone to bed and Granada closed down we would meet regularly in the bar of the old Midland Hotel and while away the small hours in endless conversation, fuelled by a steady intake of malt whisky. Tim cultivated an image of himself as a typical Oz. He was rash, brash and forthright, and exceedingly foul-mouthed, not by habit but by design, using the more pungent sex words only when they were required to shock, surprise and, if necessary, horrify his listener. His grasp of politics and the affairs of the world was basic but shrewd. He was witty. He looked nice, with an open Australian face, a long inquisitive nose and dark red hair parted near the middle. I liked him, and dearly longed for him to join Granada.

This is Tim's own account of how it came about:

> I was Editor of the *Daily Express* Northern edition, in Manchester. Beaverbrook was determined to have political editors, and although I wanted to become editor of the *Express* I was a technical, sub-editor type rather than a political animal. There was obviously no future in it for me. Because my job on the *Express* used to finish about midnight and the Granada crowd would be drinking at the Midland at that time, I used to wander down there to pick up my wife; and I met Denis Forman and got to like him.
>
> I came and saw the Granada people, had a talk with Denis, met Sidney, and I was hired. That was in May '57.
>
> Denis Forman himself produced *What the Papers Say* for about the first year, though he never took a credit for it, and during this period I was in effect understudying him.

Once Tim came aboard he moved from point to point round the company like an editorial electrical storm. As well as working on *What the Papers Say*, he assisted Sidney ('the proprietor') on several special assignments, some of them mysterious. He took on the series of late-night Outside Broadcasts, which were pretty disastrous, and immediately showed complete command of every situation, as when a televised Caesarean operation ended long before its scheduled time and he filled in by chatting to the surgeon, asking him *en passant*, 'Say, who was this guy Caesar anyway?' He made programmes about Cuba, which caused trouble with the IBA; he made programmes about India, which caused trouble with the Indian government; he made the fortnightly series *Searchlight*, which nearly always caused trouble with someone. He played a central role in Granada's crusade to get politics on the air, and all of this before he found his ultimate destiny in *World in Action*. He was a phenomenon, and was accepted as such by everyone in Manchester.

The Chanan history quotes Derek Granger as saying:

> Tim liked to pose as a headlong ruffian son of the Australian earth, an image slightly mitigated, in fact, by an Australian public school education. He presented himself as the dynamic newsman straight from Ben Hecht's *The Front Page*; he was like no newsman there had ever been since the Thirties. He was a movie version of a newspaper man, the hectic creature holding the front page for the big story. Coupled with that he liked to be the coarse, totally truth-telling, appalling, shocking, rough diamond hillbilly; the hairy ape *in excelsis*. In fact he was a few of these things, and underneath all that an enormous sentimentalist, very emotional; he could cry at the drop of a hat. He was both sensitive and insensitive. He had a characteristic habit of being brutally frank with people about themselves, a slightly unfortunate habit which I don't think does many people much good, and indeed the kind of truth that's told in those terms is not usually correct anyway. But apart from that he cared enormously for the people on the team.
>
> Beneath the surface Tim was highly sophisticated. If he was posing as a Ben Hecht-type editor he was actually an astute and clever creature of journalism, with a real journalistic flair, and it was his natural sense of story-telling that led him to make such excellent programmes. In a way I found it inspiring working with him.

Once freed from *Chelsea* and restored pretty well full-time to Manchester, I found I was gradually becoming the producer of all the programmes that were not run by Sidney or Cecil. I still had no title (and indeed, except for the formal labels of Managing Director and Chairman, never did have one). With Philip Mackie as writer, I started a drama series, the memory of which still makes me shudder: *Knight Errant* (handsome young bachelor inserts advertisement – 'Knight Errant – go anywhere, do anything ...' – which leads to a number of adventures so romantic as to make Barbara Cartland's novels seem like documentaries). Then another not so shaming, *Family Solicitor*, which gave Geoffrey Palmer his first major exposure on television. There was a series of 'Specials' opening up topics that had hitherto been taboo on television –venereal disease, birth control, euthanasia, homosexuality and the like. They were prepared with immense care, for we took such subjects very seriously. In the Chanan history I recorded the way we set about making one of these programmes, 'Homosexuality and the law'.

> I got hold of an embargoed copy of the Wolfenden Report through ITN the day before its publication, and sat up all night and marked it up for its relevance to the skeleton script we had laid out. As soon as the Stationery Office opened the next morning we picked up twenty further copies of the report. These were brought straight to Euston Station where the cast were standing by, together with the doctors, the lawyers, the sociologists. Each of them was given a copy of the report on which they duplicated my markings by page and by paragraph; they were also given a brief as to how the programme would absorb the material. I went into the compartment next to theirs and slept for a bit while they studied the report; then I rejoined them to discuss it. By the time we reached Manchester we had a pretty finalised shape for the show. 'Homosexuality and the Law' went into the studio that night, and was transmitted, therefore, the same night as the press reports on the Wolfenden appeared.

I recall that Sidney asked to see a script about four hours before we went on air and had only one comment: 'A lot of people don't know what buggery is. You must explain it.' Nonsense, thought I, but nevertheless I got the director, Silvio Narizzano, to go down one side of a corridor whilst I went down the other, walking into each office and asking the startled inmates, 'Anyone here know what the word buggery means?' Sidney was proved right. About one in five had a vague notion that it was a reprehensible male practice, but of what nature they had no inkling.

The word 'producer' was something new. It had become impossible to give the director sole charge of a show, as we had at first, if only because I did not have time to act as the producer for a dozen directors simultaneously. So it was that Philip Mackie, Tim Hewat, Barrie Heads, Derek Granger and a big cheerful newcomer from Canada –Harry Elton – took on a number of shows as producers. The directors did not like this, particularly when we ruled that in the event of disagreement the producer's view should prevail, and they produced a formal round robin asking if we thought they were mice or men, and who needed producers anyway? But soon producers were accepted first as a necessary evil, then as team leaders and organisers of the show, and later as the begetters as well. Who could produce the show became as important a question as who could direct it.

Since the titles of director and producer are variously interpreted in the world of films, theatre and television, let me make it clear that the prime job of a television director in those days was to sit in the Control Room (the Gallery) and tell people on the floor what to do. He had prepared a camera script, and while his PA (Production Assistant) called out to the cameras just before they went on air – 3 on shot 24, 2 back for shot 25 – the director gave the Vision Mixer the cue (often by snapping his fingers) where to cut from one shot to the next. Of course his contribution might be much greater than this – he might have written the show or even invented it. The producer's task was to look after the logistics of the show – budget, schedules, etc. – and to agree with the director its content and form. Often a producer would mastermind a production and a director would be driven to do it his way. Sometimes a producer was little more than a minder for a masterful director.

It is enshrined in Granada mythology that it was the emergence of the producer class that led to what became known as the Peasants' Revolt. I had gone to Japan to look at the technology used by NHK in their Tokyo studios and to make our number with Sony. Back at the ranch there was trouble. A director – Peter Plummer – had shot a scene for *Coronation Street* in which Minnie Caldwell's cat, an animal who was well known to more than half the nation, vomited in shot. The producer, Harry Elton, thought this to be in bad taste and suggested a cut. Peter, a stalwart defender of directors' rights, balked. The matter was referred to Sidney, who told Harry to make the cut. The programme went out without Peter being informed of the cut and all hell broke loose. The director's anger was directed against Sidney rather than Harry, and he was served with a round robin signed by all the directors saying that they would not continue to work for Granada unless it was agreed that no changes would be made by a senior executive without the director's consent. A management meeting took place in Manchester (not attended by Sidney) at which, in reply to Cecil's customary question, 'Who is the ringleader?' Tim Hewat replied, 'That bearded prick, Baker.' A passing secretary overheard this exchange and reported it to the said bearded prick, which did little to improve matters. Eventually a work-to-rule was agreed on the understanding there would be a full inquiry when I got back. The full inquiry took two days. The directors were told that Sidney was the boss, more or less owned the company and could do pretty well what he liked. They could lump it or leave. No one left, but an undertaking was given that a Directors' Charter would be drafted (it never was) and that two representatives of the united directors would meet Sidney and put their point of view. This was an extraordinary occasion. Sidney listened respectfully to what the directors had to say, admitted he had acted wrongly and apologised. The directors were bowled over, reported back to their brethren, and family life continued much as before.

Sidney and I were keen to find a style of programmes on the arts that sustained the old *Chelsea* tradition. Even before we went on the air we had approached Sir Thomas Beecham to be our Music Adviser. This came about because one of Tom Brownrigg's first acts had been to engage Sir John Barbirolli and the Hallé to give a series of televised concerts for Rediffusion. Sidney was infuriated at this encroachment on our patch and asked me, 'Who is the greatest British conductor after Barbirolli?' to which I replied, 'Beecham, and he's not after, he's before.'

This gave rise to a series of enjoyable but endless discussions which resulted in little more than a warm mutual regard. We did make one programme – 'Sir Thomas at Lincoln's Inn' – in which there is some precious material of Sir Thomas rehearsing the royal Philharmonic Orchestra for a concert in the Great Hall. But then Sir Thomas fell mortally ill. He was a ninety-day man and the limit of his stay in England was near. Had he overstepped it most of his total income from his worldwide activities would have been liable to UK tax. Sidney and I sought out Eddie Playfair, a senior civil servant in the Treasury, and laid before him Sir Thomas's circumstances. To his eternal credit (and one must add a plaudit for that universally disliked body, the Inland Revenue) it was agreed that Sir Thomas could stay on and die in England, with no tax penalties. Which he did.

We also made a try for opera. I worked out a proposal that the

Royal Opera House and Granada together should arrange for extended contracts for visiting artists and record extracts from operas in the repertory or complete short acts in the studio. We sent a document to David Webster, then the General Director, and in due course were bidden to lunch in the Royal Box by Lord Drogheda, then Chairman. It was not an enjoyable occasion. In addition to Webster and Drogheda there were Lionel Robbins, Freddie Ashton and Madam herself, Ninette de Valois. They chattered endlessly about the scandals and credulities of the opera and ballet world, throwing in countless names and nicknames which meant nothing to Sidney or to me. 'Have you heard who's going with Dukey for a snug week in Cannes?' one would say, and the rest would cry, 'No. Who? Who?' When the tease had run its time and the answer was given, 'Bim', they were all convulsed with laughter for several minutes. Sidney and I ate our food in isolation until coffee when Garett Drogheda said, 'Now, Sidney, tell us about your film idea.'

'Not film,' said Sidney, 'television.' And he put me in to bat. It was clear that Webster had not read the paper and that no one else was even faintly interested. People began to whisper to each other about what Teddy had said to Paul and I was glad when Drogheda cut me short by saying, 'How interesting, but if it is about television we must of course ask the BBC first.' As we went downstairs I could see Sidney was white with anger. 'Treated like servants,' he said. And then a little later, 'English gentlemen!'

But if some of our more grandiose plans never got airborne, the early years did give birth to two of the programmes that were to change the face of British television, *Coronation Street* and *World in Action*.

In November 1960 we were still working in the tobacco warehouse on the banks of the Irwell, waiting impatiently to get into the new office block which was rising up behind us. Conditions were crowded, and one day I heard a considerable stir in the open area outside my office. Harry Elton, our adopted Canadian producer, and Stuart Latham, one of our few experienced drama directors, burst in with a script in their hands. 'Read that,' they said, pushing it in front of me and standing above me like a pair of invigilators. 'Sure,' I said, 'if you'll get out of my office for twenty minutes.' They went and sat down outside. I could see the outline of their heads against the frosted glass partition. I read Episode 1 of 'Florizel Street', and called them back in. 'Good characters, good dialogue,' I said. They looked at me pityingly.

'Is that all you've got to say?' they asked. 'It's a knockout.'

'Any more?' I asked. 'Who wrote it?' Seven episodes were planned. Tony Warren was the author and he had just completed Episode 2. I knew Tony only as a willowy figure with a long cigarette holder and a cane, who affected the style and manner of speech of Noël Coward. He was unmistakably a grown-up child actor, and this was not at all the sort of stuff I would have expected from him. It was established, however, that 'Florizel Street' was autobiographical, and that the characters, especially the women, were modelled on real-life people he had lived with in his youth. 'Will viewers outside Lancashire manage the argot?' I asked.

'Of course,' said Stuart. 'Ena Sharples is no more Lancashire than Harry Lauder was Scottish. Not a minus, a plus.' I told them to distribute the two scripts to the Television Committee (it was before the days of the Programme Committee proper) and to find a better title. But I felt deficient, a doubting Thomas in the face of a modern miracle. Looking back, I can now see that the sort of faith these two had in the embryonic *Coronation Street* was a phenomenon matched only rarely in life. I saw it in Sam Wanamaker's belief in the Globe Theatre, and the unmatched assurance of Peter Dimmock and his BBC sports team when they absolutely refused to plan the coverage of the 1966 football World Cup on any basis other than that England would win. So it could be that we owe the existence of *Coronation Street* to the persistence of Harry Elton and Stuart Latham, and somewhat late in the day I hereby stake their claim for a prime place in the *Street*'s hall of fame.

The Television committee meeting took place over lunch in the penthouse-like dining room, perched in those days at the back of the Golden Square office in London. From my seat I could see down Carnaby Street. How unlike, how very unlike, the street we had on the agenda, I thought. So far as I can remember only Sidney, Cecil, Victor Peers, Alex Anson and Ken Brierley – the Committee secretary – were present. Alex was dismissive. Dreary, trivial, downbeat, boring, he thought. Victor too was against. How could the residents of Esher be expected to understand the Lancashire idiom? Cecil saw merit in the scripts. If the show was a flop on the network we could always play it locally. Sidney would express no view. It was not his cup of tea. He would like others to decide. Ken Brierley, who seldom spoke, nodded vigorously when unfavourable views were expressed. Gradually Cecil and I worked the meeting round to a reluctant agreement to let the show go ahead as a seven-parter, provided the title was changed from 'Florizel Street'.

I flashed the news to Manchester, where it was received coolly. So if the committee had not recognised the show for the miracle it was, at least they had avoided making fools of themselves by turning it down. Next came the rush and bustle of getting 'Florizel Street' on the air with the eleventh-hour decision to cast Violet Carson as Ena Sharples. Harry Kershaw, who was to become the programme's first executive producer, records in the Chanan history how the matter of title was finally settled:

> We locked ourselves in an office with a bottle of Irish whiskey vowing not to come out until we'd found a title. We decided within the first hour that as the street had been built at the turn of the century it would have coincided either with Victoria's diamond jubilee, in which case it would be called Jubilee Street, or a little later on with the coronation of Edward VII, in which case it would have been called Coronation Street. We got drunker and more argumentative about the respective merits of Jubilee and Coronation, until eventually, with great aplomb, Harry Latham reminded us that since there were three of us, if we took a vote we were bound to reach a decision. We did take a vote and we all went home. When I came in the next morning Harry Elton was already at his desk and looking at his copy of the same memo as I received. It said that the title was to be *Coronation Street*. Harry said, 'I'm damned sure I voted for Jubilee Street.' And I said, 'I'm damned sure I voted for Jubilee Street too.' The producer was boss, and to hell with democracy.

I recall a playback of the first tape to a large assembly in Manchester, with Harry Elton gleefully writing down each negative or guarded comment so that he would be able to use it at some future date against the misguided wretch who uttered it (which he did). From then on the story of the *Street*'s rise and rise to fame is documented in over a dozen accounts of variable accuracy. Ken Irwin reviewed the first episode in the *Daily Mirror* as follows: 'The programme is doomed from the outset – with its gloomy tune and grim scene of a row of terraced houses and smoking chimneys ...' Some members of the network, and especially Lew Grade, would not agree to take such parochial stuff until they were shocked into capitulation by, of all things, the London ratings. From then on, over three decades and 3,500 episodes, it was to stand, majestic and unchallenged, at the top of the Top Ten.

World in Action's period of gestation was longer. From the moment he joined Granada, Tim Hewat had wanted to run a show that would put his kind of news story on the air each week. In those days film was still stuck in its 35mm mode, with bulky cameras, tripods, dollies and all manner of supporting gear for sound. We had sent Peter Brook to the South of France to interview Gordon Craig on film, and although the results were acclaimed, and especially his recollection of the acting style of Henry Irving, the expedition had cost £300, a figure which shocked Sidney and Victor into banning the use of film absolutely. So it was when Tim, supported by Mike Wooller and myself, launched a campaign for a weekly show based on the current practices of *Panorama* and *This Week*: leading off with a ten-minute film followed by fifteen minutes of prominent persons chewing the cud in the studios. The management was divided – Cecil, Joe and Victor against, Sidney and myself for. By nefarious means I obtained the budget figures for the opposition shows and demonstrated ways in which we could cut them by 30 per cent. We conceded that there should be no shooting abroad. We agreed to a fortnightly strike rather than weekly, and we won. *Searchlight*, although better than the ponderous *Panorama* and the aimless *This Week*, was not a distinguished show.

The team of Hewat, Isaacs and Wooller picked stories that illustrated muddle, sloppiness and failure in odd corners of society: dirty food, crooked sport, slovenly British Rail, deficient child welfare, unlawful gambling. Only once or twice did they touch a nerve, as when they attacked the road system as disgracefully inadequate. This elicited an hysterically violent response from the Authority ('one-sided'), a reaction which came to be accepted as a sign we had done something worthwhile. There were twenty-seven episodes of *Searchlight* between March 1959 and June 1960, and shortly after its demise came a conference called 'Avanti', a stock-taking of Granada's performance to date and a consideration of proposals for the future, the whole running for one week. Each senior producer had a slot on the agenda, and when it came to Tim's turn he produced a happening of high theatricality. In the darkened conference room a spotlight fell on a massive 35mm camera and all the gear that went with it, whilst Tim related the precise weight and dimension of each item. 'That', said Tim, 'is the film-making of yesterday, and this' (as he whipped a sheet off a sparkling new Arriflex 16mm camera) 'is the film-making of tomorrow.' He told us that 16mm was no longer for amateurs but could give results for television quite as good as 35mm. He showed the same scenes shot on 16 and 35mm on monitors, and indeed the result seemed almost equal (although I am sure I was not the only person in the audience who suspected that, although the 16mm had been shot with the maximum skill and care, no such pains had been taken over the 35mm). Then came Tim's clincher. The costs of filming could be halved. The day was won and he was given the go-ahead.

As the first weekly programme neared the screen the matter of title was debated. Every old bromide from 'Thrust' to 'Here and Now' was passed around until I recalled that there had never been a better title than the one used by Grierson and Stuart Legg for a show they tried (and failed) to launch in the USA – *World in Action*. This was thought to be acceptable and I called Grierson , who was in Glasgow recording an edition of *This Wonderful World* for Scottish Television. 'John,' I said, 'Granada would like us to use the title *World in Action* for a show that is coming up.'

'It's mine,' he said.

'Will you sell it?' I asked.

'I need £100 for new strawberry nets for my farm in Wiltshire,' he said.

'£100? Done!' I said.

'Done,' he said. Little did he know that he had sold it for a song. *World in Action* was to be all on film with no presenter in vision. The prose style, which came naturally to Tim, was to be that of the *Daily Express*. The content was to be modelled on 'Mirrorscope', the serious four-page fold-in which the *Daily Mirror* ran over several years, much admired in Granada. Little guidance was given to Mike Wooller, who as lead director was in charge of 'the pictures'. Once the research was in Tim would tend to write a script at newspaper speed and say, 'Get some crap to go with that.' When *World in Action* hit the screen the result was sensational. Well-mannered elderly viewers accustomed to the avuncular Dimbleby and the mild-mannered *This Week* were startled by passages such as:

> Last week life in Paris was unchanged. On the Stock Exchange there was excitement – but no more excitement than usual; it's always bedlam. In the nightclubs, the girls were undressed – but no more undressed than usual. In the fashion houses it was the last week of the Spring Collections – but all the confusions were no more hectic than usual.
>
> Throughout Paris – indeed throughout France – life went on as if nothing had happened. But, of course, some-

thing of immense importance had happened. General Charles André Joseph Marie de Gaulle, properly elected and popularly chosen leader of the French people, slammed the door of Europe in Britain's face.

Or this:

Forty-five minutes ago, Members of Parliament divided after their two-day debate on Defence spending. The motion was to approve expenditure of £1,800 million.

In discussing so much money, MPs must have had several expensive memories in front of their minds.

Item – Britain's first anti-aircraft rocket is said to have cost 140 times more than the estimate.

Item – The Army spent £16 million on a vehicle before they decided it wasn't good enough.

Item – *The Financial Times* reported last week that the RAF's latest jet will have cost £400 million by the time it enters squadron service. £1,800 milliion this year – that's the sum.

World in Action had a resonance that was new to television. For two decades the BBC had spoken with the voice of the broadsheets, more particularly perhaps with the voice of *The Times*, a voice which patronised and so alienated the people of the working world who, if they read a newspaper at all, read the *Mirror*, the *Sketch* or the *Express*. To be addressed as equals in tones they did not resent and in language which was their language was a welcome change. Within a few weeks *World in Action*'s ratings were double those of *Panorama* and shot ahead of those of *This Week*.

So the show started on the long road to the present day, passing through the Hewat phase, when a team working independently as a private army within Granada pushed out the most sensational subjects at breakneck speed; then several short-stay producers – Valentine, Heads, Granger; then the Plowright era when a team of a dozen or so top-class journalists researched major stories in depth, sometimes for a year or more, giving the programme *gravitas* and punch; then the time of Ray Fitzwalter, the arch-investigator of the murky corners of society; until the 1990s when, like all current affairs programmes on television, *World in Action* fell into gentle decline. It was also the beginning of a running war of attrition with the Authority, which occupied more of their time and mine than all the other Granada programmes put together.

*

Even before *World in Action* was born, as a group of mostly ex-print journalists we were conscious that in the matter of politics television was bound and gagged in the most ridiculous manner. This was due partly to Bob Fraser's timorous interpretation of the 1954 Television Act and partly to the BBC tradition of treating politics as an activity that had to be sanitised before it could be presented to an impressionable public. In the BBC establishment's view the constituents' trust in the integrity and honour of their MP would be undermined if they learned too much about the party political game. Thus it was that the coverage of politics in the BBC was confined largely to reports of what politicians had said both in the House and elsewhere, and to the daintier sort of Round Table Forum which was more in the style of the old *Brains Trust* (whose stock-in trade was topics of such burning interest as why a dog could hear the call of the sperm whale and a human ear could not, or whether the Tudors used deodorants) than of a Tammany Hall debate. Greatly daring, they did mount a programme called *In the News* in which Michael Foot, Bob Boothby, W.J. Brown and A.J.P. Taylor were allowed a reasonable degree of freedom in a knockabout discussion of the issues of the day; but when the Conservative Party expressed discomfort they immediately withdrew it. (The same format was, however, put on the air again by ATV under the title *Free Speech*.)

Most ludicrous of all, as it seemed to us, was the BBC's behaviour at the time of a general election. It was in those days the practice of 'the prime instrument of national broadcasting' to pull down the shutters during the election period and to carry on as if nothing of any importance was taking place. The 1956 BBC Handbook explained why:

> During the period between the Dissolution [of Parliament] and polling day the BBC is careful to exclude from its programmes (apart from election [party political] broadcasts) anything which could fairly be considered likely to influence electors in recording their votes.

We, on the other hand, believed that in a democracy the most important time to expose the voter to the full force of political argument was in the run-up to an election. In January 1958 the writ was issued for a by-election in Rochdale, and we seized our chance.

As soon as the election campaign got under way in Rochdale a

Granada team, under Tim Hewat and Barrie Heads, approached the three candidates. Yes, they were willing, even eager, to take part. Ludovic Kennedy, the Liberal and a national broadcaster, was 100 per cent on our side. The Conservative Parkinson saw himself as a potentially great broadcaster and longed to get on the air, and the Labour candidate McCann fell happily into place when I told him the other two had agreed. As the news of this project seeped upwards and southwards the Regional Officers of the parties accepted it with not much demur, but when it reached London it was a different matter. Morgan Philips, a fiery Welshman then in charge of Labour Party headquarters, summoned me to his office and registered his opposition to the plan, complaining bitterly about 'you television people interfering with the proper processes of democracy'. But when the Tories were seen to be indulging in an orgy of buck-passing and evasion and when the press endorsed the Granada initiative with a tidal wave of support, he changed his tune and moved over to our side. The Liberals, of course, who had nothing to lose, were already enlisted, so now it was only the top Tories – Heath, Hailsham and the Chief Whip Whitely – who had to be convinced.

Despite assurances that the Authority had cleared all matters of law, they sheltered behind the ambiguity of the Representation of the People Act – surely the proposed broadcasts could not be legal? The press accused them of 'ludicrous dithering', and at last they sought an opinion from a noted QC which, to their great chagrin, confirmed that there were no legal obstacles. So little more than week before polling day they caved in, and the field was clear.

A discussion between the candidates was broadcast on Tuesday 4 February, a mini-public meeting, carefully controlled, on Friday 7th and an Outside Broadcast of the count and declaration on polling day, Thursday 13th. After the excitement of the chase the programmes themselves were an anticlimax. In the first one everyone except Ludovic Kennedy was paralysed with fear. The show was set in a particularly hideous corridor-like room in Rochdale Town Hall. The candidates sat in a row on three too-high chairs some ten feet away from the chairman's (Brian Inglis's) desk, looking like schoolboys called up before the beak. There were stopwatches everywhere, for we were determined not to be faulted by failing to achieve equal time for all three candidates. I remember hovering anxiously around the scene of action, as senior executives tend to do on such occasions with no real effect save to irritate the workers by constantly asking them to check things which they have already checked several times. My own personal contribution was to take Brian into the Mayor's majestic loo immediately the show was over and provide him with a sorely needed bottle of Guinness. I had brought two, one for him and one for myself, but he misconstrued the situation and drank both.

The second programme, the 'Public Meeting' (a gaggle of hand-picked supporters recruited equally from the three parties, asking carefully vetted questions) passed off without incident, as did the Outside Broadcast of the count, which was, however, much longer than we had anticipated, with the result that poor Brian was reduced to asking questions about the armorial bearing over the fireplace and the lifestyle of Gracie Fields until in an inspired moment he turned to Jim Phoenix, the Granada Press Officer in the North, and asked him if he had any experiences of by-elections. Jim had been a returning officer several times and Brian was saved. 'I just kept asking questions,' he said. 'I didn't hear the answers. I was concentrating on not asking the same question twice.' Just after midnight, on the morning of Saturday 15 February, the result was announced:

J. McCann (Labour)	22,123
L. Kennedy (Liberal)	17,603
J. Parkinson (Conservative)	9,872
Labour majority	4,530

The Liberal vote had advanced greatly since the last election. The turnout was 80 per cent, exceptionally high when measured against the 82 per cent of the previous general election. No one could say whether or not this was because of television. The programmes had been amateurish and without intrinsic interest or merit, but that did not matter. We had broken through the party political barrier and put a by-election on the air.

The press coverage throughout the campaign had been enormous and now this thing had actually happened even all the fence-sitters joined their voices to a chorus of congratulation. Sidney was naturally seen to be the person responsible for Granada's break-through: 'Granada, which is run by Mr Sidney Bernstein, who holds a Labour Party membership card, and which has the name for being the most politically conscious of the independent programme companies, had broken new ground in television broadcasting,' said the *Guardian*. 'Sidney Bernstein, a real innovator in television programming, proposed that all candidates should appear on several programmes before the election, a suggestion that broke with all tradition,' said *The Times*.

But Sidney was far away and out of touch with the happenings of

Rochdale, Manchester and London. In January he had gone on holiday with Sandra to Jamaica and went on from there early in February
to New York, where he stayed for a month, freshening up his innumerable business contacts and glittering around in the café society he
loved so much and adorned so elegantly. On 30 January – a day of
decision – I sent him a general report in which Rochdale was a casual
item amongst many:

> Here are some odd bits of news from the North and from
> Golden Square. I saw John Halas's drafts last week. One of
> them, an animation of our present card, was excellent.
>
> Saw Bernard Levin, who was interested but non-
> committal. He would not like to produce: believes he is a
> writer. I have written to ask him to do the linking
> commentary for *Chelsea*.
>
> Our plans for televising the Rochdale by-election have
> caused a very great stir.

Flushed with success and ablaze with missionary zeal, we now turned
our attention to the possibility of doing a Rochdale on the grand
scale at the next general election. We would offer every candidate in
the Granada region a chance to address the voters in his constituency,
provided, of course, that all the other candidates agreed to appear. We
would cancel daytime programmes and run our marathon (this soon
became the official title) for as long as was necessary to screen every
consenting constituency. Within Granada, Sidney had reservations
about our ability to pull off such a monstrous project and Cecil's
heart was in his boots, for he could see what *Marathon* would do to
the ratings, but in public both of them supported our 'Experiment in
Constituency Television in a General Election', as we somewhat
pompously called it.

On 20 August 1959, when an autumn election had become a
certainty, we made our formal offer. Two Granada detachments
moved out simultaneously to different destinations in Smith Square,
where we encountered much the same reactions as had greeted the
Rochdale proposal. At Tory headquarters we were asked, of course,
what the Labour reaction would be. The Labour Party wanted to
know what line the Tories were taking. The two Granada executives
telephoned each other to find out, and I can remember putting the
phone down and saying, 'Well, Morgan, if you pull out I guess the
Tories will say that they were prepared to go ahead but you funked.'
A similar speech to the other side by my opposite number assisted

both parties to reach an agreement in principle that they would take part. Then both sides began to have cold feet and to raise doubts on the legality of the operation. We then produced our rabbit out of the hat in the form of a written opinion from the most eminent constitutional lawyer available, Sir Ivor Jennings, at that time Master of Trinity Hall, Cambridge, which found that in every respect the proposal for *Marathon* was within the law.

Once the dissolution of parliament was announced, *Marathon* began to lumber towards the screen. This time we sent a prospectus both to the party headquarters and to regional offices, setting out the proposal in meticulous detail. There were few objections and on 16 September we sent a personal letter to every candidate. Two hundred and ninety-four candidates accepted, but only 221 could appear, since in 53 constituencies (out of a total of 153) there were refusals. Mercifully this was before the days of the Greens, Screaming Lord Sutch and other fringe parties, so the standard performing team was made up of a chairman and two or three candidates. Two studios leapfrogged each other to give continuity (one in Leeds, since in those days, Granadaland covered Yorkshire as well as Lancashire) and the broadcasts were mainly slotted in between noon and 4 p.m.

And so the monster *Marathon* went on the air. For a total of over twelve hours the long-suffering public could hear every cliché and every bromide in the political spectrum. There was much repetition, for candidates watched each other to learn how to perform, not to listen to what they said, and speakers tended to tread and retread the same patch of ground already flattened by the national debate. Very occasionally an original voice was heard, as when one Manchester player opened by saying, 'My stand is that what Moss Side needs is a new sewerage system and a closer association with Europe,' or when a female candidate, looking intensely at the camera, said, 'Now, children, I want you to run and tell Mummy that there is a lady on television who wants to speak to her.'

But we, the Granada pioneers, were oblivious to the fact that we had produced twelve hours of what was probably the most boring broadcasting since the fatstock prices were read out after the evening news in the early days of radio. We were jubilant. We had attempted a *Marathon* and we had completed the course. One other programme – *The Last Debate* – caused a serious shock to the system of the participants, namely Selwyn Lloyd, Barbara Castle and Arthur Holt, a genteel Liberal, and was to have serious consequences. We had filled our largest studio with an audience reflecting meticulously the balance of the parties in the House of Commons. Unfortunately an over-enthusiastic floor manager, director and executive producer (myself) led the audience to believe that we wanted the supporters of each party to behave more or less as would the Liverpool Kop in the annual local derby against Everton. They took on this idea with enthusiasm, and during the programme the cheers, counter-cheers, catcalls and whistles rose to such a pitch that no one could hear a word that was said. In vain it was explained to the speakers that thanks to close miking the viewer could hear them perfectly and that the roars that seemed so formidable in the studio had been reduced to a gentle whisper. Selwyn Lloyd (the Foreign Secretary) came off white with anger, vowing that he would never take part in any Granada programme again (he never did). Barbara Castle, for once genuinely frightened and blazing with fury, only said, 'You will hear more of this', and stomped off; Arthur Holt sat with his head in his hands repeating, 'Oh my God' at frequent intervals. It was, we thought, a great show, but hear more of it we did. The parties set up a joint committee to monitor all television proposals for the next general election, and for many years programmes with a studio audience were banned.

But overall the election shows were greeted as a great success. The press in their free estate could never understand why television was hedged around with (to them) ludicrous regulations, and so they gave us full support and warm praise. In particular, Sidney was singled out as a man of vision who had changed the face of political broadcasting in Britain.

Our next target on the political agenda was the party conferences. Should not the members of a party have the right to see how affairs were being conducted on their behalf, we asked? Once again we soon had the press and the public on our side, and once again the party machines prevaricated. This time they could not call in the law to their aid, but they deployed all the same arguments against broadcasting the conferences that were to be used to delay the coverage of the House of Commons by some two decades: television cameras would distract attention, the lights would dazzle the speakers, the conferences would become a 'personality parade' with people showing off to the camera, and it would change the nature of the conferences: they would lose their intimacy. We were favoured by fortune in that the TUC conference was taking place in the North that year (1962), some weeks before the party conferences, and naturally the TUC had no inhibitions about television coverage. So covered they were, in what was acclaimed as a technical and democratic achievement, although the thoughts of the mothers whose children were deprived of their usual afternoon fodder are not on record. Jim Callaghan, the Labour Shadow Chancellor, was enthusiastic and saw in the TUC coverage a clinching argument for televising not only the Labour conference but (much ahead of his time) the House of Commons itself. So all three were covered, and all good men and true in the parties congratulated Granada.

The next year, 1963, we were again lucky in that the Conservative conference provided the best political drama of the year. Just before the last speech of the day began, the chairman of the conference came on to say that there would be an announcement after the speech. Barrie Heads, the producer of many of our pioneering political doings, was unable to find out what it was going to be about – it might well have been that a lady's grey purse had been found behind the platform and would the owner come forward and claim it – but he had a hunch that something was up, so instead of fading out the last speech and joining the network at five o'clock, as he would normally have done, he told the central controller that he wanted to stay on the air. He suggested that the entire network stay with the conference; but they wouldn't, so it was Granada alone which was there when Lord Home came on the platform and announced that he'd seen Mr Macmillan the previous day in hospital, and that Macmillan had told him that he was tendering his resignation to the Queen: the biggest political story for years. The press benches emptied as everyone rushed for the phone. While Granada were on the air with this news, the network was showing *Criss Cross Quiz* – ironically a Granada production. 'What was important to us at Granada,' said Barrie, 'was the feeling that if you were prepared to take a flier on something that required political or journalistic judgement you always got the backing. I don't recall consulting Denis, as Controller of Programmes, on this occasion because there just wasn't the time; the decision had to be made in a matter of moments.'

While Barrie was sweating in the control room, Sidney and I were driving over to Blackpool. We discussed in detail the chances of each candidate, and I can report with some pride that we found for Alec Douglas-Home, then 8-1 against, rather than the favourite Rab Butler (6-4), Hailsham or Iain Macleod. We arrived to an evening of high drama, some of which was adroitly captured and relayed to Granada viewers over the next forty-eight hours.

For some years the BBC stood aloof from the conferences, and when at last they started to cover them with live cameras there were conspicuous notices displayed assuring the public that Granada would cover the conference as usual and they should beware of imitations.

Throughout these happenings within Granada, Sidney remained a figure in the background, a benevolent patron, always supportive of the lads in the front line but seldom interfering and never congratulatory. At Labour party conferences he would always sit alone through the whole proceedings in the gallery behind the platform, an isolated figure, notably inconspicuous. He would inspect the Outside Broadcast vehicles for cleanliness but did not take part in programme discussions. Publicly he still reaped the credit:

> Full marks for Sidney Bernstein. None for the BBC or the independent contractors in London and the Home Counties. For the second time Granada televised the TUC live. And no one in London and the South East could see it. Once again the debate proved fascinating viewing, as well as bringing democracy at work into every home . . . . This is one thing that only television can do. Granada, incidentally, did it efficiently and well. Why are the other contractors – and the BBC – afraid to do it at all?

So wrote Neville Randall in the *Daily Sketch*, and it was typical of much of what appeared in the press. From time to time Sidney published a resounding and carefully ghosted letter in *The Times* demanding that broadcasting at an election should be freed from party regulations and designed to suit the needs of the viewers rather than the party managers; at the same time, by adroitly managed disclosures and by various hints and nudges, he created the impression that he was modestly attempting to shift the credit from where it belonged (himself) to a group of meritorious workers whose efforts on his behalf deserved recognition. At the time none of us felt the slightest rancour at this treatment. It seemed to us that it was helpful to our cause to have Sidney portrayed as the great Panjandrum of media politics, and it was only much later when I looked back over Sidney's career that I saw that one of this greatest strokes of genius was his ability to conceal under a front of exceptional modesty a ruthless drive to ensure that none of his colleagues was visible to the public eye. He was quick to give unstinted praise to 'creative people' who were not on the Granada payroll, and would generously ascribe all credit for the success of a Granada programme to Tony Richardson, Charles Laughton or Arthur Miller, but it was not his custom to acknowledge that anyone within the portals, even his brother Cecil, contributed anything of significance to the onward march of Granada.

Granada coverage of politics reached its zenith in those early heady years. *Marathon* was mounted again at the general elections of 1964 and 1966, but the number of consenting candidates dwindled (mainly because more and more sitting tenants saw the folly of risking their necks) and this was the last time. The audience for blanket coverage of the party conferences was so small that we could not justify even to ourselves the loss of so many viewers to tickle the political palates of so few. The public had let us down. They were much less interested in politics than they should have been. Cecil had shown remarkable restraint in withholding any pressure to restore the daytime ratings to reasonable levels, but now we capitulated. In January 1969, in a sad little article in *The Times*, I sketched out the nature of our early ambitions and achievements and concluded, 'This initiative has failed'. But the reason I gave – 'Even people who are interested in politics are not interested in their present politicians' – was wrong. Political debate on television served up in its raw form and in real time can only break through the boredom barrier at times of great crisis or of high drama. At all other times, however important the topic, however sparky the speakers, live coverage is strictly for the birds and for the journalists, the political commentators and that now numerous and prosperous tribe, the psephologists.

So Granada gave up the pursuit of bringing live political debate into the living room and turned its energies to large-scale programmes on major topics (*The State of the Nation* series) and to inventing new and ingenious ways of enlivening the scene at general elections, such as the Granada Five Hundred, in which a body of citizens in a marginal constituency had their voting inclinations monitored as they were subjected to a series of seminars conducted by leading figures in the opposing parties. We continued to challenge the remaining restrictions on our freedom and enthusiastically supported Robin Day's campaign to broadcast the proceedings of the House of Commons. Indeed, we got the House of Lords to agree to a series of experimental sessions on closed circuit in 1968, which were well received but did not appear to accelerate the reluctant progress of the lower house towards the day of the cameras.

So it was that in the name of free speech we opened the Pandora's box that let fly the multitude of political programmes that fill our screens today and which, at times of General Elections, make even the most avid student of politics cry out for mercy.

CHAPTER SIX

It was not the style of the Bernsteins to admit business colleagues into their homes. Family was family, with the binding ties and organised intimacy of Jewry. For friends there were regular weekend parties at Coppings, Sidney's comfortable farmhouse in Kent, and occasionally also at Cecil's more urban but not quite suburban home, Five Trees, in Bognor. For Sidney, friends were mainly old friends: Gerald Barry, David Blairman, often visiting Americans – Alistair and Jane Cooke, Betty Comden and Adolf Green, Lauren Bacall – and, in later years, usually one of the two familiars, Bernard Levin and Paul Bevan. (Paul started life as a design consultant and then as employee, it is true, but soon assumed the role of honorary ADC, companion and family friend.) In a quite separate stratum of friendship Sidney consorted regularly with Solly Zuckerman and Victor Rothschild, sometimes separately, sometimes together. The relationship between this trio was cordial – they joshed each other like schoolboys – but cagey. They met not for fun but rather to update and check the state of their current knowledge of the way the world wagged. At any moment one of them might be the bearer of sensational news (for them) about what was on the agenda for Pugwash, why the French were going nuclear, why so much American gold had been turning up in Colombia. Occasionally I was included in the party, and then what I saw was three great lions at their intellectual feeding time, all eating voraciously but each one watchful lest one of the others gobbled up more speaking time than was his due.

But Sidney's most precious friendships were of a more exalted kind. He revered the best kind of Englishness and respected learning, especially learning in literature where he himself was disadvantaged. One such friend was Sir William Haley, editor of *The Times*, Chairman of the BBC, bookman extraordinary, who contributed from time to time prissy little essays on Victorian novelists to his own paper under the *nom de plume* of Oliver Edwards. Sidney corre-

144

sponded with him, lunched and dined with him, and discussed with him aspects of the world's affairs that were philosophical, political and, on a rather mundane level, artistic. Brighter even than Haley's star in Sidney's planetarium was Radcliffe – Cyril Radcliffe – whom Sidney first met when at the Ministry of Information. Lord Radcliffe, already a distinguished judge, went on to preside over the British Museum and to lead pretty well every government inquiry that required a verdict confirming the status quo, and if not the status quo then the nearest thing to it that his cautiously selected committee would wear. He was greatly respected by the right and the centre left but regarded as something of a cartoon character by the outer left. I remember Nicky Kaldor saying of him that he was 'quite useful in sniffing out communists and that sort of thing but otherwise did nothing but confirm the deep conservative instincts of the Labour Party'. He was, however, charming, and in spite of holding tenaciously to every prejudice known to High Toryism, was somehow able to impress people as an open-minded and liberal sort of chap. He and Sidney corresponded from time to time in long elegant letters about affairs in general or affairs relevant to one or the other, but never in any mode that could be described as 'professional'. After Cyril Radcliffe's death in 1977 it was Bernard Levin who filled his place. Bernard had long been closer to Sidney than any person outside his family – indeed, it could be said that he had been adopted into it, not as a son but perhaps as a younger brother.

It was with these three that Sidney entered the realm of high friendship as it was understood and practised by eminent Victorians. Such friendships, wholly male-oriented, were undemanding and unexploitative, and offered emotional as well as intellectual satisfaction. Sidney was spreading his wings in a world of erudition and culture which he had never known before. He was, in a way, enjoying an education that had eluded him in his youth. Not that there was anything of master and pupil in any of the three relationships, for Sidney had as much to teach them about his world as they had to teach him about theirs. Haley's style could be elaborate and mannered, Radcliffe had the tortuous even-handedness of a great lawyer, Levin could come at any subject the long way round. In contrast, Sidney's approach to any topic was direct and clear, his critical faculty fresh and acute, and his wit amiably deflationary.

There was a faint aura of romance over these one-to-one relationships and certainly there was no place in them for a third party. I was on good but separate terms with William Haley and Bernard Levin, but early on was excommunicated by Cyril Radcliffe. One fine morning, Sidney and I had taken a helicopter to visit the great man in his country home near Oxford to consult with him about some point concerning political broadcasts. Things went awry from the start. We went to the wrong door and a new butler did not know who Sidney was. Antonia Radcliffe, poor thing, was suffering the effects of what must have been a huge intake of alcohol over breakfast since she kept entering the room cringing and pathetically pleading for 'Just one little drinkie, Cyril, please', and, when he paid no attention, backing out of the door sobbing faintly. The English Test cricket team was in action and something terribly unsporting had happened which threatened the whole future of the game – as I remember it, a player had spoken critically and publicly about a decision by the Test and Country Cricket Board. This had thrown Cyril into a state of anger and consternation. He had already phoned the editor of *The Times*, had been busy drafting a letter to him when we arrived, and could talk of little else. When we began our serious discussion, he discerned that I was desirous of using the power of television to force politicians into more open debate with the public. After listening for some time he turned to Sidney and said, 'Just as young Compton (or Trueman or whoever) is going to ruin English cricket, unless you are careful, Sidney. Denis Forman is going to destroy the Granada you have created and love so much.' This was a bit of a conversation stopper, and since we were only halfway through the perfectly underdone roast beef the end of the meal seemed a long way off. Lady Antonia was helpful, however, for (now in possession of a little drinkie) she discovered that I had been a party to putting the Royal Ballet's *Cinderella* onto television and gushed on about Michael Somes, of whom she was a leading groupie. 'Somes! Somes!' she cried, 'so absolutely beautiful! Such Greek legs! Did you speak to him, Mr Forman? What did he say? Was he speaking to Margot?' After this, Sidney and Cyril concentrated on the economic prospects for Israel until we made an early departure.

My chief relationship with Sidney was of course that of colleague, perhaps most favoured colleague. But there was also a whiff of old friend, partly because I was Helen's husband (they had sometimes locked horns during the war, but there was a lasting mutual respect) and partly because of the good times he and I had together before I joined Granada. We were candidates for Coppings weekends and went down there from time to time. I also became, for a short time, a fringe member of the family, mainly because I became equally friendly with Sandra and would often pass her inside information about her man's health or progress in a crisis such as that caused by Mr Whipp, when

I was able to phone her after the first vote and say, 'He'll walk it. It's a happy birthday.' She would keep me informed when Sidney was out of sorts or sulking in his well-found tent in Wilton Crescent. Once a disgruntled chauffeur, who thought that for a man who earned so much Sidney paid him too little, found his way into Sandra's daughter Charlotte's twenty-first birthday party and felled him with a straight left, causing him to graze his cheek as he dropped to the floor. I rang up a week later and said, 'But surely Sandra it must be healed by now.' She replied, 'Of course it's healed but it still *shows*.'

We stayed with the Bernsteins in their villa in Ansedonia and were given the free use of the main establishment or of the neat little farmhouse Cocculuto, whenever we wanted. It was there that we found a happy association with Alan Moorehead and his family, and spent much time at sea in the yacht owned by Lucy Moorehead and Sandra Bernstein and cleverly named 'Lucandra'.

Yet although moving easily through the several strata of Sidney's friendships, I never quite entered the most exalted class of Haley, Radcliffe and Levin. Had I left Granada in the early sixties I believe that this would have come about, but any such prospect was blighted by the clash of wills which was to occur as my control over Television grew greater and his, owing to the absorption of his energies elsewhere in the Group, declined, although his desire to retain it did not. We came closest to high friendship when we travelled together abroad, to Canada several times when we were setting up our Canadian station in Ottawa, CJOH; to New York, although here our time was more socially spent; and once, in the early winter of 1958, to Moscow. Although, despite allegations to the contrary, neither of us had ever had any traffic with the Communist party, both Sidney and I were unashamedly pro-Russian. In my case it was my love of Russian literature and Russian music that lay at the root of this feeling; in Sidney's it was his admiration for a system that had moved such a huge intractable country into the twentieth century and had at least to some degree made it work. And for both of us there was the memory of the great Russian films (*October, Battleship Potemkin, Earth, The General Line, Alexander Nevsky*).

We set off to Russia all agog and prepared to believe the best of what we saw and heard. But it was not to be gas and gaiters all the way, as the following extracts from a journal I kept at that time will show.

23rd November 1958 flew in a Viscount aircraft from London to Warsaw. Met at once by small talkative Pole, friend of our friend [Jerzy] Toeplitz, and later by an Orbis courier. Complete confusion as to who is who. Warsaw 85 per cent utterly destroyed. Hotel Bristol spacious but shabby. In Warsaw hotel rooms are not vacated until 6. Both hearts sink; not yet 3.30. Talkative Pole offers person-ally conducted tour.

Personally conducted tour a limited success. Centre of Warsaw rebuilt in various styles and periods. Sit down in wine bar. Talkative Pole launches into serious talk about Poland, the Jews, Germany, Russia. Have been able to understand half of what he said until now, but percentage drops as he becomes excited. Heat intense, sweet wine horrible, Teddy boys and girls all around very noisy. Am overcome, lose all understanding of talkative Pole. At last Sidney, suffering equally, says, 'Let's get some air.'

On way back to hotel talkative Pole develops habit of calling us 'My dear'. Reflect on reasons: could be –

1. Bad knowledge of English. He could mean 'My dear fellow'. Remember Indian who used to say 'My chap' as form of address. He meant 'My dear chap'.
2. Has mixed with stage people.
3. Is homosexual. Certain odd seizures of the arm in conversation add weight to this.

Light fades as we return (4.30). Conducted tour now abhorrent. Long for room, so does Sidney who has headache. We succeed; the rooms are ready. My Dear says he will be back for supper at 6.30. Sidney says quickly, 'Too early' – 7.30 is fixed.

Am summoned by Sidney at 7.32. We go to a restaurant, 'Rabytas', selected by My Dear. Long sagas of unsuccessful attempts to finance Polish film production by Britain, France, America. Sidney absolutely valiant, implores him to make an historical spectacular. But My Dear much too interested telling us of Poland's difficulties.

Good vodka, raw herring in cream and stuffed carp. Small sauce dish put down which I take to be my property and almost empty at one dive. Was meant for all three. Sidney, always alert when waiting is in question, shouts to waiter to bring more; waiter does not understand and brings nothing.

We had decided to travel from Warsaw to Moscow by train 'in order to see more of the country'. In fact, all the way to Brest Litovsk, Sidney had his head in last week's Sunday papers whilst I looked out on a scene of utter desolation.

> At Brest Litovsk hockey-girl interpreter, young and embarrassed, enters compartment and says, 'Yan Bernsteen?' I say no, Forman, and she shepherds us about the station and offices with grace and goodwill. We are the only two Intourists. Sidney anxious about food; we have to stop at Brest from 5–7.30, there is a restaurant at the station and a dining car on the train. Sidney asks my advice; having had large breakfast at 11, lunch at 2, and having gained two hours we have only just eaten, I favour train. Sidney asks girl's advice. She says, 'You may be rushed if you eat at the station.' Intimidated, he reluctantly agrees to train. After changing money, however, it is clear that he is not easy in his mind and insists on going to inspect the restaurant. It is not uninviting with a great display of cold food on huge altar covered with rust-coloured velvet. We almost set to, but not quite. We trudge through the mud and gaze at our first Russian shop, also at what we think must be a meeting of some organisation inside a small room with curtains undrawn. On return to the station Sidney (the matter has been preying on his mind) suggests a snack just in case the train dinner is disappointing. The snack starts as a raw herring and caviare with vodka, but runs on through sprats in oil, sausage and sturgeon. Back at the train then we enter the dining car and order dinner, and as soon as we move out it is duly eaten.

Again in Moscow things started badly at the National Hotel:

> A few little hitches. I have a poor room. Mr Parker [Ralph Parker, the *Times* correspondent in Moscow and married to a Russian ballerina], hangs about. Difficult to get tickets for a theatre tonight. Both of us sluggish and tired. But the blockage shifts, my room is changed, Parker goes, tickets may be possible after all. Two blessed hours at rest. My sitting room is about as big as the dining room at home. I can see the Red Square by craning out. The room is decorated in two distinct styles: 1. Czarist (lamp, vases, mirror,

inkstand). 2. Tottenham Court Road (desk, tables, chair and all else). In the bathroom the lavatory has a Czarist bowl with a Tottenham Court Road seat. The bath is a Turkish cistern and there was no plug in the basin. (Sidney later produced Peter Brook's rubber ball with triumph.)

Sidney troubled by toothache. I go and buy Codeine in chemist. Huge queue of Muscovites mainly buying contraceptives. Young girl behind counter draws them out of a tub naked and unashamed by ones, by twos, and once a dozen.

After a snack (caviare and vodka) in Sidney's room we go to see Raikin, a recommended comic, in a Ziv car with a chauffeur. I have a vague form from Intourist to show the administrator (no ticket). It works. Theatre a small Second Empire rectangular hall holding 800 (Bernstein estimate). Show on the lines of a concert party, one or two good strokes of design, Raikin very good, very sympathetic. Leave after first act and find Ziv car gone. Board a taxi, eat a large meal and to bed by 12.

Our first encounter with the British Embassy was not impressive:

26 November 1958. Weather raw and sleety. Up early, breakfast in room, journal, and down to meet Guide. She is Zoya Kuranacheva and she has a terrible squint. But otherwise charming, deadly intelligent, and serious to help. We have a lot of talk. Sidney lingers over breakfast until Parker arrives. Go to British Embassy, crouching timidly on bank of river facing the Kremlin. To see the Kremlin first time is a knockout. Huge, sprawling, full of its own citadels and temples, a renaissance front here, a Moslem tower there, all on different levels, crowded, spacious, terrifying, and surrounded by the high stone wall the colour of a dead man's blood. It has grown through the accidents of history, a little of the Tower of London, a little of Athenian Edinburgh, a little of the London Zoo, but mostly it is like the ruins, also red, of Akbar's great palace at Delhi.

Saw Paul Holmer. Nice young establishment man, cut out to be a virgin monk. But he has strayed into marriage. He knows less about the people we want to see than we do. We talk about the weather. It is warm for the time of year. He doesn't know that Russia will soon perhaps be on

EBU. He doesn't know Russia is interested in colour TV. He doesn't know that George Gale of the *Express* is in town. Really pretty hard not to know this. He is the Information Officer. I ask if we can send scripts by the bag. He says no bag until Monday. I say, 'You must use the 'phone a lot.' He misses the joke and says, 'Oh no, not much really; not so much.' I could forgive him everything except that he thinks being stationed in Russia is a bad joke. ('Oh yes, I keep trying to learn the lingo but I find it jolly hard to find time for my prep.')

Within a couple of days we had made our own contacts:

At 5.45 Sam Russell (*Daily Worker* correspondent in Moscow) comes in, collars a huge whisky, and says Sidney wants me because Alexandrove [Eisenstein's one-time producer] has arrived. Join the party, drinking old red vodka and eating caviare and toast. Splendid gossip with Alexandrov, dear man, until 7. Alexandrov insists party is on him. Sidney says no, on him. We are now halfway downstairs, and waitress runs down with bill for 104 roubles, which I pay. Walk to the Bolshoi theatre in sleet. Alex says what nonsense forecasters talk – they had predicted 18 degrees frost. We agree forecasters pretty contemptible people.

We make our formal visit to the TV studios and to the British Embassy on 27 November:

Meet Zoya. Sidney comes down. Slight hitch – no Intourist cars owing to cold. Cannot see studios this morning, must first see Chapligin, Deputy President Committee Radio and TV. He is responsible for TV in Russia. After long tramp through Ministry corridors we see him, tough, shrewd and humorous. He asks the right questions. Sidney leads with the answers and I support, a little too much. We say, can we see studios? He says, yes, of course. But he can't get through to them on the telephone. He takes this well. We part warmly and drive via the hotel to lunch at the Embassy.

We are the last to arrive and after clambering up wide Czarist staircase are met by Sir Patrick Reilly, KCMG, Her

Majesty's Ambassador. He says, 'How do you do.' And as he says it I reckon he doesn't look as if he was doing very well himself. Lank sandy hair, big codfish face, a badly cut suit.

Ambassador's lady stoutish little soul, leads us into crowded drawing room and takes Sidney round the full circle leaving me stranded in the middle facing, of all things, the then popular concert pianist Eileen Joyce. Am angry, not because of the affront, not because of Eileen Joyce, but because of the sheer inefficiency of it. After all, we are paying good taxpayers' money for Ambassadors' wives to do a job, which is almost exclusively confined to introducing people to other people. And she hasn't introduced me to a soul. Take a few threatening paces after her; she looks over her shoulder in a hunted way and goes on with Sidney. I fall back on Eileen Joyce, who suspects that I have attempted to escape her and failed. Gulp some tepid sweet sherry and square my shoulders.

Lunch is agony. On my right, and most talkative, is the naval attaché's wife. She rattles on. 'We had to buy a whole year's supply of tinned goods when we came.' (Why, in God's name, why?) 'They [the Russians] live in indescribable squalor. You visitors don't see that. But they seem to prefer it that way. Of course our flat is completely wired. We know that. We go to church every Sunday and it's so awful, nothing but old people.'

'Like England?' I say, and she doesn't know quite what I mean. So I talk to a nice young engineer on my left who is on a visit to install plastic presses in a tyre factory. After lunch we chat with the Ambassador, who was astonished to hear of Russian TV developments. (I didn't think he believed us, just thought we were 'alarmist'.) Later note with chagrin that Sidney has got charming young girl Miss Stone, journalist, who is travelling Brussels–Peking by rail to spend Christmas with her family in China, where she was born, and I have drawn, once again, Eileen Joyce. We talk about Russian orchestras, aren't they bad? But the audiences, my dear, are wonderful. (Know this to be untrue of Moscow). Ambassadress breaks it up and we talk of *The Cranes Are Flying*. She says, 'Such an old-fashioned film, I thought. People ran up and downstairs so much faster than in real life.' (Verbatim.) At last we leave. In the car Sidney turns to Eileen Joyce, still warm from the ambassadorial flattery, and says, 'Abominable lunch'. He means the food; she is not quite sure what he means. Long drive to Eileen Joyce's hotel, with Eileen and Sidney talking about how to deal with a rouble balance.

Later the same day we reached our first goal:

To the TV studios with dear Zoya. (She is well versed: was John Gunther's guide and has just finished with a delegation of American TV and radio men.) After a slow start we get into control rooms and studios. I get excited, shout a bit and want to find out more details than Sidney has patience for. They are about the size, in floor space, of the Manchester TV Centre. Not so well equipped, but some interesting things.

From the TV centre to Mosfilm studios where Alexandrov awaits us. We see his new experimental film: the experiment (optical marriage of foreground and background through use of infra-red instead of BP [back projection] is sensationally good). The film itself, a singing travelogue, is vulgar. He never was a good director, just a part of the Eisenstein troupe and a very nice man.

From Mosfilm to the hotel (now after 7), a meal, and on to the circus, where we catch the last act of the first part and see the whole of the second. Circus good beyond all expectation: final magician act left Sidney and self embarrassedly saying, 'They must be doubles', and 'They must have traps,' but not really having the faintest idea how the highly spectacular tricks were done. Circus housed in permanent open-stage building: very attractive, capacity 2,000 (Bernstein estimate).

But things were not to go on so happily:

Disaster and frustration. Zoya sick, Victoria, her substitute, a stupid Armenian cow. All morning she fails to make appointments, is fobbed off on to subordinates, fails to understand what an audition is in spite of elaborate pantomime. Four hours of misery and the shades deepen when Victoria takes me a long drive to get my camera mended and the shop is shut for lunch. We give up.

To the Pekin Restaurant. We make five false starts. We

get to (a) the first floor of the hotel, (b) a staff canteen, (c) ladies' hairdressing, (d) about three flights of stairs, complete with corridors, (e) a huge room set for a Chinese feast. We are told that this is the restaurant and it is closed. Spirits drop, but we see large numbers of Chinese gentlemen in blue uniforms eating behind a curtain. We ask if we can join them: the request is granted. We sit in a howling draught at a small table with one of the largest blue Chinese eating in very rudimentary way and at very close range. We move to another table; draught worse. We give order to bungling waiter (in a Russian Chinese restaurant the clientele are Chinese and the waiters Russians, in England the waiters are Chinese and the clientele English) and move to a third table. Sidney is shivering; my cold sits more heavily upon me every moment. We wait and wait. Bungling waiter makes the appalling mistake of bringing our food where Sidney can see it and then potters off on some other errand. This is the low point of the tour. Sidney nearly frantic, only with great effort of will restrains himself from leaping up to capture the food. I am past caring whether the food comes or not. I want to go to bed and get warm.

We were surprised to find more legitimate theatre playing in central Moscow than in London's West End. Some nights we went to only one show; twice we managed three, one act apiece; the norm was two:

First theatre, *The Bedbug*, a 1930s Soviet farce, coarse, broad and very funny. Although book and actors good, the real contribution comes from the production. Great use of a revolve, characters leaping out of the audience, gauze back-drop to interiors, allowing fade through to exterior scene. Who would think of staging a Whitehall farce this way? Laugh heartily and leave at interval; house capacity 800 (Bernstein estimate). Proceed to the Tchaikovsky Hall, new and I thought very good, though Sidney was a bit sniffy and found the decor cold. Here the Red Army are at work; last act of first part a good dancing ensemble of 24 men. Second part singing; solo and choral which is good of its kind but soon a deadly bore. Hall capacity 1,500 (Bernstein estimate).

Find car deserted by driver: no amount of beating out nearby stores (shopping still going full swing) flushes him. After so many years of the Dixon-Daft [Sidney's London chauffeurs'] regime Sidney bears this situation (it has happened before) with great phlegm. Taxi and to bed.

Victoria was to become the bane of the visit:

29 November 1958. Another bout of frustration with the fat and unctuous Victoria. Sidney has taken a great dislike to her and says she is the kind of woman who is always looking into her bag. Take her to find fur. Victoria worse, takes us to bad shops, is not alert. No fur found. At last we get message we can go to the studio. We complete our nose-round; this time I take many photos, although my stock not fast enough. At one point this seems to embarrass guides, which makes Sidney uneasy. I feel rather callously that photos more important than embarrassment, but ask permission before taking next shot. I want a picture of woman on a camera and explain through Victoria that in England, backward old place that it is, we have no lady cameramen. Would like to take back to comrades in Manchester progressive photograph of Russian lady cameraman. This offer is not well received, and soon I learn the reason: there are no lady cameramen in Russia either.

We had a further meeting with British Officialdom:

Lunch with Peter Holmer, the first secretary British Embassy, in his home. He is really the senior information officer (I imagine this means spy). He explains that this is not a helpful title in Moscow. About twelve people, all English, six birds of passage, five respectable connections of H.M. and myself. Sit next to hostess and love her. Vague, faded middle-aged-one-time deb, worried by two little daughters in a hostile capital and complete exile from her hairdresser, dressmaker, Mummy, *Vogue* and summer holidays in Aberdeenshire. Has been checked so often by pedantic husband that she qualifies every statement to the hilt. 'Didn't Kruschev or someone say …?' 'Wasn't it at the Bolshoi or somewhere …?' Appalling lunch: cheese souf-

flé, consistency of crème caramel, roast pork, not enough
to go round and either dogs' or children's dinner pillaged
to spread over last two guests, and finally 'shape', white,
tasteless and shapeless. She tells me that Russian cooking is
quite impossible. As I say goodbye I ask Paul Holmer
where I can buy a bottle of whisky. The Embassy? He is
thrown; no, not the Embassy; the Americans do that sort of
thing but we are given an allowance for entertainment on
the Embassy premises only. Would I accept a bottle of his
own? (Well, yes.)

Tonight getting coats after the ballet we have difficulty
in locating correct cloakroom. Sidney picks one, I have
doubts, go upstairs along corridor, downstairs and see
another, which pleases me more. I go in and see Sidney. It
was the same one; I have walked in a circle and he has lost
his place in the queue. This will not be forgotten.

Victoria continued to be unsatisfactory:

We visit the Kremlin with Victoria. She showed us round
the Kremlin Museum, a splendid collection of gold, silver,
armour, costumes and coaches, with great complacency. I
asked her the date of an object; she said 18th century. I said
yes, but what date, early or late? She said, 'I do not give
dates, the century is considered to be enough.'

Sometimes we found it difficult to communicate our enthusiasm
for Russian culture:

There was nearly one ugly incident. To be uncultured in
Russia today means to behave like a peasant (or a capital-
ist) and not in the best Soviet manner. It is uncultured to
get drunk, to drop orange peel in the street, to blow your
nose without a handkerchief, to push in a queue. This
became one of the running gags of the trip. In the book-
shop a schoolmistressy type of young woman had been
pushing like a buffalo at my buttocks for some minutes. I
was squeezed against the counter (the shop, like most
Moscow shops, was like a tube train at rush hour). Sidney
was looking at a children's book in which a rabbit was shot
by a man with a gun. He disapproved of this violence. I
agreed with him by saying, 'Very uncultured.' The

schoolmistress heard this clearly and understood English.

'Who are you calling uncultured?' she said, scarlet and hostile. I began to explain to her that my friend thought that to use violence to kill a rabbit was in bad taste, but realised as I was speaking that it sounded too like a Thurber story and lacked the power to convince. She snorted, and charged away into a group of diminutive Japanese men, scattering them like marbles.

The final crunch with Victoria came on 1 December:

Waiting for Victoria to fix time of appointment already fixed in principle. She bungles interminably. Eventually we drive to the offices of the Cultural Relations Committee where we wanted to see Zhukov, of whom we had heard good things. He had proved to be absent in America, so we got an introduction to his deputy Krukov, of whom we had heard fairly good things. On arrival, we were told that Krukov's deputy would see us (of whom we had heard nothing at all). Whilst this to-ing and fro-ing was going on Sidney and self roamed the premises. Some people can walk down a street without a moment's diversion from their main purpose, which is purposeful travel. Not so either of us, who are both inveterate potterers. Sidney has a passionate addiction to architectural pottering. This big Tsarist house which had been cut and chopped about to make government offices presented him with just the sort of puzzle to tickle his fancy.

We started in the waiting room where we had been put working out where the original entrance had led to the main reception room. But soon we were ranging far and wide along corridors and up and down stairs tapping walls, taking measurements, poking our heads into cupboards and yelling out to each other, 'I think I see traces of the original stairhead here', or 'This must be a partition to screen the fireplace.' When Victoria eventually finds us, strayed far from where we should be, I am on my hands and knees looking into a kind of horizontal flue and Sidney is measuring the width of a doorway putting one foot in front of the other in the manner of a tightrope walker and with his arms stretched out for balance. Victoria announced with great aplomb that Zhukov's

deputy's deputy's deputy will see us now. Sidney sends me
to tell this inferior person, in the politest possible term, to
stuff it up, which I do, and in the piece of time gained we
drive to see the Museum of Fine Arts.

To Victoria's immeasurable satisfaction this proves to be
closed. I resent her pleasure; the slow burn of the past few
days bursts into flames. I say will she please get us in, it is
her duty to do so. She says impossible. She will, if we like,
ring the Ministry of Culture and see if they will issue us
with a pass for tomorrow, but she says this in the way
Nannies used to say 'We'll have to ask your father about
that.' I leave her and Sidney with the car, and walk furiously round the gallery, aggressive and pertinacious. I
discover a small door in the basement which yields to pressure. Inside there are signs of activity, an army of women
hammering up packing cases and parties of schoolchildren
eating sandwiches, also a policeman (soldier). I explain I
am English and want to see the Administrator. Soon a man
appears whom I take to be the administrator and I explain
that two important English art scholars are knocking at the
door. We go out and get the car. Driven to another door.
Get into a wooden hut and wait for what seems like half
an hour while our passes are made out. We drive back to
the basement door. Then we get in. I wink at Victoria but
she will not meet my eye, nor even speak. She is mortally
affronted. We get a guide, a straggly art-crazed spinster who
can be found in the precincts of any museum in the world
living on one and fourpence a week. The galleries are full
of activity; the German art treasures, pinched during the
war, are being sent back to their owners. We want to see
the collection of Impressionist paintings which Sidney
remembers from a previous visit when they used to hang
in the Sugar King's Palace. They are immense, in quantity
and quality, and the fact that they are crowded higgledy-
piggledy in a storeroom makes it all the more exciting.
Picasso, Matisse, Gauguin, Renoir, Cézanne, Manet, all
splendidly represented by some of their richest work. We
spend a happy hour.

The morning after this event Victoria rather sourly said
to me, 'You and Mr Bernstein were like two schoolboys
running about looking at pictures and making exclama-
tions.' I reported Victoria's disapproval of us to Sidney who

sent for her and said, 'Victoria, you are not a good communist. It was your duty to get us in to see the pictures and
you failed. Mr Forman did not fail because he had determination.' That was the last we saw of Victoria. For the last
two days we had an agreeable scatterbrain called Sophie.

We flew to Brussels where our connection to London was
cancelled because of fog. I managed to get the last stateroom for two
on the Hook–Harwich night boat but when we embarked we saw
two familiar figures – Michael Somes and Margot Fonteyn, who had
been dancing in some charity event in Berlin. Sidney instantly turned
to Margot and said, 'Would you please accept our cabin', which she
most graciously did. Sidney and I returned to the bar, curious to
know how the word 'you' would be interpreted, but the matter was
soon settled by the appearance of Somes seeking hot brandy and milk
and asking rather petulantly for a warm rug to spread over his knees.

We came back from this trip with our admiration for Russia
undimmed. We were not as euphoric as the great lions – Bernard
Shaw and H.G. Wells, who had visited Russia before the war – but
we had met some remarkable people and seen some wonderfully
good theatre. Although we picked up unspoken fears about Stalin's
regime, we had no knowledge of the monstrosities that were soon to
come to light. And there was a bonus for me. In the late evening, in
the many hours of waiting to see self-important people, over the
many snacks of vodka and caviare and in cars and trains, Sidney
would talk to me about his early life, about what had made him a
socialist, and about what he thought of men and matters today.

It was from these talks and from information gleaned from some inti-
mate outside sources that I was able to piece together a picture of
Sidney's life before television. I should say that the facts as I came to
know them do not always agree with the authorised version of
Sidney's life which was current within Granada and was later
enshrined in Caroline Moorehead's biography. The arrival of the
Bernstein family in England, for instance, is described in the biography as follows:

> It was to Ilford that Alexander Bernstein had come from
> Sweden in the 1880s, together with his mother and sister
> Annie. Why he chose to come to England, or why he
> settled in Essex, is unknown. Neither parent ever spoke to
> Sidney of the past. He discovered that his father was a

naturalised Swedish subject only when, already grown up, he saw his passport. All he knew as a boy was that on 6 August 1893 his father married Jane Lazarus, daughter of two Russian immigrants, and that, as children multiplied and family finances grew, so the family had moved into ever larger houses, always in Ilford.

The facts are somewhat different. Sidney's father Alexander and his brother Julius arrived in London's East End from Riga in Latvia in the early 1890s. Julius had been trained as a tailor, and from the age of seven had travelled round from house to house with a sewing machine on his back doing odd tailoring jobs. Alexander had been apprenticed as a shoemaker. Neither had been registered at birth for fear of being conscripted into the Russian army when they reached military age; hence neither knew his true age. These two penniless young men set up shop in the East end and soon married two sisters, daughters of an earlier immigrant from Riga known as Isaiah Lazarus, who also practised as a tailor. This little cell of orthodox Jews from the other side of the Baltic stuck closely together. As the children started to arrive (in considerable numbers) Julius would provide the clothes for both families, Alexander the boots and shoes. Their businesses prospered and Alexander soon set up a boot factory which expanded greatly when he made a lucrative contract to supply boots to the Boers in South Africa. Once again fact and fiction diverge, for in the official biography Alexander is represented as a prosperous businessman with a stone quarry in Wales, an office in Finsbury Square and a housing estate in Ilford. In fact, when the Boer War broke out the boot business collapsed and he was declared a bankrupt. No doubt the family cell united to bale him out and set him up in the next venture, which was the manufacture of carborundum wheels. Next he set up a factory in Upton Park and the family moved to Ilford, and from this point on the official version of his life begins to run nearer to actuality. In this period the stone quarry and the housing estate may have some substance, although surviving relatives of Sidney's generation have no recollection of either. What is certain is that Alexander prospered and in 1908 he built the first of the Bernstein Theatres, the Edmonton Empire, and ran it as a music hall; it was soon to be followed by the purchase of two other halls.

Sidney was born in 1899, the fourth of nine children. He spent most of his early childhood in Ilford, where he went to a private school and won a scholarship to the Coopers' Company School at Bow. But he had no love of scholarship and opted to leave school at the age of fifteen, with the intention of joining his father's business. At first Alexander resisted. Sidney was despatched to become an apprentice in an engineering firm, but within a year he got his way and was allowed to join the film company which supplied the music halls with the film segments that now made up a substantial part of each night's bill.

Sidney and his father did not live and work together harmoniously. In all the years he and I were together he told me only two things about his father: that at eleven o'clock every morning he had an imperial pint of champagne brought to his office (of which Sidney disapproved), and that on one occasion at a Sunday lunch, during a heated argument between father and son, Alexander lifted the stack of plates awaiting cuts from the Sunday joint and dashed them to the floor, and then, glaring at Sidney, said, 'Now apologise to your mother', which Sidney refused to do.

From Ilford the family moved to Bow and then to Cricklewood, where for many years they occupied a commodious house (which, according to the Moorehead biography, was equipped with a sauna 'recalling his [Alexander's[Swedish childhood'.) There is no doubt that Alexander was now a prosperous businessman, an impresario, a risk-taker who, like his son after him, had an expert eye for a deal.

In 1915, Sidney's elder brother Selim was killed at Gallipoli. This had a profound effect on him and he is recorded as having attempted to join up at the age of sixteen, but he was found medically unfit, owing to an impaired ability to breathe through a nose that had been partially flattened by a kick on the football field. It is reported that Sidney underwent a long and painful operation in order to achieve a sufficient passage of breath to satisfy military standards, but the operation failed.

In March 1922, Alexander Bernstein died and at the age of twenty-three Sidney became head of the family business. He let all his father's other varied interests go and set about building up the music hall and film business. He loved the live theatre, and long after the music halls became cinemas in the 1930s he rather quaintly clung on to their live performance image by calling every cinema a 'theatre' (a title they all retained in the 50s and 60s when they became, one by one, bingo halls) and by presenting in them live acts, including ballet and orchestral concerts, mainly at weekends. His success was rapid and spectacular. Before his father died he had visited New York and Hollywood and had instantly absorbed the bold and brash American style of showmanship which he applied in his own 'theatres'. Indeed his affinity with America and Americans was refreshed by numerous visits and grew stronger and stronger until he went to work with Hitchcock in Hollywood in 1946.

In 1925 Sidney was one of a group of highbrow film buffs who started the Film Society, whose purpose was to make available to selected London audiences the great films of the world, especially of Russia. This brought him into touch with many heavyweights who were keen supporters of the enterprise, such as Shaw, Wells, Keynes, Julius Huxley, Augustus John, James Agate, Epstein, T.S. Eliot, Wyndham Lewis and Ivor Montagu. This group found him perhaps amusingly *outré*, but also charming, rich and generous. His acceptance by this circle was one of the turning points in Sidney's life. Some would come down to spend a weekend at his rented 'cottage in the country'; others would meet regularly in the Café Royal in informal club-like gatherings. Sidney would say little in these high-powered discussions but kept his end up with an occasional one-liner, and would assiduously follow up leads that were dropped concerning an introduction to some mogul in America, support for some artistic enterprise or the publication of a pamphlet or manifesto. 'Whilst we talked,' one of them said to me in later years, 'he would get things done.'

At the same time, and no doubt to a different group, Sidney appeared as a dashing young man about town. To quote from the Moorehead biography:

> On his return to London he moved at last into a house of his own at 46 Albemarle Street. It was here that his style became more marked. He hired a butler-cum-valet, and rode every morning in Rotten Row, returning home to find his bath run and North waiting to pull off his boots. While he breakfasted, a secretary arrived with the mail, after which he would walk to his office at 197 Wardour Street – the Bernsteins had moved there in 1923 – smoking Sullivan and Powell cigarettes, a special mixture of Turkish and Virginian tobacco. In the afternoon, when not working or visiting theatres, he went to *thés dansant*; in the evening, he danced at Ciro's or the 400.

Sidney's vision of himself as a young blade sounds convincing enough except for the reference to early morning rides. Throughout his life he had a horror of proximity to any animal. If a cat were to jump on his lap he would go into a state of minor shock, an approach from a friendly dog would cause him to panic and look in the opposite direction whilst patting the air somewhere in the neighbourhood of the dog's head and saying rather quickly, 'Good fellow, good fellow.' The idea of Sidney coming to terms with a horse, to say nothing of being prepared to sit on its back, does not seem credible.

Another bizarre aspect of Sidney's life at this time which seems equally unlikely but is undoubtedly true is that he was addicted to going on walking tours in several European countries, usually with David Blairman, with whom he jointly rented his country house, Long Barn in the Weald of Kent, from Harold Nicolson. The image of the sybaritic Sidney striding over mountains, rucksack on his back, water bottles strapped to his belt, and roughing it in an overnight chalet, would again challenge credibility were it not for the documentary evidence of contemporary photographs. Granada mythology has it that it was on one of these walking tours in Spain that Sidney was inspired to select the title Granada for his company and for his theatres.

Meanwhile the theatre continued to exercise its magnetic attraction for Sidney. He went into partnership with Arnold Bennett and put on an unsuccessful series of plays at the Court Theatre in Sloane Square. He saw on the board of the National Theatre-to-be with eminent persons such as Bernard Shaw – but his great moment of triumph came in 1930 when, in partnership with the Bovis construction firm, he built the Phoenix Theatre in Charing Cross Road and opened it with a new play by Nöel Coward, *Private Lives*, featuring the young Laurence Olivier, Gertrude Lawrence and the author himself. It was – to use Bernstein terminology – a smash.

Sidney's main work lay in developing the 'theatre' chain. All over Britain Odeons, Majestics, Empires, Grands, Rexes and Roxys were springing up, but none could compete in grandeur and style with the Granadas. In partnership with the flamboyant Russian interior designer Komisarjevsky he built and built. Smallish sites were bought up in outer London, along with some larger ones such as Walthamstow and Slough, and further afield lay Dover and Shrewsbury. At the heart of the Bernstein empire stood the great Granada Tooting, with its majestic muddle of styles – Moorish, Renaissance and classical; a lasting and now listed monument to the Bernstein/Komisarjevsky genius.

When war broke out Sidney offered his services to the Ministry of Information, but it was not until Churchill replaced Chamberlain in May 1940, and appointed Duff Cooper as Minister, that Sidney was formally appointed as Governor Film Adviser. He was not suited by nature to the status of adviser and immediately took on an executive role, setting about the task of swinging American opinion round to support the Allied cause. His energy and his methods of using direct action made him many enemies, but his influence was decisive in persuading the Ministry to use American journalists, such as Quentin Reynolds and Ed Murrow, in their propaganda films, and in animating the British publicity campaign in the USA. Later, with the honorary rank and in the uniform of a Lieutenant Colonel (which must have delighted him), he visited North Africa; and he was amongst the first to see the captured concentration camps of Buchenwald and Belsen in all their horror. This was undoubtedly the greatest shock of Sidney's life, and he subsequently told me that whenever the camps were mentioned he suffered from a sense of nausea. He strove to make a film to show the world the extent of the 'greatest crime ever committed against humanity', but for political reasons the film was never shown ('Don't let's be beastly to the Germans'). In 1985 Sidney instigated the production of a film made from his original material, then lying in the Imperial War Museum. It was called *A Painful Reminder*.

Throughout the war, Sidney's brother Cecil had been in charge of the theatres and had done a thoroughly competent job. After the war there were no building permits and no possibilities of expansion. Thus Sidney, always unable to stand still, decided after lengthy, friendly but cautious discussions with his old friend Alfred Hitchcock, that he would join him in a partnership as independent producers. Hitch was already a top director, with *Rebecca*, *The Man Who Knew Too Much* and *The Thirty-nine Steps*, to his credit, but he disliked front office interference and longed for creative freedom, or rather creative autonomy. Under the title of Transatlantic Pictures Corporation, he and Sidney made one moderately successful film, *Rope*, one flop, *Under Capricorn*, and one artistic but not financial success, *I Confess*, whilst discussing, as is the practice in the film industry, a myriad other subjects. In 1951 Sidney and Hitch decided, surprisingly amicably considering that both were umbrageous by nature, to split up. Hitch went on to make *Rear Window*; Sidney returned to London.

Back in London, Sidney once again faced the disagreeable prospect of inertia. The cinema business was in decline and Cecil was managing the beginning of the end game with his customary shrewdness and skill. Sidney did not want to be in the front line of politics. British film production was in the doldrums. Thus it was that, after a couple of restless years, the prospect of television found him ready to spring like a greyhound from the slips at a new and mighty challenge.

This period also saw the end of another relationship, Sidney's marriage to Zoë Farmer. No one knows how Sidney really felt about his first marriage, but in public he always treated it as incidental. He seldom mentioned it, and when he did he gave nothing away. Zoë, a journalist, was generally described as 'bright' and 'pretty', and it is clear that after their marriage in 1936 they both briefly glittered happily in the sort of café society they frequented; but by the outbreak of war things had gone awry and by the time Sidney went to Hollywood, and long before he formed a relationship with his second wife Sandra, the marriage was effectively over.

It was at this point in his life that Sidney and I became colleagues. From the first we had taken to each other, but it was mainly as a result of our jaunts abroad that our working relationship became even closer and more cordial. When he was unfair or outrageous I could more quickly persuade him to see reason, when angry more easily cajole him into good temper. On his side he could put a stopper on my more madcap ideas with less opposition, and could more easily overcome my conviction that I was always right on those occasions when I was wrong. Those who were not on such easy terms with him saw in our relationship something of patron and courtier, but this was to mistake its nature entirely. It is true that I admired him for his extraordinary abilities and that he was perhaps a little flattered to be so admired, but at work we were absolute equals and at leisure we were equally friends.

The 1960s were probably the happiest years of Sidney's life. As Chairman he ruled over Granada Television as it became the most successful and the most admired television company in Britain, and while others were becoming the doers he still retained his status of figurehead and his image as the only begetter of anything and everything good that Granada produced. In truth he had now arranged things so that he could spend most of his time and energies in developing the Group, which he did brilliantly.

Over the years of this golden autumn, although the visits to Manchester became fewer, his ménage remained much the same. He would travel from London in the Granada private plane with one or perhaps two secretaries, with a producer or two – Derek Granger or Julian Amyes – and perhaps with a senior engineer. Lowly engineers fell below the line drawn by Sidney's redoubtable Miss Haselwood between those who were *persona* sufficiently *Granada* to travel by plane and those who were not. The Haselwood line would, for instance, include a little-known writer who was working on a play, but would exclude the stars who were to act in it, unless of course they happened to be personal friends of Mr Sidney. It would leave the representative of an important advertising agency to travel by train, and offer a seat to a retired theatre manager who was travelling to mount a charity show.

On touchdown, a car would drive up to the plane and whisk Sidney with one or two favoured companions off to the TV Centre, where he would usually arrive just before dinner. He would then go straight to his bedroom, make a number of telephone calls, perhaps take a shower, and time his entry into the ante-room to perfection. Here, in a cardigan and open-necked shirt, a file of papers under one arm, he would call for a dry martini whilst taking stock of the company present. There were very few martini-makers whom he trusted, and I often found myself having to put a glass into the freezer, place two cubes of ice into a retort – already frozen – drop in four drops of Noilly Prat and a slice of lemon peel, pour in a tumbler half-full of cold vodka and stir vigorously. Sidney would despatch two doses of this mixture very quickly and then – saying 'I'm getting drunk already' – if there was any left ('the bonus') he would drink that too.

There would be from six to twelve people for dinner, mainly producers and directors, including all the senior hands in town and free that night – Tim Hewat, Philip Mackie, David Plowright, Mike Scott and so on. Discussion would start immediately. It would always be general and Sidney would always hold the ring. Then in to eat Miss Thorne's excellent plain dinner – Morecambe Bay shrimps, roast lamb, Stilton, fruit. The decibels increased as the good but not extravagant claret was consumed, and it became harder and harder for the weaker speakers to get a hearing – for Granada diners were not prone to give way easily – until a halt was called to watch a show off air, or perhaps a tape. The debate would start again in the ante-room, usually by now jollier, but sometimes intense and occasionally heated. Claret would give way to whisky. Headlines of *News at Ten* would be watched briefly and around midnight Sidney would say, 'Well, I'm for bed', and disappear abruptly. Often the talk would go on well into the small hours, and on one or two rather disgraceful occasions drowsiness overcame the last two or three participants and they were found asleep next morning by Miss Thorne, recumbent and redolent of strong liquor.

Before going to bed, if it were not yet 11.30, Sidney would make the daily fraternal telephone call to Cecil; if later, the call would be postponed until 7.30 next morning. And so – glass of water, two sleeping pills, open notepad and two sharp pencils to hand – to bed.

Next morning Miss Roper, Sidney's senior travelling secretary, would appear before he was out of his dressing gown and overnight notes would be dictated, early telephone calls made, the day's diary confirmed. Then breakfast in the dining room with the day's papers strewn over the table, a quick session in the office, and the morning safari with Mr Pook. Intelligence as to its destination was flashed around the building at the speed of lightning and all other departments heaved a sigh of relief. The day would be spent seeing people, as many as possible: the Town Clerk about improving Manchester's cleanliness; Bill Grundy, who last night on a local programme had been visibly affected by drink; David Plowright over a *World in Action* row; Mr James, who looked after the cleaners; Julian Amyes about a costume in his last play that had not pleased; Fred Boud, the general manager, about a multitude of items; the graphics man to demonstrate a new trick table; Sebastian de Ferranti about some Northern charity. I would be in attendance for much of the time.

For lunch he went to what he called the Festival Café and everyone else to the Canteen, to take pot luck. But Miss Longhurst, an old Granada hand, had been tipped off and Sidney would find to his surprise that amongst the standard array of pies and puddings today there were soft roes on toast, for which he had a passion, and after that a perfectly ripened Comice pear. It is possible that Sidney actually believed that he also took pot luck at finding a place at table, but here again Miss Longhurst, who, although a perfectly respectable woman, had all the arts of a procuress, would have arranged that there would be an empty place at a nearby table where would be seated one or two of Sidney's special buddies from amongst the workforce, a pretty young woman, plus an up-and-coming director or two. Sometime during the late afternoon he would disappear to London as suddenly as he had arrived.

Sidney was on easy terms with anyone he met around the studios. In the lift he would ask secretaries about the shopping they were carrying. He would stop opposite anyone at work and invariably ask, 'What is your name? What do you do? How long have you been with Granada?' and if time permitted he would get down to the nitty-gritty of the job in question. Was the equipment well-designed? Was there enough light? Why were the metal filings on the floor? There could be a cradle to catch them? How often had the machine needed maintenance in the last year?

But all departments were not treated alike. Below the level of Reg Hammans, engineering middle management were all Misters – Mr Holt, Mr Gower – and the lower echelons were Christian name plus surname – George Eagle, Geoff White. In contrast, producers and directors were all Christian names unless temporarily or permanently *non Granada* – not Herbie but Mr Wise, after a poor *Make up Your Mind*, and, alas, Mr Butler throughout his producing career. Rarely, very rarely, Sidney would use what he imagined to be a person's nickname which he had invented himself. Thus he would refer to Ray Fitzwalter of *World in Action* as Fitz. No one else called him that. The nomenclature he used, and also his tone of voice, indicated precisely where the person referred to stood in the *persona* scale that day. There was no disapproval in referring to Alan Gilbert, the number two in the accounts department, as Mr Gilbert. All jacket workers, be they in or out of favour, were 'Mister'. But a pause before the 'Mister' and a slow and clear articulation of Gilbert was not a good sign. And if by any chance he was referred to as Mr Gilbey, then he had better look out. Engineers had a special terminology because Sidney did not much care for engineers as a class. Knowing little of the mysteries of their trade, he was unable to check the accuracy of what they told him, and so he found it safer to distrust them all, Reg Hammans usually, but not always, excepted.

Sidney had a good rapport with the heads of all departments (otherwise they would not have been there), especially perhaps with Bill Dickson, head of finance, and Alex Anson, head of sales; but his friends lay amongst the creative people. Philip Mackie and Tim Hewat liked to make a show of independence by striking a macho stance ('I'll show everyone I can stand up to Sidney'). The truth is that they and Sidney relished their combative encounters, which could lead to arguments on every point but were often overcome by sudden mutual enthusiasm or by Sidney's generous support for their more risky ventures. Beneath the posturing there was a fundament of mutual respect and many of their most ferocious displays were no more than shadow boxing, until latterly a genuine feud developed between Sidney and Philip.

Two of Sidney's closest colleagues were Derek Granger and Julian Amyes. Both had the urbanity and the shrewdness to sum him up with total accuracy, both kept their own personae intact and would not allow him to bully them, both enormously enjoyed his company, and both successfully ran the play department under his aegis. Of Sidney in the early days Derek Granger wrote:

> Sidney was very exhilarating. He had this enormous eupeptic quality, buoyant quality of enthusiasm and zest. He was everywhere; I've never known a man so ubiquitous. One moment he was in the canteen sampling the

soused herring, the next moment he was checking the fire buckets to see that the lettering on them was of the right type; then all of a sudden he was in his office amidst a production team, discussing what horrors had been perpetrated in their last show. Wherever the action was there he was, and wherever he was there was the action.

During the 1960s two members of the home team, David Plowright and Barrie Heads, moved steadily onwards and upwards among the Manchester band of producers. Both at different times ran all the local programmes with the support of the diverse talents of Bill Grundy, Michael Parkinson, Peter Eckersley and Mike Scott, all of whom were soon to make their mark on the network. David Plowright then took on *World in Action* as his principal charge amongst many, and stuck with it, first as producer, then as executive producer, and then continuing as its internal inquisitor and public protagonist and finally its *eminence grise* until his chairmanship ended in 1992. After Tim Hewat's initial coup of bringing tabloid journalism to television it was David who gave *World in Action* its *gravitas* and its penetrative power. He had a nose for a story, insisted on absolute accuracy and combined a dashing style of journalism with canny editorial judgement. It was due to him that the programme went to the top of the investigative field and stayed there for nearly three decades. Part of its success was owed to the fact that the top Granada team (Sidney, David, myself) refused to succumb to the moral blackmail through which the British establishment seeks to smother any story that could cause them embarrassment. Time and again we were told that a forthcoming *World in Action* programme would be against the national interest, would damage irrevocably our foreign trade, or would cause a loss of confidence in the police force, the army or the navy, and we became accustomed to listening to heavy breathing from top civil servants, from Ministers, and sometimes from lawyers. Only when the dreaded Official Secrets Act was called in did we sometimes have to give up. Like Harry Evans of the *Sunday Times*, with whom on some stories we worked in tandem, David was the ideal boss for a team of investigative journalists. Everyone who worked for either of these two knew that no story would be trimmed, fudged or spiked because of outside pressure and that guilty men, no matter how highly placed, would get their comeuppance.

Temperamentally Sidney Bernstein and David Plowright had little in common. David concealed acute sensibility behind a bluff Yorkshireman's front. Except in anger, and he had a short fuse, he never spoke too soon. His quick wit allowed him to play for time in reaching a decision for, unlike Sidney's, his pace was deliberate. Both were well endowed with charm. For Sidney's world of café society, painting, ballet, the arts generally, David cared little. His own world was that of his father, the editor of the *Scunthorpe Gazette*, expanded to the nth degree, and only later in life did he find his way into the theatrical set of his sister Joan and her husband Laurence Olivier. Yet although there was little intimacy between them, David and Sidney trusted each other. When they faced one another across Sidney's desk they each had a twinkle in the eye as they embarked on a brief contest to deliver the best one-liner in the cause of resolving whatever the problem of the hour might be. David was one of the few people who could wear Sidney down by sheer immovability. He would state his position and gaze steadily into Sidney's eyes as arguments darted and flashed around his head, until eventually the pace slackened and Sidney would concede, usually with good grace.

With Barrie Heads there was no such rapport. Although Barrie had all the qualities calculated to commend a man to Sidney, something was amiss with the chemistry, and for nearly three decades Barrie remained a *persona* not really *Granada*. But only so far as Sidney was concerned: Cecil thought the world of him and from the first he was, with David, my most dependable Manchester colleague. It was he who played a decisive role in bringing the Rochdale by-election to television, and who carried out the experiments in televising the House of Lords. He was universally liked and respected by journalists and politicians – but not by Sidney. Barrie possessed, however, along with a wry sense of humour, an inexhaustible reserve of Yorkshire doggedness. He decided to sit it out and, whilst others like James Butler thought it wise to chuck in the sponge when Sidney's displeasure was writ clearly on the wall, sit it out he did. When the time came to make the difficult decision as to who should be my successor as head of programmes in Manchester – either Barrie or David – one thing that had to count against Barrie, although not decisively, was the lack of good feeling between him and Sidney, for neither of them was going to give any ground.

So Barrie became head of Granada International, the company that sold Granada programmes and sought co-productions abroad, and thus worked to Cecil and to me; but there was no refuge for anyone within the boundaries of Granada when Sidney chose to cast a baleful eye. Once Barrie was dissatisfied with the performance of our New York representative, and he brought her over to Manchester so that David and I could make our own assessment. At dinner, she made a poor impression and next day she was given what today is called a negative appraisal. Soon after that she told Barrie she had been offered another job. Barrie did nothing to persuade her to stay, and she left. But not before she had been on the phone to Sidney, with whom she had ingratiated herself, not only by providing him with the customary lampshades, socks, film stock and cheesecake that it was the lot of any Granada person in New York to procure, but by relaying to him gossip which was more up to date and spicier than was generally available. She had also stayed as his guest at his home in Barbados, a singular privilege and one enjoyed by very few of his more senior Granada colleagues.

Sidney called Barrie. What was he thinking of? He must immediately set out to persuade the lady to stay. Barrie said no and reported that Forman and Plowright had been parties to the decision to let her go. Sidney then called what amounted to a top-level Group meeting in London to make the case that a brilliant, loyal and hard-working Granada employee had been subject to constructive dismissal solely because she had incurred the dislike of her boss. Some of those present – and especially Joe Warton – wondered what the fuss was all about, but as the afternoon wore on and everyone longed to escape to their offices, it became clear that the row was not so much about the lady in question as about Barrie. Was such a man fit to hold high office? For once Sidney found himself on his own. The lady went, and from then on Sidney knew that Barrie was unassailable. Indeed, as Managing Director of Granada International, Barrie outlasted Sidney as Chairman of Granada Group.

With the top band of Manchester producers and performers Sidney's relations varied. Bill Grundy, brilliant, mercurial and inclined to imbibe alcohol rather freely, adopted a macho-type of teasing which Sidney did not much relish. With Michael Parkinson he was friendly – who could be anything but friendly with Barnsley's most amiable and most famous son? There was a degree of incomprehension between Sidney and Peter Eckersley, an erstwhile *Guardian* man, who revelled in D.C. Thompson's comics, frequently quoting Korky the Cat or Tiger Tim and making jokes about serious subjects such as Granada's Good Housekeeping policy, and death. This was strange ground for Sidney, but although never at home with Peter socially, when he saw his programmes – and especially *Hard Times* – he bowed his head in acknowledgement of a great producing talent.

Mike Scott was one of the family, not the Bernstein Bernstein family but the Bernstein Granada family, perhaps a favoured nephew. Mike could be cheeky to Sidney in a way that Sidney liked, and of all those around him he was perhaps the best able to get a direct answer to a personal question.

The many other producers and directors in Manchester treated Sidney with cautious respect. A few, a very few – perhaps only Denis Mitchell and Ivor Montagu – spoke with him as equals. Some – Silvio Narizzano, Derek Granger and Julian Amyes – could share creative problems with him. Others – Bill Gaskell, Herbert Wise, James Butler – found him a pain. For the rest he was comparatively remote but much feared. When they were called into a close encounter they were always surprised by the accuracy of his criticism and usually disarmed by the directness of his approach and, when applied, his charm.

Although Sidney could hound a producer or a director unmercifully he had a veneration for 'creative people' as a class. This included writers, with whom Sidney never really got to grips. Uncharacteristically, and in total contrast to my own attitude, he tended to regard their work not as raw material to be moulded into a television show but as a finished product, the 'text'. Designers fared differently. There was many a summons up to the sixth floor when with blue and red pencils Sidney would hack away at set drawings, usually, it must be confessed, to demonstrate how money could be saved. But amongst 'creative people' directors and producers were the most venerated and their creative welfare was always one of Sidney's cares. They were encouraged to go to the theatre by the gift of two top-price tickets for any show in town. If something sensational hit the stage in Paris someone would be selected to go to see it and report. Because Sidney and I had got such value out of our trip to Moscow we arranged trips for 'creative people' to European capitals in pairs for a couple of weeks. They saw all the shows that were running, visited the local television station and otherwise had no obligation except to write a report on their return for domestic circulation. This scheme was popular and Berlin, Prague, Budapest, Vienna, Rome, Paris and Madrid were all duly visited, and later the Scandinavian capitals. Sidney, although not in any way concerned with its execution, fully supported the very substantial sums spent on the Production Trainee scheme, which is described in the next chapter. He was in effect the champion of creative power against all-comers, sales persons, administrators, engineers and bureaucrats. Financial control there must be, but within the parameters of the budget the producer should be king.

In the early days Sidney's closest encounter with the creative side was as chairman of the Programme Committee. This met sometimes weekly, sometimes fortnightly, and it was the forum in which all important decisions were taken. The committee was both discursive and executive, having something in common with the BBC's Board of Programme Review, some of the powers of a company board, sometimes indulging for an hour or two in pure brainstorming, always argumentative and never boring. It began at 11 a.m. and finished as the Londoners began to pack their papers for the 4.30 train. Although there was a certain amount of lobbying for pet ideas, the debate was remarkably open. Many of my own pet projects bit the dust in the face of Programme Committee disapproval, and no programme was safe from a critical appraisal more searching and often more painful than any that came from the professional critics. Each member had his role: Tim Hewat and Philip Mackie unashamedly promoted their own interests; Barrie Heads was the champion of regional programmes, David Plowright of current affairs; Sidney and myself encouraged wider perspectives – where was the Labour Party going? Was the Beeching axe a national disaster? – and often, when we all got carried away by some majestic concept such as documenting the anatomy of Britain in fifty-two one-hour programmes, Cecil's plaintive voice would be heard calling out, 'But S–Sidney, where's the slot?' He was the realist, and unlike the rest of us saw the week parcelled out into a patchwork of little squares which made up a comparatively immutable schedule. Sidney was impatient with this pettifogging approach. 'The ideas come first, the slot second, Cecil,' he would say. But of course Cecil was right and he often left a meeting which had approved half a dozen programmes, all of them impossible to schedule, in despair. The writing of the minutes was the key to the interpretation of what had happened at the Programme Committee and it was here that I had the whip hand, since the committee secretary, the honest Ken Brierley, would consult with me after the event to assist him towards a draft. He would not allow any departure from fact, but in the interpretation of opinion he was more flexible.

As Sidney's presence in Manchester became less and less frequent he found ingenious ways of casting his shadow over territory he once patrolled on foot. One morning he would get into Golden Square early, perhaps by nine o'clock. His secretary would then make half a dozen telephone calls to Manchester executives, leaving a message at each still empty desk for the occupant to call Sidney 'as soon as he got in.' This could have a disturbing effect on those who did not surface until mid-morning. Then there were Sunday morning Coppings calls. Sidney had constructed an office in one of the farm outhouses and he would stride out there and take up station on Sunday mornings to make perhaps three or four telephone calls to people he felt had not had enough of his attention in recent weeks. Sunday morning calls were never jolly and they could be gruesome, as I had reason to know. Sidney would pick a victim, perhaps Fred Boud, the General Manager, or Mike Murphy, a brilliant writer who for some time has been conscripted into service as press officer. Sidney would weigh in with a list of delinquencies and omissions and give the wretched man at the other end a hard time. Coppings calls could last for up to forty-five minutes and I can remember Mike saying that of all Sidney's wickednesses he found this practice the hardest to forgive. To be put through the wringer in the office was bad enough, but to be bullied to the point of breakdown in your own home in front of your wife and children was just too much. And yet the next time they met Sidney would charm him into good humour within minutes and Mike would soon be chatting happily to him about the howlers in yesterday's *Daily Telegraph*.

Towards the end of his chairmanship Sidney felt Television was slipping from his grasp, and he resented it. The early days were the happiest days, both in his working life in Television generally and in our partnership together. I joined the Television Board in 1959 and the Group Board on the same day as Alex Bernstein in 1964. And then came the ultimate accolade. Sidney mysteriously asked me out to lunch at a little-known restaurant. As we sat down, a bottle of champagne was produced. Then Sidney, rather coyly, asked me if I would become a trustee of his family trusts. I had now become an honorary Bernstein.

During this otherwise harmonious decade there was one event which was to put my trust in Sidney under severe strain. It arose from his devotion to his brother Cecil. In their business life at that time the two were as close as identical twins with an almost extrasensory power of communicating with each other. In their private lives there was no such bond. Sidney on a spree in New York would not be thinking much about Cecil, and Cecil, as he reclined on a sun bed by the pool at Five Trees, would be quite unmindful of Sidney. But if one of them were to step into the shadow of a cinema which could be for sale, see a preview of a 'smash', hear of a threatened bankruptcy, he instantly became a part of the business unit which was the sum of the Bernstein brothers, thinking and acting as one person.

It was not the sort of partnership that demanded physical proximity: they could never have worked together over a partners' desk, as did Val Parnell and Lew Grade, for their temperaments were so different that they would have driven each other mad in minutes. Communication was confined to the occasional visit to each other's office and to the daily phone call, often lasting for up to an hour. The exchanges between them were informative and reflective. The party of the first part would impart a piece of news and this would be followed by his considered reaction to it. The party of the second part would first absorb the news, perhaps seeking some further and better particulars, and then give his own view in turn, often a mirror image of the first. If that were the case, they would move on through the agenda, ensuring that they were like-minded on each item. Sometimes there would be a debate. Sidney, always impatient, would brush aside some of Cecil's forebodings, perhaps about the decline in Saturday cinema attendances, or the fear that some major debtor was going broke. Give it another week, he would say, it could be the weather, or let's ring round and see who else has not been paid. But Cecil could be dogged, and if he wanted Sidney to take an item seriously he had a phrase to stop him in his tracks. 'But S-Sidney,' he would say, 'it goes deeper than that', and he would adumbrate the disasters that would arise if they did not change the weekend booking tomorrow or cut all credit to the shaky debtor at once. To really major items – should we pull out of bowling? could we trust Tom Brownrigg to stand by a certain deal? – they would revert night after night, each having taken soundings during the day, and Cecil always reporting Joe Warton's views, which formed a sort of continuous ground-bass to their nightly duet.

Occasionally Cecil could get angry with Sidney. He would try to cajole or persuade him to give up some risky or, as he thought, foolish project and when he failed he would sit very still and go grey and silent. Sidney, on the other hand, would shush and override Cecil shamelessly, often to the embarrassment of those present, and this habit is enshrined in one of the most enduring Golden Square myths.

The scene is set in Sidney's office during a planning meeting with architects, draughtsmen, surveyors and the like, all clustered round his desk. Cecil puts his head round the door, takes in the scene, and calls out in a stage whisper, 'Sidney'. Sidney wordlessly waves him away without raising his head and continues his dialogue with the planners. 'S-Sidney,' calls Cecil, louder and more urgently. Again Sidney does not raise his head but says, 'Can't you see I'm busy, Cecil? Come back later.'

Cecil does not move but calls out again, this time in a tone not to be denied: 'S-S-Sidney!' At last Sidney gives up. 'What is it, Cecil?' he asks.

'Have you seen the share price this morning?' asks Cecil.

'No,' says Sidney.

'Well, I don't know about you, Sidney,' says Cecil, 'but I'm gettin' out.'

Both Bernsteins had a chronic fear of illness and in particular a dread of the surgeon's knife. On one occasion, when Sidney was to undergo an operation (which turned out to be quite minor), he saw the shadow of the grave ahead and set about making provisions for a Granada without him. Assuming Cecil would be Chairman, he appointed Cecil's son Alex, Brian Wolfson and myself as the three joint managing directors of Granada Group. Twenty-four hours after the operation he bitterly regretted this move, but it was not for some years that he could summon up the courage to write us each a note pointing out that times had changed and would we kindly relinquish a title that now signified little? Which we all did; but one of our number, Brian Wolfson, still records in his CV that he was at one time the Joint Managing Director of Granada Group, which, without fully explaining the circumstances, sounds singularly impressive.

Cecil had a congenital limp, the origin of which was never fully explained to me, and Sidney, who did not like to loiter, was never happy to walk at his pace. Thus faced with a short walk, say from the office block to the staff canteen in Manchester, the brothers would always time their trips separately, the one setting out two or three minutes ahead of the other, although their destination was the same.

I always imagined that any ailment in one brother had a sympathetic bodily response in the other. When Sidney got serious arthritis it was in the left knee, the same as Cecil's poorly one; when Cecil had earache, Sidney would keep dabbing his ears with a handkerchief as if in pain. But the prime example of bodily empathy took place one day at a programme committee lunch. Cecil suddenly stopped eating, put his napkin to his mouth and hurried out of the room. After a minute or two he returned with his napkin still in place and gave Sidney an agonised distress signal. It was clear he was suffering from some dental calamity. Sidney followed him out and in a little while I popped into the ante-room to see if help was needed. Cecil was seated by a table in the attitude of a man in the stocks, arms dangling out, head down and in front of him on a spotless white handkerchief a fragment of broken tooth. Sidney was on the phone talking to one of the leaders of Northern industry to discover which Manchester dentist could be trusted to work inside a Bernstein mouth. But the surprising thing was that as he spoke he held his own spotless handkerchief to his gums, which forced him to talk out of the side of his mouth. 'Have you broken a tooth too?' I asked. He came to with a jump, stuffed the handkerchief away, said to Cecil, 'Mr Brown, John Street', and swept back into the meeting, leaving me wondering whether I should get an ambulance to transport Cecil to Mr Brown or whether the station car would suffice.

The brothers had the same doctor, Joe Stone, their brother-in-law, who counted Harold Wilson as one of his more eminent clients. Joe would be inclined to recommend to them the same hearing aids, and this was to lead to another well-remembered Granada event, the howlround lunch.

Both Sidney and Cecil were somewhat hard of hearing and each dealt with this affliction in his own way. Cecil would lean forward, cup his ear, say, 'I beg your pardon', or, amongst Granada folk, 'What?', never attempting to conceal that he was more than a little deaf. Sidney, on the other hand, was loath to betray any physical deficiency, and particularly this one. He was assisted by an uncanny sense of intuition which helped him to pick up the drift of almost any conversation, and time and again at a meeting or a party I marvelled at his ability to keep his end up, even though he might have only the haziest impression of what was being said. He was a past master of the quick riposte which appeared relevant but which, when one came to examine it, could have sounded suitable in almost any situation. When absolutely gravelled he would draw himself up, look immensely dignified and change the subject. Both brothers, guided by Joe Stone, employed specialists to keep them supplied with the latest thing in hearing aids. Sometimes for a week or two they wore the same model until one or other came across something fresh, when they would once again go their separate ways. Here again Cecil was prepared to use larger chunky devices which were the wrong shade of pink and stood out from the side of his head. Sidney's apparatus was always discreet and almost invisible except to the knowing eye. There was a turbulent period when he had a microphone embedded in the earpiece of his spectacles, and since he tended to carry three or four pairs about his person there was often a bout of feverish fumbling before he identified the hearing pair. At another time there was a thin filament which ran up the back of his neck and disappeared into his hair. But what happened after that no one ever knew.

The hearing aid event of all time occurred at a lunch in Golden Square. The brothers had both recently adopted a newly invented item which consisted of a multi-directional mike, housed in something that looked like a small pencil case, which they laid on the table or desk in front of them. This transmitted radio signals to an invisible earpiece, again controlled by radio from a discreet black box housed in the side jacket pocket. The guests that day were Americans (I forget who) and the topic was of burning interest – the dismemberment of the great Music Corporation of America, for the reason that it had fallen foul of the anti-trust laws. Granada had long been a client of MCA and scarcely a day passed without one or other of us calling Burle Adams or more occasionally Lew Wasserman, the high priest (or perhaps the Chief Rabbi) of the American entertainment business.

There was only one thing that interested the Bernsteins more than success in business and that was failure; hence they listened to this tale of corporate disaster with breathless attention, tempered with a slight but discernible degree of *schadenfreude*. One of the Americans, the main narrator, spoke quietly, too quietly for the black boxes, so one Bernstein, or perhaps both Bernsteins simultaneously, stuck a hand into his jacket pocket and turned up the volume. The result was a piercing electronic scream. The brothers had howlround: each fiddled feverishly within his pocket, but neither being of a mechanical turn of mind and both lacking manual dexterity in the face of the simplest electrical device, instead of turning the volume down one, or both, turned it up. The caterwauling redoubled in volume and now it was backed by a noise as of a thousand chattering monkeys. In the Golden Square dining room all life stood still. The howlround went on for what seemed like an eternity, until at last a Bernstein finger stumbled across an off switch. Now there was silence, which was broken by the quiet American, still in shock, saying, 'What in the hell was that?' Cecil, shaking with distress, looked at Sidney pleadingly. Sidney, unruffled, looked piercingly at the quiet American and said, 'You were telling us of the possibility of an Appeal to the Supreme Court', and then with a masterly sense of timing he turned to the waitress and said, 'Would you please bring some fresh Pellegrino water: this bottle is not cold.' It was a virtuoso performance, and I had never admired him more.

After the howlround lunch the black boxes, although continuing to appear singly, were never observed in the same room. But they too had a limited life, and it was not long before the brothers were exploring new frontiers of aural technology. Yet like many deaf people the Bernsteins never had any problem with a one-to-one conversation, and when I found myself speaking too loudly to Sidney, as one so often does with the hard of hearing, he would look at me with the hooded eyes of a llama peering over the top of a wire fence, at which signal I would immediately moderate my tones and never once, so far as I recall, caused him to descend to the vulgarity of telling me not to shout.

The event that tested brotherly love to its limits came in March 1965. I do not know who it was who first thought of making a *World in Action* special about the Freemasons. What I can remember is that from time to time Tim, Barrie, David and maybe others would say to me, 'Isn't it time we did the masons?' They were clearly a prime target. Here was a secret society supported, even led, by the highest in the land, whose prime object was to look after its own under a cloak of philanthropy. Our editorial view was that this was monstrous and should be exposed. We knew that masonry was rife in the police and the civil service, and that there were pockets of it everywhere, even in the most unlikely places such as Granada, where it was rumoured that Cecil was a very high official, and Joe Warton too, though not so grand. Our Finance Director and the General Manager in Manchester were known to proselytise actively. But we, the programme people, found the way they used religion as a cover for self-interest nauseating, and the tribal mumbo-jumbo of their rituals ludicrous.

So the show was got under way, masterminded by myself and wholeheartedly supported by Sidney. Naturally research was hard, but after a month or two, with so many masons around and, more important, so many former masons, and with the help of a secret handbook cataloguing all the masonic rituals discovered by chance on a barrow in Westbourne Grove, the vows of secrecy were well and truly breached and we had a substantial dossier on masonry from the rolling up of the initiate's trouser leg to a chart of the masonic high command in the United Kingdom.

As the film rolled towards the screen Sidney and I became aware that Cecil and Joe were showing distinct signs of anxiety. But whenever Cecil raised the subject Sidney would shush him or say, 'I don't see why you should worry over a programme about your silly little boy scout games.' We had both seriously underestimated the strength of the opposition. Unknown to Sidney and to myself, Cecil, accompanied by a posse of leading masons, arranged for a screening of the rough cut in Golden Square. The next day Sidney called me into his office in Manchester. His face was white and drained and he stared stonily in front of him. 'Denis,' he said, and he was not talking to me, he was merely identifying the next and painful topic on the agenda. After a pause and without looking up he said, 'Denis, read that', and he pushed a letter across his desk. It was from Cecil and as I remember it it read as follows:

Dear Sidney,
I have been a mason for more than thirty years and hold

the position of Grand Master of my Lodge. I have seen the rough cut of the show about masons that you and Denis are preparing, and I have to tell you that if it is transmitted I shall have to resign from the boards of Granada Group and Granada Television.

Yours ever,
Cecil

'Oh,' I said, and sat looking at Sidney and then at the letter. 'Oh.' There was a long silence. 'He is my brother, Denis,' said Sidney. 'He and I have worked together since we started.'

'I know,' I said, 'it's going to be a hard job to bring him round. And there's Joe in there too.'

'Forget Joe,' said Sidney. 'Cecil means what he says.' And then, 'Denis, I love my brother.' This was a shock. I had never before known Sidney to speak like this of any other human being. I suddenly realised that we were no longer on the same side. I thought of all that Sidney, Granada and especially myself had said and done in the face of threatened censorship from governments, boards and proprietors, and of how editorial independence had been Granada's holy grail. 'If the show does not go out, Sidney,' I said, 'you may keep Cecil but you may lose me.' And I got up and walked slowly out of his office, collected my papers and caught the London train, arriving at Stansted that night unexpectedly early.

The next day I phoned the team. But Sidney had been in there before me. Not surprisingly there are no papers about the masons film remaining in the Granada archive. It might never have existed but for the evidence of one document which must have been overlooked. The form of this document is unusual since it is a transcription of a telephone call taken down by a secretary listening in on an extension and subsequently typed – a very rare occurrence in Granada. The call was between Sidney and Alex Valentine, the producer of the programme, and is dated 4 March 1965. It was probably made just after I had walked out of Sidney's office in Manchester. Hodges was the director of the programme. The reference to a 'scoop' relates to the fact that the BBC were also working on a programme about the masons. I do not remember 'the programme about the BBC' which is mentioned. Sidney's phone call went as follows:

re: *World in Action*
SLB   I can't explain to you in detail but we cannot do the Masonic programme.

AV   Oh, God.

SLB   It is not the Masons that have moved in. We cannot do it. I am embarrassed. You and I will discuss with Hodges on Monday.

We must get the programme about the BBC out on Tuesday evening instead. Have you seen *Time and Tide*? It is very good and will help you. There is a picture of Hugh Greene on the front and all that they say about him inside. On the question of the other programme I think the BBC will probably scoop you and I know how awful that will be. It is not censorship. I am opposed to censorship.

AV   Can you tell me why we can't do it. Are you saying that it is being postponed or cancelled?

SLB   Let's say this to you, we cannot do anything more on it … Hodges and you should stop all work on it and don't say anything about it, but get on with the BBC programme. I can't say anything more for the moment. I shall be in Manchester tomorrow, Leeds tomorrow evening and Saturday morning. I will be back in London or at Coppings Saturday afternoon. Telephone and we will talk..

The following day Alex Valentine and Mike Hodges were flown up to Manchester and met Sidney in the flat. He was distressed and told them that the stop put on the masons programme was 'for family reasons' and he could tell them no more than that. In recalling this meeting, Mike Hodges says that both he and Alex Valentine felt deeply sorry for Sidney, who at one point broke down and cried. Subsequently, however, their natural resentment slowly turned to anger, and as the story spread through the building it was met with incredulity. No one could believe that such a thing could happen in Granada and those less affected became even more indignant than the team. Yet nobody blew the whistle and to this day there has never been any mention of the masons story in the public prints. Many years later some of the 1965 material was used in a Granada series of six programmes about the masons, but by now masonic secrecy had been much eroded and the series had little impact.

Early the next week I tried to quell the universal outrage by pointing out that Sidney had no option. We could not expect him to break with Cecil. Our problem was different: how to get the show on the air, perhaps through the BBC, as we had done before when a *World in Action* had been censored by the Authority. I was prepared to do this without Sidney's knowledge. But they, naturally, put out their programme, a poor thing, and scooped us.

No matter how I rationalised Sidney's decision I could not help feeling betrayed. Nothing could hurt more than that the show should be blocked by the very power it was designed to challenge. I should resign? But why? I would have acted just as Sidney had done. What would be gained by anyone from my resignation, except some private solace. For five days I stayed at home and took no calls. Then I found my normal equilibrium was returning. On a Wednesday morning I drove into Golden Square and started to pick up the threads. Just before lunch I was asked to go to Sidney's office. 'Denis,' he said, 'the graphics in last night's *Scene at Six-Thirty* were quite disgraceful. Did you approve them?'

'No,' I said, 'I'll go and take a look at them now.' The masons programme was never mentioned between us again.

CHAPTER SEVEN

For some twenty years, from the mid-60s to the mid-80s, Granada's programmes were my concern. In the beginning, even as the producer of my own shows such as *Under Fire* and *What the Papers Say*, I felt I was Sidney's deputy. Cecil had his own corner and stuck to it for nearly ten years. But when the head of the play department began to look to me rather than to Sidney for guidance, and after Cecil had launched his last network show in *Cinema* (1964), gradually the whole portfolio came my way. Sidney the critic stood in the wings ready to pounce. Sidney the proprietor, if and when he moved in, had the last word: Cecil faded from the scene save for a godfatherly interest in light entertainment and a continuing role as the supremo of *Coronation Street. World in Action* might be in the throes of a seismic eruption, there might be a root-and-branch review of programme policy in progress and Cecil would not stir from Golden Square, but if a cry of alarm went up from the *Street* Cecil would be in Manchester in a trice, to take tea with Violet Carson in the Midland Hotel or to offer a little quiet advice to Peter Adamson.

My main activity was seeking out subjects and talent and matching the two together. When a writer, a producer or a director had finished a show (and often when he was still working on one) he would come to my office with a proposal for his next assignment, or conversely I would ask him to come to listen to an idea of mine. The debate would often pass rapidly to a string of options, some practical, some fantastical, some outrageous, until we parted, often having rejected each other's ideas but carrying away the germ of a programme that might come to life some time in the future. Often we would summon a kindred spirit to add his or her pennyworth to the debate, or David Plowright, Derek Granger or Julian Amyes would see the group round my desk through the glass panel of my door and join the debate unbidden. Every morning by 9.30 or so there would be one or two people sitting in the lobby outside my office and they would drift in and out as the traffic of the day permitted. Also a great deal of programme talk derived from casual encounters throughout the day in the corridors, in the canteen (where I had lunch every day) and even in the lavatories. As Granada grew, programme decisions about plays, light entertainment and main-line current affairs began to be taken by the people who produced them: Julian, David, or Johnny Hamp – a cheerful ex-Granada Theatres man, a born showman and our impresario for most light entertainment programmes. My own patch, where I had hands-on control, became more or less confined to drama series and serials, the arts, 'special' current affairs programmes and maverick ideas of all kinds such as a study entitled *Eight Weeks in the Life of a Car Park* or a series of three *Slight White Papers on Love*, an inquiry conducted in mock civil service style on the status and nature of love in British society (a flop).

The Programme Committee was the other great source of programme ideas. Here the proposals were better formulated and each one was presented by its own champion. Some survived the critical ordeal and duly came into being; many were changed beyond all recognition, and many more were strangled at birth (amongst them some of the best), the most common reasons being lack of support, no slot or too costly. But any really good idea had a habit of reaching the screen, whatever fate for it had been recorded in the minutes.

The Sales Department was rigidly excluded from any discussion of programmes. Sidney and I had seen the disastrous consequences in America of allowing marketing men to take programme decisions. Whilst it was perfectly permissible for the Sales Department to say, 'We want a rating of sixty at eight o'clock on Wednesday', it was not admissible for it to say, 'Why don't we move *Coronation Street* to eight on Wednesday', or, 'We should develop a strong quiz for late peak-time on Saturday.' 'We will give you the ratings you want,' we would say, 'and you sell the time.' The rationale for this rule was that in programme thinking marketing men are yesterday's men. When they spot a success they immediately want to replicate it. They would follow *Lassie* by *Son of Lassie*, *Lassie Afloat*, *Lassie up the Khyber*, until the sawdust ran out of the *Lassie* brand and the ratings slumped. And there would still be half a dozen more *Lassies* queuing up in the production line. Marketing men and money men see success by looking backwards and they should never be allowed to influence creative people, who must look forward. And when the creative people do deliver fresh delights they must be careful lest the marketing men make them stale by over-exposure. And what is true of marketing men and money men is almost equally true of committee men and women (for here the sensible sex are more freely admitted), who are bound by all the laws of collective decision-taking to take a safer course rather than a riskier one, and to back experienced talent rather than to fan a spark of genius as yet untried.

I would claim that Granada proved this thesis decisively, for in the years between 1956 and 1987 Granada held, on average, a clear ratings lead over all the other companies in ITV and for over two decades by far the highest number of programmes in the Top Ten. Those companies that were sales-led or committee-ridden, in particular Rediffusion and ABC, fared worst.

But the greatest gain to emerge from the lack of any hierarchy in Granada, coupled with the system of growing programmes out of the people who were going to make them, was the building up over the years of a company of like-minded individuals who knew each other, trusted each other, and liked working together. The tone had been set by the early recruitment of people like David Plowright, Barrie Heads, Mike Scott, Mike and Joyce Wooller, Derek Granger, Julian Amyes and Mike Parkinson. A dud could not survive in this company and a shit would not be tolerated. The body of good sense and good feeling was powerful enough to absorb a buccaneer like Tim Hewat or an eccentric like Bill Grundy. Tim used to say, 'Everyone in Granada is too nice. What we want are some clever shits.' To which I would reply, 'No, Tim, the world is knocking at our door. We can pick decent people who will outwit the shits any day.' Later we set about the recruitment of the next generation of talent in a serious way through the Production Training Scheme.

There was no segregation of people into departments. A director might be doing a play one week, a *World in Action* the next, and then move on to some local Outside Broadcast. There were a few, a very few, specialist directors, mainly in sport and drama. There were no specialist producers. yet assignments were far from haphazard. Frequently a programme claimed a person because he had the right talent to do it, and very often a person claimed a programme because it was his idea, but the central aim was to direct talent onwards and upwards to its limit.

Joyce Wooller was my closest colleague and adviser in assigning people to programmes. Without her instinctive ability to judge character and talent Granada would never have succeeded in training and developing the people who were to be the foundation of our success in the 60s and 70s and who in later years would populate the upper realms of British broadcasting. They included a Director General of the BBC, the first Chief Executive of Channel 4, Programme Controllers in several ITV companies and the Chairmen of two, and numerous heads of department both in the BBC and ITV. Joyce filed everything that was known about our producers and directors in her memory. She could recount the work history of any one of them since he joined. She knew which designer could work with him and which production assistant could not. She recalled that a certain producer required an extra-vigilant cost clerk. She was up to date with the shifting scene of marital and extra-marital relationships that can be decisive in building a good working team in a closed community. People spoke to her with complete confidence, as they would to a priest. She knew what was in each person's contract, for she had drawn it up. We pondered over assignments for many hours each week: if I said, 'What about John to direct the next episode, with Margaret as producer?' and she frowned, I knew I'd got it wrong; if she said, 'Yes, that's a good idea', I knew I was safe. We seldom disagreed. When we did it was usually because I tended to have a greater belief in a person's potential talent than she had. I have found that many people are able to do things of which they never dreamt themselves to be capable. 'It's true that you have never handled actors before,' I would say, 'but I *know* (and here I would gaze steadfastly into their eyes) you can do it.' And often they could, and did. But I would never address a person to a task unless I truly believed it was within their power, and I would never challenge an absolute veto by Joyce.

In the Chanan history I am recorded as saying:

> One of the absorbing tasks was following each individual from stage to stage and trying to find where he would flower best, where his real aptitudes and real talents lay, which were very often different from the ones he thought he had. You found yourself applying a rather strange yard-stick: instead of saying that the company was going to make the following portfolio of programmes, and asking yourself who should be assigned to them, in many instances you would ask somebody what they wanted to do next, thrash it through with him until it was absolutely clearly defined and practical and then *that* would go into the portfolio. Of course, if he didn't come up with a good idea he'd have to do something else and perhaps be rather cheesed off.

*

There were a few who did not live up to expectations, there were many about whom expectations were limited: the bus-driver directors, as Joyce and I labelled them, who were condemned to work on routine and repetitious shows where to have ambition was a positive disadvantage and even to have imagination was a drawback.

It is possible that those hours spent in dialogue with directors were not so golden as in retrospect they seemed. Always I had to explain to my companions not to take seriously every idea I threw into the pot; they must realise that nine out of ten were impractical or just ludicrous and it was up to them to spot those few that were absolutely brilliant. Sometimes discussions were indulgent, and often they would lead to a dead end, but even today I see those many hours spent in debate with writers, producers and directors as my core contribution to the developing art of television.

Our structure as a company was designed to support the programme people. Lines of communication were short. A person had only to talk to their producer or to me, with no intervening layers of heads of department, and no committees. A decision could be taken on the spot, often within the hour, but only if it was before lunch, for there was a firm rule that no important decision was taken after twelve noon and no decision at all after 7 p.m. Evening decisions were quasi-decisions until they were confirmed first thing next morning. Disagreement could cause delay, but disagreements were only given elbowroom if they were profound and needed persuasion, reflection or time for the losing party to save face. Disagreements over whether a show with a heavy overspend should go ahead or be dumped could be taken at once, although the hurt might be considerable. The costing system kept a producer up to the minute in the matters of spend against budget. The craft department (Design, Graphics, Construction, Make-up, Wardrobe) were run by enthusiastic and collaborative people, not (as sometimes happens) by sullen barons who make petty rules and raise protocol difficulties that can become the bane of a producer's life.

The Story and Casting departments, too, were supportive and creative: they contributed critically to Granada's success. Communication was rapid, either by viva voce or telephone, seldom by memo, where the rule was that a memo of ten lines or fewer would be read and acted upon at once, one of a full page would be read on the evening of receipt, and one of two pages or more at the weekend.

We had, of course, our full quota of flops, cock-ups and abortions but although always disappointed and often mortified, we took our punishment in our stride. From the midst of the delightful turmoil which made up life in television in those days I would pluck one or two programmes to nurture myself, for in television there is no joy so great as playing a central part in a successful production. Current affairs was in the main a matter of report and comment, but drama – especially in the form of series drama – was a field where a producer could make the world jump to his command. In series drama characters could be grown and cherished until half the nation loved them, They could then develop cancer, marry a schizophrenic, lose all their money, die in a holocaust, anything except live happily ever after. I relished this power.

I first tasted blood as a *deus ex machina* in a show called *The Verdict is Yours*. Cecil had spotted it in *Variety*, the show-business journal. It was put on in America by CBS, and the next time I was in New York I saw it and instantly realised it was one for us. As adapted by Granada it had a simple formula. A court case was selected (or invented) which turned more on the character of the witnesses than on matters of fact and dealt in situations that were always highly dramatic, but never quite melodramatic. Witnesses were then fully briefed as to their own nature, character, life history and part in the story, but no more. Counsel was briefed as in a real-life case, and we all went into court in Studio 2 with no script and our fingers crossed. At first the actors were terrified, but soon they came to regard extempore performance as a challenge and a test of nerve where success carried great *réclame*, and the show became fashionable within the profession.

Devising the programmes gave unalloyed pleasure to the trio who were the joint authors – John Whitney, later to become Director General of the Independent Broadcasting Authority and Chairman of the Really Useful Company; his partner Geoffrey Bellman; and myself. In developing stories we would consider, say, the situation of a young woman who had the misfortune to marry a rich and handsome master of foxhounds who turned out to have two wives alive, well and undivorced.

'I think it would improve matters if he had met the woman on a visit to his daughter in a convent,' one would say. (Yes, indeed, and she would immediately become a nun.)

'What about a physical affliction?' another would suggest. (So the poor lady acquired a club foot.)

'Marrying a number of women is rather macho and rather admirable,' someone would volunteer. 'The man should have some despicable trait that makes him a real nasty.' (So the unlucky husband was discovered to have been habitually cruel to hounds, often beating them secretly and unmercifully behind the hunt kennels.) To make such bold decisions about other people's lives was heady stuff.

The Verdict is Yours was played over two evenings with the real-life jury pronouncing their verdict (which even we, as authors of the show, could not foretell) after the commercial break on the last night. It was a huge success, running for over seventy editions and coming off only because (egged on by Cecil) we became too greedy and tried to cram two stories into three nights.

Another form of participation in programme-making which gave satisfaction was to become the partner, confidant or familiar of some leading talent who was looking for a talking mate. One of these was Eddie Boyd, a Glasgow writer of high style, mordant wit and commanding personality. Eddie's stock in trade was the thriller, but a thriller that led us into his own private world, dark and mysterious, where menace was always in the air, where all men and women were blessed with the ability to deliver a string of the driest of dry one-liners and where every character was so ambivalent that the hero could suddenly commit the act of a shit and the baddie surprise us with a burst of nobility – and yet remain credible. His first series for Granada, *The Odd Man*, puzzled many viewers but was a hit. During the making of its successors, however, there began to be hints of trouble: Eddie would vanish from time to time in a haze of alcohol; and at last the time came when he could no longer deliver. This was a great sorrow, for I loved working with Eddie and indeed loved the man himself, especially for his wry courage in his battle against the demon drink, which alas he lost so decisively.

With Denis Mitchell there was a sunnier relationship. We had met whilst I was the Director of the Film Institute. Helen and I heard a radio programme about the railway king, John Hudson, which we thought a piece of magic, so we wrote a fan letter to the anonymous producer. Denis replied; we met for a lunch that lasted until ten o'clock that night, thus laying the foundation for a dialogue that never really ceased until he died in 1990. Denis and his colleague Norman Swallow joined us from the BBC to explore the delights of the newly available videotape on location. They made the famous programme on working men's clubs, *The Entertainers*, which was banned and later unbanned by the Authority. Norman Swallow made *A Wedding on Saturday*, which won the Prix Italia. Then together they set up a master class or school for young directors who were given the chance to direct a half-hour film on a subject of their own choosing. Over a period of five years some thirty films were made under the general title *This England*. None of them was a masterpiece but all were interesting, and they offered an early chance of direction to, amongst others, Mike Grigsby, Frank Cvitanovich, Leslie Woodhead, Michael Apted and Mike Newell.

Denis never managed to channel his talent, which was considerable, into a major work for television. His best piece was probably *Morning in the Streets*, originally a radio programme, and he brought from radio to television the sort of virtuosity in handling the soundtrack that Stewart McAlister had applied to the films of Humphrey Jennings. Alas, try as I would, I could not get the younger generation to learn from him. In their time they were all to produce the standard picture-orientated, character-reflecting, plot-dictated soundtrack that has become the pervasive Muzak of the feature film and the television show. Denis's track could take the lead, prepare the mind for what was to come, send the ear into sudden shock, or change the meaning of a scene by giving an undertone of menace, joy or nostalgia in counter-point to the message taken in by the eye. He was never my partner, for he worked on his own; but he treated me as an equal, which is the greatest compliment a talent can pay to an executive.

He would, however, use me as a talking block when he was angry, sometimes about the performance of those around him, sometimes about his own shortcomings, always about the world in general. His best work for Granada was probably *Seven Men*, a series of character studies of a number of great eccentrics including Quentin Crisp, Ivor Montagu, and Réné Cutforth. He loved the bizarre, the original, the nonconformist. And any person who had those qualities was his friend and soon his client, for with his casual chatty approach he had an uncanny knack of unlocking the inhibitions of even the most private and secret of people, who found in him something of a father confessor and something of a witch doctor.

More memorable than the hits amongst my personal projects are the flops. The greatest flop of my life was *Judge Dee*. This series was based on a number of best-selling books by Robert van Gulik, trans-lated from the Dutch, which I read whilst on holiday in Greece and thought would make stunning television. I did a deal for the rights with Charles Pick of Heinemann and set about adapting these dramatic and bloodthirsty doings of a mediaeval Chinese judge for the screen. I enlisted two directors – Howard Baker (dubbed the 'bearded prick' by Tim Hewat at the time of the Peasants' Revolt, in fact a talented if somewhat solemn director), and Richard Doubleday, a highly experienced drama man. During the early months of 1969 the three of us worked in almost total isolation. With such a winner on our hands we felt no need to consult anybody.

When the first episode was complete I showed it to the Programme Committee. As the lights went up (always the most daunting moment in a producer's life) there was dead silence. I had expected the usual chorus of abuse and appreciation, but there was nothing. It soon dawned on me that the silence was caused by compassion. They were sorry for me. No one dared to say that the show was an unmitigated disaster. I sat in the theatre in shock for what seemed like five minutes before honest Ken Brierley, ever anxious to ease a situation, spoke a line that will forever be etched on my memory. 'The beards on the extras,' he said, 'were surely a little too long.' We then passed on to the next item of business.

Later in the day Julian Amyes, the sensible all-seeing Julian, Julian my friend, came up to my office where I sat gloomily alone. He told me he had often lost perspective on a show. He too had failed to see a flop when it was staring him in the eye. He told me what was wrong with the show – the plot arcane, the characters wooden, the stylised Chinese dialogue unbearable, the whole concept pretentious and hollow. I began to feel a little better, and as Julian's therapy took effect had the strength to pick up the phone and cancel all further work on *Judge Dee*. But we had three in the can and were committed to more. The critics and the viewers unanimously confirmed the Programme Committee's unspoken verdict. Ratings sank like a stone and I was forced to invent a new late-night drama slot where the fruits of a managing director's folly could be decently and inauspiciously buried.

Another kind of disaster befell me in the same year (1969) over a show of much higher calibre, *Big Breadwinner Hogg*. Many of us had been alarmed at the revelation of torture and killings carried out by the Richardson and Kray gangs in London and I enlisted Robin Chapman as writer and Mike Newall (later to make *Four Weddings and a Funeral*) and Mike Apted (now of Hollywood) as directors to make an eight-part series that would display to one and all the full horror of what was going on in our very own law-abiding London. A huge research effort was made to give us an authentic feel of our subject. It was a good script, a good cast and the two Mikes were becoming smart directors. It was, in fact, a really good show. Unfortunately, in our zeal to shock our audience into a state of alarm and fury about the iniquities taking place on their doorstep we depicted a gangland fight outside a nightclub in which there was some very nasty work with a knife, ending with phials of acid being thrown into a poor wretch's eyes whilst the camera lingered on his stricken face to show its deadly effect. Even today such a scene would be best transmitted after midnight and hedged about with warnings for those with nervous dispositions. In those days nothing like it had ever been seen before. All hell broke out. Switchboards were jammed. Fleet Street was abuzz, the Authority's duty officers alerted their seniors, and Bernard Sendall phoned me at about eleven o'clock, almost speechless in shock.

The next morning there were headlines. Editors rang up Sidney. Sidney flew to Manchester, where Robin and I met him. Sidney was in shock too. How could we have done such a thing? We viewed the offending tape, and viewed it again, and yet again. Robin and I watched it uncomfortably but with some pride. This was exactly what we had wanted to do and we had done it in spades. Too many spades. It had never crossed our minds that public outage would be directed against us, not the horrid gangland life of London; that we would have half the viewers in Britain reaching for the phone, children crying out with terror and elderly persons fainting away in shock. I remember that when we had viewed the tape before transmission I had said to Robin with some satisfaction, 'That should frighten the horses.'

But it was not the horses we had to deal with now. It was a raging and ranting Bob Fraser. Sidney sought wildly for some respectable reason to justify such a lapse from grace by Granada, but since there was none I preferred to come clean and say, 'Sorry, it was a failure of judgement.' We argued a good deal, but Sidney got his way and some lame but high-sounding press release was issued. Meanwhile all transmissions were postponed. Sadly Robin and I went off to sanitise the remaining episodes. Rediffusion smugly announced they would drop the show. The rest of the network, with great trepidation, agreed to put it out somewhere just before the midnight hour. So a truncated version of *Hogg*, suitable for children and entirely free from menace to horses or any human being, crept back on the air ignominiously and played out its time to a handful of insomniacs. The final twist came when we received our official wigging from the Authority. Their letter made little of the shock to viewers but much of the fact that the précis of the show I had sent them in advance had a misleading description of the incident that had set the nation by the ears. 'Outside the nightclub a fracas takes place.' They thought this inadequate, and I suppose it was.

Almost as painful as a flop is a misjudgement, the killing of a winner because you think it won't come right. One of these was *Singing in the Brain*, a fantastic comedy developed by Denis Pitts, John Glashan and myself. The show was introduced by the lugubrious Ivor Cutler accompanying himself on his dreary portable organ and singing some McGonagall-like truisms to what could have passed for the musical setting for a Scottish paraphrase. Then into a series of sketches, such as one which featured a competition to read an oculist's eye chart between two world champions working in bath chairs from a range of fifty yards in front of a packed audience and accompanied by a David Coleman-like commentary – 'He's got E! He's got E! Now he's moving down to the third line! It's Z, it's Z. He's got it. He's got Z!' Another demonstrated how to train Sloane Rangers as gun dogs. We saw them trotting out across the moor in twin-sets and pearls, picking up grouse and bringing them back in their mouths to the guns. Again the hectic commentator described their every move: 'She's casting about downwind – no, no – yes, she's on the scent – now she's moving across – No! No! not what way – Yes, that's better – she's very near – she's got it.'

The central character in this idiotic but charming string of fantasies was David Langdon, who gave a performance that was quite beautiful. Alas, I convinced myself that the show did not hold up for half an hour, and on the principle that no comedy is better than its worst five minutes, after weeks of striving to find enough top-class material I cancelled it. The absolute folly of this decision became clear when, some fifteen years later, I looked at the first two unfinished shows and found them to be funnier than any fantasy comedy I had ever seen, always excepting *Fawlty Towers* and the best of *Monty Python*, a series which certainly had many more *longueurs* per half-hour than the unseen *Singing in the Brain*. It was *Chelsea at Nine* all over again.

But as the 1960s wore on and labour relations and the politics of the television industry took up more and more of my time, it became necessary to hand over great chunks of programming to others. By the mid-60s the Manchester team, most of them in their mid-thirties, were fully-armed professionals, and indeed in the context of those days pretty well veterans. David Plowright was now at the top of his form, masterminding *World in Action* and doing battle with the Authority in the front line. His sagacity and wit were a constant joy, and every time he put his head round my door (which was frequently) my spirits gave an upward jump. It was all fun for him and for me, but not always so jolly, I guessed, for those who worked for him, for he could be a hard taskmaster and was unforgiving of sloppy work or – the worst sin in his book – imperfect research. And he had a short fuse. But he was an instinctive leader and exerted iron control over the crew of self-confident and self-assertive journalists who worked for him and with many of whom he formed close personal bonds. *World in Action* moved in dangerous territory and danger demands total trust between the men in the field and the top men at home; and it is fair to say that the show operated on a basis of absolute trust between the team and David, and David and myself. Sometimes when we had a really hot number coming up, such as sending a couple of members of the team to Geneva acting as arms dealers to negotiate with representatives of an Arab state, or when we were about to reveal some improprieties in Reginald Maudling's business life, we would go together to Sidney's office and tell him all. At such times we encountered a different Sidney. He very seldom asked any questions but would listen impassively to all we had to say. When we had finished he would rise silently and offer us a whisky. This we felt was Sidney at his most magnificent.

The tiny portion of David's life not filled by Granada and its affairs was taken up by his pursuit of seamanship. He studied navigation at home, passed exams, and eventually bought a boat which spent most of its time anchored in front of the yacht club in Abersoch, where he could often be seen seated behind the plate-glass window of the club gazing thoughtfully at the boat through the rain and the wind, a gin and tonic in his hand. Occasionally he and his crew set out to sea, but this was a rare event and would rate as a topic of conversation for a twelvemonth.

As a colleague David was quick in doing business, but Barrie Heads was even quicker. He would sail into the room, a large child's exercise book – in those days of foolscap size – under his arm, open it at the appropriate page and run down his shopping list at a gallop. A lot of the points required only a yes or a no. Often after only five minutes he would say, 'Well, that's it then', snap his book shut and rise to his feet. 'Hold on a minute,' I would cry, 'tell me how the House of Lords show went last Tuesday.'

'It went OK,' Barrie would reply, and gaze at me to see if further and better particulars were required. He was perfectly able to give them if they were; indeed he would sit there for half an hour and recount events in detail if necessary, but not unless he was asked to do so. This was a very great virtue. Like David he was the author of pungent and often comical memos, and like him could quickly take command of a team. The ratio of women to men in his territory tended to be higher than elsewhere in Granada, not because he was a feminist, nor because he had a more highly developed libido than the rest of us, but because he liked working with women (as I did), a propensity which, protestations to the contrary, not many men in Granada shared, Sidney himself being inclined to be uneasy, over-courteous or else coyly gallant with females unless he was angry, when he would treat them as normal human beings. Both sexes liked working for Barrie because he made quick decisions and came out upfront with his views about individuals' work and prospects. Indeed sometimes he was a little too upfront and certainly never able to flatter, cajole or crawl to gain the favour of any person, however important he might be. He was impatient with swank of any kind and unable to conceal his contempt for those who carried a heavy load of personal vanity, or for practically any member of the acting profession. Whatever it is that may be the opposite of a sycophant, Barrie was it.

Derek Granger, by contrast, the great polymath of Granada, could live with the vanities of individuals and of the world at large with an easy grace. He regarded human folly with an affectionate amusement, and the greater the folly the better he was entertained. As he recounted the horrors of some ghastly lunch party he had attended or an encounter with the union strike committee, his narration would be punctuated by an obbligato of bubbling laughter which would sometimes rise and quench the flow of words until he had regained his composure. His knowledge of literature was wide and deep and ran right through the ages up to the present day, where he was particularly strong on recent fashionable books like *The Naked Lunch*, which he always seemed to have read before anyone else. Derek would undertake anything, whether it was a mission to find a one-armed signalman for an item on *Scene at Six Thirty*, making a précis of *War and Peace* by Tuesday, producing a comedy for Arthur Lowe or taking over *Coronation Street*. He had immense confidence in the power of the *Street* and used to claim that if he were to will it *Coronation Street*, properly deployed, could bring down the government.

But there were to be defections. In February 1967 the long-delayed new round of television franchises was announced. Yorkshire and Lancashire were to be separated: Granadaland was to be split in half. There were two immediate consequences: Sidney announced that he would appeal to the United Nations, and Tim Hewat and Philip Mackie decided to make a bid for the Yorkshire contract. For some time both had been restive, for both were ambitious, and neither could see any prospect of upward advancement into the solid wedge of the Granada leadership.

So Tim and Philip, who was now a freelance but working mainly for Granada, joined a powerful consortium led by Arnold Goodman. We gave them six months' leave with pay to make the application, and a promise of a welcome back if their application failed. But they told me it would not fail. They were certain of success; and as they scavenged around my mind to learn about those parts of television their experience had not reached, they made it clear that the brave new Yorkshire company would avoid many of the deficiencies in structure and working methods that they had identified in Granada. A few days before the announcement of the award, Tim rang me to say that Lord Hill had tipped him off that it was in the fucking bag. Such an indiscretion from the Chairman of the Authority, even if expressed in more parliamentary language, seemed highly unlikely and I bided my time, apprehensively. Sure enough the contract went to the *Yorkshire Post* consortium. The decision was a disaster for both Tim and Philip. After talking so long and protesting so much, their pride made it impossible for them to come back to Granada Television. Tim went back to Fleet Street for a short time and then returned to Australia, where he had an equal lack of success in attempting to launch a new journal. His departure from the scene was a huge loss to Granada and to British television.

For Philip, we had set up a feature film company of which he would be the chief executive if he failed in the Yorkshire bid and which would fade away if he succeeded. Its brief was to produce low-budget feature films, mainly comedies, hopefully in the Ealing tradition. But it was no go. Sidney, uninvited but with the *droit de seigneur* of Group Chairman and the authority of one who had made all of three pictures with Hitch, sent for every script, scrutinised every budget and vetoed every leading actor whom Philip proposed. It was the television play scene all over again, with Sidney more negative and Philip more belligerent. Project after project bit the dust, and it was clear that their stock of mutual tolerance was running out when at last a script based on the play *Semi-Detached* was agreed and went into production.

The stage production had been something of a triumph. In the film, after seemingly endless wrangles, Warren Mitchell was given the lead. Sidney kept away whilst the film was shot and completed, and one wet and dismal afternoon we all trooped down to the Granada Slough for what Sidney insisted on calling a 'sneak'. As the lights went down a dinner-jacketed manager announced to an indifferent audience of perhaps a hundred souls that instead of seeing the current release they were going to have the privilege of sampling a spanking new major production fresh from the studios. There were no laughs in the first ten minutes. There were no laughs in the following half-hour. Indeed there were no laughs in the whole film, save once when a paper boy held out his hand for a tip and Warren Mitchell told him to piss off. The Granada top brass strode out of the cinema grim-faced and silent. Sidney and Cecil sped back to London in their separate Rovers. As I walked out of the cinema, Philip turned to me and quoted the last line of *Pagliacci*, '*La commedia è finita.*' The next morning he sent Sidney a letter of resignation in which he exorcised the frustrations of the past months by explaining to him in prose of devastating clarity why it was impossible for any creative person to work with him.

But in the big world there was always plenty of work for Philip. His roll of honour at Granada was long and immensely distinguished, incorporating nearly a hundred plays and series made up from adaptations of Saki, Maupassant and Feydeau, and culminating in perhaps the best thing he ever did, *The Caesars*, a six-part series written and produced by himself, in its day an all-studio production of stunning virtuosity. Some time after the débâcle of Granada Films and the Yorkshire contract, he wrote and produced a series called *The Organisation* for the new Yorkshire company which was alleged to contain unflattering portraits of Sidney and myself, as well as of other Granada ex-colleagues. I asked Joyce Wooller, a reliable judge, to tell me whether the rumours were true, and when she said yes, I decided not to see the show since it was likely to cause nothing but pain and grief. Philip, of course, publicly denied that his characters had had any foundation in real life. But I was deeply hurt. Philip was my oldest friend in the business. We first met when we sat at a table together in the old MOI in 1946, waiting for Helen to give us our first assignments. We had shared a house together, written reviews together, above all worked together happily and harmoniously for more than ten years. There had been no row, no falling out. I reflected that he might feel that I had failed to use my full powers to help him win the battle of Granada Films (which was impossible), or – more likely – that the Yorkshire disappointment had bred in him a resentment of Granada's success, but to this day this fit of malice towards an old mate remains a puzzle.

There were others ready to move into the space vacated by Philip and Tim. Peter Eckerssley, with his high, domed forehead, shiny bald head and large circular spectacles, would have looked owlish had he been a solemn person, but this was far from his nature: he surveyed the world with benevolent irony. He was a *Guardian* man through and through, and believed that to write a good piece was the summit of man's ambition. After a period as one of the lead writers on *Coronation Street* he surfaced as a producer (and writer) of comedies, and later of plays and drama series, culminating in his great production of *Hard Times*, surely the best adaptation of Dickens ever to reach the small screen. Peter was a buddy to most people on the station, but was a little afraid of me, catching, I suspect, a whiff of public school, Oxbridge and army that was foreign to his lifestyle. But I admired him greatly and we got on well, save once. He was producing a dramatisation of Ford Madox Ford's *The Good Soldier*, to me a very special book, and I wanted to iron out the multitude of flashbacks (as I was later to do with *The Raj Quartet*) and tell the story in consecutive time. He wanted to keep several of the time planes in play. The director, Kevin Billington, a determined young man, cut through between us like a knife through butter, and the resulting show looked expensive and elegant, and was well received. But it was no masterpiece, as it could have been, and Peter and I shared a degree of guilt and sorrow – but without any mutual recrimination.

This episode proved that it was best for Peter to work for David Plowright and indeed the benefit was mutual for it was largely through Peter that David got a taste for drama and later went on to produce his brother-in-law Laurence Olivier in several great epics. With Sidney, Peter had no meeting point: they admired each other from afar, but each was unable to speak the other's language. Peter had many special qualities. He was a walking thesaurus, and always ready with perms, options and alternatives for any writer looking for the *mot juste*. He was a scholar in the field of D.C. Thompson's children's comics and his conversation was laced with references to Korky the Cat and Tiger Tim. He could fire off one-liners at speed, and never in all the time I knew him did he recount a funny thing that had happened to him or tell a set-piece joke.

Derek Granger now strode the decks of Granada with assurance, his time of hunting one-armed signalmen and canvassing the commissionaires for their opinion of the jokes in his shows long over. His successful reign over *Coronation Street* had made him king of the walk. He now felt capable of doing anything and was usually engaged in multifarious activities as he ranged the corridors at speed, talking in a high baritone with occasional bursts of fortissimo, perhaps eating nuts as he talked and stressing his points with emphatic but precise gestures. His appearance was that of a highly intelligent small mammal, bright of eye, alert, quickly reactive. He had the liveliest of minds and an extraordinary degree of verbal facility. He could persuade Sidney that he was wrong when no one else would dare try, and charm Cecil into a budget increase and leave him smiling. He could be the presenter of *Cinema* in addition to producing his own shows, which after several years in the galleys he could do brilliantly. He simultaneously filled the roles of Granada's universally available

critic, literary conscience and court jester, throwing himself mercilessly into whatever work he was doing, scarcely ever pausing to let
himself catch his breath. He took no holiday and would sit across my
desk and say, 'It's hopeless. I've had no holiday in eighteen months
except for one Saturday afternoon at the Manchester YMCA baths.'
'But, Derek,' I would say, 'you are due seven weeks' holiday and can
take it when you like.'

'I know,' he would say listlessly. 'It's so difficult to find time. I must
get away after the dry run next week.' But he never did. It was this
dedication to the task in hand that was to see him through the rough
days – and they were rough days indeed – of *Brideshead Revisited*.

Of all my colleagues during this period Julian Amyes was the closest, the most versatile and the most staunch. He was by vocation a
director. In the Chanan history, Derek Granger says of him:

> As a director Julian was one of the most exemplary in
> British television. Julian's preparation was absolutely
> legendary, and his camera script was more detailed than an
> ordnance survey map. There was no doubt in anybody's
> mind on the whole of the technical staff, cameramen,
> vision mixer, PA and what have you, but that every single
> detail of the play was pre-arranged and fore-ordained. Yet
> funnily enough, this didn't produce a strict effect at all, and
> Julian, who is the most passionate man, became in the
> studio the most calm and docile. I once remarked on this
> to him and he said that the whole reason why he had to
> be such a fastidious preparer of his scripts and his cameras
> was the fact that he couldn't otherwise have contained
> himself in the control room. It was the only thing that
> could keep him calm, because he is not normally a calm
> man, but a man of marvellous vehemence.

But Julian as a director was more than a brilliant executant. He had a
unique understanding of actors and acting. To quote Derek again:

> Julian was trained as a classical actor and had, in fact, spent
> three years at Stratford. Had he gone on I think he would
> have made an absolutely definitive character among
> Shakespeare's lean and hungry types. He might easily have
> been a definitive Malvolio or Jacques, Thersites or Timon of
> Athens. He had the wonderfully lean, almost skeletal appear-
> ance, topped by a face of fervid intent, of a man who seems

of absolutely Calvinist rigour; but when you got to know him he revealed a most extraordinary sparkling humour. A lapsed Leavisite, Julian had picked up, from Leavis I think, something of that vehement utterance on the side of the real right thing, and truth and integrity in art.

Behind his appreciation of the actors' part in making drama, Julian had a deep respect for the basic stuff of drama, the text. Whereas I was always happy to cut, embellish and if necessary rewrite a piece to make it work on the screen, Julian would seek for the author's true meaning and interpret this as best as could be without alteration. If it was good enough to do at all, it should be done the way the author intended. He and his wife Anne had a wide knowledge of dramatic literature. Julian was a classicist, and responded best to contemporary writers who were masters of form such as Harold Pinter or Peter Nicholls. He disliked impressionism and was suspicious of cleverness.

But to me and Granada, Julian Amyes was more than a drama director and a dramaturge. He shared with me the personal problems that surround the head of any creative organisation, was my partner in coping with Sidney, and for several years took on his shoulders the huge weight of the company's (and later the industry's) labour relations.

From the mid-60s labour relations tended to dominate the life of the managing directors of the independent television companies. The militant mood of the times, coupled with the unions' knowledge that (as with newspapers) even the shortest stoppage would cost the management far more than it would take to buy them off, gave them the whip hand. In ten years they had secured working conditions that Fleet Street had gained only after half a century of struggle. Within Granada the realisation that here was a force that could have the power to strangle television dawned slowly. In the bad old days of the pre-war film industry, with its Quota Quickies, sweated labour, unpaid overtime and exploited talents, Sidney had been a party to the foundation of the film technicians' union, the ACT.

When Independent Television started up this same union took aboard the television technicians, and under its new banner of the Association of Cinematograph and Television Technicians it quickly became the leader in handling the industry's labour relations. Sidney was still remembered as something of a saintly figure, particularly by George Elvin, one of his associates in the early days and now the union's boss. Personal bonds, although not so strong, had also been formed with heads of the other two unions representing the electricians and (broadly speaking) the craftsmen. Thus in the early days, as the unions struck roots in Manchester and began to formulate demands for rights and recognition, if any point had to be referred to the top Sidney would invite George Elvin round to Golden Square for a drink and in the haze of reminiscence over the bad old days the problem would disappear. Occasionally a union boss would have to make a visit to Manchester or a shop steward would travel to London, but in the end the problem would be resolved without any trouble at the coalface. But things were to change. The shop stewards began to disregard the advice sent down from above. The General Secretaries began to find compelling reasons why they could not keep an appointment at Golden Square. Arguments began to rage between management and unions in Manchester. Victor Peers was at his wits' end. And then in 1958 there was our first strike.

Sidney was shocked. Here he was, a champion of the trade unions, with his own people, his own union, in revolt against him. 'Look at those cars, Denis,' he would say as he gazed down at the car park from his office window. 'Everyone is well paid. We in Granada believe in the trade unions and will help them to set up good trade union practices. But this is unreasonable.' Unreasonable or not, it was the *realpolitik* of the day and, as Sidney gradually became disillusioned and the unions began to see him no longer as a founding father but as a domineering and inimical old-fashioned mill-owner.

At first, Victor coped manfully with the sullen civil war that was spreading across the face of ITV. Local agreements, some of them foolish, were made by different companies. The unions were quick to seize on the best of the regional deals and to impose them throughout the industry. The companies saw that they must combine, and combine they did, showing as much acrimony to each other as they did to the unions. Accusations of selling out (particularly by Lew Grade) and bad faith (by all against all) were commonplace. Victor lost confidence in his industry colleagues and began to run out of steam. By the mid-60s I found myself in the thick of it: the local shops at the door, the unions nationally combining to outwit the companies collectively, the companies, usually in some disarray, mounting one rearguard operation after another, always too late, nearly always ineffectual. And in the background lay the most formidable hazard of all, Sidney. Sometimes he would sulk in his tent, sometimes he would emerge in a rage, insisting that his way was the right way and that the failure to impose his will upon the unions argued a lack of skill or, more likely, a lack of moral fibre in those delegated to do the task. This was made all the harder to tolerate since labour relations was

one of those areas of human activity for which Sidney had no understanding, no feeling and no talent. Hence (as with engineering) he
distrusted everyone.

As the battle rumbled on in the trenches a serious labour relations
crisis would blow up two or three times a year. The sequence of
events was always the same. If a deal could not be reached in
Manchester, Julian and I would carry the negotiations to the point
where the demands of the two sides were absolutely clear and then
report the situation to our masters in London and tell them what
options were open to them. Nearly always, doing a deal meant spending a certain sum of money for ever, and often not doing a deal meant
a strike which would cost a much greater but unquantifiable amount
of money now. Julian and I would trail down to Golden Square and
address ourselves to Sidney, Cecil and Joe. As we deployed the union
case there would be short explosive comments from the trinity.
'Quite unreasonable.' 'Ridiculous.' 'Disgraceful.' As we laid out the
management options we would be quizzed closely, particularly on
any point relating to the expenditure of money. At this stage we never
made a recommendation, but waited until what we called the hunting noises had died down. The sentiments most commonly expressed
in the chorus were Stand Firm, Show of Strength, No Compromise
and Management Must Manage. Julian and I would then slowly and
patiently run over the advantages of what we saw as the best practi-
cable deal. Again most commonly, we would be sent back to
Manchester with the words of the hunting chorus ringing in our ears
and no agreement to any movement on our side.

If things got really tough the union would issue notice of industrial
action, and as soon as this was reached the Golden Square mood
would change. Panic would set in and far-fetched solutions would be
suggested in lengthy phone calls. Other companies would be
consulted ('What does Lew think?' – most commonly, 'Pay up and
keep the show on the air.') 'Can the Authority do anything?' (No, they
never can.) 'Has the Minister been advised?' (Yes, the Minister has
been told but that won't help.) 'Have we made sure that our side will
be fully reported in the press?' (We have issued a factual press release:
the tabloids will certainly back the union.) 'Can we travel down for a
meeting in Golden Square at seven o'clock tonight?' (Well, yes.)

And so, in a very different climate, we would meet for a second
time and listen to a variety of proposals, some of them quite wild,
some devious and all designed to prevent a strike but without spending any money. The company secretary might be called in, other
Group directors who happened to be in the building, the Head of

Sales, and there would always be one or two people standing in corners talking into phones. Meanwhile Julian and I would ruefully reflect that this same scene was probably being played out in every ITV boardroom. Sometimes we would get a decision. Sometimes we would have to reconvene the next day. If the strike went ahead the whole management team would come together as a band of brothers, if it were averted by means of a deal both Sidney and Joe would let it be known that the terms of the deal had been forced on them against their better judgement and only Cecil would stand staunchly behind the negotiators. After a particularly stressful encounter in 1968 I decided I had had enough, and wrote to Sidney:

> The matter I wish to raise is, of course, labour relations. It must be very galling for you to have people like myself and Julian – and from time to time Cecil – acting as your lieutenants and not winning nearly as many battles as you would like. I know you are impatient with us, and I am sorry. But I would point out that, when it comes to the tactics of labour relations, you yourself are much worse than any of us.
>
> It has always been a sorrow for me that your interest in music did not match your interest in painting. Even your best friends could scarcely claim that you are musically gifted. But then, you don't play the violin in my office all day. I do suggest to you that there is an area in labour relations where you suffer from an equal colour-blindness, tone-deafness or whatever, and this is the tactical area. Even when it comes to strategy, your instincts, although often as splendid as usual, would confuse anyone who knew you less well than Cecil, Julian and myself. They often appear to be contradictory, the impulse to generosity is frequently cancelled out by the instinct for good housekeeping which often takes you to the brink of nearness. The desire for a happy and democratic company is often overcome by a flash of the domineering spirit which works so well in getting a big building enterprise under way but which is fatal in industrial relations.
>
> Perhaps the most tedious aspect of my work at Granada at the moment is to have to listen to the ritual war dance of management in times of labour crisis. The well-known cries (Stand Firm etc.) seldom mean what they imply. They are parts of a well-worn routine which is played out in

boardrooms and in executive suites all over Britain and which belong to the period before the Viennese psychologists explained to us a thing or two about human reactions and human behaviour. We should be a little more sophisticated. Apart from being bad art, and tedious, this ritual war dance is positively harmful because, after going through its first few cycles, reason is diminished and propaganda clichés take over.

I beg you, dear Sidney, to believe me that the quality of firm management is to be found in the day-to-day demeanour of the executives in charge of labour. By the time that crisis is reached, the only practical issue is to gauge the realities of power and to pursue the course that will sustain the respect for management and hence its continuing authority.

I don't apologise for this lecture because I feel in Granada I am in the privileged position of being allowed to lecture the Chairman whenever I feel inclined. But I do want to conclude by saying that I know I don't live up to the lofty tone of the preceding paragraphs. I am not very good at labour relations either, but I am better than you and learning.

I don't think that we can continue to engage the attention of six Company Directors in our labour crises. I don't think we could easily stand another period of dissension such as we have just passed through. I would like to suggest changes, but not unless, when you have read this letter, you feel you can accept it with a smile.

Your affectionate Colleague,
Denis

Sidney never made any reply, but it was noticeable that he began to delegate all but multi-million pound labour relations issues to Cecil, who left more to me, who in turn left as much as possible in the sensible and safe hands of Julian.

Another call on my time came with the gradual transfer of control over the internal economy of the company from Golden Square to Manchester. In the earliest days the Bernsteins' personal writ ran across the board. Sidney himself monitored the purchase of writing paper, the cost of a cup of tea and the layout of all forms. Cecil would know the footage of each commercial transmitted and Joe would

each day ponder a schedule of proposed expenditure on items costing £50 or more. The explanation for this bizarre but highly effective method of cost control was as follows. The Bernstein system of
running a cinema chain was enshrined in a bulky procedure manual
which was followed to the letter by every cinema manager. It told
him how to indent for lavatory paper, how much to pay the cleaning
ladies per square foot and what a uniform could cost for a small,
medium and outsize commissionaire. If a form of expenditure was
not in the manual it could not happen without reference to head
office. This system was perfected and replicated over some four dozen
cinemas until the Bernsteins were satisfied that it was virtually spend-
proof. Unfortunately this method could not be applied to television
because there were no cinema managers and very little was replicated. So the bosses had to do it themselves. A great volume and variety of miscellaneous expenditure had to be approved rather urgently.
Joe and Victor would toil long hours, with a mass of requisitions, as
they were quaintly called, passing from one side of the desk to the
other. Sidney undertook spot checks. I had no authority to spend
anything and so in the early days took each programme to Sidney or
Cecil, who after due diligence would give it the green light.
Something had to be done and I suggested to Sidney that we should
introduce programme budgets. Sidney was against. Budgets did not
stop people spending money. Indeed if the budget was generously
drawn it could encourage them to spend more, a horrifying prospect.

The Chanan history records Reg Hammans' heartrending account
of how Sidney's anti-budget views were seen by the Engineering
Department:

> I found Sidney to be generous to a fault on a personal basis
> and ruthless to a degree on a business basis. I believe that
> he calibrated the effectiveness of any organisation in which
> he was concerned by the amount of money it made. One
> aspect of Sidney's way of working which I deplored more
> than any was his utter refusal ever to work to budgets. He
> never, for example, gave the engineering department an
> annual budget, and this is unique in television broadcast-
> ing. In the early years of Granada nobody could spend
> more than £50 without going outside the department for
> approval, and I found that quite extraordinary. One of the
> biggest headaches I had to meet with was not knowing
> what kind of expenditure would be possible over the next
> x months. While that helped to ensure that the department

was cost-conscious, it was stifling to initiative too, because it meant that you had the enormous trouble of trying to convince people who were absolutely ignorant in engineering terms of what it was you were talking about. If there'd been an annual budget there were things you'd have gone ahead with on your own initiative.

But in the field of programmes Cecil was persuaded, and then Joe, and budgets became the accepted thing soon after we went on the air. But a budget by no means took the producer all the way. The money could not be spent unless the production office, the construction department, the casting office and so on were permitted by Sidney to release the cash. We were pretty well back to square one until, with the onset of the great cash crisis in the late summer of 1956, Sidney became so wholly preoccupied with other matters that budgets began to slip through on my say-so.

The move from the Bernstein system of preventing people from spending any money at all to the Forman system of authorising them to spend a little spread very slowly through the Granada Television economy. To begin with there was no interest in the notion of an annual budget for the programme department. If Sidney or Cecil wanted an estimate of next year's spend they would ask Joe for it. He would then cover several pages of blue-lined foolscap with scrawls from his Swan fountain pen, discover what we were spending now, ask me how much more we had to produce in the next year and turn in a figure of astonishing accuracy.

But soon I was to find an ally. Even before we went on the air Bill Dickson, a cheerful and alert Geordie, had been recruited from our auditors, then known as Peat Marwick Mitchell, to work as number two in the accounts department in Manchester. He was familiar with methods of cost control (used by his more advanced clients) and the two of us put together a system that could be adopted to cover the field of all programme production. When Bill became number one in Manchester we worked together independently of the Group, developing our own thing until, mercifully, Joe came to see that he could trust Bill and that there was good sense in our system.

From then on we had an almost clear field. At the same time as introducing budgets to cover expenditure we set up a system of cost control which was over the years to make Granada by far the most economical producer of television programmes in ITV. The system, not unlike the one used in the production of feature films, was simple. We appointed a cost clerk to shadow every major production

– indeed a major play might have two clerks – whilst some of the smaller programmes would be grouped together under one. Each day when shooting was over the cost clerk would report the day's expenditure against budget. If trouble threatened, Bill would warn me immediately. If necessary the producer, or he and I, would move in and sort things out. An overspend would be checked and authorised, or in extreme cases the show would be cancelled. As a result there were no major financial disasters, very few overspends, and a respect for the sanctity of the budget. We refined the methods of drawing a budget, often controlling costs not only by putting a ceiling on spending but by limiting the availability of time and space. 'Two days shooting on location and two days in Studio 6 with two main sets and four corners' would be a common brief for the producer of a drama series, and the main lines of his budget were pretty well set. As Bill's confidence grew the whole of Granada television became our oyster. Production manuals were out, as were committees (except for capital expenditure). Delegation went deep down, reference up was at the referrer's discretion. Decisions must be immediately available, lines of communication short, control of expenditure rigid, the number of forms minimal.

One important tool in the system was the Blue Book, which set out programme planning and personnel assignments for all creative staff up to one year ahead and had emblazoned on its cover the following inscription:

PRACTICALLY NOTHING SHOWN IN THESE
SCHEDULES IS A FACT
NEARLY EVERYTHING IS AN ASSUMPTION
THIS IS PLANNING

(I was secretly chuffed to learn that Sidney had circulated a copy of the Blue Book to every Managing Director in the Group. He must now think planning, at least, a good thing.)

Each Manchester morning at 8.30, Bill would greet me cheerfully in my office for a review of the affairs of the industry, the company and the problems of the hour. The decisions we took in the first ten minutes of the day quickly worked their way through the company by phone and by personal encounter. I do not recall that over some thirty years Bill and I ever wrote a single memo to each other. Every successful company has its unsung achievers who are obscured by the men in front. Bill was one of them, and he progressed steadily from senior accountant to Chief Accountant to Company Secretary, to a seat on the Board, to Finance Director, and then went on to chair the finance Committee of the ITV companies. Finally, and this was enormously valuable to Granada, he became the privy adviser and consultant to the Authority on the financial affairs of the industry.

Bill was a paragon within his own field. He also had another and more private side of which many people knew nothing. If a member of the staff had a problem too personal to expose to the general management, whether it was legal, marital or financial, they would seek out Bill, who as a freelance father confessor would gently steer them towards a solution. He was a persistent visitor of the sick and gave much of his time and his talent to supporting charities. With Sidney his technique was impeccable: he had the answer to every question at his fingertips, never lost his equanimity even under the most severe attack, and when Sidney became unfair or unreasonable he could check him by sheer moral authority. 'Ah, come now, sir, not quite that,' he would say, looking at him like a judge calling to order an unruly counsel. He never lost his cheerfulness, his Geordie accent or his ability to play 1930s jazz on the piano at the drop of a hat. We had two matters we never mentioned. One was the fact that despite all our checks and safeguards and to our great shame the head of our recorded music department (who was known to keep a pair of greyhounds) skipped with £15,000 of the company's money. The other was that Bill was a committed mason.

In the early days the sentiment most often expressed in our industry (along with 'Television is the medium of the future') was 'Television is a young man's game.' The second motto was uttered mainly by young men, and as the century rolled on and as the young grew older it was heard less frequently. But in the late 1950s, as the average age of our creative people rose from twenty-six or so to thirty or more, a sort of panic set in. What were we doing about the leaders of the future, the young whose game television was alleged to be: where were they going to come from? All the world was seeking a job in Granada, or if not with us with the BBC, and after that the more commercially minded of the ITV companies. Why did we not make a major effort to skim off the best young talent available and ensure Granada's pre-eminence for another generation?

We decided to do just that. Julian and I brewed up the Production Training Scheme. It was ambitious and very expensive. We took it to Sidney, who endorsed it on sight and surprisingly suggested some improvements that would make it even more expensive. Cecil and Joe were told it was going to happen and realised the wind was blowing too strongly to allow any resistance.

There were over a thousand replies to the advertisements for the first course (1,700 for the third). One hundred and thirty-eight applicants were interviewed by two senior producers who travelled to the most central venues – Oxford, Cambridge, Newcastle, Edinburgh, Bristol. Twenty young men and women came to Manchester and spent three days in the studios (to go through a programme not a million miles away from the one developed by the War Office Selection Boards for officers), all were interviewed by the full board (a terrible mistake), and eight were taken on as trainees.

Derek Granger masterminded the selection process and the syllabus for the early courses in 1959 and 1961, and later the head-masters included Mike Wooller, Julian Amyes, Barrie Heads and Peter Heinze. The early trainees thought little of our efforts. The course lasted nine months and began with four weeks in a Granada cinema, taking the tickets and helping the manager with his returns, which the trainees hated. They could see no point in this kind of assignment and neither could we, but to Sidney it was an essential way of introducing the *jeunesse dorée* of our universities to the common facts of life in the great world. Subsequently the unions would not permit the trainees to do much hands-on training, much less let them take part in a real show. They hung around, listening to lectures disconsolately, grumbling quite a lot, playing hockey with walking sticks and waiting eagerly for the end of their indenture.

Later courses were better organised, with a mock-up studio and programme of film-making on 8mm. Despite the grumbling the trainee scheme must be rated a success, producing as it did four internationally famous film directors and at least a dozen men and women who were to become the backbone of the Granada programme team, including Peter Plummer, Mike Beckham, Leslie Woodhead, Mike Apted, Mike Newell, Gordon McDougall, Peter Jones, Andy Mayer, Andrea Duncan (later Wonfer), Nick Eliot, Charlie Nairn, Chris Pye, Jonathan Powell and Charles Sturridge. Some went elsewhere, and I used to say that many of the best people leave Granada – only the very best stayed. Two – John Birt and Alex Bernstein – were destined for greater things.

It was hard to make out what lay behind John Birt's moonlike smile. This, stretching almost from ear to ear beneath a pair of huge circular spectacles, gave him an air of smug amusement at the follies of the world around him. He reminded me of the wartime graffiti character Chad whom one would encounter peering over walls or round corners asking 'Wot, No Tea?' (or vino, or bints, petrol, loo paper or whatever item was not there when it was wanted). At that time it was not yet clear, however, what it was that John wanted. After directing a zany comedy called *Nice Time* with Andy Mayer and Germaine Greeer, he came to ask for some money to subsidize a group of actors for three months. He was going to develop with them the comedy show to end all comedy shows. He got the money and after three months came and asked for more. The show was not ready. This was more grudgingly given and again after perhaps a further month he came to me and said there was no show. 'No dry run?' I asked. 'No scripts?' 'No, nothing,' he said. It hadn't worked. As I see him reorganising the BBC today with much the same degree of confidence and much larger sums of money, I hope the end result will be better.

So John was switched to *World in Action*, where he did well enough as Joint Editor, and was well liked by his mates. Even then he had such a passionate belief in his own intellectual prowess that he could persuade others he was as clever as he believed himself to be, which was a matter open to some doubt. He had no talent for the management of people, which in the end is the sort of management that matters most. The thesis he wrote with Peter Jay on the 'Bias against Understanding', although it set the television world by the ears, turned out simply to make the case that television's current affairs journalism did not treat its subjects in depth – something we all knew. He was not one to admire the mighty achievements of the *Daily Mirror* in the late 50s, which alone of popular newspapers succeeded in combining a mass circulation with a modicum of information in depth.

Alex Bernstein was a trainee on the course of '61. Educated at Stowe and Cambridge, and with the prospect of the Granada succession hanging round his neck like an albatross, his path was not easy. He had already done time in the cinemas, for since the cinemas were the foundation of the Granada Group they must also be the foundation for the training of the man who was the heir apparent. Other trainees did four weeks in the cinemas. Alex, because he was a Bernstein, did three years, after which the move to Manchester must have seemed like an escape from jail.

Alex lacked the flamboyance of his uncle Sidney but had inherited the shrewdness and wit of his father Cecil, and the dogged determination of both. He managed his passage through the course and his relations with his fellow trainees with elegance. I realised with some relief that the man who was likely to become one of my closest colleagues and perhaps my boss was a Bernstein to be reckoned with, and not one of the lesser breed of Bernsteins, Sidney's brothers, who after fumbling their chances in the motorways or catering divisions had been pushed off to the Channel Islands with a curt goodbye and a bundle of shares.

And so it was that as the 70s hove into view the roles of Granada Television's top persons had shifted imperceptibly but decisively. I was now carrying most of the cans that once were carried by Sidney, Cecil, Joe and Victor. But Sidney was still very much the Chairman of the Board, still interventionist on any matters where his whim might take him, sometimes a Torquemada, sometimes a gadfly, still regarding it as his duty to keep us on our toes, still prone to pepper us with flying missiles such as:

> I met Felix Fenston [property tycoon] some time ago. He told me that there is a big gathering of geese in Scotland – not sure where – at the end of October or early November. Would this be worth while filming?

and again

> Royal Ballet Company
> Shame on Lancashire. Shame on Manchester. Shame on Liverpool. Shame on polo-playing Cheshire.
> Last night, Tuesday, the Royal Ballet Company from Covent Garden gave an evening of grand ballet at The Opera House, Manchester. But where were the audience? Where were those who always complain that Grand entertainment does not come North? In similar civilised cities to Manchester in Italy, France, Germany, and dare I say it Russia, the theatre would have been filled. It is not too late for the North to make amends. The Royal Ballet Company is at The Opera House, Manchester until December 5.

He had other ways of enlivening the scene. On two different occasions he flew up his old friends Charles Laughton and Alfred Hitchcock to talk to our people in Manchester. Laughton's trip was a success and we made a couple of programmes with him. Hitch's trip was something of a disaster since at a press conference (called by Sidney) a journalist asked what the press conference was for, to which neither Sidney nor Hitch had an answer. Subsequently Hitch gave an address to a mixed audience in which he developed even more coarsely than usual his thesis that all actors are cattle, at which a number of actors in the audience walked out.

Sidney now left the territory of finance and administration that lay under Bill's control almost entirely alone, but he kept a line open to the station's housekeeper, the General Manager – at first Fred Boud and later Leslie Diamond – plaguing them with queries about the sand in the firebuckets, the relative prices of cling film for sandwiches, the telephone bills and the mode of dress of the 'young gels' who roamed the corridors. Poor Fred, an excellent manager in every way and a man of almost infinite patience, was driven pretty near to the wire by Sidney's unending inquisition. For, alas, Sidney did not share the universal high regard for his General Manager, who ominously slipped from 'Fred' to 'Mr Boud'. Once he said to me, 'Denis, I am beginning to lose confidence in Mr Boud.' To which I replied, 'Then you had better get on your knees Sidney and pray to have it restored, for there is no better manager in all television.' This had the effect of halting Sidney's relentless progress towards 'I think we should let Mr Boyd go,' but in the end Fred had to move with Philip Mackie to Granada Films.

Cecil too had handed over to me most of the tedious and time-wasting industry matters. He continued to buy the films and all the American shows, but his interest in the schedule slackened and his dislike of travel to Manchester grew more pronounced. Indeed at the opening of one board meeting in Manchester an embarrassed Bill Dickson had to point out that Cecil was no longer a director of the company, for he had been absent for a greater number of meetings than was permitted by the articles. Needless to say some solution was found, but from then on Cecil had to go to Manchester not only when a crisis on *Coronation Street* called, but to attend at least two board meetings a year.

Joe Warton now pretty well regarded Television as outwith his bailiwick. He had total confidence in Bill and a few set meetings a year with him were enough to satisfy him. He noted that we were now by far the most profitable company in ITV but it is by no means certain that he knew why. No doubt he put it down to our adherence to the Bernstein policy of good housekeeping and to Cecil's shrewdness in buying programmes, which was true but only in part. He never interfered in programmes and regarded the whole area of programme-making as a far-off world in which strange people moved in mysterious ways.

In today's world of media affairs and media folk it must be hard to understand how a major television company could prosper when it had no job specifications for its top executives, no mission statement, no committees below board level save one, the Programme Committee, and that more of a debating society than an executive body, and no formalised relationship with its parent company. In 1955 Eddie Pola (then Head of Light Entertainment) used to introduce me with the words, 'This is Denis Forman. He's in charge of the serious programmes.' Now, fifteen years later, I was managing the company, dealing with the Authority, the industry, labour relations, the sales department, all programmes and a major revamp of the whole of our engineering installation to make way for colour. The movement upwards and onwards had been uncharted and unremarked; it had just happened. My salary had notably failed to keep pace with my increased responsibilities. I had no targets, no set ambition. I felt no sense of achievement, no sense of having reached any destination; indeed the most pervasive feeling I can recall is one of perpetual discontent that the programmes were not as good as they should be. I was, it is true, now called Joint Managing Director, as required by the Authority, Cecil being my other half, but the title signified little and was seen almost exclusively at the bottom of letters. In the early years I had had one close colleague – Sidney. I had spent all my time working with him and for him. Now I saw him perhaps once a week.

Meanwhile in Manchester I had gathered round me a varied company of like-minded spirits who together formed Granada's new persona. The stamp of Sidney was still there and so, occasionally, was Sidney himself, but Granada's programmes went far beyond the Bernstein canon. *The Stones in the Park*, a large enterprise to cover Britain's biggest open-air concert; *Johnny Cash in San Quentin* – emotional and evocative numbers sung to the inmates of America's toughest jail; and in preparation the wonderful *Country Matters*, short stories mainly by H.E. Bates, English inhibitions and preoccupations with sex at their heart – none of these would have passed muster ten years earlier. We were different from other companies, and with uninhibited arrogance we thought we were better. We worked all day and talked for much of the night. Life went on in London, but it was an outstation where Cecil operated and the sales department sold time. We were a sovereign state. We had the freedom and the resources to make pretty well any programme we wanted to make. It was a glorious state of affairs and one almost unique in the history of show business. And yet, as I shoved away in the front row of this scrummage, if anyone had asked me if I was happy I would probably have answered, 'I'll tell you after I've seen Monday's *World in Action*.'

CHAPTER EIGHT

By the early 1960s Granada was seen as the good boy of ITV: public-spirited, adventurous, cultured and generally superior to the other companies, who were interested only in ratings. This picture was not entirely false, reflecting as it did a programme performance that was certainly more lively than others, but it owed a great deal to Sidney's masterly projection of himself and the Granada image, the two having much in common. The other companies did not like this too much, but the Authority did. They purred with pleasure as our plays got good notices, and as we picked our way through the political minefields of *Rochdale* and *Marathon*. We would have been the apple of their eye but for a canker that was to remain malignant for over two decades. The Authority believed that Granada's current affairs programmes were not impartial.

We, of course, held that they were. After the exploratory rows over *What the Papers Say* and *Under Fire* the first serious clash with the Authority came with Tim Hewat's four programmes on Cuba, which were transmitted in autumn 1961. In a note to Sidney (The Proprietor) immediately on his return from shooting, Tim had written:

> Cuba is a bastard and that's a fact. For many reasons. They are, apparently, the most Latin of Latin Americans; therefore totally unreliable, charmingly dishonest. They are lazy and expect you to be too. They live in a weakening climate – not very hot (80 to 90) but intensely humid.
>
> They held me in custody for nearly five hours the day before we were due to leave – and that gave me a bad fright. So I didn't find the assignment congenial. Just the same it was fascinating and successful.
>
> The revolution was long overdue, is a good thing, and is popular with most of the people. It is now a Marxist revolution and aims to be more so. Cuba probably needed a

214

hefty dose of Marxism. The country had been outrageously and stupidly exploited by the Americans.

And so on for three breathless pages. The programmes themselves reflected Tim's euphoria and shocked not only the Officers but also the Members of the Authority to whom they were shown. Sidney was hauled up before the Board to receive a wigging, the nature of which I never discovered for he would never speak about it. Immediately, as a slight act of defiance, he wrote to the Chairman, Sir Ivone Kirkpatrick, requesting that he should be officially informed under what section of the Act the programmes had been faulted. Sir Ivone had no difficulty in complying and, with the formal letter, thinking perhaps to lighten what was becoming a heavy exchange, enclosed the following whimsical note:

A short Socratic Dialogue written in an idle moment.

Socrates: Conceive a freedom-loving Englishman who for years has been cut off from news of the outside world. If such a man were asked to choose whether he would live in France or Cuba purely on the basis of these programmes, would he not elect to live in Cuba?

I.K.   Undoubtedly he would.

Socrates: Then loving truth as you do, can you affirm that it is truthful to depict Cuba as a more desirable residence than France?

I.K.   O Socrates, you have hit the nail on the head and I shall not fail to write to Mr S.B.

After Cuba came *Searchlight*. Bob Fraser told us after the first series that 'As presently constituted every issue broke the Act because it expresses a point of view', and he went on to say, 'Ideally at the end of any edition of *Searchlight* I should be unable to say what is Granada's attitude on the issue.' To our ears this was anathema. We despised the journalism of the two-handed lawyer ('on the one hand, on the other hand'), which had been the BBC's stock-in-trade for years. We believed that our job was to find a good story, to research it, to copperbottom it and then, if it lay safely within the parameters of the law, and particularly the law of libel, to transmit it without fear or favour. A good story we defined as something that someone didn't want you to publish. It should be remembered that these were the days before journalism of this kind came to be called 'investigative' or 'campaigning' and recognised by some as an essential tool of democracy and by others as the lowest known form of media activity. This difference between our view of what television should do and the view held by Bob Fraser led to long years of relentless warfare between Granada and the Authority.

The lines were drawn over a fairly standard issue of *Searchlight*, entitled 'Crawling Highways', which deplored the dreadful state of British roads. Ernest Marples, the Transport Minister of the day, had read the script and agreed to appear, which he did. We saw nothing wrong with the performance save that it was perhaps a little dull. Bob Fraser found it 'a programme of opinion which was meant to "take a line" and I should be staggered if anyone said it was not. In our view this programme contravened the Act' and much more. He ended by saying, 'Perhaps you would let us know how you see this problem. We really must solve it.' I reasoned with him in vain. If we made a programme saying the royal family was a good thing or drunken driving a bad one, no one would object. Yet these were opinions. Similarly to say in 1960 that the state of our roads was deplorable was an opinion which no sensible person would challenge. Controversial opinions were another thing to be sure, and were going to be much more difficult.

Indeed in the days to come problems over controversial subjects in *World in Action* were to drive Bob Fraser to the verge of despair. In only its second issue *World in Action* ran foul of the Authority. The topic was waste in the defence services. The House of Commons was debating this issue on the day of transmission and we wanted to check with the Authority that this would not run counter to an agreement made with the Government (at the time the ridiculous Fourteen-Day rule – which forbade the discussion of any matters which were going to arise in Parliament in the next Fourteen Days – was dropped) that television would not interfere with the workings of the House. The programme was cleared on this head, but the Authority was dismayed to find that the script was little more than a catalogue of examples of gross ineptitude and waste in the services, particularly in the Navy. Sir John Carmichael, the acting Chairman of the Authority, saw the programme and banned it immediately.

I sat in my office in Golden Square with an enraged Tim Hewat. 'The fuckers,' said Tim, and again and again, 'The fuckers.'

'It's no go Tim,' I said. 'We can't transmit it. We can show it to the press and that's about it.'

'The BBC?' said Tim.

I called Paul Fox, the producer of *Panorama* and told him the full story. Without a moment's hesitation he said, 'Sure. Let me call Tim Hewat.' And so it was that the BBC's *Panorama* showed the central ten minutes of an ITV programme. Just before *Panorama* went on the air I had the pleasure of calling Bob Fraser at home. 'I thought you should know, Bob,' I said, 'that part of our Defence *World in Action* is going out on *Panorama* tonight.' There was a long pause.

'Thank you for telling me, Denis,' said Bob slowly. I waited for more but there was only the sound of breathing and perhaps a faint sigh before the receiver was slowly replaced.

Sidney's recollection of this event is a little different:

> Tim was very cross, and in the end I had to say to him, 'That's a decision, Tim, and this is the end of the meeting. Good day to you.'
>
> The programme on defence spending was an exceptional case. I didn't give a damn about the Fourteen-Day Rule, but I felt rather reluctant to fight on an issue which involved national security. However, in the face of the Authority ban I did finally allow Tim to make contact with the BBC and, if I recall, Sir Hugh Carleton Greene, the Director General, phoned me. Hugh Carleton Greene and I had great public arguments about television and about the respective merits of our two systems, but underneath that we both took the same kind of attitude towards authority, so I permitted the BBC to show a section of the banned *World in Action* film on *Panorama*.

As I recall it, Sidney knew nothing of this affair until I called him just before *Panorama* went out.

The Authority was flabbergasted. Collaboration between broadcasters to defeat censorship was something new. Some time later Bob Fraser wrote to Sidney saying:

> I have long been meaning to tell you that the BBC's stunt with your programme on certain aspects of defence expenditure made me feel sick, because I was perfectly well aware that there was never the smallest possibility that the Corporation would run the whole programme as one of its own.

And he went on to quote an article published by an old BBC current affairs hand supporting his view. In the official Granada history Bernard Sendall records that within the ITA camp they regarded the BBC's action as 'a rather shameful stunt'.

Things were soon to get worse. A programme about Angola which depicted the Portuguese rulers as ruthless imperialists (which undoubtedly they were) caused thunderous missives to fly around the diplomatic world and a mighty official protest by the Foreign Office to the Authority. Charles Hill, now Chairman of the Authority and ever pleased to be seen as a man of action, decided that enough was enough. From now on every edition of *World in Action* must be vetted by the officers of the Authority before it went out. The Authority could lay down the law but we could make terms too, and instead of the production being a collaborative effort at working level, as the Authority had hoped, it was laid down within Granada that the programmes would be produced just as before and shown to the officers when completed. If they found anything amiss they must take the matter up with either Sidney or myself. Bernard Sendall puts a respectable gloss on this bit of gamesmanship as follows:

> It was hoped that it [this ruling] could lead to more regular interchanges between themselves [the Officers of the Authority] and Granada current affairs producers, and that these, in their turn, could perhaps contribute in time to greater mutual understanding so that otherwise laudable journalistic zeal could be more closely aligned with inescapable statutory responsibilities. But for the time being at least that was not to be. For one thing, the Granada Board's high sense of personal involvement and responsibility did not allow them to countenance policy discussions and decisions about their programmes with production executives rather than with themselves.

Sendall goes on:

> In the very nature of television current affairs production, preview of transmission-ready programmes, or even scrutiny of transmission scripts, could not be a very sensible or practical way of obviating lapses. It would seldom be possible to do either far ahead of scheduled transmission. Time to discuss and to make consequent changes would therefore be limited. Banning or postponement of the programme could easily become the only available option. Such factors tended to make the ITA men appear to company production staff as busybody bureaucrats.

Things ground along uneasily until June 1964, when a programme on the preparation for the Olympic Games got stuck in the works. The editorial line was clear. The British team had been shamefully underfinanced and undersupported by our government compared with the teams of other major competing nations. The Authority deemed that this was an opinion. We replied that it was a fact. Once again Bob Fraser returned to the breach and repeated: 'A programme must not itself adopt one point of view rather than another . . .'

Needless to say this rebarbative message was greeted with howls of derision in the *World in Action* loft where, commando-like, the team worked privately and in isolation from the common folk of Granada. But accompanying the broadside which was addressed in all formality to Sidney there was a private note to the now semi-retired Victor Peers, who Bob surmised (rightly) to have more sympathy with the Authority's way of thinking than either Sidney or myself. Bob admitted to 'very real anxiety' and suggested an effort should be made to 'reach a better understanding'. Victor responded positively and a 'goodwill' meeting was arranged at which it was agreed to drop the Authority's requirement to preview. But no amount of goodwill could bridge the chasm between us, and in October, when we transmitted a revised version of the Olympics programme, we were told that once again we had contravened the Act. In the official history Bernard Sendall, in mentioning that I had now taken over from Sidney all dealings with the Authority, adds, 'Although relations remained friendly . . . Granada were very obviously far from convinced that the ITA's understanding of due impartiality was the right one.' This was an understatement.

In August 1965 came another crisis. *World in Action* made a programme accusing the drugs industry of grossly overcharging for drugs supplied to the National Health Service and giving misleading information in their advertisements. The drugs lobby was one to be reckoned with and they put all their power behind an assault on Granada and the Authority. A voluminous case was made against the programme and they demanded a public apology. Granada refused to apologise but offered a second programme in which the industry could state their side of the case more fully. The drugs lobby (in the form of the Association of the British Pharmaceutical Industry) refused.

Now the Authority examined the programme again and found it to be biased. They insisted that Granada should apologise. Once again we refused. Bob Fraser said in that case the Authority must apologise on our behalf, to which I replied:

> We feel that the ABPI is not owed an apology for this programme. If you feel the Authority has to make an

apology we would have to consider seriously whether we should not make a number of points in public which, so far, we have only made in the private comments to you.

The first is that we have had no reply to our offer of debate.

The second, that we would welcome the threatened legal action.

The third, the curious offer to our researcher.

I cannot for the life of me remember the nature of the 'curious offer to our researcher', but clearly it was something not creditable to the Association. I also included some comments on what seemed to us to be the fairness of the commentary which Bob Fraser had questioned. Now exasperated, he wrote to me on 2 December 1965:

> You wrote to me on the 22nd November, enclosing Granada's comments on the ABPI's comments on the *World in Action* programme on the 3rd August. What you do is this. You take a highly controversial subject. You then arrange that the critics whom you invite into the programme have a field day, and that those who are being attacked are boxed into relatively short contributions. And then you run throughout the programme a commentary which (I'll eat my hat if it doesn't) sides plainly with the critics.
>
> I enclose the letter I have today sent to the ABPI. It lets you down lightly.

His letter to the ABPI was a bromide. But I felt that his description of our programme was a caricature and told him that I proposed to place it before the Granada board. Subsequently Sidney wrote to Bob Fraser:

> My Board have considered your letter. We are shocked by it.
>
> We don't accept that there is justification for the general aspersion contained in your second paragraph. I suggest that the Authority may have been led into the error of considering facts of an adverse character as a reflection of hostile opinion. In the case of the Drug Industry I submit that the presentation of an entirely objective picture does create a most unfavourable impression. This is not due to

any editorial bias; it is a case of the facts speaking for themselves. You suggest that our commentary was tendentious.
Again, it simply states facts and by doing so may embarrass
some sections of the Drug Industry but it does not embellish the facts nor put any gloss on them in any way which
is at all unfair.

If for the British public to hear the truth from an independent television company is an infringement of the
Television Act, then we admit to such an infringement
with pride.

I hope that the apology to the Pharmaceutical
Association was not sent. If you stand by the terms of your
letter, then I suggest it is time that we met Members of the
Authority once again for a free and open discussion. They
are, after all, at the same time our prosecuting counsel, our
judge and our jury.

The meeting when it finally took place was a bit of a fiasco. The
Authority staff had spent weeks preparing a case that covered the
whole field of *World in Action* misdemeanours since it began. The
Granada team had come expecting to discuss only the drugs
programme. On this last item both sides stood firm on their respective patches. Towards the end we dropped a time bomb. We had taken
advice from a leading QC. He had found that the drugs programme
did not contravene the section of the Act on due impartiality and
hence did not break the law.

This threw the officers of the Authority into consternation, for the
idea that anyone but they themselves were entitled to interpret the
Act was a new one. The ensuing legal wrangle dragged on for nearly
a year, indeed until in December 1966 Bob Fraser sent Sidney a
formal note saying that the Authority could not accept the Granada
legal opinion and formally recorded that the drugs programme had
been in breach of Sections 3(1) and 3(2) of the Act. Sidney immediately wrote asking what procedures were available for appeal against
this finding. Bob Fraser replied that there were no such procedures
and there, at last, the matter ended.

The drugs programme had an unhappy personal consequence for
me. Some four years later I gave a lecture in Glasgow on the subject
of television censorship in which I said:

All that happened [to conclude the drugs saga] was that a
letter of apology was sent to the Association of the British

Pharmaceutical Association by the Chairman of Laportes, one of the Association's member companies, who happened to be Lord Hill, who also happened at that time to be Chairman of the ITA, and previously to have held the posts of Secretary of the BMA and Radio Doctor.

Alas, although the general thrust of this charge was true, namely that Hill had a foot in both camps, Laportes were not members of the APBI. My researcher, usually the most reliable of men, had made a terrible mistake. Lord Hill wrote to Sidney pointing out that this was a serious libel. I found that everyone in the building had gone quiet. Sidney and Cecil cast their eyes down whenever I came into the room. No one had any advice to offer. I rang Arnold Goodman. He suggested an immediate personal apology. I wrote a few abject lines and had them hustled round to Brompton Road. It seemed to work: Hill did not demand any public statement. But I had to pay a price. From then on, when at any social gathering Charles Hill approached me with his Wallace Beery voice resounding with bonhomie, and buttonholed me in jolly conversation, I felt constrained to exchange pleasantries with him for longer than I would ever have tolerated had he not done the decent thing by me over drugs.

The years 1966-9 saw a period of trench warfare. Occasionally the big guns behind the front line would rumble, a foray would be met by a counter-attack and minor skirmishes at tactical level would affect some programmes. There were major confrontations over another eight programmes. After one or other of these encounters late in 1969 Bob Fraser said in a letter. 'I really would like to know what exactly is Granada's interpretation of the Act.' We took up this invitation. I sent him a paper, 'Due Impartiality', which defined the causes of our differences and ran to some twelve pages. Its main thrust lies in the following two extracts:

> If the Authority's interpretation is accepted root and branch, then current affairs television moves into the sphere of the two-handed lawyer. We do not believe that this concept of equipoise on all matters of importance can be sustained. The Authority clings to this principle as a sanction to superimpose its own editorial judgement over that of the programme contractors. Since the Authority has absolute power over the contractor we would prefer to work upon the basis of frank reality — namely that the contractor's editorial judgement sometimes has to defer to

the editorial judgement of the Authority. We would like to abandon the shadow play around the concept of absolute balance.

Finally, we do believe that the extended debate between Granada and the ITA over *World in Action* may have become obsessive. We feel that the degree of consternation expressed concerning the first three programmes of the new series was unmerited. We hope that the temperature can drop, and that the indirect pressures of censorship which have affected our team very seriously from time to time in the past can be removed.

The ensuing meeting to discuss this paper between the two heavies of each side (Fraser and Sendall: Forman and Plowright) was to lead to a crisis in the relationship between Bob Fraser and myself. Extracts from my *aide-mémoire* of the meeting of 23 January 1970 show that Bob was in a belligerent mood:

We arrived at Brompton Road just after 1. At 1.15 we moved from the cocktail annexe into the dining room. Conversation was general. At 2.10 Fraser said, 'Well now, let's get around to the unpleasant subject of Granada and the Authority.' I said, 'Not unpleasant.' Sir Robert said, 'Well . . .' He then said that the last paper ('Due Impartiality') I had sent him showed the gap between Granada's view and that of the Authority to be wider than ever. There were two sides to all questions and it was the duty of a responsible broadcaster to give a fair hearing to both. Except on two subjects (and here he agreed with Carleton Greene) race relations and democracy. Here the broadcaster should adopt an editorial attitude which was one-sided.

Sir Robert then left the subject of the paper and said that what worried him was that Granada's current affairs output showed a persistent left-wing bias. What alarmed him was a certain element of Marxist/Communist and anti-democratic views in Granada's recent programmes, especially *World in Action*. He said if he were a communist he would have no doubt as to where to look for a job in television (Granada) and he enumerated what such a person would seek to do. Bernard Sendall said, 'You see, it all fits in to the pattern of your own views as expressed in *The Times* article (an article advocating a more radical approach to current affairs television which had alarmed several people). I replied that the article contained no anti-democratic implication. After a pause I said, 'I hope this is not necessary, but I feel I have to say that I have never been a communist nor a Marxist and have never held anti-democratic views.' Sir Robert made no reply.

Sir Robert continued with the thesis that if he were a communist working for *World in Action* he would not try directly to bring about a victory for the proletariat in Britain. Instead he would denigrate the United States wherever possible, point out the deficiencies in our society [which enjoyed the highest standard of living in the world], dwell on the efficiency of communist forces in Africa which opposed regimes for which no one had much sympathy, and find even Hong Kong, a prosperous and successful colony, something to the discredit of Britain. [All of these subjects had been covered in *World in Action* at one time of another.] We said there was nothing 'communist' in journalism of this kind. Half of the subjects could have been selected by Peregrine Worsthorne. All of them by many journalists writing for socialist or liberal papers. If we started looking for communist in everything, we were approaching a state of McCarthyism. Sir Richard said he had been expecting a charge of McCarthyism.

Sir Robert indicated that the claim in Granada's paper that there were 'pockets of Marxists in the Conservative and Labour parties' was ridiculous. I said there was no such statement. The paper said that elements of the Marxist *economic* theory were now in different degrees accepted by all parties, which I believed could be easily demonstrated, and gave examples. Sir Robert recalled that the phrase was 'Marxist theory'. I referred to the paper, which I had with me, and established that the words were Marxist economic theory.

Sir Robert reverted to certain personalities in Granada whose presence worried him, mentioning names and in particular one person who had recently joined *World in Action*. We said we had spelled out to the persons named, in writing, the requirements of impartiality and loyalty and were confident that they would observe them.

Sir Robert recapitulated some of the *World in Action* subjects and said that the two Northern Ireland programmes had worried him most. The only comment made came from Marxists. We reminded him that this had been raised at the previous meeting and we had established that one of the speakers he referred to was a leading trade union representative and was not a communist. We pointed out that if anti-capitalist sentiment were the index of Marxist/Communist/anti-Democratic views, then perhaps half of the trade unionists in Britain were of this persuasion.

Several times I asked what was the specific allegation that the ITA were making. Sir Robert said, 'In the late thirties I was often called a fascist because I would not publish what certain people wanted me to publish. In that sense, and only in that sense, is there an allegation.' More generally, he confirmed his view that Granada's current affairs programmes had an undue proportion of communist, Marxist, anti-democratic sentiment. We were playing with fire.

I called Sidney (who was on holiday in Barbados) over the weekend. He was angry but cool. 'I have had to live with plenty of this kind of rubbish in my time,' he said. 'Do nothing until next week.' So I did no more than prepare a draft letter.

Dear Bob,

After knowing each other for some twenty-four years I don't know whether I should apologise for writing this letter to you, or whether you should apologise to me for making me feel it is necessary to do so.

At last Friday's meeting you said that in your view Granada's current affairs programmes tended to be coloured by Communist, Marxist, and anti-Democratic views. There was an implication that I personally endorsed, even inspired, these views. I felt compelled to state categorically that I did not hold and had never held such views. You remained silent.

I therefore find myself in the (for me) ridiculous position of having to ask you whether or not you accept my word on this matter.

My *aide-mémoire* for Monday 26 and Tuesday 27 January goes as follows:

26 January: Shortly after 10 a.m. Sir Robert phoned me to say that he was not happy about the meeting on Friday and would like to come round and see me any time at my convenience. He thought it unnecessary for anyone else to be there. I replied that I would call Sir Robert back as soon as possible. SLB was just back from Barbados and had not yet reached the office.

At approximately 12.30 I discussed my *aide-mémoire* of Friday's meeting with SLB and JW [Joe Warton]. I suggested that I should consult Lord Goodman and they endorsed the idea.

I called Sir Robert back and said unfortunately it was not possible to see him that day, but I would be available any time on Tuesday. He said he would like to come as soon as possible because he was very unhappy about the way the meeting went on Friday. Could he come immediately after he had seen the Minister for Posts and Telecommunications on the following day? We fixed a date for 3 p.m. on Tuesday 27 January.

I saw Lord Goodman for half an hour after lunch. He was astonished at the *aide-mémoire*, and puzzled. He thought Sir Robert's behaviour reprehensible. I showed him the draft letter. He thought it would be unwise to confirm in writing an accusation which might not have existed, and, if it did, might have been made by an individual not fully aware of what he was saying. He thought it better to send a milder letter.

On return to the office I showed a milder draft to SLB who felt that it did not match the occasion. We consulted Lord Goodman on the telephone and decided to send no letter until I had seen Sir Robert. We agreed that I should open the meeting by saying to Sir Robert that I could not discuss the matter with him unless he withdrew what seemed to have been an insinuation or an allegation about myself. Having received a complete retraction I would then proceed to ask for the same assurance in respect of Granada management. If I did not receive this assurance I would ask Sir Robert to speak with SLB, who would be standing by.

In fact Arnold Goodman, the great pacifier, was keen to insinuate that Bob Fraser's intemperate behaviour was the result of too good a lunch. But he took the point that there might be an *aide-mémoire* of the meeting on the Authority's files which could seriously affect a renewal of our contract, and agreed that the record must be set straight. I wrote of the meeting with Fraser on the next day:

I opened the conversation by saying to Sir Robert that it seemed to me that there were certain allegations or insinuations in the air at our meeting last Friday. We had known each other for 24 years and I apologised for having to ask him this question, but before discussing anything else I must know whether or not he personally believed any of the allegations as concerning myself. He said, 'No, absolutely none, unequivocally.'

I then asked him whether he or the Authority would use any of the three words (Communist/Marxist/anti-Democratic) about the people concerned with the management of Granada programmes or with the Management as a collective group. He said, 'Of course not. I don't know David Plowright very well.' I said, 'Would you accept my assurance in respect of David Plowright and Mike Scott.' He said, yes, he would.

I asked him whether he would convey my questions and his answers to the members of his staff who attended our meeting on Friday. He said he would. I asked him if there were any record of Friday's meeting or if there was going to be one. He replied there would be no record.

He said in his defence that a lot of people might have been thrown by my *Times* article. He was not thrown because he knew me so well. I said the article was written with the intention of puncturing the complacency about political broadcasting and I hoped it had done that.

We then settled down to a long and detailed discussion on *World in Action* subjects transmitted in the past year.

The meeting lasted an hour and a half.

The next major explosion took place in September 1970, when Charles Denton (later to become the Chief Executive of Central Television) produced an edition of *World in Action*, 'The Quiet Mutiny', in which John Pilger visited the scene of the Vietnam war and, by talking to GIs and others, reflected the universal disillusion, discontent and war-sickness of the American army. This was much milder stuff than James Cameron was writing in the *Guardian* but it threw the Authority into a frenzy of concern over 'another example of Granada's left-wing propaganda'. We surmised they were under heavy pressure from the Foreign Office and the American Embassy in London, for news of the broadcast had reached the Pentagon where he had heard that certain high personages were expressing outrage and calling for blood. There happened to be a routine meeting with the Authority about *World in Action* fixed for the day after 'The Quiet Mutiny' had been transmitted. Bob Fraser opened. He had found that the programmes was 'outrageous left-wing propaganda, that John Pilger's views were savagely opposed to American policy in Vietnam and that the programme was edited to make the official viewpoint absurd.'

Granada rejected the allegation of left-wing bias. Pilger had reported what the GIs had said. Did anyone doubt that this was untruthful? Pilger was a left-wing journalist, it was true, but Richard Dimbleby was a middle-of-the-road, middle-class journalist and he was allowed to pontificate on any subject without let or hindrance. And so on. But Granada had one bull point. The programme had been seen by Jack Harrison, the Authority's regional officer in Manchester, and he had approved it (or so the team believed).

After the meeting I wrote to Bob Fraser, who was about to retire in a matter of weeks: as follows:

> Before you leave Brompton Road and hand the baton over to your successor, I send you this valedictory note.
>
> Over the recent years, as I think you will agree, Granada's relationship with the officers of the Authority has been very good and has helped to bring the companies together and to form what was much desired, a Programme Controllers' Committee and some other measures of corporate planning within the industry. You have also said some very kind things about the programmes we have transmitted in recent months and all in all the retrospect is fair and pleasant, except for one thing. Except for *World in Action*.
>
> Again you were kind enough to say that the officers of the Authority felt that *World in Action* was going along happily. Then came the programme 'The Quiet Mutiny'. In describing this you used strong words such as 'outra-

geous', 'propaganda' and 'left-wing'.

The charge of left-wing we refute absolutely. The innuendo that certain groups of television makers, of whom
Granada is one, are working at some kind of conspiracy
against the democratic system we regard as too absurd to
be taken seriously.

A programme like 'The Quiet Mutiny' is accepted
unanimously by Granada management (Sidney, Cecil,
David Plowright, myself), as well as the *World in Action*
team, as containing something new and something important which the public has a right to hear. Two members of
your own staff shared that view. I have reason to believe
that the BBC would have shared that view also.

You will remember that Bernard [Sendall] suggested
the possibility of a 'balancing' programme which would
trace the history of the special relationship between the
US Army and America, and hook this upon Nixon's
European tour. We think what he had in mind was a USA
government propaganda film. The news services and
many current affairs programmes, particularly when they
deal with governments at home and abroad, often
inevitably (and sometimes unwittingly) become apologists
for the 'official line'. Television resounds with the official
views of politicians, governments and institutions. Perhaps
it is right that it should. But if this is so, surely it is also
right that the public should see the other side of the
picture.

My second point. 'The Quiet Mutiny' was shown to
members of the Authority's regional staff, who passed it.
And yet the programme was subsequently denounced by
senior members of the staff of the Authority. This is not
good enough. Bernard said he did not wish top members
of the Authority's staff to become implicated in editorial
decisions before transmission. But the Act doesn't read this
way. (Section 3(1): 'It is the duty of the Authority to satisfy
themselves, *so far as possible . . .*') It doesn't seem unreasonable, since the Authority has created a regional system, that
we should have on call in Manchester the voice of the
Authority, be it Friday, Saturday or Sunday. And that we
should get a clear and unequivocal view before transmission whether or not a programme meets with the
Authority's requirements.

We have to make editorial decisions daily and at short notice. It is part of the television business. We do not think the Authority can evade sharing this responsibility.

It has been a long, varied and usually happy relationship, and before you take your final bow I would indeed be grateful for one last effort to solve our only intractable problem.

To which Bob replied:

There was no hope that I could reply to your letter to me in the time between its arrival and my departure, and for this I am very sorry.

It is a big letter, raising big issues and asking big questions.

I can only leave it in other hands, saying nothing but this. I do not see how there can ever be peace between Granada and the requirements of the Television Act as long as Granada thinks it proper to produce programmes confined to the expression of one view when there is more than one view to be found among those who believe in democratic governments.

But from the 'other hands' I received the angriest and possibly the longest letter I had ever received from Bernard Sendall. He had already sent me the usual mild but firm missive recording our meeting. But now he was deeply offended:

Your description of my concept of a possible balancing programme is nothing short of a travesty . . .

I am quite unable to agree with the view that the news services and run-of-the-mill current affairs programmes are apologists for the 'official line' . . .

Neither of the two members of the Authority's staff [who passed it in Manchester] were wholly satisfied that it was a programme which should be transmitted . . .

It is absurd to infer from what I said at lunch that I do not wish top members of the Authority's staff to become implicated in editorial decisions before transmission. Give me the credit for knowing after fifteen years that this is just the sort of thing that top members of the Authority's staff have to be implicated in from time to time.'

★

The longest-running serial ever: early days on
Coronation Street.

The worst television series ever:
Judge Dee.

Television people: Joyce Wooller (not holding a cigar).

Three stalwarts of the early days of ITV: Bernard Sendall (*standing*), Cecil Bernstein and Lew Grade.

Julian Amyes, off duty.

Derek Granger, on-screen
presenter of *Cinema*.

The Jewel in the Crown, with Peggy Ashcroft
and Geraldine James.

The Jewel in the Crown: on location with Christopher Morahan in Udaipur.

The Jewel in the Crown: on parade at BAFTA.

Mr Bernstein leaves the Forman country residence by the back door, minded to become a peer of the realm.

Granada Television's heir apparent:
David Plowright.

The Television Board, 1981. *Clockwise*: Paul Bryan, Don Harker, Peter Rennie, David Plowright, Alex Bernstein, myself, Bill Dickson, Andrew Quinn, Joyce Wooller, Barrie Heads, Mike Scott
(absent: Leslie Diamond and Leslie Young, non-executive).

The Group Board, 1978. *Clockwise*: Desmond James, Alex, Joe, Cecil, Sidney, Mark Littman (non-executive), myself, Chris Stanton, Bob Carr, Bryan Quilter.

Sidney at 90. Among those present (*back row from left*): 1. Julian Amyes, 2. Paul Bevan, 5. Alex, 6. David (Sidney's son), 7. Muriel Haselwood, 9. Josephine Weston, 11. Derek Granger, 12. Jeremy Isaacs, 14. Caroline Moorehead, 15. myself; (*middle row from left*): 1. Sandra, 2. Peggy Ashcroft, 3. Sidney, 4. Joe Warton, 5. Charlotte (Sandra's daughter); (*front row from left*): 3. Bernard Levin, 4. Jane Wells (Sidney's daughter), 5. Jonathan Wells (her husband).

Now I had to deal with the fury of the *World in Action* team, who insisted that the Authority's officers in Manchester had given them the clear go-ahead for transmission. My reply to Bernard did not give much ground, and ended:

> Discussions over *World in Action* have involved a lot of meetings, a lot of people, and a great deal of that precious commodity, time. We have gradually reached the conclusion over the years that censure in retrospect is more damaging to the quality of television journalism than consultation in advance. I therefore do ask you again if the Authority cannot be available to say yes or no, even if it means taking a northbound train at the weekend. I did not mean to imply that the officers of the Authority shirk taking a decision before transmission but I do suggest there is a preference for a playback down the line to London followed by a group consultation rather than delegating the power of decision to someone on the spot. It is hard to explain to people who often work three weekends in a row, and sit up through the night editing a film, that the Authority can only consider their work within office hours and in London.

Three weeks passed in silence. Then we had a call from Bernard. He would like to visit us in Manchester. On 23 November he had dined in the flat with David Plowright, Jeremy Wallington, the incumbent producer, and myself. I noted that before dinner Bernard drank three gin and tonics, for him a positively reckless level of consumption. The dinner was amicable, sometimes even jolly. We found that the Authority had read certain scenes in 'The Quiet Mutiny' in a way that was not intended. They were not going to insist on a pro-American *World in Action* to balance the series. We suggested we should keep a spare edition of *World in Action* on the shelf to give some flexibility in a crisis. Bernard understood our problem of consultation at the weekend. In extreme cases he or another senior officer of the Authority would of course be prepared to take the train to Manchester. (No one ever did.) A diary note of this occasion ends: 'There was a marked change of attitude in Sendall's demeanour: he appeared to want to bring the debate to an amicable close.'

What had caused this change of heart? Did he feel he had gone too far in his cross letter? Had the last paragraph of the piece on 'Due Impartiality' struck a chord? More likely the change of mood was due to the fact that there was a new Director General standing on the threshold of the Authority, a man of a different kidney from Bob Fraser and with a different vision of the job that lay before him. Had the *World in Action* problem already been discussed with him and had he advised Bernard to go north and seek an armistice to give him time to make his own appreciation of how the Authority, the Television Act and *World in Action* could live together? However that may be, Bernard and I now exchanged notes of effusive cordiality.

So we reached the end of another chapter in the saga of Granada versus the Authority, which had begun with their objections to *What the Papers Say* in November 1956 and was destined to grind on for yet another two decades. In the early days 'coping with the Authority' had been regarded as a minor and specialist function which was delegated to Victor Peers. The programme people did not take seriously a complaint from this quarter. It was Victor's job to keep them off their backs, and I recall that when Bernard Sendall wrote complaining of bias in a Tim Hewat programme about some aspect of the armed services and enclosed a furious letter from a general (whom we may here call Knightly Dempster), Tim replied to Victor's request for his observations: 'General Knightly Dempster is less than frank and Bernard Sendall is a prick.' Victor came to me wringing his hands in despair: 'What can I say to the Authority?' I told him he would get no more from Tim and that he and I would have to cobble up something together: which we did.

Tim's view of the Authority in the Chanan history is summarised as follows:

> But then nearly all the handling of *World in Action* problems by the Authority was nonsensical because the silly people never realised *how* you slanted television. They thought that the slant occurred in the words uttered, whereas in fact it occurred in the subjects chosen. The choice of subject *dictated* what the show said. Once you've decided to do a programme on litter, or on defence spending, or on alcoholism, there's no way in which it's going to be an even-handed argument, because they are things which are outrageous in themselves, and so you just expose them. We used to spend hour after hour going through the scripts with the silly buggers. 'Would you please look at page thirteen of the script? Would you change the third word on line five to so and so.' Yes, sure we changed them. Why not?

*

But producers were not to get so debonair an approval for long, and soon the editor, the producer and the whole team would become involved in the struggle to keep the Authority at bay. When, occasionally, they could prove a programme was factually incorrect or, worse, contained data that had been manipulated to support our case (this happened on two occasions), we acknowledged our errors with, I fear, a minimum of grace. When they made a palpable misjudgement we crowed, and indeed there were two own goals that the Authority were never allowed to forget.

The first was a programme called *The Entertainers*, made by that old master of documentary, Denis Mitchell, which featured an act in a Northern working men's club of some striptease artists whose progress towards nudity he documented a little further than was acceptable to Lord Hill and his colleagues. Cuts were requested by the Authority and refused by Granada and the programme did not go out. A year later it was resubmitted to the Authority who, under the impression that this was a new version, declared it to be much better and passed it for transmission. In fact it was exactly the same programme. When Lord Hill was told this, he had the grace to say he could not see why it had been faulted the first time. This was pure gold for us, for it showed that the Authority's interpretation of the Act could vary with the whim of the moment.

Much later, in 1971, the Authority fell into an ever greater elephant trap when they condemned a *World in Action* programme on Idi Amin entitled 'The Man Who Stole a Million'. The team had spent enough time in Uganda to satisfy themselves that Amin was a crook, a hoodlum and a political pirate, and spared no pains to make this apparent to the British public. The result was an explosion of fury in the Foreign Office for whom Amin, British Army-trained and apparently friendly to the Brits, was a golden boy and a defence against his dreaded Communist rival Milton Obote. As news of the impending exposure, leaked out, I became the target for telephone calls from all quarters of the Old Boy network, including ministers, editors, and a tearful and aghast Lady Cohen, the widow of the late High Commissioner and a personal friend. But we transmitted the programme without showing it to the Authority and took our subsequent punishment cheerfully, for we knew that time was on our side, and indeed within a year the same people who had been so outraged by the programme could find nothing bad enough to say about Amin.

Now that Bob Fraser was on his way out we hoped that all would be sweetness and light between the Granada team and Brian Young, the new incumbent at the Authority, but his regime was to bring conflict just as dogged and much more public than in the Fraser years. Although the days of the old slogging match were over, the state of warfare with the Authority over *World in Action* was to continue throughout the 1970s on a more sophisticated plane. As Jeremy Potter puts it in the official history of Granada:

> Within ITV the most expert practitioners of the adventurous committed programmes were to be found in Granada's *World in Action* team. This history has recorded how no single ITV series was the occasion of more discussion between Authority and company, and this dialogue of the 1960s continued unabated through the 1970s. The Authority alternated between sorrow and anger. Granada, valiant for truth, remained aggressively unrepentant. But both parties strove to avoid a revival of earlier acerbity.

With Brian Young, we did indeed develop a much friendlier relationship. Bob Fraser had, I believe, been motivated by fear – fear of what the press would say, fear of public opinion, fear of displeasing our lords and masters in Westminster. This drove him to adopt his doctrinaire interpretation of the Act. Brian Young was a man of very different mettle. Educated at Eton, and after a double first in Classics at Cambridge going back to become a beak at his old school, he then became headmaster of Charterhouse and later the Director of the Nuffield Foundation before landing up at the Authority. He was, one might speculate, the best-educated Director General ever to preside over any broadcasting institution.

Brian ruled by debate and discussion. He believed that by reasoned argument he could persuade an opponent to accept the right view (his) on any topic. His approach was not doctrinaire but based on what one might call the doctrine of fairness with a dash of Christian morality thrown in, for he is a committed believer. Wartime service in the Navy as the commander of a destroyer gave him one deep-seated prejudice. He would not countenance any programme that might impinge on national security. He regarded the Official Secrets Act with awe. We saw it as the civil servants' last resort when in need of a cover-up. He was determined to avoid the danger of giving any information to the enemy. We believed that what our security services knew about our defences the Russians had usually known long before; he was a stickler for observing protocol. We regarded the D-Notice system (an official warning to journalists to keep off the grass) as a joke. There was, therefore, a marked difference of view between us on the matter of security, and also on many other topics where streetwise journalists were apt to take a more cynical view of human nature than did Brian, who believed that on the whole governments were good, democracy worked and civil servants were not corrupt.

On many a Sunday morning Brian would ring me at home to argue the toss about the following day's edition of *World in Action*. In the course of a lengthy and usually enjoyable debate we would warily size each other up, wondering whether a point given here or there would gain us our main objective. As I remember it, few editions failed to go out and most of the concessions were minor. Once we had an argument over a still picture of GCHQ in Cheltenham. 'But Brian,' I said, 'the picture has been published. It is common currency already. Any half-decent Russian spy would have filed it months ago.' 'It doesn't matter,' replied Brian. 'You are giving wider currency to an image which might be harmful to the interest of National Security.' And on Monday the picture did not appear. Had the request come from Bob Fraser there would have been no compliance, but with Brian, even when the team thought he was at his most lunatic, there was room for a bit of give and take.

If most *World in Action*'s problems were now about defence, by far the biggest row took place early in 1973 over 'The Friends and Influence of John G.L. Poulson'. This enterprising architect and developer had built up a network of business connections which stretched across the North of England, and indeed into parts of Europe. With his running-mate Dan Smith he had 'influenced' councillors, MPs, trade unionists and all manner of people in high places to help him in his crooked ways, and despite all this help he had gone bust. The bankruptcy proceedings were long-drawn-out and revealed a fascinating saga of skulduggery, deceit and corruption. Raymond Fitzwalter, a News Editor on the *Bradford Telegraph and Argus*, had made a comprehensive study of the case. He joined Granada to make a one-hour special *World in Action* based on the Poulson bankruptcy hearings, a subject on which he was by now the world authority. It was to be his *chef d'oeuvre* and ours, and it turned out to be a stunning indictment of local government in the North-East in general and of Poulson and Dan Smith in particular.

When the officers of the Authority saw it, their reaction was one of shock and disbelief. They banned the programme, due for transmission in January, on sight. They could not comprehend that it could be lawful to transmit so many defamatory and damaging statements about public figures. There was, however, no legal problem because a bankruptcy hearing is not a court case and we had copper-bottomed legal advice that the programme was in the clear. Brian, less dictatorial than Bob Fraser, referred the matter to the members of the Authority, who confirmed that the programme should be banned 'permanently' and 'irreversibly'. This was because the members, like the officers, found it hard to believe the revelations of widespread bribery and corruption in local government. Two powerful women on the board, Baroness Sharp, once the Civil Service queen of the Ministry of Housing, and Baroness Macleod, Iain Macleod's widow and a lay magistrate, felt the programme would undermine public confidence in local government nationally. Trial by television, character assassination and many other of the usual war cries of censorship were all trotted out. Meanwhile in place of *World in Action* on 29 January a film was shown - *The Flight of the Snow Goose*.

I asked Bert Aylestone, the Chairman of the Authority, for a meeting. This was brusquely refused. The whole industry was shaken by the Authority's intransigence and the unions threatened industrial action. In spite of our opposition to this, pickets appeared outside the Authority's headquarters in Brompton Road. The technicians' union said they would black out the screen on the ensuing Monday unless discussions between Granada and the Authority took place. Bert Aylestone then agreed that David and I could meet the Authority (on Thursday 1 February). We viewed the programme with Bert, Brian and one or two Members of the Authority, including Dame Evelyn Sharp. She had worked closely with Dan Smith at the Ministry and had given character evidence for him in court when he was accused of corruption over a development in Wandsworth. As the lights went up she said, 'Poor Dan, this film will ruin him' (little did she know that regardless of our film poor Dan would shortly be behind bars). In that tiny theatre the sense of unease and distress was palpable. It was clear that the posse from the Authority were casting about desperately for reasons to justify the ban. We gave no ground but in the end agreed to 'give some thought to their objections'. The next day the Authority issued a somewhat woolly press release. Both the Authority and Granada, it said, were giving thought to the points made at the meeting and the Authority were 'considering whether the programme might be shown at a later stage'.

We did not think this was good enough. We showed the programme to the press, giving them the full factual background to its production and its banning. But once again we discouraged industrial action. Our press release ended:

In banning the Poulson film the Authority acted within

their legal powers . . . We, as a management, did everything in our power to persuade the IBA that they were wrong and we were right. We failed to do this and we have to accept their verdict. Within the last fortnight there have been suggestions that the judiciary and the House of Commons should take over certain powers exercised by the IBA. Granada believed that the right way to run ITV is to have a broadcasting authority that is independent of parliament and independent of the companies. The ACTT are known to take the same view. The company therefore deplores the union's intention to take action which challenges the IBA.

But on the next Monday, during the scheduled *World in Action* slot, the screens were blank.

Now the bandwagon began to roll. From the *Socialist Worker* to the *Sunday Times* a tidal wave of support for Granada engulfed the Authority. The press pointed to some significant relationships between Members of the Authority and the protagonists in the Poulson affair – between Dame Evelyn and Dan Smith, Sir Frederick Hayday and his close friend and fellow union official Alderman Andrew Cunningham, who was mentioned in the programme, and between Baroness Macleod and Reginal Maudling, who had to resign as Home Secretary because of his close business associations with Poulson. It was quite unheard of for the *bona fides* of the great and good members of an august public body to be called into question. Was the Authority as at present constituted competent to rule over ITV? The *New Statesman* pointed out that of the forty-six Members of the Authority since 1954, twenty-eight had been to public schools and twenty-six had titles, and that their average age had been just under sixty.

On 13 February I wrote to Brian suggesting some changes to the programme. A revised script was sent on 2 March to be considered at a special meeting a few days later. The changes were cosmetic. The actors who had represented the leading parties in the hearing were no longer seen in vision but were heard in voice over still pictures of Poulson himself or of Muir Hunter, the QC acting for the creditors. A new and rather pompous introduction was added calling for an obligatory register of outside business interests by councillors and MPs. There were some minor cuts and additions. The title was changed from 'The Friends and Influence of John Poulson' to 'The Rise and Fall of John Poulson.'

The special meeting reached no decision, so it was deferred to the next regular meeting on 22 March. Once again I quote from the Official History:

> After its meeting on 22nd March the Authority announced that the revised programme had been approved for transmission, subject to a check on certain points of detail. No hint was given of the argument which had taken place round the table. Evelyn Sharp was not to be deflected from her conviction that the programme would damage the reputation of local government and ruin Dan Smith. Indeed the conflict had developed, to some extent, into a duel between her and Forman: the one determined that the programme should not be shown, the other equally determined that it should. Another Member of the Authority, Lady Macleod, held to the view that, as a magistrate, she could not in conscience sanction a broadcast containing defamatory statements. This was a point of principle, and it made no difference that those defamed had already been widely discredited and the risk of a libel action was negligible. When the matter was put to the vote it was a tie at five-all. The missing Member was absent on a business trip overseas. He was telephoned by the Director General and the programme was saved by his casting vote from South Africa.

So the Poulson programme was broadcast on 30 April and the press was universally favourable, describing the programme as a model of its kind. 'No longer can any accusation be made of innuendo and unfairness,' reported the *Guardian*, although its television critic, Peter Fiddick, regretted that the long delay had blunted its impact. *The Times* praised the programme for having 'cleverly pieced the Poulson story together and told an extremely complex tale in a simple and easily understood form.' It was a famous victory.

There was a follow-up to the Poulson programme. In the course of his scrutiny of Poulson's affairs Ray Fitzwalter had unearthed the story of how Poulson came to get a contract to build a hospital on Gozo, a small island near Malta. In this he was greatly assisted in gaining Maltese government support and a British government grant by Reginald Maudling, who wrote to the Maltese Ministry of Works and to the Prime Minister of Malta emphasising the need for a hospital in Gozo and pressing the claims of Poulson as the developer. But in his letters Reginald Maudling failed to mention the fact that he was a close business associate of Poulson, being the chairman of one of his companies and a director of another. Poulson had given a job to Maudling's son and had made a generous donation to Mrs Maudling's pet charity, the Adeline Genée Theatre. Lawyers thought hard and long before clearing the programme for transmission and so did we. It was clearly damaging to Maudling and our defence against a charge of libel could only be one of truth. But we had total confidence in Ray and the programme went out in the spring of 1974.

For some months there was no action. Then in October 1974, on the day the general election was called, Maudling issued a writ. We were ready for this and stood by for proceedings to begin. It was a long wait, and indeed it extended until Maudling died in 1979. His reason for not bringing the case must have been, of course, the fear that a great deal of evidence discreditable to him would come to the surface. It was better to sit tight and keep mum. This did not, however, prevent his widow seeking 'compensation' from Granada after his death for the damage that had been done to her husband's reputation, a request which was rejected.

In retrospect one can only have a good deal of sympathy with the officers of the Authority for what they endured throughout the long war with Granada. Every other ITV company stood to attention when hauled up before the Authority. Occasionally there might be a token show of resistance, but for the most part they would pull their forelocks and vow not to sin again. So it was that Granada's exceptional arrogance, obduracy and plain insubordination gave the Authority so much pain and grief. The officers also had to endure confrontations with their own Members, when seeking to justify their craven (as many Members thought) conduct towards Granada. The more macho right-wing Members bayed for our blood. They could not see why Granada was not brought to heel but comforted themselves with the thought that at the next contract round, if they could not prevent Granada having its licence renewed, at least they could see that stiff conditions were imposed.

Yet neither Sidney nor I ever felt the slightest apprehension that our rebellious ways would threaten the renewal of our licence. When we were up for interview before Members of the Authority in 1967 for a renewal of our licence, Sir Sidney Caine, the Deputy Chairman of the Authority, Director of the London School of Economics and our deadly enemy, pointed out that the file of complaints against Granada programmes was larger than the combined files of all the other companies, to which Sidney retorted, 'We consider that a compliment.' This raised a laugh with the other Members, and indeed the last laugh was with Granada for our contract was renewed *cum laude*. It was true that we had to listen to a short lecture from Bert Aylestone, but it was clear from the look in the eye of that wily old politician that he knew that we knew that this was a formality required by his Members, and unlikely to have much effect on Granada's future behaviour – an assumption that was, of course, correct.

In all our problems with the Authority we had, ostensibly at least, the total support of both the Television Board and the Group Board. This, of course, was entirely due to Sidney. Sometimes when the heat was on Joe and Cecil would look glum. They seldom spoke their minds to me but I thought it likely that in the nightly telephone call between the brothers Cecil would, from time to time, summon up courage to beg Sidney not to go too far, and once when Joe and I were in adjacent lavatory stalls during a recess from a board meeting, he turned to me and said, 'Look, old lad, why not leave the Authority alone for a while?'

Sometimes an uneasy non-executive director who had been got at by some Authority-influenced VIP would appeal to Sidney to moderate Granada's line, but Sidney would have none of it. When relations with the Authority cropped up at board meetings (a rare event) Sidney would draw himself up in his chair in his grandest manner and open by stating the Granada position in uncompromising terms, thereby quelling any opposition before it was voiced, much as I imagined a prime minister would impose his will upon a potentially recalcitrant cabinet.

In Sidney's view Granada was a sovereign state, proudly independent and morally at least the equal of any Broadcasting Authority. He appeared to take no account of the fact that we were franchise holders and that there was a Television Act which gave the Authority all manner of powers over us. Indeed a study of the correspondence between Sidney and the Authority, especially in the early years, demonstrates that if there were any subservience in the air it was not from him to them but from them to him. Yet none of us who toiled in the front line seemed to formulate any sentiments of admiration or gratitude towards him, much less to express them. He was Sidney, and we expected it of him.

CHAPTER NINE

When in 1969 Sidney was first approached by Harold Wilson on the matter of his ennoblement he said nothing to anyone, not even to Cecil. But his response must have been sufficiently positive for the long grey-green envelope to arrive from Number Ten with its formal proposal. Now his reaction was ambivalent. A part of him was apprehensive. What would his old friends in the Labour Party say? Especially those with whom he had so often discussed the desirability, nay the need, to abolish the House of Lords? What would Granada employees think? Would anyone laugh at him? Did Lord Bernstein sound all right?

The other part of him (and it was by far the greater part) glowed with pride that he, Sidney Bernstein, son of a Jewish immigrant from Sweden or Latvia (what matter?) should be singled out to serve Her Majesty as a Peer of the Realm. Although dismissive of English gentlemen in the sense of the set of Old Etonian cronies who hung around the City, he loved the best of Englishness and there was a lot that was very English about the House of Lords. It was the ultimate acceptance of the outsider into the heart of British family life. He was honoured. And so, in typical Sidney fashion, although he had decided to accept from the very first, he set about a long and elaborate programme of taking advice. In each case the decision was presented as an open option and in each case he was strongly urged to accept. This was thoroughly satisfactory.

His visit to Helen and myself was arranged with extreme formality. To meet in London over lunch, or even at his home in Wilton Crescent, would not have been appropriate to the requirements of the occasion. Accordingly an overnight visit to Little Garnetts, our home in Essex, was arranged. At 6.30 precisely a helicopter hove into view and duly landed in a adjacent field, sending several tons of newly dried hay flying to festoon the fences and cover the surface of the moat that lay in front of the house. Sidney, in a dark blue fresco suit and with shoes shining like a guardsman's scabbard, picked his way from the chopper past the dung-heaps and cabbages in the vegetable garden, blanched visibly as two large Labradors shot out of their kennel barking noisily, and entered the house as spick and as span as could be.

We had a very happy evening, but of advice there was little since Helen opened the proceedings by saying, 'Come on, Sidney, we all know you're going to accept, the only question is whether you are going to take the whip.' He told us he had complete freedom to do as he chose and he had decided to be a cross-bencher. Helen, a dedicated local politician, regarded this as dereliction of duty and the debate raged with Sidney quite clearly unwilling to take orders from any superior body. When Helen asked him what, as a cross-bencher, he would stand for, he said, 'I will represent Granada.' He made it sound as if it were the most important political party in Europe.

In the same year, however, Sidney was to face another change, this time not so pleasant. It was laid down by the Authority that all members of the boards of contracting companies should retire at seventy. Sidney, Cecil and Joe pondered. Should they, since Sidney was quite clearly a special case, ask for an extension? Perhaps for five years? They consulted me. Of course, I said, by all means. All of us thought that a five-year extension would be a formality. I am not sure what happened next, for I was never told. Sidney either spoke or wrote to Bert Aylestone, the Chairman of the Authority, and he must have replied that he must consult his Members. In due course the verdict was given. Sidney was told he could continue as Chairman of Granada Television for one year only, until he was seventy-one years of age; he could, however, remain as a board member up to the age of seventy-five. This was a great blow, not so much because Sidney wanted to continue in the Chair (although this was certainly true) but because the Authority had failed to recognise his unique contribution to Independent Television and had equally failed to appreciate that his powers were at their zenith and that he was ten times more capable of running a television company than most men half his age. Sidney never mentioned the matter to me – the mortification was too great. But Cecil said to me naïvely, 'Sidney's decided to hand over the Chair to me next year.' We both knew that this was because of *force majeur*, and Joe let the cat out of the bag as we were (this time) drying our hands in the men's room by saying, 'Heard about Sidney and the Authority? Disgraceful!'

This snub, as he thought it, by the Authority hurt Sidney more than at first I understood. Here he was, the man who had fathered

the company, fostered it, made it a shining example of what a television company should be, defended it against all comers; and now, at
the very height of his powers, he was told he must give it up. It was
his company, his property. And more than that. Sidney was Granada
personified, *persona Granada*. Granada was a part of him and he was a
part of it. For an outside body to take it away from him was an act of
violence against his person. As Group Chairman he could, of course,
have carried on dominating the board pretty well as before, but under
Cecil's chairmanship he seemed to feel that he should not throw his
weight about but must act as a board member equal to others.

Cecil did not change his life one jot after his promotion to
Chairman. He still minded those parts of Granada's estate that had
traditionally been in his care, he still took a keen interest in the politics of the industry, but the internal affairs of Manchester he was
happy to leave entirely to others. For him the only penalty of promotion lay in the requirement to travel to Manchester to chair, if not
every board meeting, at least a respectable number. This task was alle-
viated, however, by the provision of a wheelchair which stood outside
his first-class compartment as the train pulled into Manchester
Piccadilly and whisked him down to the awaiting Granada car. The
greatest change brought about by Sidney's enforced abdication was
the arrival in Manchester of Alex. Cecil and I had been Joint
Managing Directors for many years, but now I had father Cecil as
Chairman, son Alex as my Joint Managing Director and uncle Sidney
as a member of the board.

I had, of course, observed Alex getting through the production
trainee course as a person in his own right and successfully living
down the stigma of being the heir apparent – the other trainees liked
him. He had built a do-it-yourself Lotus car with one of his running
mate, Leslie Woodhead, and it actually worked. In the intervening
years as Managing Director of Granada TV Rental he had developed
the rental business with great success. Unlike his uncle he was no
extrovert, but beneath a much calmer exterior he had the same will
of iron. He also had his father's wit and charm, and a degree of
sophistication greater than either his father's or his uncle's. Although
he was nearly twenty years younger than I was, I never felt godfatherly or avuncular towards him. He was a joy to work with from
the start, for despite the disparity in age we were as Joint Managing
Directors working equals. Later, of course, as Chairman of the
Group and my boss, he became more equal than I. I can honestly say
that only once did a cross word pass between Alex and myself, and
that was when he sent me a memo containing a few of the buzz

words in common use between sharp young business-school trained executives at the time. In an idle moment I struck some of them out and substituted plain Anglo-Saxon alternatives, and foolishly sent back the amended version attached to my reply. It was a ghastly thing to do and Alex was furious. I can no longer remember exactly what he said, but I do remember the phrase 'behaving like a fucking schoolmaster'. I never heard him use such colourful language before or since.

Alex and I were appointed to the Granada Group Board on the same day in 1964, from which coign of vantage we observed our elders and betters trying with all their might to diversify our interest beyond the two money-makers, Television and Television Rental. Actually Television Rental was not a money-maker for a long time because, although it was profitable, we ploughed back all the profits into buying more and more shops which took several years to pay off. Just as it would seem that at last our large investment was going to bring in some bacon, Wham! – an opportunity we could not ignore would offer itself and another purchase of several millions would be approved by the Board. How to diversify puzzled everyone.

I have said that we got into Television Rental by pure chance, and this is my version of how it happened. There were a lot of viewers living on the coastline over the rim of East Yorkshire who could not get our signal off air, and there were a number of small cable companies who took it to them. We bought these companies to extend our coverage and two of them brought with them tiny but highly profitable rental businesses. Someone on the spot saw the light and went on buying rental businesses whether or not they had cable. So from little acorns are mighty oaks grown. But every time I mentioned this piece of (as I thought) early Granada history I was shouted down by the Bernsteins and Joe, who preferred to believe that the choice of the rental business was due solely to their good business judgement. Indeed they denied my version so vociferously that I came to the conclusion that they thought there must be something in it.

But now where to look? There was no Group diversification policy. Phrases like 'potential synergy' or 'cross-sector interdependence' were unknown. People talked to people, and it was always worth listening to Bernie Delfont, the Black brothers in Blackpool. C.O. Stanley of Pye, Jules Thorne, and Arnie Weinstock of GEC, who was thought to be a clever fellow. So if rental worked for Television why not for other articles? We bought a firm that rented artificial flowers mainly for weddings and funerals, and a furniture rental company from Brian Wolfson, whose managerial services came with it. Both companies sank slowly into the sand. Flowers and furniture were no good. But both Bernie Delfont and Lew Grade thought the new thing was going to be bowling, which was going great guns in America. So we bought the very complex machinery required for some half a dozen bowling alleys at enormous expense from an American company. But bowling did not go great guns in the UK. It was, on its first coming, a flop. Only one of our original bowling places survived, at Bellevue in Manchester.

So what about Motorway Service Stations? We started with three, spending far too much on bricks and mortar, at least on Toddington, soon to become the great mother ship of Granada's roadside enterprises. They didn't make much money. It was clear that we should either sell them or replicate them across the land. We did neither. Films were no longer drawing a public and the only profitable use for most of our cinemas was to turn them into bingo halls. But was bingo ethical? Gambling was something that had no place in the Bernstein canon. But was bingo *really* gambling? Wasn't it more of a game, a game of chance perhaps but one that had had the stamp of approval of the British army for decades? And was there not great social value in offering housewives an opportunity to meet over a cup of tea in well-appointed club premises during the afternoons? So the Granada Social Clubs gradually took over the cinemas, and it was a feature of the Social Clubs that the members could play bingo at them – but only, of course, if they wished to do so.

More meaningful was the move into publishing, for here Sidney found a fresh outlet for his energy. In the early 60s we had bought the publishing house of Rupert Hart-Davis, which produced a limited annual output of distinguished hardbacks. Other acquisitions followed, but it was not until we obtained the paperback imprint Panther in 1965 that Granada Publishing became of any real significance. From the first this new development felt the keen edge of Sidney's interest in its management and in the appearance, price and occasionally the content of the books it produced. But as his central position in television began to slip away from him he found in publishing, and in particular in a young man named Tony Richardson, a fresh stimulus to create something new. Together he and Tony Richardson dreamt up a new concept for a series of books. They should be beautiful to look at and to handle, short, exquisitely written, relevant to the day, not too expensive, and they would be called Paladin. Only recently an experienced publisher told me that he had come across the specification that Tony Richardson had produced for Paladin. It almost amounted to a short book in itself, he said, and he had been astounded by its attention to detail and the clarity of its overall vision. It was, he said, as relevant today as on the day it was written.

The story ended sadly. Tony Richardson suffered from an incurable disease, and only one year after the launch of Paladin he died. The first dozen books produced under his aegis caused a considerable stir and the series continued successfully for many years under different editors including, for a while, Sonny Mehta. But for Sidney it was not the same, and the creative management of the whole company, including Paladin, was taken over by Aelwyn Birch, with whom Sidney continued to work closely and usually harmoniously until Publishing was sold to Collins in 1982. When the decision to sell was taken there were only two dissenting voices on the Group Board: those of Sidney, now President, and myself.

Although I was firmly excluded from Publishing, our purchase of Novello gave me a chance to work with Sidney again. Novello was a small music publishing company, founded by Vincent Novello in 1811 and run for over a hundred years by the Lyttelton family. During that century it had published the bulk of all the church music sung in Britain, and it was one of the most respected names in the business. Alas, what with the advent of the xerox machine and the increasing age of the one surviving Lyttelton, the business had fallen upon bad times and in 1970 an American predator made a bid for it. How it happened I do not know, but an appeal was made to Sidney to move in as a white knight and save this treasure for the nation. Sidney and I had one or two excited meetings, and despite Joe Warton pulling a face like a disgruntled walrus we bought it – I shall never quite know why. It was a combination perhaps of a burst of patriotism, the fact that the press release would read well, that it would appear to complement our book publishing business (it didn't) and that it was very cheap. Years later Sidney used to say, 'I bought Novello for Denis,' but I do not think that my interests were uppermost in his mind at the time.

I found Novello an enchanted community, frozen in time. There was the elderly John Lyttelton sitting in the Study Room to open the post himself and enter each letter in the Journal Book with not quite a quill pen but a dip-in-the-inkwell pen with a Relief nib. There were two engravers each with a set of fifty chisels and a wooden mallet, engraving notes on to copperplate to produce sheet music of the most exquisite beauty. There were half a dozen monster printing machines, miracles of mechanical technology, looking as if they had come straight out of the Great Exhibition of 1851. There was a cast of the Abbé Liszt's hand, taken when he stayed with the enterprising Vincent Novello in Soho, a letter from Brahms in the library, and the original manuscripts of many of Elgar's major works.

It was not possible to transform this living museum into a cost-effective, competitive, modern publishing business without a measure of pain and grief. I wanted to go gently: Sidney wanted to go fast. We compromised, and our working relationship was enormously eased by the recruitment of George Rizza from the publishing house of Chester, who very soon settled in and did all the right things in the right way. But there was one conflict that preceded George's arrival. The neat cottage-like set of offices and the roomy warehouses that housed Novello at Borough Green in Kent were slowly but inexorably sliding into an adjacent sandpit. My instincts were to shore them up as best we could or to get out, but Sidney sniffed the smell of bricks and mortar. The architect in him found irresistible the prospect of building afresh an intricate structure standing on a concrete raft of novel design. We argued that the investment in such a grand project would impoverish poor Novello for years to come, but at a stroke of the pen he somehow had the major cost transferred to the Group building company, where it was written off. So a new warehouse rose from the sand, large enough to contain the biggest music hire library in Europe, Goodwin and Tabb, which we had, conveniently, just acquired.

Novello prospered in a modest way, making a decent profit and doing its best to serve its thirty or so composers and to sell and hire out as much sheet and bound music as was still required in the age of the xerox. Whereas I was inclined to treat writers as equals I approached composers with reverence, mainly because I was too ignorant to meet them on their own ground. I especially admired John McCabe, Richard Rodney Bennett and Thea Musgrave, who became friends. Every day I made it my business to listen to one hour of music from new composers. For one brought up on Bach, Beethoven and the diatonic scale this was a severe shock to the system. It was not unlike learning a new language, but not a single new language, rather one for each composer. After ten years I felt I could master any idiom and I reached the conclusion that, all considerations of tonality or atonality aside, if music is not accessible to the intelligent ear after three hearings it is usually bunk. A great deal of musical porridge is served up behind a barrage of assertive sound. And yet in this territory it is wise to tread carefully. I remember I recoiled against the first Harrison Birtwhistle piece I heard, and today I bow before *Gawain* as one of the great operas of the century. Sidney did not like meeting composers. He did not have the lingo. But at a first night he would sit through many a piece that much have given him nothing but pain, and backstage, after the show, he would be as gracious and gallant as only he could be.

A much less successful musical acquisition was Transatlantic Records. I was an advocate of Granada Group developing a strong arts and publishing arm – television, book publishing, music publishing and more. The only way of making money in the music business seemed to be in records. I sought out Transatlantic, a small enterprising record company specialising in jazz and blues as well as striving to find a place in the pop market. The company's founder and impresario was a highly plausible young man, Nat Joseph, not immediately recognisable as a *persona Granada* but fast-talking, quick-witted and with a genuine flair for spotting talent. I bulldozed the Group Board into buying Transatlantic. It was a small amount and there was little opposition. A meeting between Sidney and Nat had of course taken place and it seemed to me that Sidney responded well to Nat's street-trader chatter and warmed to his cheeky cockney-sparrow style. Before we took over Transatlantic I had told Sidney that it was, like all small record companies, a pretty ramshackle outfit. The main premises were in a shed in the deserts of West London; there was a tiny office in Marylebone, no ready cash and everything depended on getting a hit. A hit could see the company solvent for some six months, so a reasonable strike rate of hits was rather important. Transatlantic's record in the matter of hits was quite good but they had not had one for some time. Sidney listened carefully and said nothing. Alas, I failed to pick up any warning signals.

For the first month or two life within Granada went quite merrily for Transatlantic. Alex joined me on the board and our policy was simply to let Nat continue to run the company as he had done before the take-over with the minimum of adjustments needed to make it a subsidiary of Granada. But soon questions began to be asked by Group headquarters. Were we satisfied that Transatlantic's employment policy met with Group standards? Well no, I was in no way satisfied of this because I had been down at the warehouse and seen the workers paid off in cash at the end of each shift – mainly women from the West Indian community. Matters such as tax, national insurance and the like were quite foreign to this sort of transaction. Next, we were requested to provide regular financial information in the standard form required by the Group. I went to discuss this matter with Transatlantic's Finance Director, a student-like youth, and found him in an unfurnished attic room above the warehouse with pieces of the company's sole computer strewn across the floor. He had taken it to pieces and had found, unfortunately, that he was unable to put it together again. I went to see Joe and told him that if we were going to Granada-ise Transatlantic the company could never be viable. 'I know, old lad,' said Joe, 'but Sidney's getting after you.' This set Alex and myself the difficult problem of protecting Transatlantic from the legitimate pressures of the Group.

One day the board of Transatlantic was sitting round a table in a box-like room in Marylebone when suddenly and silently, as if by stage magic, Sidney stood framed in the doorway. There had been no advance indication of any visit. He was not a member of the Transatlantic board and had no status whatsoever vis-à-vis the company, except that he was Group Chairman and that he was Sidney. Without speaking a word he advanced and sat down at the table. In that moment of shock I was at the point of saying, 'Hello, Sidney, nice of you to drop in,' but thought better of it. The silence held for what seemed like several minutes until Sidney said, 'Carry on.' The business of the meeting was brought to a lame conclusion whilst Sidney sat looking straight in front of him. Then he said, 'I have some questions to ask', and proceeded to probe with deadly accuracy all the most vulnerable parts of the operation, and all the most questionable management decisions, and to point out that other firms of our size had had a number of hits in the last three months and we had had none for nearly a year.

After that Alex and I knew that Transatlantic was doomed. It was decided to sell it. When this had been done at a subsequent Group Board meeting Sidney asked the Company Secretary to inform us of the full cost of the Transatlantic Venture (as I remember it, some £400,000). When I pointed out that this could all be charged as a tax loss and would cost the Group not one penny, he gave me his angry put-down look and said, 'Because some people in the Group are money earners, this does not excuse those who are money losers.' Of all people it was Joe alone who showed some sympathy. 'Could have been all right if we'd left it alone,' he said. But I now realised it was an act of folly to take on an un-Granada company like Transatlantic at all, and to do it without first making sure that Sidney was on my side was madness. I was an old enough Granada hand to regret but not to resent his way of punishing me for my folly.

Alex suffered a similar but less humiliating baptism of fire over the matter of car-washes. They were then a novelty and he wanted to add a number to our motorway service areas. He and Bob Carr, who had long been the group's legal adviser and had recently joined the group board, were certain they would be a success. Sidney was not convinced. For months the argument ebbed and flowed until at last it was agreed that a limited number (I believe it was only two) should be installed to test the market. From then on the matter of car-washes tended to crop up regularly at Group Board meetings. Sidney, with apparent unconcern, would say to the Company Secretary – now Joe's successor, Desmond James, 'By the way, what are the figures on the car-washes?' This, of course, was a set-up. Sidney would not ask for figures unless they were bad. Desmond would duly quote figures that sounded pretty dismal. Alex would immediately question the basis on which the figures rested, or come up with much better figures relating to the bank holiday weekend. The rest of us would sit back and wait for the shadow-boxing to end and pray that car-washes would come to stay or go away altogether. In the event, they went away.

Yet it was perhaps Sidney himself who led us into our biggest disaster in the matter of diversification. He had always wanted to use the Rental shops, where people came regularly to pay their money, for other purposes. His request to start a Granada bank was turned down by whatever authority it was that controlled the number of banks. He thought of a building society and finally he thought about insurance. Nothing could remove from his mind the notion that people could conveniently pay in their regular insurance premiums at the same time as they paid their rental bills.

After several years of casting about in the UK without success, an insurance company, L'Etoile, SA, was identified in Brussels. By now Bob Carr had been encouraged by Sidney to buy into insurance. Sidney sent Alex and myself across to make our assessment of the business. We spent a lot of time with the exceedingly boring proprietor, who talked ceaselessly in broken English through a small mouth like a rat-trap. We spent even more time with the equally boring son, who did not talk at all and gave us a poor lunch. We examined buildings. We gazed at sheets and sheets of computer print-outs and, of course, we could make neither head nor tail of the business prospects which could only have been assessed by an expert after several months' study. Alex and I gave an indifferent report. We could make no estimate of the business prospects. The owners, although boring, did not appear to be crooks. The buildings were impressively sited in Brussels. By now all association between the Belgian insurance company and the Television Rental shops seemed to have been forgotten. We were into insurance for insurance's sake. There could be some side benefits in using L'Etoile to carry some of the Granada UK insurances, and it was believed (but not very strongly) that L'Etoile might one day be used as a stepping stone to a car insurance business in the UK.

We bought the company and so began the most tedious, the most baffling and the most confusing saga in the history of Granada Group. When L'Etoile cropped up on the agenda, Bob would explain that although the company was technically making a profit it would be advisable at this point to invest several millions of Belgian francs in the future underwriting of risks two years ahead, which action would in the fullness of time bring rich rewards. As millions followed millions, some board members got a little restive. Both Sidney and Joe felt they must support Bob, who spent many hours explaining to them the inner workings of the insurance market. It was clear that neither of them fully grasped what he was going on about but that they did not dare to admit it. I began to doubt whether Bob understood it himself. Then I became certain he didn't. Indeed I privately formed the view that no one understood the workings of the insurance market, a man-made maze where a few bluffers put on a good show of knowing their way about (this view was to gain some credibility when in later years unthinkable things happened to Lloyd's of London). As the millions mounted even Sidney and Joe became uneasy, but when it was decided to sell L'Etoile it appeared that no one wanted to buy it. The disagreeable task of touting our sinking star round the insurance markets of Europe was delegated to Desmond James, who struggled nobly for some two years before he could rid us of the unwanted L'Etoile. This time the costs were not added up and read out to the Group Board.

Apart from the dreadful incident of Transatlantic there was a remarkable degree of harmony between Sidney and myself on Group matters. Although occasionally I was to find myself taking Alex's view rather than Sidney's, in general there was little contention between us. Alas this was not to be the case with the company we both knew best – Television.

After Sidney left the Programme Committee he used to say, 'I may no longer be with you but I can still be your critic.' This did not appear to signal any great change for within the committee – drama excepted, he had never been an initiator, nor had he been the source of many programme ideas. In the arena of public affairs he had several enthusiasms, such as clean food, questioning those in authority, and better housing, and also many antipathies – racial intolerance, country house snobbery, and a lasting vendetta against British Rail, the cause of which will be explained later. His main positive contribution had been in quick and generous support for the ideas of others and in his power to overcome the caution and lurking fear that the play-safe members of the committee (and especially Cecil) might hold. But it was his criticism – constructive, witty and to the point – that killed off many of the weaker programme ideas at birth and gave some of the survivors new strength.

'What about this notion of interviewing six cabinet ministers' wives about their husbands in the closed period before the election?' someone would ask (politics at one time was banned from the screen for twenty-four hours in the run-up to polling day). 'Hopeless. They would all say the same thing. And most of them are boringly good women,' said Sidney. 'No man is a hero to his valet. Who said that?' (Shouts of Oscar Wilde, Johnson, Walpole, Trollope from round the table and a brief diversion until the Oxford Dictionary of Quotations settled the matter in favour of Madame Cornuel.) 'Find out who were the cabinet ministers' political valets – not in their present private office but the one before. And the one before that. Get hold of their speech writers. Offer anonymity if you have to.'

After he left the Committee, Sidney would sometimes seize hold of a programme (certainly any programme about Israel) and spend an afternoon anatomising it with an embattled producer and director and David Plowright and myself round a table. These were invigorating encounters and usually resulted in a much improved show. During this period I would still ring him up to report on particularly bright programmes ideas, a scandal unearthed by *World in Action* or a major risk we were about to take. But these moments of communication grew fewer, as did his visits to Manchester.

In the early 1970s he would visit the flat for an evening with programme people perhaps once in six weeks. At dinner his conversation would be as lively and witty as ever. After dinner, as was the custom, we would watch a programme off air, or the video of a dry run or rough cut. Sidney would drop off to sleep within the first five or ten minutes and wake with a start as the show ended. His automatic reaction was always negative – 'Pretty sloppy work', 'Well, I hope we can do better than that' or 'Not up to standard.' If it were a small family party someone would say, 'Oh come on, Sidney, you slept through the whole thing, how can you possibly know?' and he would join in the general laughter against himself. If there were guests present his awakening thoughts would be drowned by one of other of us who knew what was coming, or simply ignored.

The first indication of hostility towards the new management came to the surface over the Stables Theatre at a time when Sidney was still Chairman of the Television company. Julian Amyes and I had invited Gordon McDougall, then running the Traverse Theatre in Edinburgh, to set up a theatre company in the old railway stables behind our studios. Here they would put on one play every month in their own small theatre. The same play would then be adapted and recorded for television. Gordon was a diligent worker and recruited a talented company, including the then comparatively unknown Maureen Lipman, Richard Wilson and John Shrapnell.

The intention was to make The Stables a writers' theatre, just as Glen Byam Shaw had done with the Royal Court in Sloane Square in its early days, and several young writers were set to work. It was a hazardous but worthwhile enterprise and its chances of success depended on wholehearted backing from the Granada board. Even with all the support in the world it was a project that could have failed, but Sidney made failure certain by submitting The Stables to the same treatment that he had meted out to Transatlantic. Every management decision was questioned, every budget cut, every call on Television's facilities was first reduced and then grudgingly granted, and no nit went unpicked. After two years of desperate struggle with some promising and some indifferent productions behind us, Julian and I had to accept that this jig was up. With Sidney, Cecil and Joe against us there was no contest. Although they might be outnumbered on the Television board, they spoke with the unacknowledged power of the Group. Group and Television had never been in conflict, and we knew it would be an evil day if they were. So we caved in, a little disconsolate and a little regretful that a project which would have been close to Sidney's heart had he fathered it himself, had been crushed so unmercifully. But then, as I said to Julian, if Sidney had taken it on himself he might have done it better.

As time passed Sidney's criticisms became less creative and more schoolmasterish. He would mark up passages critical of a Granada programme in notices by critics for whom none of us – including Sidney himself – had the slightest respect and would scrawl on them, 'In case you didn't see this.' He would send scripts back with corrections to the grammar and punctuation which were wildly out of kilter with the author's style and manner of writing. But worst of all, he took to sending me two or three times a week nasty little notes implying ineptitude, indifference or just plain bad judgement by the production team.

At first, as soon as I received one of these notes, I would drop into his office waving it in front of me saying, 'Sidney, what *is* this? You can't think that the show was as bad as that. Let's look at it together.' But the Venetian blinds would come down behind his eyes, he would put on his camel's face and say very quietly, 'I'm sorry but that's my opinion.' It was no good, and I soon gave up.

The hostility towards the new regime reached a new peak with a show called *A Point in Time*, the work of a young director, Carlos Pasini. I had always longed to introduce something in the spirit of Dadaism, something of the wild extravagances of a Buñuel or a Salvador Dali into television, and in Carlos I thought I had found a man with a stunning visual sense and an ability to handle a range of outrageous imagery that went far beyond the humdrum vision of British documentary and drama in those days. I gave him his head and hoped for the best. The result was a one-hour impressionist essay, weak on narrative, strong on striking images, with no clear message for the viewer. There was also some high-minded nudity in it which upset the Authority (but not too much) and which diverted most critics from any serious consideration of the piece. *A Point in Time* was a mistake, my mistake, but it was a well-intentioned mistake made in an attempt to give new talent a chance to flower. It infuriated Sidney beyond all measure. He saw it, not altogether unfairly, as a load of pretentious rubbish which had cost a lot of money. I think he felt that we in Manchester were losing our marbles and it was time that he put them back in their proper place. The spattering of little notes became a steady drizzle.

After my first failure to make personal contact, I replied to each note in terms of sweet reason, but now the flow was too great, so I tried ignoring them. This led to telephone reminders: 'SLB wonders if you received his note of 1.2.73 about *Coronation Street*', and so on. At last my patience gave out. Sidney complained about a play, *Captain Doughty*, in the following terms.

> To: Forman Alex Bernstein Plowright From: SLB/HB
>
> subject: *Captain Doughty*   date: 1.3.75
>
> I saw this programme in the flat on 17 January.
>
> I understand it will be transmitted on 28 March. I urge you to think again before this is done. I don't know what alterations you eventually made, but I thought it was a pretentious production and very nearly in the class of *A Point in Time*.

To which I replied:

> To: SLB cc AB Plowright   Private
> from: Forman/SW   2.3.75

I have your note about *Captain Doughty*. I liked the play very much, so did Alex, David and Peter. I am affronted by your practice of micturating from on high on certain Granada programmes. Between colleagues, and on matters of taste, written criticism is usually ill-received, or so I have found it, when it takes the form of terse little notes, spiked with uric acid. I, for one, do not wish to be any other man's urinal, and particularly I do not relish the role of chamber-pot-in-waiting for a senior colleague with whom I have worked so closely and (despite many good rows) so happily for nearly twenty years. Our creative part- nership is the longest you have had in all your life: there has been an amazing degree of tolerance on both sides: whatever there is of value in my work for television mainly derives from your leadership and your inspiration in the early days. So please consider: if you want to challenge current television standards in terms of this show or that, please send me no more horrid little notes but call us to your office for discussion. We will pre-empt other work and be available. In matters of taste and judgement which touch us deeply, you cannot pull rank or issue *ex cathedra* statements. You must treat us as equals, persuade us if you can, perhaps compromise, perhaps agree to differ. Please do not accuse me of delivering a lecture. This is not a lecture, it is an outburst.

Sidney made no reply to this. He did not challenge it, nor did he try to laugh it off. In retrospect I was ashamed that I had used such brutish language. I wished I had not sent copies to Alex and David, for this was now a personal and not a family affair.

From now on the rift with Sidney widened. There were still to be moments – precious ones – of communion between us when his delight in a good show overcame all his inhibitions, and socially we could still switch into another gear and have a good time together. But things were no longer the same between us.

For a few months after *Captain Doughty* there was a decrease in the number of little notes. Then they started again, sometimes a crit- icism of a particular person or show, of Mike Parkinson for example, who was now becoming a famous figure: 'Mr Parkinson was over- relaxed, too casual and spoke an excess of generalizations, some bordering on clichés.' Others were more general and reflected his deep conviction that since his departure Granada Television had gone into a slow decline. He sought to arrest this by sending us philosophical messages of a generalised nature, usually carrying an indirect rebuke:

A THOUGHT FOR TODAY
Experience in television (this includes films and theatre) suggests that the policy of a studio is dictated less by written statements of intent, no matter how complex or considered they are, than by the day-to-day 'crises' that arrive on someone's desk in the morning, demand a solution immediately or at least after lunch.

The policy of any studio is the accumulation of these daily decisions – decisions which reveal priorities, create precedents and eventually map out a course for future action.

Alas, it is in precisely that area that no committee of absentee directors or management can possibly participate with success and establish and maintain essential standards.

But then came a period of set-piece rows. One of them was over *The Christians*, a series on the history of Christianity. We had tried to get co-production money from the Italian state television service RAI, and, after interminable discussions, had failed. Barrie Heads had, however, rustled up some good advance sales. Whether it was the close involvement of Barrie, the nature of the subject matter, or just a general feeling that I was indulging a personal whim, I do not know, but Sidney got his knife into *The Christians* from the start. We had some problems in shooting the first few episodes. One of the directors favoured eccentric shots of architectural features which sometimes filled the screen with images more like Braque than Canaletto. I had a stern tussle with the team over the opening and closing shots: they wanted an elaborate moving mosaic culminating, as I remember, in a stained glass window, while I wanted a simple sunrise and sunset for the beginning and end, and eventually prevailed but only after a lot of money had been spent. Apart from that the rushes were good, the team harmonious, Bamber Gascoigne splendid as the presenter, and the costs well under control. Sidney called for a video of a rough-cut of one of the early episodes. He also read a synopsis of the series prepared for Jonathan Cape, who were considering the possibility of an accompanying book.

I received a note from Sidney:

From: SLB/FML   To: Forman
subject: *The Christians*   22.11.76

I feel sure you have not read the copy attached.

I understood from Heads that this is to be used by Granada International (presume also Granada TV who will transmit in UK) and will be sent to Capes. The writing is not worthy of Granada. This I think will become self-evident when you read it. It will not be worthy of Granada even if used in a corrected form. We need a new writer or new writers.

Do you think it worth mentioning the 2 or 3 stations that have a minor financial contribution? It will not help you to flatter them in a synopsis and story like this. It may confuse readers and take away some of the credit which Granada hope to get for their million pounds (approximately) project. A project on which we embarked after confused debate and some differences of opinion on what was agreed. But we are now embarked. It is therefore essential that the thousand and one details that make good programmes and which could help to exploit this programme successfully should be seriously considered. You know my view of the filming. As production continues, I hope the necessary action can be taken to ensure quality and remakes done, wherever essential, even at some cost.

To which I replied on 1 December:

1. Your memo of 22.11.76 imputes against those responsible for *The Christians* almost every sin in the calendar except Gluttony and Lust. Sorry for the delay in responding – not due to Sloth but to other priorities. Taking your points.

2. I had read the copy for the booklet.

3. The purpose of the piece is to provide Capes with a description of the TV series.

4. I have re-read the copy. It needs subbing for spelling, and punctuation. Because of the strength of your feelings I will also work it over editorially but I cannot guarantee that you will think that this modest package will thereby be transformed from something 'unworthy' to something 'worthy'.

5. The co-producers were included at Barrie Heads' suggestion. I thought it a good one. If they are not mentioned then distribution abroad might be inhibited.

6. I do not recall any confused debates and would only say that there have been fewer differences of opinion on this series than most major television programmes.

7. The budget for the series is £520,000 direct and £754,000 including indirects. We are receiving contributions of £155,000 (at today's rates) from overseas partners, total net cost to Granada £600,000. If the programme receives its present rate-card potential of £45,300 per episode we would get back £473,300 from the majors (this excludes the Granada share) and £206,000 from the Regions, total £679,300. Thus we are budgeting for a profit of some £80,000 before overseas sales (excluding Holland and Germany). As reported at the last International Board meeting, we are currently on target.

8. The problems of shooting architecture have been overcome and the offending scenes removed. We have plenty of problems left but this is no longer one of them.

9. Of course I agree that all details have to be watched.

10. Finally, and reverting to paragraph 1, I sympathise with your feeling that nobody is doing anything right unless you are actually in there seeing that they do it. I have this feeling myself, frequently. When we were toiling together in television production you never had this feeling. I am therefore appending two of the notes that I have sent to the team in the past so that you may understand better the nature of the problems we face, and the ways in which we are tackling them. I would be grateful if you would read them through.

The notes I referred to were addressed to the producer, concerned many small details and instructed him pithily to do certain things differently. Sidney then sent me a 1,200-word memo, perhaps the longest I ever received from him, from which the following are extracts:

> I take it your paragraph 1 was not meant seriously – I cannot see how you drew that inference, even for satire. Regarding the booklet I suggested:
>
> That you had not read the copy that was sent to me by Heads.
>
> That the writing was not worthy of Granada.
>
> That I did not think the two or three overseas stations (that made a minor financial contribution to costs) to be included.
>
> In your memo of 31.8.76 you said 'any troubles that lie therein are only little ones'. [I had not said this] I profoundly disagree. In the rough cut that I was shown, the problems were *not* little ones: they were basic and it was obvious would affect the total quality of the programme.
>
> Anyhow memos, however well-written ones such as yours, do not necessarily produce action or revisions and the effort required to make better programmes. The points you made were very good (chiefly because of the quality of your writing) but it was like a slap on the wrist with a feather. Did you get any replies? Have the producers agreed to act (without qualifications) on the points you so carefully made?
>
> As far as the budget is concerned, to get things clear, I still hold the view that the total costs (that's including below the lines costs) will be about a million pounds. Time will tell how near I will be to this figure (Forgive me if I say in parenthesis that lately I have reason to be sceptical about budgets for some of our other companies.) We cannot deduct from production costs what we may receive in sales or from advances from others. It's the total cost figure and this I think will be about a million pounds.
>
> I suggested that the project had been embarked upon 'after confused debate'. I stand by that.
>
> In your last paragraph you suggest that I wish to do the job myself. [I never said this.] You're wrong. Not in my thoughts or in my frustrations have I ever considered that I was capable, or wished to do the job myself. That is not the feeling I have about our productions, but to be a

prophet in the wilderness it is not necessary to be a mistaken prophet, and while there can always be more than one opinion about the merits of a production, a consensus of adverse opinion among ourselves, professional critics and viewing figures alike would seem to indicate poor grasp of what makes a good programme suited to contemporary taste. (Don't quote me too frequently on this.)

What I do care about is the production of a programme of a quality of which Granada can be proud, equal for instance to those of Kenneth Clark and Alistair Cooke for the BBC. There is nothing so far to suggest to me that we are going to get into that class.

Finally, I have no doubt that most of our memos and reports and the minutes of proposal were well written and are good pieces of 'literature' but the question arises were they productive? I have never believed that a wordy diagnosis necessarily implies the cure. In retrospect I can't remember any minutes of mine that produced better results than straight discussion with the people involved. They knew exactly what my criticisms were and understood what changes had to be made. My recollection is that the creative people on the other side of the table were appreciative of clear directives.

Along with this monster memo Sidney sent me a private note:

I've had many memos and notes from you in the last few years about TV productions etc.; some were more agreeable than others. But whatever thoughts I had when they were received they did not disturb me. I didn't answer them. Time has, I think, done that.

I think, however, your memo of 1.12.76 regarding *The Christians* calls for us to talk and I would like you to read the attached as a kind of agenda.

To which I replied:

Yes, let's talk. But lest we get off on the wrong foot I'd like to say in advance that my note about *The Christians* was an answer in kind to yours – this degree of difference that I had hoped by giving you some account of our problems

and progress we might recapture something of the partnership we enjoyed so often in the early years. The note
clearly failed in its mission. I am sorry.

The first paragraph about Sin was a rather simple joke.

The talk that then took place did not lead to complete harmony over
the matter of *The Christians* but it did at least bring about a period of
greater mutual civility. It should be recorded that *The Christians*
turned out to be a success. It got decent ratings, a good press and cost
slightly less and earned a little more than I had forecast to Sidney. I
did not think it appropriate to point out these facts to Sidney, for I
knew that he would only want to hear news of the show if it were
bad, and that he would already have studied every bit of available
evidence and held his peace because it was predominantly favourable.

The truce after *The Christians* did not last for long. Sidney began
to wage a series of campaigns which took the form of picking on a
show or person and bombarding me with evidence that the show
should be cancelled or the person fired. One of the objects of his
displeasure was Don Harker, head of Granada's political and public
relations. His transformation into a *persona non Granada* was surprising because he had only recently rejoined the company at Sidney's
invitation (he had asked him to return no fewer than five times in a
dozen years). Before rejoining Granada, Don had directed the Rank
Organisation's publicity and government relations and run PR at
Conservative Central Office for the life of a Parliament. Now he was
back with a broader brief, and very welcome he was. In 1974 Sidney
had agreed that Don on his second coming should join the Television
board. One night in the flat he told Don over a whisky that 'some
people are trying to take Granada away from me.' (Who? Alex?
David? Me?) He asked Don to keep his eyes and ears open and to
report any evidence of disloyalty to him. When Don failed to respond
positively to this suggestion, he began to give him a hard time and he
gave me an even harder one.

Each week dozens of press releases describing forthcoming
programmes were issued from the Manchester press office. This was
run-of-the-mill stuff and neither Don nor I expected them to be
gems of English literature. But Sidney marked up each one of these
in blue pencil, making detailed corrections to their grammar and
syntax. Sometimes the corrections were pedantic, often they
attempted to turn what was no more than a message from one journalist to another into something more literary. 'How could Granada
put up with such sloppy work?' he asked. 'Who was responsible?'

(Don Harker) Why could things not be put right at once? I reasoned with him, but the avalanche of blue-pencilled releases continued to flow over my desk until I sent him a memo saying that his criticisms of Don Harker were unfounded, that Don was the best public relations man in Independent Television, that if he cared to refer to the members of the Television board he would find that they unanimously supported my view. Would he please get off my back and leave Don alone? There was no reply to this, but the flow of notes about the press releases ceased, which I suppose in one way was a victory but in another was a set-back for it made all the more remote any chance of a rapprochement. As for Don, he went from strength to strength and became one of the longest-serving members of the Television board.

It was some while after the Harker affair that I received what might be called the Doomsday memo from Sidney. As he saw it, things were going from bad to worse. In order to set them to rights, and so that we might regain some of our former glory, we should shut down all production for at least a month. This would allow us to rethink and to replan forward programmes and get things 'straightened out'. If no such action was taken he could see nothing but disaster ahead. I told him such a stoppage was impossible. The plaudits for *Hard Times* and *The Christians* were still ringing in our ears, *World in Action* was firing shot and shell as effectively as ever it had done, *Coronation Street* stood at number one and number two in the Top Ten, we had won more prizes in the last two years than ever before, and the ratings were uncommonly strong. I also spoke frankly with Cecil and deduced from his reaction that he had not been consulted over Sidney's recent guerrilla war against Television or about the Doomsday memo. This was unusual. For whatever reason, however, the stream of memos from Sidney dried up.

From 1976, the relationship between Sidney and myself reached its lowest point. He felt that the great company he had built up, and the great reputation that it (and he) had gained were threatened by the incompetence of a louche management who were distracted from their main task by external affairs. Things were not as they used to be, or as they should be. Within Granada he was accustomed to getting his own way. Now, it seemed, he could not get his way. He could no longer impose his will on the company that meant the most to him.

Some of Sidney's disenchantment can be put down to our different styles of management. Although ready to interfere with anyone or anything if need be, I was a delegator and he was not. I was content to leave Current Affairs to David Plowright because I knew he was

262

more capable than I to run them, to leave the daily grind of labour relations to Julian Amyes, sales to Peter Rennie, finance to Bill Dickson and engineering to Leslie Diamond. I did not pick about within my colleagues' bailiwicks. I did not write a memo if I found that a nameplate had dropped off a camera, I did not send notes to every producer after every show I saw, although I would telephone them if it was outstandingly good. If anything bothered me I talked to the boss and not directly to the person concerned, and this was not Sidney's way. He was, of course, a brilliant practitioner in the art of setting up a new company and seeing it through the first phase of its development. But when it reached a size that outran the capability of his one-man do-it-yourself style he would perforce have to hand over to a managing director who employed more conventional methods, such as delegating responsibility to colleagues and giving a higher priority to a regular meeting with departmental heads rather than to inspecting personally the interior of the lift shaft. In Television, Publishing and Television Rental, Sidney felt that the men who took over from him were not really up to the job. During this time Alex was in charge of Rental, and he suffered as much from this syndrome as I did – perhaps more.

I was saddened by this estrangement. Try as I might, I could find no route that would lead us back towards the easy friendship of earlier days. Sidney, once my mentor, my companion and the person who in all the world I most wanted to please, was now something very like an enemy. One day in Golden Square after a board meeting, when Joe and I were ascending together in the lift, he said to me casually, 'By the way, Sidney is making some adjustments to the family trusts and he asked me to tell you that you will no longer be required as a trustee.' I cast my mind back to the champagne ceremony of the initiatory lunch and wondered whether it was the message itself or the curt manner of its delivery that hurt most.

CHAPTER TEN

It was in July 1960 that we learned that a committee under the chairmanship of Sir Harry Pilkington, of glass-making fame, was to be set up to examine the performance of the Independent Television system. In sharp contrast to the announcement of the Annan Committee some fifteen years later, this caused no great stir. The industry made no effort at a collective response: each company put in its evidence in its own style, regarding the Committee as one of those time-consuming bureaucratic bodies whose needs had to be satisfied as quickly as possible. Sidney, in those days still fully involved in all the affairs of the industry, masterminded the Granada evidence, which consisted of a plea for less interference from the Authority and more editorial freedom.

In June 1962 I was on holiday in Ullapool with Helen and our two boys when one morning a solid packet thumped through the letter-box onto the floor. I sat down and started to read the Pilkington Report with mounting horror. It seemed to find everything to do with ITV bad, everything to do with the BBC good. Until now any article that was critical of Independent Television, no matter how hard it had slammed into quiz shows, advertisements and so on, had always qualified its condemnation with the words 'except for Granada'. But in the Pilkington Report there was no 'except for Granada': there was no Granada, for individual companies were not mentioned. No programmes were named. The whole report was based on generalisations about the nation's universal disquiet and dissatisfaction over ITV's light entertainment 'American imports', 'game shows' and so on. Granada's dedication to politics and to serious social issues were not mentioned. Nor were Granada's plays. That night, as my fury mounted, I called Sidney. 'I know, I know, I know,' he said, 'it's disgraceful. But don't let's fool ourselves – it's going to change the face of television.'

That night the whole industry seethed with indignation.

Chairmen were telephoning Ministers, Managing Directors drafting letters to *The Times*. Peter Cadbury, Chief Executive of Westward Television, burnt Sir Harry Pilkington in effigy in the grounds of his house at Preston Candover. At the Authority, Bernard Sendall and Bob Fraser were in a state of shock and taking no calls.

A more careful reading of the Report made it clear that the Committee had been dominated by the views of Richard Hoggart, a well-meaning liberal media sociologist. He strove to establish in the opening essay 'the purposes of broadcasting', and found that these were not 'to give the public what it wants' but to 'broaden and deepen public taste'. This the Authority had failed to do. The whole structure of ITV was wrong. The Authority should sell the advertising time and plan the programmes, and the companies would then be commissioned to produce them to the Authority's specification.

None of the report's main recommendations was adopted and the system jogged on much as before, but Sidney was right: the doctrine of original sin had descended on us like a damp cloud and Independent Television was never the same again. I used to call the pre-Pilkington years the Age of Innocence. Froth, fun and profit had been the order of the day – Lew Grade could go to the limit with quiz shows, variety and comedy without let or hindrance. The ratio of viewing between ITV and BBC was 70:30; but now when the Authority came out of its trauma it set about imposing a new puritanism across the spectrum of ITV. The number of quiz shows was cut, the amount of prize money was cut, the number of American imports was cut, and it was made plain to the companies that they had better set about broadening and deepening public taste right away.

To be honest, although the Report itself had done us no good, in the aftermath Granada gained a pole position in the matter of serious programmes. A two-hour study of some social malaise which we would never have dared to offer to our network colleagues before Pilkington would now be accepted meekly by all, or, if not, the Authority would sort them out. The truth is that although we would never admit it even to ourselves there was a lot in common between the views of Richard Hoggart and those of Granada Television. But the jolly days of a private network run by Cecil or Lew were over. 'Brownie points' became as important as ratings. The network schedule became a matter of concern; the network committee took on a new importance. Each company had to ensure a place in the sun to show what good boys they were, and when a little later the days of the licence to print money were over and the dreaded Levy began to bite, the industry realised even more clearly that it must make common cause against the Treasury, and full collaboration became the order of the day.

Committees proliferated. By the early 1970s there were two main committees run by the Authority – the PPC (Programme Policy Committee, chaired by their Chairman) and the SCC (Standing Consultative Committee, chaired by their Director General). Within the industry there was the Council, attended by the Managing Directors of all fifteen companies; the NPC (Network Planning Committee), attended by all the majors and representatives of the regional companies; Programme Controllers, attended by the five majors only (Thames, London Weekend, Associated Television, Yorkshire, Granada); plus a dozen or more specialist committees. For several years I had to attend my full quota of these meetings and I can remember writing in despair to the Authority, who were contemplating setting up yet another committee, 'Where once there stood an executive and his secretary there now stands a committee and a secretariat. Half of our lives is spent talking to each other. Can we not become a little less democratic?'

After Yorkshire Television had joined the majors I was charged with the job of setting up the new Programme Controllers committee. Its function was to agree on a division of network time between the Big Five, and at the first meeting the temperature soon reached boiling point. Most of the time two or more of the Controllers were on the phone talking to their principals. Cyril Bennett of LWT took of his jacket off and challenged Donald Baverstock of Yorkshire to come outside over the matter of an allegedly broken promise concerning Friday evening peak-time. When the combatants had calmed down, the telephoning seemed to get less and through the smoke of battle I could see that the room was filling up. In the shadows behind each controller the figure of their respective managing director loomed. Soon the controllers were elbowed to the rear and the principals took over, with Lew Grade in the van pounding the table in his customary style as the debate raged. Subsequently they all told me that they happened to have been in the building attending another meeting. After the meeting had broken up in disarray, new ground rules were laid down which firmly excluded outsiders. I also requested the presence of an invigilator from the Authority to ensure a better standard of behaviour in the classroom.

Sidney had by now opted out of industry affairs entirely, regarding them as boring. Cecil too was losing his first enthusiasm, now network territory was no longer the domain of Lew and himself. Yet network committee life was enjoyable in its fashion. Independent

Television in those days was run by a very good class of person, perhaps because in order to obtain the franchise the companies had to present a top deck of executives who had at least a whiff of the great and the good about them. There were, of course, shifting alliances and combinations but on the whole the Big Five fought amongst themselves in private, as did the middle five – Scotland, Tyne Tees, Anglia, Southern and Harlech. The public confrontations were between these two groups. (The five smallest companies were little more than spectators). This conflict was always with us and always in the news. The Regionals wanted to make more programmes for the network and enlisted public sympathy in their campaign to challenge 'the network carve-up'. The majors did not want to give up their role as the network's main producers. Bob Fraser had designed the system on the basis that network programmes should be provided 'by the five to the ten'. We had set up our business on the assumption that this happy state would continue indefinitely.

Each year there was a major negotiation to fix the amount the Regionals must pay for the programmes they received from the majors. On one such occasion – I think it was on Cecil's last appearance in the network arena – he, Lew and myself represented the majors. The debate was long and heated. At one point David Wilson of Southern, the chief Regional spokesman, said, 'My people could never accept a figure of that kind.' 'I don't care about what your people think,' Cecil replied, 'what I care about is the money.'

'That's all you ever care about, Cecil,' said David. 'You only care about the money. People don't matter to you.' Cecil was seriously affronted. He snapped his mouth shut and cocked his head up in the air and walked out of the room. When he returned, he left it to Lew and myself to finish the negotiation.

After the meeting we went to our separate destinations, but that evening Sidney called me to his office. Cecil was sitting by his desk, grey-faced, the hand holding his stick shaking a little. 'Cecil tells me he was insulted by David Weston' ('Wilson, Sidney,' I said) '– by David Wilson and he feels he should demand an apology from him. Do you agree?' I had thought that David's remarks were fair enough in the rough and tumble of television life, but now I saw Cecil so deeply unhappy I agreed at once. Draft after draft passed across our desks and eventually Cecil's letter, curt and to the point, was despatched. David responded generously and a copy of both letters was sent to all who had been present at the meeting. Cecil was reasonably happy again, but I noted that David Wilson's name was dropped from Cecil's vocabulary. From now on he was to be called 'Southern'.

Granada executives were prominent amongst the members of the club that steered Independent Television life through its maze of committees. The major committees followed the rule of Buggins' turn in appointing their chairmen, but the specialist committees were inclined to select the best man for the job. There was a time in the early 1970s when it was my turn to chair the Network Planning Committee, David was chairing the Programme Controllers, Julian Labour Relations, Peter Rennie Sales and Bill Dickson Finance, a post he seemed to hold indefinitely, and even when he was not the titular chairman people still treated him as if he were. Once, during this period, Bernard Sendall sidled up to me at an industry gathering and said, 'The Authority are a little worried by Granada's dominance in the affairs of the industry.'

'Why?' I asked belligerently, ready to refute any allegations of self-interest.

'Because we think it is dangerous for the industry to become too dependent upon half a dozen people from one company,' said Bernard, and I was disarmed.

In 1970 I was persuaded to become the Chairman of the British Film Institute. The Institute had gone from strength to strength during the late 50s and early 60s, mainly due to the qualities of its director, the excellent Stanley Reed. But now Stanley was to retire, it was student revolt time and the Institute was in turmoil. Semiology and Cohn-Bendit politics were the order of the day. Little groups of staff and members defied the Governors, working day and night to make trouble for everyone. I was subjected to a trumpet call of duty. The Institute you built, cherished and loved is in mortal danger, they said, only you can save it now. This, of course, was rubbish, but like a fool I fell for it and found the Institute in an even greater mess than I had expected.

The dominant figure on the Institute Board was John Davis, Führer of the Rank Organisation and indeed of the whole British film industry. A more unlikely person to bridge the gap between the governing body and the seething mass of semiologists and semioticians there could not have been. It was as if General Dyer had been put in to cope with the Jarrow hunger marchers. His method of dealing with the insurgents was to employ gunboat diplomacy – threatening dismissal, legal action and if necessary police intervention. Moreover, John Davis had virtually acquired life tenure; as the decades rolled on, each time his term of office expired he expected to be, and was, reappointed. Eventually he was dislodged when we enlisted the support of the responsible Minister, the excellent David

Eccles. The whole basis of appointing Governors would be revised: some would be elected by the Institute's members, others would be appointed by the Minister, all would have a maximum term of office.

So John Davis went; but the new system had the side effect of unseating Helen, my wife, another long-serving Governor, but one who was greatly valued by the saner elements of the staff. She, however, cheerfully accepted that what the Institute suffered in losing her would be compensated for tenfold by the departure of John Davis. A minor hazard lay in the close relationship between John Davis and the Bernstein brothers. When looking at some new business enterprise the most common question after 'What does Lew think?' was 'What does John think?' I knew that if John and I were to come to loggerheads he could call Sidney and Cecil to his aid, which, with Cecil unwell and Sidney trembling before the prospect of surgery, was the last thing I wanted (from his demeanour we assumed he was to have a lung removed or to undergo some major restructuring of his intestines – in fact it turned out to be a minor operation to correct a hernia). Fortunately I managed to remain friends with John throughout the period of his planned expulsion, laying the responsibility for his banishment, in a cowardly way, on to David Eccles. Similarly when Sidney and Cecil asked me, 'Why are you losing John from the Institute?' I replied that it was the work of the Minister.

Before he left, however, John Davis and his squad of toadies managed to block the appointment of Sandy (Alexander) MacKendrick to succeed Stanley Reed in the post of Director by telling horrid stories of what went on in the long past when he had directed a film for him at Pinewood. This was sad, because Sandy was revered as a great leader in the film school in Los Angeles and would, I believe, have been able to cope with the mutineers satisfactorily, since he was pretty well one himself. Granada called, and I could no longer spend time striving to extricate the Institute from its slough of ideological anarchy. It was the failure of a mission, and I regretted my folly in taking on such an intractable task. In due course time, and the arrival on the scene of that great achiever Anthony Smith, pulled the Institute round and in the late 70s and 80s it went on to become the mighty force in the film world that it is today.

The television industry was also making even heavier claims on my time. Jeremy Potter in the Official History says, flatteringly but untruthfully:

During the 1970s Granada Television was run by Denis Forman, whose talents and experience were outstanding among the leaders of Independent Television. His influence and stature in the industry were recognised by colleagues in his appointment as Chairman of the steering committees which presented the companies' case to the National Board of Prices and Incomes in 1970 and the Annan Committee on the Future of Broadcasting in 1975.

Unfortunately Jeremy entirely misconstrued my colleagues' motives in so frequently appointing me their chairman. Throughout my life I have been plagued by the inability to say no to any invitation to take on a public service job that appeared to be interesting or challenging. Thus I have spent many hours planning the future of television, promoting the interests of young photographers, supporting the preservation of Essex's heritage of ancient monuments, sponsoring groups of young musicians, stimulating film production in Scotland, backing an organisation seeking to find redress for victims of torture worldwide, sitting on the board of the Royal Opera House, raising funds for a decent common room for the students of an agricultural college, and assisting a small group of idealists to launch a pro-field sports movement within the Labour Party. How much this reckless expenditure of time has achieved must be open to doubt, but one thing is certain: time so spent, although it may bring happiness and sometimes satisfaction, is not in any sense of the word profitable.

It was with this sensible thought in my mind that my colleagues in the industry – John Freeman of LWT, David Windlesham of ATV, Bill Brown of Scottish Television, who were every whit as capable as myself of leading the committees that were set up to steer the industry into the future – persuaded me time after time to respond to the call of duty and take on yet another chore whilst they, like sensible folk, concentrated their energies on running their own companies.

The struggle with the National Board for Prices and Incomes I remember as a number-crunching affair. It was our aim to find a formula which would fix the amount of Levy to be paid. Hitherto it had been left to a somewhat unworldly Authority to argue our case each year with the highly skilled and rapacious representatives of the Treasury. They had done reasonably well, we felt, but not well enough. The companies were tougher. We must move in and find some permanent basis that would allow us to plan ahead with certainty. The debate moved slowly towards a definition of what might be a reasonable rate on return of capital employed in the television industry. At that time (1970) the accepted rate of return over industry generally was from 12 to 15 per cent, but it was agreed that the risk of losing one's franchise every seven years or so must greatly increase the margin of profit needed to ensure that the business was sound.

The final stage of the contest took the form of single combat between myself and the then Minister, Sir John Eden. My memory, fallible as ever, would have me believe that we met alone with no aides present in a dark oak-panelled office and that over a glass of malt whisky we embarked on an elegant and almost academic debate, leading to agreement that 23.5 per cent must be the appropriate figure. I thought this result to be a triumph for the industry and went about commending Sir John as a most intelligent and gentlemanlike person. In retrospect, I imagine that the level was fixed some weeks before by shadowy figures in the corridors of the Treasury who allowed us to play out our comedy in the tradition that it is Ministers, and not civil servants, who take decisions.

When the Annan Committee was set up in 1974, ITV decided to make a collective effort to present them with a far-sighted, wise and fair view of what the future shape of British broadcasting should be, namely their own. The greatest issue was the Fourth Channel, who should operate it and what nature of programmes it should broadcast. A small committee (the Future of broadcasting Committee) was set up (and here I quote from the Official History):

> ITCA's Committee was composed of six company chief executives: William Brown (Scottish), Sir Denis Forman (Granada), John Freeman (LWT), Peter Paine (Tyne Tees), Jeremy Potter (ITP) and Lord Windlesham (ATV). Forman was Chairman of the committee and its mastermind. Freeman and Windlesham were politicians as well as communicators: one had been a Labour, the other a Conservative, minister. Brown, a senior figure in the industry, had a special responsibility for the interests of the nine regional companies. Advertising was Paine's particular expertise. Potters was the scribe.

Chairing this committee proved to be the most agreeable and stimulating task that fell to my lot in my long participation in the hurly-burly of ITV's affairs. My fellow members were all outstanding people and the Future of Broadcasting Committee came to be a select club. We looked forward to our meetings, whether it was a long morning session, a quick get-together in the early evening, or over a working lunch – a meal that took on a special style known as an FOB lunch, in which a complete meal of delicious cold food was served on a single large plate, leaving the rest of the table bare to accommodate papers.

We took a schoolboy pride in our final submission, which was delivered in a smart volume printed in two colours, whereas the BBC's offering was a tatty, typed document delivered seriatim in a number of bits and pieces. The Annan Committee, too, liked our submission and we had a series of friendly, even jolly, discussions with them under the avuncular chairmanship of Noel Annan. In retrospect I do not think that our evidence had the slightest influence on the main issue of the day – the Fourth Channel. We advocated ITV2, the Committee preferred a channel run by a new Open Broadcasting Authority. In the end it was Willie Whitelaw in his great wisdom, acting on a seminal idea put forward by Anthony Smith, then of St Anthony's College, Oxford, that hit on the notion of Channel Four, an independently managed channel charged to do new things in broadcasting with finance guaranteed by the ITV companies. Our report did, however, raise the status and reputation of the companies within the small world that centred around broadcasting affairs, and some of its better jokes passed into civil service folklore, frequently to be regurgitated coyly by Home Office officials at meetings in years to come.

Throughout my time with Granada there was a state of cold war between the ITV companies and the BBC. Each side never ceased to plot and scheme ways of outsmarting the other. Although I was always ready to challenge the BBC's belief that as the nation's premier instrument of broadcasting they had a divine right to cover exclusively any event which might be remotely claimed as 'national', and apart from the inevitable battle of the ratings, I was a collaborator. I found my ITV colleagues' attitude childish and often counterproductive. I did my best to seek ways of working with the BBC when it was obvious that this would result in a better deal for the viewer, as with the Olympic Games, which we both had the right to cover. In this I was greatly assisted by three people – Huw Wheldon, David Attenborough and Paul Fox – all three great broadcasters and all prepared to put the viewers' interest ahead of any feelings of petty rivalry, which were even more rife within the BBC than in ITV. I often wondered if they were sometimes regarded as quislings by their colleagues, as I often was in ITV. Through my friendship with these three key BBC men I gradually became a *persona Beeb-grata*, and when I finally retired from television I was touched when they arranged a totally unexpected farewell party for me. In many ways I had more in common with the BBC's attitude to broadcasting than with that of some of my more commercially minded colleagues in ITV.

By the time the Annan Committee was at work it was not possible to arouse the slightest interest in Sidney about the industry's affairs. When I told him of the state of our discussions on the Levy, where the outcome might affect Granada's fortunes by several millions of pounds a year, he would look out of the window, abstracted and unresponsive. He would take telephone calls whilst I was talking, a clear sign of indifference, for if he was truly concerned with the matter in hand no phone would ring. I sent him a draft of our submission to Annan, which he returned next day, clearly unread. Had the discussions involved Granada alone, it would have been a different matter. The reputation of his company would have been at stake and Granada was still a part of his own persona. But for the doings of a group of run-of-the-mill television companies he cared little. Again, had he been conducting affairs himself he would have been at the centre of the fray, eyes flashing, telexes flying, phones ringing, but he was not. Someone else was doing it. So he simply turned his back on the whole of television's business outside Granada, and through indifference gradually lost his understanding of what was going on. He would grumpily complain that the London companies now had two slots that used to belong to Granada, but it was no longer possible to explain to him the workings of a complex deal wherein Granada, by giving up a little in one place, had gained more elsewhere.

Where once Sidney and I had shared in everything that happened in the whole spectrum of Granada's affairs, he was now opting out of huge tracts of strategically important territory. These he left to me perhaps because he felt that if he could not mastermind the affairs of ITV himself, it was beneath his dignity to be no more than the auditor of some other person who seemed to be doing it all right anyway. And he knew that the watchful eyes of Cecil would allow nothing to slip by that might in any way be detrimental to the interests of Granada, or of Sidney Bernstein. To some degree this was also now true of labour relations, where he had begun to leave the conduct of affairs to Cecil and myself. Only when there was a major threat to the profitability of Television did the urge to intervene become irresistible, as when in 1979 ITV suffered the most damaging strike in its history. Union power was at its zenith. Pay restrictions had led to all manner of phoney productivity deals. When these were lifted, the dam burst and the ACTT came forward with an opening bid for a pay increase of 50 per cent over two years. The strike which followed lasted for seven weeks and ended in an ignominious climb-down by management.

Julian Amyes had now left Granada to become a freelance director. This was without doubt the right decision for him, for he was much in demand by both ITV and BBC and continued to direct brilliantly and happily until his death in 1992, but it was a great loss to me. His place in labour relations had been taken by Andrew Quinn, a long-time Granada manager noted for his great ability coupled with a high degree of caution, who much later briefly succeeded David Plowright as Chief Executive. At this time he was the quiet and efficient General Manager, supreme within his own territory but when called in to take gunpoint decisions on programme matters prone to examine each case so deliberately as to earn the title of Stopper Quinn. He was at the centre of affairs during the turmoil of 1979, and it was through no fault of his that the strike, which cost the industry dearly and incidentally imperilled the very existence of *Brideshead Revisited*, went on so long or ended so badly. It was the old story of brave talk in the boardrooms ('time for a showdown') giving way in due course to panic in the face of unacceptable losses and a final scramble for the best deal that could be got.

Sidney was understandably appalled by the abysmal performance of the company managements in settling the strike. It was no good telling him that Granada had taken the right line but had been overwhelmed by the lemming-like final rush of the other companies to reach a deal at any price. I was subjected to an hour-long telephone harangue in which the two main themes were Granada's poor communications – our failure to talk directly and frankly to our staff (Sidney could never understand that letters sent to union members at home, so bypassing the shop stewards, were counter-productive) – and secondly that loyalty to the company had disappeared, now the staff looked only to the unions and this allowed them to run the whole show. I sent him a memo, of which the following are extracts:

So what about communications? I can only quote a newspaper manager's reply to this most trite of all labour relations questions. 'Much too good' – and it is true of the communications business that unions often get information as soon as, or before, management. Communications cannot mean telling all of the truth all of the time, otherwise we would see many more management messages on the following lines: 'We are glad to report 50 per cent rise in profits but sorry to tell you that not a penny of this will be passed on in increased salaries because we want to give a healthy dollop to the shareholders in order to increase our stock exchange rating and put us in a better position to take over rather an interesting little company which, if we are successful, will in fact mean that most of you will be out of a job. We thought you should know this.'

Are television management methods out of date? Perhaps they are, but then what about the unions' methods? I can reflect on earlier times when one could say with some truth that television managements got the unions they deserved. Last summer, as I observed managements driven to actions outside their usual character, it seemed perhaps now unions were getting the managements they deserved, and not liking it much.

A union member has at least three faces. At a shop meeting he is a member of the Trades Union Movement, at pains to show, above all, solidarity. This, so far as we have one in our studio, is the first article of faith. He is a different fellow, however, working in his management relationship. He is good at his job; he likes his manager; his manager likes him. It is a good relationship. Third, although it should perhaps be first, is his private persona, the person he is in his home and with friends and family where he will show his true attitude to life and work. The man who is a happy man is consistent in all three compartments of his life, except in times of industrial strife when he is not so happy. There is no choice open to him: he must support the union. Even if he thinks they are wrong he can only vote against in a safe protest vote. In a shop of 100, it is comfortable to vote against in a minority of 30. Once the margin gets below 10, a vote against the motion can be a vote against solidarity. Most female union members, by contrast, have only one face. A campaigning woman is much the same at breakfast, in the manager's offices or at a shop meeting. This does not necessarily mean that women are superior to men but that men have learned from centuries of industrial conflict how to live in different camps at the same time.

Management is usually only two-faced, one the outward-looking visage confronting the union, the press and the rest of the world, and the other seen only within executive territory and at home.

This was to be the last of our exchanges on labour relations, and from now on, whatever other hazards might lie ahead in the unending struggle with the unions, a sudden and imperious intervention from Golden Square was not one of them.

Despite the pressure of affairs of management, labour relations and television industry, I still kept a few pet projects under my hand. One of them was *Disappearing World*. Some twenty years earlier, whilst still at the Film Institute, I had seen the silent film *Grass*, made in 1925 by Ernest B. Schoedsack and Merian C. Cooper, covering the transhumance of the sheep and cattle of a nomadic tribe in Iran. The image of a whole community moving several hundred miles, and especially the scenes of hordes of animals attempting to swim across rivers swollen with flood waters while their owners in rafts of inflated ox skins desperately try to round them up, came to be fixed in my memory. At the Institute we used to share out the agreeable chore of putting a music track to silent films before showing them in the National Film Theatre, and I laid my finger on *Grass* and gave it a score made up from the music of Smetana. To this day his tone-poem *Moldlau* conjures up before my eyes hordes of animals swimming against the tide.

It struck me that here was a priceless record of the way of life of a tribal society that soon would disappear for ever. I got in touch with the great anthropologist and film-maker Jean Rouch at the Musée de L'Homme in Paris with the thought of setting up an archive of films recording tribal life, and had I stayed at the Institute a little longer I have no doubt that something would have come of it.

Years passed and one day in Golden Square a young man with exceptionally bright blue eyes, Brian Moser, walked into my office. He was a budding anthropologist and an adventurer and he showed me a film of an expedition he had led up one of the tributaries of the Orinoco, then over the watershed by porterage to join a feeder of the Amazon. The technical quality was amateur but the content was stunning. I persuaded Brian to join Granada with the long-term aim of making a series of anthropological films, on condition that he first learnt his trade by doing a spell on *World in Action*. This held things up, for Brian, being an enthusiast in anything he undertook, became committed to *World in Action* and wanted to do nothing else. There was an episode in South Africa when one night he had heard village women ululating for the death of Verwoerd (goodness knows why they should have found this a matter for regret), and since he had no lights he very sensibly paid them a small sum to repeat the performance in daylight, a transaction which caused the South African police, suspecting some media skulduggery, to clap him in jail. It was not easy to prise him away from such adventures and back to his destined task, but it was done, and he set off on several consecutive expeditions to central South America, sometimes accompanied by his wife, also an anthropologist, with their baby slung papoose-style on her back. The material he brought back was pure gold and his first three films (*The Last of the Cuiva, The End of the Road* and *The Wars of the Gods*) laid the foundation for a series which today numbers some fifty titles, many of them documenting tribal practices which would otherwise already have passed into oblivion. Leslie Woodhead, one of the great contributors to the series, some ten years after he had made his famous study of the Masai in East Africa, returned and played the original material back to them. They were in no way thrown by seeing themselves on the screen, but tribal life could never again be quite the same.

Over the years that *Disappearing World* was being produced I had a hard time in holding the directors to the original brief. They longed to extend the series to cover peasant life, the shanty towns surrounding the great cities of Latin America and picturesque semi-industrialised Eskimo communities. Later, when I had moved on to other things, the brief was relaxed because it was alleged that there were no more primitive societies left. Nevertheless I would class *Disappearing World*, along with *Jewel in the Crown* and *Brideshead Revisited*, as one of the three more lasting monuments that Granada contributed to television in the 1970s and 80s.

The series *Family at War* was a more ephemeral affair. It was first suggested by John Finch, one of the lead writers of *Coronation Street*, as a short series covering the life and adventures of a Liverpool family throughout World War II. But I saw it as a long-runner, and we had the greatest satisfaction in spinning out the yarn to some fifty one-hour episodes. This show was on a homely scale, well cast, shot in four days – two in the studios and two on location – and it cost £12,500 per episode, even in those days something of a miracle. Jonathan Powell, later to become a great figure in television drama, then a newly graduated production trainee, was assigned as second writer. John would delegate to him the task of writing the odd script, and when the draft came in he would look at it and say, 'I'd like to make one or two amendments', and take it away. A week later he would reappear with an entirely new script. This was not egoism but simply writer's itch. John likes writing, and if offered an hour of television time he would fill it, regardless that someone else had already done so. Jonathan, a good-natured fellow, put up with successive disappointments with great patience and was rewarded by getting one half of a whole show entirely written by himself on the air before the series ended.

Family at War was a success at home and a smash hit in Sweden, where it regularly came number one in the ratings under the title *The Family Ashton*. We were all puzzled by this and could only conclude that as neutrals throughout the conflict the Swedes got a vicarious buzz from watching the horrors of the war they never had. *Family at War* was an example of one of the prime rules of television drama – that with a good script and a good cast there is no need to spend money on anything else. Cecil, who loved a copper-bottomed success, especially when it cost so little, was heartbroken when we reached the end of the road and pleaded with us to make at least another thirteen episodes. But John and I were adamant. To lead the Family into peace-time would be an anticlimax, and Cecil had to lump it.

Another of my pets was *Adam Smith*, a half-hour drama series designed for the God-slot on Sunday evenings. The title came from the Christian name of my father and of many Formans before him, most of them ministers in the Church of Scotland, and from the surname of my mother's family who similarly had generously supplied the kirk with divines. The story was set in a Scottish country parish, and Adam's faith came to be tested by encounters with the modern world which caused him to wonder whether there might be a more rational explanation of the affairs of the universe than were to be found in Christianity. But the churchmen who watched over Independent Television's religious programmes became uneasy, and after a run of thirty-nine episodes it seemed wise to terminate the programme before Adam became an out-and-out atheist. The series was notable for an outstanding early performance as a country doctor by Tom Conti, clearly a star in the making, and for scripts, written under assumed names, by James McTaggart and Trevor Griffiths, two of the leading scriptwriters of the day.

A much more ambitious exercise was the translation of the format used by the Harvard Law School for instruction, and known as 'a Hypothetical', from the lecture room to the television screen. I had known Fred Friendly for many years, first as a colleague of Ed Murrow and later as head of news and current affairs at CBS. Now, as a visiting professor at Columbia University, he invited me to Santa

Barbara to witness a 'Hypothetical' on the ethics of press journalism sponsored by the *Los Angeles Times*. I saw a skilled Harvard moderator quizzing the leading journalists of the day about hypothetical situations which step by step became more fraught and more testing. Most of the victims began by acting a part, but as the pressure mounted the inquisitor began to induce in them the illusion of reality. I persuaded Fred and the *Sunday Times* to mount a similar evening in England, and as I sat watching the 'Hypothetical' I suddenly saw its potential for television. At first Fred was sceptical, but we persuaded him to give it a try.

So he and Brian Lapping together produced the first in a long series of 'Hypotheticals' that served Granada well over a span of some eight years. Viewers got considerable pleasure from seeing politicians, civil servants, captains of industry and journalists pushed remorselessly against the wire by the moderator as they groped with a nightmare-like succession of problems. No skilled television techniques could save them now, for life in a 'Hypothetical' was real and made each participant unwittingly display what manner of man or woman they were. Latterly the series owed its success as much to Brian, a brilliant producer, as it did to Harvard. He trained several British QCs and others as moderators but none, it must be admitted, ever matched the skill of the old American masters.

A series which was to run into trouble with Sidney (as has been recounted), the Authority and once again the Religious Advisers was *The Christians*. I had the notion that it would be an interesting adventure to produce a history of Christianity that was, as far as it could be, objective. Christianity would not be treated as if it were the only true religion; indeed the series would not be on the side of Christianity, nor would it be against it. The civilising influence of the Christian ethic over the centuries would be placed alongside the catalogue of war, political intrigue and torture which had been motivated by a belief in Christianity. My partner in this enterprise was Bamber Gascoigne, well-known as the dean and quiz-master of *University Challenge*. Working with Bamber was pure joy. At Eton, I believe, he had been known as a swot, a derogatory word used by stupid boys for their more scholarly schoolmates, and Bamber was indeed a scholar, with a scholar's mind and a scholar's appetite for knowledge. He had an astoundingly retentive memory and his curiosity in the study of history, particularly for the bizarre and the outré, was far beyond the ordinary. He was the ideal person to write the script and to present the series on the screen. I recall discussing with him one evening the problem of some recalcitrant episode, I think on the Borgias. We agreed that the structure was wrong, that we would have to scrap the script as it stood and start all over again. It was about 7.30 when Bamber picked up his papers and went off to his hotel, as I thought for dinner. Next morning when I came down to my office at about 8.15 there was a neatly typed new script lying on my blotting pad. I read it through quickly. It was a completely fresh piece of work and exactly what we wanted.

The Christians was not of course designed for the Sunday 'closed period', but because of its quasi-religious nature we thought it wise to seek the support of Robert Runcie, the chairman of the committee that advised the Authority on religious affairs. This he gave in full measure when the programmes, as we had anticipated, caused alarm and some dismay amongst the good churchmen of all denominations who had been expecting the usual bland treatment of the Christian story. We also had the backing of Brian Young, another committed Christian, and between the two of them we rode the rough water with ease.

The industry as a whole found Brian to be schoolmasterly and somewhat unsupportive of their business interests. I did not. For me he was a doughty sparring partner who cared about the quality of the television service he controlled, and this was rare. It was even more unusual to have a Director General of the IBA who, when overcome by boredom in a meeting, would while away the time by writing Latin verses.

When, in the mid-70s, Bert Aylestone was succeeded as Chairman of the Authority by Bridget Plowden, more famous for crusading in the cause of gypsies and small children than for her worldly wisdom, she became in industry parlance the headmistress to complement Brian's headmaster. It is true that in business affairs they were a couple of innocents. I remember once, when pointing out that one of their high-principled schemes would put the companies into the red, one of them replied, 'Well, you have been making good profits over the past years, you could surely stand a small loss now.' And yet Brian slowly built a good rapport with the senior figures in the industry, and only occasionally did their uneasiness with his grand manner and superior intellectual powers show above the surface. Mainly to amuse Sidney, I made a diary note of one such occasion:

> Scene: The Royal Television Society dinner in the majestic 15th-century hall of King's College. Seated round the NE corner of the top table are Huw Wheldon, Helen Forman, DF, Brian Young and Hugh Cudlipp. Cudlipp

arrives late and launches into matters at once.

Cudlipp: Bloody good coverage of the TUC this week, Denis. (To Young) You don't know how lucky you are, Brian. If it hadn't been for Sidney Bernstein independent television would never have been taken seriously.

Young: We all know that, Hugh, but don't say it *in front of Denis*. It's bad for Granada to get so much praise.

Cudlipp: Well, it's true and you know it's true and all you do is harass them. Why should a big handsome upper-class man like you walk in and mess about with television?

Young: Well, I see all the companies as complementary. ATV, for instance, provides the show-biz.

Cudlipp: ATV provides crap.

Young: But that's disloyal, Hugh.

Cudlipp: I don't care what it is, but it's the case. ATV provides crap from America and crap squared from Elstree. And you just sit there with your big handsome face and say the companies are complementary or some such balls.

DF (desperate): Stop it, Hugh. One thing you must give Brian credit for – he takes decisions on the basis of what he thinks is right. You can't say that for most.

Young: Thank you, Denis, thank you . . .

(Conversation more general: everyone preoccupied by attempting to chip a mouthful off their partridge, as hard as any stone.) Later:

Cudlipp: Mind you, Brian, if I was in your job I would be a lot tougher, but about important things like violence. I would be really tough. I'd get my Managing Directors around me and say to them, 'Now, you buggers, listen to me!' I'd soon get them to take my line.

Young: But you are a director of ATV. Why don't you take that line there?

Cudlipp: You must be crazy. Do you think an outside director of ATV has the slightest influence on Lew? You have far more influence than I do because you speak posh and you're big and handsome, and I'm not.

But nothing could daunt Brian and he steamed steadily on his course unperturbed by the slings and arrows of such as Hugh Cudlipp.

Gradually the managing directors came to see that the moral authority he gave to ITV was their greatest asset, and I recall that at his
retirement party in 1982 there was a demonstration of respect and
affection for him from all the company principals, the like of which
I had seldom seen.

All the other ITV companies had non-executive directors on their
boards, often representing minority shareholders, as Hugh Cudlipp
represented the *Daily Mirror* interest in ATV, or else appointed in the
belief that the wisdom and experience of some disinterested outsider
would help to keep the executive directors on the straight and
narrow. Granada Television was a wholly owned subsidiary of
Granada Group and therefore had no minority interests, and since we
felt we had an adequate supply of wisdom and experience amongst
ourselves we had no non-executive directors. Then in the later 1960s
the Authority began to press us to remedy this lack. Such men, they
thought, by bringing their balanced judgement and wider experience
of the world to the board, would help to moderate Granada's
excesses, and when it came to a row with the Authority were more
likely to support their view than that of Granada's tearaway lefty
programme-makers.

We resented this attempt to intrude into our private affairs.
Initially the Television board had been made up of Sidney, Cecil, Joe
Warton and Victor Peers, plus one or two cronies left over from
Theatre days. Then I had joined the family party and the cronies had
gone. We were perfectly content with the status quo. On one occasion Sidney had invited Peter Brook, whom we all admired as a
producer, to join us as a non-executive director, but this was not a
success. Sidney's gesture had been partly because he felt that the
director's fee might help Peter to spend more time on experimental
work in the theatre. Perhaps it did, and perhaps because it did Peter
seldom seemed able to attend board meetings. After a year or more
had passed, the more protocol-minded members of the board insisted
that Peter should be asked to stand down. Sidney reluctantly agreed
and cavalierly delegated to me the disagreeable task of imparting this
news, which was received explosively.

But by 1969 persuasion gave way to instruction. We were *ordered*
to appoint two non-executive directors, but the Authority had overlooked one thing. It was an absolute rule in Granada that programme
matters were never discussed at the Television board. This was left to
the Programme Committee, who were largely the same people wearing a different hat. So non-execs would sit at the board table somewhat bemused whilst the Granada in-group swept through at light-

ning speed an agenda that was concerned only with administrative matters, indulging freely in family arguments conducted in the family jargon which must often have been well-nigh unintelligible to an outsider.

There were some exceptions, of whom latterly Simon Towneley, then the Lord Lieutenant of Lancashire, was one. He became a stalwart champion in protecting our interests in the North. Another was my old wartime friend Paul Bryan, who figured extensively in my earlier book *To Reason Why*. I thought Paul would make an ideal non-executive director for Granada Television and arranged for Sidney to see him – although I did have qualms. No two men could be more different in temperament, background and lifestyle: Paul, public school, Cambridge, a rugby footballer, a brilliant wartime soldier, now a Conservative MP and a gentlemanly businessman in Yorkshire; and Sidney, second-generation Latvian immigrant made good, a showman and a socialist. I need not have worried. Sidney instantly recognised Paul's qualities, and Paul, although slightly overwhelmed by the first encounter, was to become one of Sidney's greatest admirers.

But there was a snag. No sooner had Paul accepted a seat on the Television board than he was appointed shadow Postmaster General by Ted Heath. The two roles clearly conflicted, and sadly we had to accept that Paul would have to fade from the Television scene. To my surprise, Sidney immediately invited him to join the Television Rental board and later the board of Granada Theatres. There was no obvious role for Paul in either of these companies, and when he asked Sidney what his contribution to the Theatre company might be, Sidney replied, 'I think the bingo operation needs tightening up a bit', and Paul left the room wondering how a non-executive Yorkshire clothier could effectively tighten up the administration of some forty or fifty bingo halls scattered across the country.

The truth is that Sidney's instinct, accurate as ever, told him that Paul was not only a *persona Granada* but a valuable scout to watch over Granada's interests in the regions, a freelance personnel officer and a point of contact for the Group at Westminster. Paul quickly became an invaluable counsellor and friend to half the companies in the Group and formed, along with Don Harker and myself, a triumvirate with a better insider knowledge of the political scene than any other television company, and, I suspect, most newspapers. Later, Paul served as a Whip in Heath's Conservative government, but by 1974 he had shed all political office and at last could join the Television board, where our happy partnership was given a fresh lease of life. On one occasion Brian Young sidled up to Paul and began to quiz him on how it could be that, as a director of Granada with Conservative affiliations, he could live easily within a company which produced such markedly left-wing programmes, in particular *World in Action*. He got no change from Paul, who instantly reported this episode to me. And so, in the course of a conversation with Brian, I was able to drop in a casual aside about his lobbying a Granada non-executive director behind my back. After that I do not think that there were any approaches made to Paul or to any other of our non-executives.

Sidney's friendship with Paul was important to him for another reason. He felt that all over the Group new managements were trying to take away from him the companies which he had ruled over for so long with absolute dominion. In Television Rental, by far the biggest company, Alex had introduced a new deck of senior executives, and although they were known to Sidney and in many cases – but not all – liked by him, they were Alex's men, not his. Publishing had been taken over by Bob Carr; the Theatre company, of which he had once known every root and branch, although still run by an old Granada man now consisted of a string of bingo halls each run by a stranger. Alex had set up a Group Services company, manned, as far as Sidney was concerned, by men from Mars. So Sidney treasured more and more his relationship with old Granada hands who would keep him abreast of what was going on inside Granada and, with non-executive directors such as Mark Littman on the Group board and Paul Bryan in Television (and with continuing contact with Rental and Theatres), could give him some insight – and often much-needed reassurance – about how things were going at the top.

CHAPTER ELEVEN

Despite the widening rift between Sidney and myself over management of Television I had no feeling of excommunication. From time to time sunshine broke through and we were back in our old relationship, discovering a new film, dashing off to a first night together or calling each other to compare notes on the latest big event in politics. Shortly after he had given up as chairman of Television he set up a fellowship in music at Edinburgh University in my name. As an amateur musicologist I found this embarrassing, and he was a little miffed when I asked if I might change the title to that of my aunt Jean Turnbull Forman, who had read music in Edinburgh and became an assistant to the great Professor Tovey. And in 1975, on the twenty-first anniversary of my joining Granada, Sidney phoned Helen and asked what I would like as a twenty-first birthday present. Without hesitation she replied, 'The piano in the flat in Manchester'. Sidney responded nobly to this outrageous request, and on the anniversary of the day I joined Granada a Bluthner grand piano appeared outside the French windows of our new home, The Mill House. I sent Sidney, who was in Italy, a cable:

> Twenty-one thousand thanks for the magnificent Bluthner. The secret was kept piano but I send my thanks forte. I am quite delighted to have the best domestic piano I have encountered in our drawing room. What do the really long-serving members get after 50 years service? A private orchestra?

And out of the blue and only shortly after my curt dismissal as family trustee, I received a letter from Sidney asking me to be an executor of his will. I pondered this for some time and decided that it would be too much of a responsibility. I wrote to Sidney in the friendliest terms saying that I was really too old for the job since he might well live longer than I. He replied:

> I didn't answer your letter about being an executor of my will before this because I was searching for a logical argument that I could put to you that might help to change your mind. I can't find one. I overlooked your age when I approached you. You do not – to me – look any older than when we first started in television.
>
> I have to search for a 'young' Denis – or accept that there is no such person. Again thanks for the many years of friendship from you and Helen.
>
> Your older friend,
Sidney

But such flashbacks to old friendship became ever more occasional. I have recalled how Sidney, wrongly assuming that a hernia operation imperilled his life, had rashly appointed three of us to be Joint Managing Directors of the Group. Now, nearly ten years later, he wrote:

> Despite the fact that you are now Executive Chairman of Granada Television, you are still (for some reasons not now clear) a Managing Director of the Group based on a resolution passed in 1968.
>
> I think it would be more practical if you, as the Executive Chairman of a major subsidiary, ceased to be Managing Director of a Group based upon an out of date idea we had nearly 10 years ago.
>
> I therefore ask that you resign as a Managing Director of Group and I hope that you will agree.

To which I replied:

> I remember the circumstances when three of the Group Board were appointed Managing Directors and agree that things have changed a lot since then. I have no objection to dropping a title which means little and is never used but would like to know who the present officers of the Group actually are and what is proposed for the future.

Sidney replied inaccurately and vaguely: 'Good point. Joe and Alex *were* also joint MDs. Only MDs left are Cecil and myself appointed, I think, 1949. Future unknown.'

The third Managing Director who had been appointed with Alex and myself was not Joe but Brian Wolfson. Nobody else seemed to know that Sidney and Cecil were joint Managing Directors of the Group. It was clear that Sidney was anxious to avoid defining the status of Alex. I had no ambitions for office in the Group. I was happy to continue as Chairman of Television, but only if I could work on programmes at the same time. I wrote an unusually long memo to Sidney, from which the following are extracts:

> You have kindly said that you would like me to stay on as Chairman of Granada Television as long as I wish (though I must remind you that at the age of 70 this is no longer a matter of choice). It would seem to be only civil to offer some indication of my thoughts about the future.
>
> As I have said to you on frequent occasions, I have been carrying the can for long enough. Indeed, I have been carrying the bloody can all my life, in the Army, at the Film Institute, and in Granada for 25 years – and this despite a lasting conviction that I should be, and am always shortly about to become, a producer, a director, a writer. Indeed last year, at the age of 62, when I should have been turning my attention to Mozart's wind serenades, what was I doing? Carrying the can vis-à-vis British Steel and the contract renewal. To illustrate this anti-can mood I will remind you that the IBA offered me the Chairmanship of the Fourth channel, which has in a way been my baby for nearly a decade. This was an empty invitation in that Granada was on the run-up to the franchise renewal, but even if it had been a free choice, I would not have wanted it.
>
> I would like to get back to production. Specifically I would like to produce *The Raj Quartet* and to set up the *History of Music* as General Editor (always assuming we go forward with these projects). Both items could be very fine. I believe that *The Raj* is the greatest long novel of the century, and the *History of Music* could carry into the new software age something of the magic that Walter Legge brought through to the age of the LP. If it was thought that I could and should continue as Chairman, alongside these responsibilities, I would gladly do so.
>
> Travel. Time is slipping by and whereas we know that

Robert Mayer went round the world at 101, he did it in a wheelchair and I want to go when I can still ride a yak. The Caucasus, the Andes, Australia, China, Mongolia. This must be a private enterprise, and if travel schedules inflate the statutory quota of holidays by a week or so I hope this can be regarded as a counterweight to those early years in television when holidays were short and often at the end of a phone.

Which leads me to the last point. We know that inflation has halved the value of the pound in five years. Is this going on? I think, thanks to my Granada shares, I shall be all right for money. But I recall Sundays in the early fifties which I spent walking round the garden trying to decide how to fend off the garage so that we could still have credit with the grocer. I never want that again. I end on this note because it would be foolish to imply that money is not a factor in choosing a path through the future.

Before following up the story of *Jewel in the Crown* is may be amusing to give some account of my treatment by Granada in the matter of pay. Throughout my long Granada years I never asked for a rise, save once. When I joined in 1955 my salary was £3,000 a year. By 1962, when I joined the board of Television, it was £7,750. In 1964 I was appointed to the Group Board and in 1965 became Joint Managing Director of Television with a salary of £11,600. In 1966 it went up to £15,000, or rather I thought it had until I received the following note from Joe:

> The Board has decided to reduce your salary by £1,000 from £15,000 to £14,000 with effect from 1st October 1966. I look forward to receiving your acceptance of these terms in due course.

Since I was a member of the board and I had heard nothing about a salary cut, I sought out Joe in his lair in Golden Square and brandished the letter in front of him. 'No need to worry about that, old lad,' he said. 'It's just an adjustment I had to make to your Top Hat.' Top Hat was an obscure form of top persons' pension which none of us understood and which in those days seemed about as remote from reality as the National Debt, but it was a perk, and those, for Granada executives, were rare indeed. In 1967 I sent a rather pathetic memo to Joe:

I have been in the habit of paying a number of expenses incurred on behalf of Granada out of my own pocket. This partly out of a vague desire to set an example, partly out of laziness, partly to avoid any possibility of embarrassing colleagues by claiming for items which they do not.

I really must be fairer to myself. I list below certain items for your consideration.

Definitely Granada expenses:

a) Entertainment at Little Garnetts on behalf of Granada:
Examples:
Tom Mayer – Managing Director Production Division, Marconi.
Ed Saxe – CBS Vice President.
Mr and Mrs Alexandrov – advised on *Ten Days That Shook the World*.

b) Visits to theatres including opera and ballet. I have seldom availed myself of free tickets and often entertain a party.

c) Meals outside with senior staff where their future is under discussion. Generally on a scale which I would not authorise for others.

d) Overnight stays for my wife and self in London caused by business.

Marginal cases – We entertain on a substantial scale at Little Garnetts and some of the guests are invited because of television interests, and, conversely, only accept because of my position in television. Largely, however, it is a matter of keeping in touch with the world, which is part of my job. Some recent examples:

Nikki Kaldor – Government Adviser on economics.
Andrew Carnworth – partner in Barings.
Albert Sloman – Vice Chancellor of Essex University.
Kenneth Robinson – Minister of Health.
Viscount Caldecott – Director of EE.
Lady Plummer – member of ITA.
Lord Sainsbury – head of the firm.

A dinner party for 12 can cost £35. I would suggest it would be proper to charge at least a proportion of such entertaining.

★

Joe's reply is not recorded, but as I recall it all marginals were out, as were overnights in London. The other items were acknowledged as unavoidable Granada expenses, but so grudgingly as to make one feel like a petty criminal For some regrettable reason, in the matter of pay and perks I felt an obligation to set an example to others in the interests of keeping costs down, for the size of the salary bill was a major factor in the profitability of a television company. Not only did Granada employ fewer people than the other majors but, above Union grades, we paid up to 20 per cent less. I would tell producers or directors who were considering joining us that to concede so little for the privilege of working for Granada was a bargain, and I honestly do not think we ever lost a talent that we really wanted over money. In addition to keeping my salary and expenses down, the furnishing of my office was spartan. For over twenty-five years I sat in the same battered chair behind a plain desk – for the rest there was a table and a dozen hard-arse chairs. The pictures were on loan from the Civic Art Gallery. I always ate in the canteen except on days of over-lunch meetings, and dined in the flat. Drink was consumed in considerable quantities but never in the office. My family, and especially Helen, thought this high-minded stuff was simply lunatic and perhaps it was, but my eccentric behaviour did help to keep salaries down and was a huge asset when negotiating with the unions. And no one dared to furnish their office on more than a utility level.

By the time of the 1967 television franchise renewal my salary was still £14,000, and once the contract was secured I asked to see Sidney and Cecil together. During the run-up to the contract, I told them, all three other major companies had made me an offer to join them, and two of them had mentioned a salary of roughly 50 per cent more than I got from Granada; there had also been talk of shares. I had also been approached by two of the larger Regionals. Of course my loyalty to Granada never wavered but I suggested that there might be something here that they would like to think about. Think about it they did. My salary went up to £17,000 and they would present me with £30,000 worth of Granada shares, although they were not exactly for me but were put in a trust for my sons. This cautious move was prompted by what had happened some ten years earlier when Sidney and Cecil had sanctioned a modest distribution of shares to the senior workers in Television, nearly all of whom were young married couples, many of them starting a family. Nearly all of us cashed in our shares at once in order to buy a house, including myself. Sidney and Cecil were chagrined: they had given the shares to have and to hold. It was a sort of sacred trust. By selling the shares those employees had broken that trust and shown no confidence in Granada's future. The brothers were, of course, right in that had we all clung on to our Granada shares we would today be seriously rich. What they could not understand was that at a certain stage in life the urge to own a family house comes before everything else, including such matters as prudent financial management, loyalty to Granada or the distant prospect of untold wealth.

The 1967 offer of shares I accepted gratefully and duly put them in trust. When I became Chairman of Television in 1974 my salary had risen to £24,250 and some share options were granted. During the late 1970s the Top Hat contributions were added to my salary. What had happened to all the Top Hats that had floated down the river for me for twenty years I never quite discovered. Then, after Alex took over the Group, my salary advanced to a more realistic level, although when I was both Chairman of Television and Deputy Chairman of the Group my salary still appeared to the outside world to be comparatively on the low side, as evidenced in an article in the *Manchester Evening News* of 3 February 1986, in which Keith McDonald wrote:

THE MONEY THEY MAKE

Piccadilly Radio boss Colin Walters is in the same pay bracket as Granada Television's long-service chairman Sir Denis Forman, according to a new survey of salaries in broadcasting.

Walters, managing director and chief executive of the Manchester radio station earns '£50,000-plus' said *Broadcast* magazine's annual round-up of who gets paid what in the industry.

Sir Denis – presumably as Granada's 'highest paid director' – earns £57,000 a year. In fact, as William Phillips, who compiled the report, writes: 'The going rate for an ITV chief is £50,000–£70,000 with Granada's Sir Denis Forman continuing to set a lonely example of restraint.'

Bryan Cowgill, who last year left Thames TV, where he was managing director, after a row about his poaching of the *Dallas* serial from BBC, was ITV's top earner in 1984–5 with £87,000.

But the breakfast TV company TV-AM paid Kerry Packer's Consolidated Press £90,000 for the services of

Bruce Gyngell, which implicitly makes him broadcasting's best-paid employee.

Seeking to take full advantage of this piece I sent it to a number of colleagues with the following covering note:

> No doubt you paid particular attention to the reference to myself in the attached piece under the byline of Keith Mcdonald (admittedly my nephew) in the *Manchester Evening News*.
>
> I suggest to you that it might improve morale considerably throughout the company if this clipping were blown up, framed and hung in every office, where it would replace the few remaining Barnums and set new standards for recently joined staff.
>
> I would welcome your observation on this suggestion.
>
> PS: Do you think the staff would respond to an appeal for a collection to finance my summer holiday?

To which Barrie Heads replied:

> Indeed, sir, all of us have been much taken by the example set by you to us all and reported in the public prints. I believe I can speak for all when I say that your modest suggestion for some sort of preliminary canonisation is long overdue.
>
> I have already had installed in the offices of Granada International a life-size facsimile of your good self. It is in the full-dress uniform of an officer of the Argyll and Sutherland Highlanders, as equipped for the Battle of Malplaquet, and stands in a glass case under a tasteful spotlight. The staff welcomed, with some enthusiasm, the introduction of a daily ceremony in which they file past the case, saluting or curtsying as appropriate.
>
> For the time being, and until I hear further about your proposals, I hope you will accept the enclosed postage stamp as a small heartfelt gesture.

And David Plowright:

> I'm afraid I must resist your appeal to fund your summer holiday on the following grounds:

1. *Broadcast*'s and Keith McDonald's article was out of date; salaries quoted as far as Granada was concerned referred to 79/80.
2. It is well known that you travel extensively and in a manner appropriate to your station
and
3. You frequently shoot helpless animals.

I suggest that any funds that materialise from this selfish appeal should be passed on to the other ranks' mess for their annual sunshine coach outing to Blackpool.

David was right: my salary by February 1986 had risen to the giddy heights of £80,000.

Only occasionally did I feel any resentment that my elders and seniors should take my contribution to Granada for granted without considering that there was any relationship between my workload and the matter of pay. In any closed community the clichés go by fashion, and there was a time when Sidney frequently used the expression 'to use your good offices' when politely asking a person to undertake some task that lay outside his normal duties. This phrase caught on and in one week I had memos from Sidney, Cecil and Joe all beginning, 'I wonder whether you could use your good offices.' I cannot recall for what reasons my good offices were sought but it might well have been to advise the son of one of Sidney's American friends how to get into Oxford, to persuade some VIP to perform some function for Cecil at the Royal Command Performance, and to get tickets for the Cup Final for a party of Joe's friends.

Owing to building works at home I was going through a period of domestic poverty and felt a slight flash of resentment at my colleagues' assumption that my good offices were always there on tap. I therefore pinned copies of the three memos together, underlining the words 'good offices', and sent them to Sidney's home address together with the following poem:

I have lent my good offices from time to time
Now I come to think of it, very frequently.
Indeed my good offices have become
A public convenience.

There is a man who roams the world
Offering his good offices
To extinguish oil-well fires.

For money.
In considerable amounts.
Lord Goodman has excellent offices,
But he charges those who use them egregious fees
Per occasion
Even to put a foot across the doorstep.

I will not lend my good offices again free gratis.
I will put them up for hire.
To stop a strike
I will demand in recompense
Eleven Caucasian dancing girls.
For a tea lady plucked back
From wrongful dismissal
I shall require ten pounds of fragrant Dharput tea.
A milk-white Arab stallion will be exacted
From any director or producer or writer or anyone
Who occupies my offices with his
Conjugal complexities.
The most distinguished tenant
Of my good offices
Often abuses them most dreadfully.
He shouts orders at my beloved office manager
Who sits stunned with grief
And yet he continues to use my good offices
Again and again and again.

I will not lend my good offices any more.
I have decided
They will not be available at all
For any consideration.
I will withdraw
My good offices
And sit beneath a sycamore tree
In Tuscany, where
I will listen to diatonic music
And sip the smooth Soave.

What Sidney thought of this effusion I do not know. He may have
shown it to Cecil, or more likely to Joe Stone, his doctor brother-in-
law, perhaps seeking his views as to whether he should call in a
psychiatrist.

But soon I was to earn my pay, however inadequate it may have been, the hard way, for shortly after the 1979 strike Granada Television became involved in the most serious legal action in its history. In January 1980 the workers at British Steel were on strike. *World in Action* decided to cover the strike in a programme billed to go out in February 1980. In the course of its preparation they received an unsolicited gift of some 250 highly sensitive documents, including Board minutes from a source within British Steel whose only condition was that his identity should not be revealed. The documents showed conclusively that the case which the Board had presented to the unions and to the public was based upon statements that in many cases were untrue. They also indicated that the strike had been brought about by government pressure against the wishes of the British Steel management.

The team informed British Steel that we had confidential papers in our possession and sent them a draft script of the proposed programme. They invited the Chairman, Sir Charles Villiers, to do an interview in Manchester, which he accepted. The day after transmission of the programme the penny dropped, and British Steel filed an injunction requiring Granada to return the documents. We returned the documents but only after cutting off any marks that could identify the source. British Steel then sought a High Court order requiring us to name our source. The chips were down. The order was granted and subsequently served on David Plowright and myself. Granada's appeal was heard by three judges, amongst whom Lord Denning seemed to predominate. They found that the order against Granada should stand. We appealed to the House of Lords, who, in their good time, found against. David and I were now in an awkward position. If we revealed the name of the mole we would commit the greatest sin in the journalists' canon; if we did not we would incur an escalating fine and might go to prison. The press was loud in our support. 'The effect of the judgement is to give protection to those who may have something to hide contrary to the public interest,' said *The Times*. 'The courts have done a disservice to the cause of press freedom,' wrote the *Guardian*, while the *Mirror* advised that 'prison should be preferred to paralysis.'

David and I had many problems in the later stages of the hearing, not the least being from enterprising members of our staff who, wishing to share in the glory of martyrdom, would tell us darkly that they too had some knowledge of the identity of the mole. We did not believe them, and indeed could not afford to do so since our defence rested on the fact that the only person who could name the mole would not, on principle, pass the information on to us. We therefore told any Johnny-come-lately volunteer to shut up and go away just in case he might have had some crumb of real information.

As the crisis approached I spent hours with my friend and long-time adviser Arnold Goodman (who has given a full account of the mole affair in his autobiography, *Tell Them I'm on My Way*). Eventually the impasse was resolved by a stroke of luck. At the very moment of crisis Villiers retired as Chairman of the Steel board and was replaced by Ian MacGregor, a rough, tough Canadian who, in Arnold Goodman's words, 'realised that to conduct a war to the bitter end against a popular television company defending the public's right to know was not, from the point of view of sensible public relations, either wise or in the best interests of the Steel Corporation'.

By another stroke of luck Mark Littman, a leading QC, was at that time a director both of Granada Group and British Steel. Through his good offices a meeting was arranged between Arnold and the Corporation's legal advisers. This went well, and I was summoned at short notice to Arnold's flat in Portland Place. Here we went through his three-roomed conciliation routine, both parties meeting in one room, party A withdrawing when necessary to room two, party B to room three, with Arnold himself flitting from room to room. In the course of the day we reached agreement. The name of the mole would not be revealed, Granada would pay their own and British Steel's costs. We thought this to be a victory, albeit an expensive one, costing the company, as I remember it, a sum not unadjacent to £200,000.

It had been a tough time. To quote the Goodman biography:

> Granada was required to disclose the name of the 'mole' under pain of condign penalties, which if expressed in terms of a daily fine could have been financially damaging to the point of ruin. It is to Granada's great credit that at no time did it waver in its determination to fight the issue on grounds of public policy, or fail to give support to all the executives concerned.

The case left me in a state of suppressed fury over the general ineffi-ciency of the law and over its cavalier treatment of litigants. Many hours were spent in court in referring to precedents. These prece-dents were contained in up to two dozen books on the law which were brought into the court in a sort of wheelbarrow pushed by an aged verger-like figure. A pile of volumes would be placed in front of each judge, counsel and junior counsel before the case began. When on his feet counsel would ask M'Lud to refer to Houston on Tort, Johnston versus Johnston, page 367. The M'Luds would shuffle about amongst the books in front of them and on failing to find Houston on Tort would summon the verger. Sometimes the verger would find the book and hand it to the M'Luds. Sometimes he would scuffle about in the wheelbarrow and failing to find it there secure a copy from a junior counsel and deliver it to the bench. Then would begin what in artillery parlance would be called ranging on target. 'On page 267 I have Smith versus Jones,' M'Lud would say in some perplexity.

'Page 367 M'Lud,' counsel would reply.

'Samson versus Armstrong?' M'Lud would ask.

'Two pages further on M'Lud,' counsel would say.

'Ah, you meant to say Johnston versus Johnston,' would say M'Lud, on target at last, and after a minute or two of study he would raise his head and say, 'I do not see how this aspect of the law on Tort can be applicable to the case before us,' and a cosy little debate, much enjoyed by the lawyers, would ensue. I reflected that if the books were replaced by video screens and the verger by a technician in a control room punching up the required extract on cue, many costly hours of courtroom time would be saved. But this might not suit the best interests of the profession.

There were, however, two improvements that would give the client a fighting chance of keeping abreast of the case without in any way threatening counsel's pockets: first to mike the judges and counsel so that they were audible to one and all, and second to replace the short-hand writer with a bank of tape-recorders so that instead of having to wait several days to learn what had been said one could pick up a cassette of the day's proceedings on the way out of court.

The style of proceedings in the House of Lords showed an even greater contempt for the interests of the client. At one end of a long and lofty room, huddled around a long table, there were on the one side the law lords, looking like a bunch of beardless Father Christmases, and facing them one could see the black and bewigged behinds of a line of counsel who would carry on private conversations with their Lordships well out of earshot of the client, seated far away at the opposite end of the room.

Shortly after his retirement Lord Denning produced a volume of memoirs in which he said, in the debonair style that lawyers can adopt when dealing with matters of life and death, that in retrospect he thought he had reached the wrong decision in the matter of British Steel. Freedom of information was more important than discovery of the source. He should have found for Granada. Just after the book appeared I met Lord Denning at a party. He said, 'I think I owe Granada an apology.' It was no time for civilities and I replied, 'Yes, also £200,000 and compensation for several months of sleepless nights.' He was in no way thrown by this and continued to smile in the genial way of doctors when telling colleagues about some little mishap in the theatre which had terminal consequences for the patient.

Throughout the British Steel case Sidney, by now Group President, was supportive but fearful. Like all of us he dreaded the consequences of our contempt of court, which most certainly must lead to either a fine escalating daily until the burden became intolerable or the incarceration of two of his closest colleagues and friends. Perhaps it was an unworthy thought, but it crossed my mind that he might prefer the second option to the first.

It had always been an assumption throughout Granada that when the day came for Sidney to step down from the Chairmanship, Alex would take over. The question was, when? As Sidney reached his eightieth year there was still no sign that he could see any reason why he should vacate the chair he had occupied for some forty-five years. The relations between Alex and Sidney had always been somewhat distant. From the first Alex had accurately assessed Sidney's strengths and weaknesses. He recognised his drive and authority but often questioned his business judgement, and while acknowledging his ability as a manager on the spot he knew that this was not matched by the same ability to design any long-term strategy. There were many clashes of will between them, and neither was inclined to give way easily.

When it became clear that the video-player had a great future, Alex wanted to stock up with the new VHS machines quickly and on a substantial scale. Sidney opposed him: it was too early, we did not know if the VHS system would prevail, we should wait and see. Eventually, instead of several thousand some 600 machines were ordered. When they went like hot cakes there was a struggle to acquire enough machines to meet the demand. This was just one of many cases where Alex's judgement was right and Sidney's wrong. In these conflicts the Queensberry rules were meticulously observed, but civility on the surface masked the sharp displeasure of each of the contestants at the wilful stubbornness of the other.

Sidney treated Alex, as he reached the age of forty, as a young boy who needed constant guidance and correction. It was a form of negative nepotism: because Alex was his nephew and destined to be his successor he treated him more harshly than any other managing director. As a result Alex suffered more from Sidney's oppressive tendencies than I did. He could not treat Sidney as an equal, as I did, nor could he blow his top so easily, for he could not fall back on the bedrock of remembered friendship that allowed me a special licence.

Within the Bernstein family, and indeed within Granada itself, they treated each other with consideration and extremely good manners. Only rarely did Alex turn on Sidney in public, and when he did so it was a memorable event. One small incident lives in the memory. On a certain occasion in Manchester, Sidney had allowed a pre-lunch meeting to overrun by some forty-five minutes and at lunch had been faced with an unappetising plate of tepid roast beef. He held his plate out to the waitress and said, 'This meat is over-cooked and quite cold. Disgraceful. Take it away and bring me some cold ham.' When the meeting resumed upstairs, in the first moment of silence Alex turned to Sidney and said, 'Before the meeting starts I want to say that you were very rude to that girl. The lunch was spoiled because we were so late and that was your fault. I suggest you should apologise.' Sidney received this rebuke silently while the rest of us looked on with no little admiration for Alex.

Sidney never discussed Alex with me, whereas Alex and I frequently talked about Sidney. As first my Joint Managing Director and then Deputy Chairman in Television I got to know Alex well. Later, when he was Chairman of the Group, I was to become his Deputy Chairman. I found in him many of Sidney's qualities and many of those of his father, together with others they both lacked. But they were hidden beneath a cool exterior and often lay undiscovered except by those who knew him well. When the old triumvirate – Sidney, Cecil, Joe – were at their zenith their combined and complementary abilities made them a formidable management team. But none of them singly – not even Sidney – could have succeeded on his own, and none of them could have taken the Group through the decade of the 80s with such adroitness and certainty of touch as did Alex.

In the late 1970s, by reason of his slow withdrawal from the television scene, Sidney became less of a burden for me but more of a problem for Alex, now the Deputy Chairman of the Group. He would oppose new projects approved by Alex, sometimes with good reason but more often not; he would thwart new initiatives, and in existing businesses he would interfere endlessly. Alex began to wonder if the game was worth the candle. Many years earlier, with Leslie Waddington as his partner, he had set up the Waddington

Galleries. The world of contemporary art interested him. He was not short of money. He had no ambitions to become a captain of industry. Sidney was making his life within Granada well-nigh intolerable. Why should he put up with it?

One day Alex went to see Sidney and told him he had decided to leave Granada. At first Sidney was incredulous, but when Alex convinced him it was his true intention he went into a state of shock. No doubt there were immediate consultations with Cecil and Joe, and now Sidney received a second shock. Cecil took the view that Alex should be allowed to do what he wanted. If he wished to leave Granada, good enough, let him go. This led to what was only the second major disagreement between the brothers in a partnership of forty-five years, the first being over the Masons. Sidney's state of mind now moved from shock to panic. What had he done to deserve this terrible blow? What had made Alex reach such a perverse and disastrous decision? (The answer – that *he* had – I am sure never entered his mind.) Was the name of Bernstein to disappear from the Granada masthead? He would resign the Chairmanship rather than allow this to happen, not perhaps just yet but in the foreseeable future.

He called for Joe Warton and sent him to Alex as his plenipotentiary. Joe told Alex that in principle Sidney was prepared to resign. Alex said he was not interested. Joe reported back to Sidney, then went to see Alex again. Sidney was prepared to resign on a date in the near future to be agreed between them. Again Alex said nothing doing. Joe came a third time and said Sidney was prepared to resign now, at the end of the financial year, and would be satisfied with the honorary title of President. Well now, thought Alex, there must be something here.

So began a round of seemingly interminable negotiations, with Joe as the middleman. The President's powers, his right to attend board meetings, his expenses, his honorarium, his office, his perks, all were debated at one remove and in detail between Sidney and Alex, neither of whom was without considerable tenacity when it came to such important personal issues. At last the deal was done and on 9 July 1979 Sidney issued a statement to all shareholders. He would retire on 30 September. Alex would succeed him. He listed the achievements of the Group under his Chairmanship from its beginning in 1934 (capital and reserves £300,000, profit £31,500) to its present size and state of prosperity in 1979 (capital and reserves £102 million, profit £34 million) all of this in large type covering two pages, whereas an account of Alex's career in the Group was confined to a footnote in very small type.

An outsider reading this account might well assume that Alex's decision to resign was a ploy in the game to secure the Chairmanship, but with my knowledge of the parties concerned I am certain that Alex genuinely intended to leave Granada until he found, to his surprise, that Sidney was prepared to go at once.

As Granada's President, Sidney's attitude towards me changed noticeably. Some of the old warmth crept back into our exchange of memos and I began to drop in for a gossip to his office in Golden Square. This rapprochement was assisted by his reaction to two programmes – *Brideshead Revisited* and *The Jewel in the Crown*. I can take little credit for the success of *Brideshead*, which was due almost entirely to Derek Granger, the producer, staunchly supported by David Plowright. The only contribution I made was in finding at the rough-cut stage that the pace was too slow. I was only partly right about this, for part of *Brideshead*'s magic lies in its leisurely pace, but no doubt Derek, in his wisdom, took aboard only as much of my view as he thought fit.

I later became a player in the efforts to save the show when its existence was threatened by the ACTT strike of 1979. When work on *Brideshead* began again after the strike, the three leading actors – Jeremy Irons, Anthony Andrews and Diana Quick – had run out of contract. Their next engagements fell within the time needed to complete *Brideshead*, and this called for difficult and delicate negoti-ations. I shall always be grateful to all three for their patience and understanding, but especially to Jeremy Irons, who found himself in an impossible position. In Manchester, Derek was pleading with him to stay on the set and finish *Brideshead*, which he wanted to do, while at the same time Karel Reisz, phoning from London, insisted that he kept his commitment to *The French Lieutenant's Woman,* his first major film, which was due to start shooting. A somewhat troubled Jeremy came to my office in Golden Square. We spoke with both producers, and Karel, who luckily was an old friend and colleague from Film Institute days, agreed to juggle his schedule to allow Jeremy windows of two or three days at a time to work on *Brideshead*. Within an hour a deal was done leaving Jeremy (and myself) mightily relieved.

In 1979, when on holiday in Greece, I read Paul Scott's *Raj Quartet* and (to quote from my introduction to *The Making of The Jewel in the Crown*):

> The sun rose on Paul Scott's literary reputation when *Staying On* won the Booker Prize in 1977. Along with

thousands of others I read it with delight, and recognised that here was a natural for television. *Staying On* led me to *The Raj Quartet*, and immediately I was back in the India that I had known in the years before Independence. As I made my way through the labyrinthine narrative, it became clear that the Quartet was an epic story on the scale of *War and Peace*, introducing a galère of characters every bit as real as those in Tolsty's novel, and like them playing out their parts within a greater plot concerned with national politics and a world war. On second reading I wondered if the Quartet might be susceptible to television. The rights were free. It could be the chance of a lifetime.

Could it be done on television? The narrative was told in a form so complex as to make all the flashbackery of Conrad and Ford Madox Ford look like a children's game. The book was heavy with references to a political scene that was never familiar and today almost wholly forgotten by the Western world. At least four months' shooting in India would be needed, and no unit from the United Kingdom or America had at that time attempted anything on such a scale (Richard Attenborough's *Gandhi* was not shot until 1981).

It seemed sensible, indeed necessary, to do two things before committing Granada to such a major operation. First, we would make *Staying On* in Simla as a single play and so gain some experience to help us decide whether the logistics and cost of a lengthy shoot in a distant subcontinent were within our reach. Also, before recruiting a production team, we must be satisfied that it was possible to do justice to the Quartet if it were translated into the form of a television series.

Staying On, with Trevor Howard and Celia Johnson, was a hit. The logistics worked. This gave me the amber light for the Quartet and I set out to satisfy myself that the story could be adapted into its narrative form:

The first step was to arrange all the events in the story into chronological order, starting from the riots of 1942 and continuing until Guy Perron flew towards Delhi in the week of Independence in August 1947. It was not a simple task. Some incidents were told and retold a second and third time. There were no fewer than thirteen separate references to the rape, each one throwing some new emphasis or a different interpretation upon it. There were excursions off the main track (notably the opening tragic story of Miss Crane). There were a great number of direct references to the political scene. There were seven main geographical locations, and, worst of all, we lost our first hero and heroine, Hari Kumar and Daphne Manners, just as they had aroused our interest and engaged our sympathy.

The next move was to see how the chronological narrative would break down into sequences each of which would form a one-hour episode for the television screen. This was done by chopping a roll of wallpaper into thirteen segments about one yard square, pinning them round the walls of a room and writing down on each the outline of scenes for each episode. After walking some miles around this gallery, touching, retouching, shifting and deliberating, it did, at last, seem feasible that Paul Scott's great book could be made into a television series that would not betray the quality of the original work.

It seemed to work. Ken Taylor agreed to write the scripts and Christopher Morahan to produce, and in these two appointments the foundation for the success of the series was laid. As the scripts came in and Christopher assembled his team, we began to cast. Christopher, working with Doreen Jones, the head of Granada casting, took the lead. Doreen had already made a huge contribution to the success of Granada's drama over the years, and this was to be her finest hour. She was supported by Susie Bruffin and Priscilla John, both of whom were blessed with that gift of insight into character that mark out the casting director of quality from the efficient hack.

This was the team that assembled the most dazzling cast ever to play in a major television series. There were forty-six important roles, one of them predominating – that of Ronald Merrick, played by Tim Piggott-Smith. When the show was finished there were only two one might have wished to recast. The others had indelibly printed Paul Scott's characters on the viewer's mind. To me, and I believe to most viewers, they were no longer actors – they had become real people. The cast were all deeply committed to the show. As soon as she had heard that the *Raj Quartet* was to be made, Peggy Ashcroft rang

Christopher and told him she must play Barbie. Some of the main parts – Daphne Manners (Susan Wooldridge), Hari Kumar (Art Malik), Guy Perron (Charles Dance) – were played by actors who were then comparatively unknown. As the move towards production gained impetus there was only one major obstacle – money.

Jewel was budgeted at something just under half a million pounds per episode. Without sponsorship it would bring back less than half of that sum from the UK and normal overseas sales. No sponsor would look at it, including the American oil companies Exxon and Mobil, who had underwritten most of Granada's major drama output over recent years. America had never been a colonial power, they said. India was a far-off continent of which Americans knew nothing, the series was very expensive and looked like being a total write-off. And who had ever heard of Paul Scott? As the point of no return grew nearer I was faced with the option of taking the prudent course of postponing the production until the money was raised, or of going ahead in the hope that a sponsor would come in at a later stage.

I have written earlier of the way in which the total confidence of *Coronation Street*'s originators overcame the doubts and fears of their masters. Similarly I now knew beyond all doubt that *Jewel* was going to be a winner. So I put my head on the block, knowing the axe would never fall. I told no one outside of Television what we were doing because any Group Board worth its salt would immediately have put a stopper on such a reckless investment.

We had already spent some £2 million, and were committed to twice that again when I showed a rough-cut of the first two hours of *Jewel* to Herb Schmertz of Mobil in the Golden Square preview theatre. I knew Herb to be a good man and one who would always respond to quality. He would like it, of course he would. Nevertheless I will admit that I felt an agreeable surge of relief when the lights went up and he leapt from his seat, clasped my hand and said, 'It's great. We're on!'

The story of the making of *The Jewel in the Crown* has been chronicled elsewhere, so I will only say that it was for me the happiest, most rewarding and the most generally satisfactory experience of my life in television. The crew worked hard and long under the Indian sun; the cast got on together so well that they became a sort of club, members of which still meet together some fifteen years later; the production team, led by the unflappable Christopher, went calmly and with great determination along the road to post-production, dubbing and at last completion. We had one setback, when one night the *Jewel* studio in Manchester was burnt to the ground together with all the costumes, props and scenery. But we picked ourselves up and a week later we were nearly back on schedule, held back only because of the difficulty in replacing Tim Piggott-Smith's artificial arm, necessarily an intricate mechanism since most artificial limbs are designed to replace an arm or a leg that is missing, whereas this one was a supernumerary to an arm that was still there.

The crowning moment for me came when, once again in the Golden Square theatre, we were showing the first two hours of *Jewel* to a miscellaneous audience representing the sponsors, our own press and sales department, and other people with a special interest. I had also invited Sidney, our Group President. As the light went up I expected the usual moment of total silence broken after some few seconds by a rising crescendo of the softly spoken reactions. To my surprise I did not hear this at all. I heard one person clapping. It was Sidney, from his seat on the front row. Others joined him, and slowly he raised himself to his feet and continued to clap vigorously. There was no sign of him stopping, and now the whole audience was on its feet and I could hear Sidney shouting 'Bravo' in a high and slightly cracked voice. The cheering spread and the noise was enough to disturb Joe Warton in the dining room across the corridor. It was all too much for me and I slipped into the projection booth, where the two operators were somewhat surprised to see their Chairman propping himself against the rewind bench with tears streaming down his face.

Jewel received many awards and many accolades, perhaps more than any other television show ever made, but none was so precious to me as Sidney's personal salute given on that memorable day in the basement of Golden Square.

My next encounter with Sidney was not so pleasant but fortunately, since the going was rough, it was at one remove through the intermediary offices of Joe. The Group was in the process of fixing up an agreed takeover of Rediffusion's rental business. In order to do this we had to have the backing of the Institutions, and they were not happy with Granada's current share structure. For many years they had pressed all major companies to have only one class of share, on the principle that one share one vote was fair to all. But the 'Bernstein family and friends' had long been the owners of Granada Ordinary shares, which carried ten votes to one for each of the 'A' ordinary shares held by the common shareholders. If the takeover was to go ahead they must be persuaded to give up their Ordinary shares. Since the voting power of the Ordinary shares was some 40 per cent of the total this dilution meant a significant loss of power, which meant compensation – but how much? Alex, sensibly wishing to keep out of a family fray, delegated the task of reaching an agreed figure to me.

On Sidney's side the decision nominally rested with his trustees; on our side, with the Group Board. In fact Joe and I were the runners between our respective principals, Sidney and Alex. In the first round Joe mentioned a figure that was astronomically high and I responded with one that was ludicrously low. It was clearly going to be a long business, and a good deal of time was wasted trying to find rational reasons to support our respective bids when we both knew that we were doing no more than playing poker, but without any cards. Once when I bumped into Sidney in the corridor he asked me innocently how I was getting on with his trustees. Every bit as well as your trustees are getting along with the Group Board, I replied.

It began to look like deadlock. The trustees were defending the last rampart of Sidney's empire. Long ago his majority shareholding had gone. Recently I had taken over Television. Alex was now in absolute control over all of Granada. Sidney was a departed leader whose power base had shrunk almost to vanishing point. In his long retreat no ground had been given up without a struggle, and now he was going to cling on to this last symbol of power with all the tenacity he could muster. In his mind this was as important as the amount of cash. There was also the question of dignity. Years earlier, when Piccadilly Radio was being set up, Granada was offered a small shareholding – as I recall it, some 5 per cent. Sidney rejected this proposal out of hand as 'undignified'. When asked what level of holding would confer an acceptable degree of dignity, he replied 'Let them make a proper offer and I will tell them.' In this way he probably substantially increased the size of any shareholding that could have been gained by negotiation.

But now the considerations of dignity and power were reinforced by a slightly mischievous pleasure in holding up the whole machinery of takeover until he gained his point. It was a stick-up, and he knew it. On the other side, the Group Board's view was in no way adamantine. They felt that the sum they agreed to pay in compensation for loss of voting rights must be seen by the Ordinary shareholders to be fair and reasonable. As new deadlines loomed up, I suggested to Joe that we forget our briefs, agree a figure between us that we two thought reasonable and then work backwards and upwards from that, or alternatively that we abandon our shadow play and each write down on a piece of paper the real amount that our masters would accept, and take it from there. But such suggestions were too unconventional for Joe and I could see no way out of the deadlock.

One day one of the trustees telephoned me. Nothing of significance was said, neither of us sought concessions and no figures were mentioned, but I could tell from the tone of voice that in their camp they were seeking a solution as desperately as we were. It seemed that Joe and Sidney were as much their problem as ours. Next day I met a different Joe. Yes, they were prepared to consider our latest offer but only if it could be improved by a more direct method of payments (and here he went into a number of technicalities, some of them quite beyond me). I went post-haste to Alex with the good news, and within a few hours the deal was done. Or rather I thought it was done, but as the minutes ticked away before the Extraordinary General Meeting I still had not received the document with the necessary signatures. After an urgent bout of telephoning, it arrived in the nick of time. What had caused this unseemly last-minute delay, I wondered: was it that Sidney still found it hard to accept that the final sum was dignified enough?

So it was that Sidney became no more than a small minority shareholder in the company he had founded and under the guise of 'the Bernstein family and friends' had virtually owned, the company he had built into a great international conglomerate and had dominated as Chairman for nearly half a century. This was the final step in the long and hard-fought retreat from absolute power to impotence. Now, as President, a meaningless title, he was no more than a bystander watching others do what he could have done so much better himself. He had begun to age visibly, and when he came to Golden Square people would say to him, 'Good morning, Lord Bernstein, you look very well.' One day when he was so greeted he turned to me and said, 'They would never have dared to say that to me when it was true.'

CHAPTER TWELVE

As President, Sidney exercised his right to attend Group Board meetings, but he would have been wiser to have deployed his presidential role more privately. Whilst he was still Chairman, the need to be in command, to put on a good show, made the adrenalin run and he was able to get by with only occasional lapses of memory or failure to follow the points made in debate. But now he was a backbencher, nervously waiting for an opportunity to intervene, and often bungling it when he did. As time went by he began to find it difficult to follow the agenda. Long after others had begun to discuss an item he would still be shuffling his papers, desperately searching for the relevant page. Desmond James, who sat close by him, would come to his aid, find the right paper and place it in front of him. At first Alex would hold up the debate until Sidney found his place, but soon this began to occur so often that he had to move the business along regardless of whether Sidney was on board or not.

Then, as his powers failed still further, his presence began to be an embarrassment. Quite often he would intervene, for instance, in a discussion about our television rental business in Canada with an observation which made it clear he thought we were talking about our furniture retail business in Spain. 'We are discussing Canada, not furniture, Sidney,' Alex would say, and Sidney, flushed and mortified, would put on his camel's face and gaze sightlessly across the board-room table towards a huge and particularly ghastly colour photograph of himself which hung on the opposite wall. At such times I felt, along with embarrassment, an overpowering sense of compassion for the person I had known so long and admired so much. As I watched him isolated, desperately trying to keep in the swim, fumbling his papers, searching for his spectacles and turning pathetically to Desmond for help, I reflected on what manner of man he once had been.

I remembered his dash and gaiety in the early days of our friendship, the urgency in his voice on the phone when he persuaded me to join him on some jaunt, the hustle and bustle of travelling together, the rapid fire of crosstalk and the shouts of laughter as we drove to theatres, cinemas, studios, the late suppers often with a string of guests he had picked up in the course of the evening like a human magnet. Then he would bring into play the full range of his charm, never flattering directly but by a thousand subtle and indirect hints, making each guest feel, for the moment at least, that they were one of his intimates, talking brilliantly about the people of the world they knew best until every person present felt a little more important, a little wittier and more of a *bella figura* than they had done only an hour or two before. On these golden evenings bright people shone with a special brilliance, quite ordinary people became amusing – and bores had no chance.

Similarly, when Sidney entered a roomful of people for a meeting a surge of electricity came in with him. Suddenly everyone was more alert, the adrenalin began to flow and it was as if the curtain had gone up and we were all on a stage playing up to the great actor manager who had cast himself in the central role. Yet he did not behave like one of the great lions of the stage or literature. He was no Monty MacKenzie, who would hold court at the Savile with an unceasing flow of wit and wisdom; no Jack Priestley, who could keep a dinner table in fits of laughter for a hour or more with what was no less than a one-man show. Sidney never dominated the conversation, never contributed more than his fair share of jokes, but as well as being witty himself he could be, as Falstaff claimed to be, the cause of wit in others.

But the Sidney of café society was only one of many Sidneys. I recalled the workaday Sidney, brusque, incisive, moving through the day at full speed and with maximum efficiency. Unlike me he was not an early riser, but immediately he woke up he was consolidating on the pad by his pillow the list of things he must do that day. By nine o'clock he was in full swing, making perhaps twenty telephone calls in the first hour, all outwards, for it was from him I learned never to take an incoming call until one knew not only who it was from but also what it was the caller wanted. He treated the telephone as a viva voce telegraphic service, as a method of sending and receiving messages, not as a medium for debate or discussion and certainly not for any kind of chit-chat.

He was equally economical of his time when it came to visitors. An important guest would be received with full honours. Sidney would leave his desk, greet his guest and sit down on the sofa, his guest in an armchair, and after some preliminary chat, coffee, and a joke or two he would move elegantly into the business of the day. But if the visitor were of lower status he would ask Cecil or myself to see them in our office and would then drop in with a disarming statement – 'I have just left a meeting for a few minutes in order to meet you, Mr Smith' – and then if the person did not seem worthy of the expenditure of much time he would slip out after only two or three minutes; but if he became interested in him the mythical meeting would be forgotten and he might stay for half an hour. Again to save time, he was exceedingly reluctant to attend any meeting away from Golden Square. He would go to Warburgs or to the Authority, but generally everyone else was required to meet him on his home ground.

It would be a mistake to assume that Sidney's day always ran its course with untroubled efficiency. Disruption was common, caused perhaps by an article in the morning press which, if it was not exactly critical of Granada, did not praise Granada enough. All work would stop in order to draft a letter for publication, or perhaps just to put the editor right. Or it might be a burst of fury over some 'unworthy' programme that had gone out the night before which called for an immediate post mortem, or a sudden blitz on the engineering department because the sound had been inaudible in London on Granada's programmes. (This was a cross the engineering department had to bear; owing to the brothers' heightened interest in a Granada programme and their impaired sense of hearing, they remained convinced in the face of all scientific evidence to the contrary that the sound level dropped every time a Granada programme came on the screen.)

Sidney's rages were of two kinds – red and white. A red rage was spontaneous. Perhaps at a meeting someone, usually a *persona non Granada*, would say something under questioning that smacked of cover-up, evasion or – worst of all – deceit. Sidney's ire would mount, his face would redden and he would address the offending person in a voice coarsened with anger – sometimes he would shout. A red rage could disappear as quickly as it came, or it could lead to brooding, which in turn might lead to a white rage. Then Sidney would go very quiet. He would call the unfortunate victim to his office, sometimes with Cecil or myself as a witness, and speaking in a voice scarcely above a whisper he would start his interrogation. The questions would be interspersed with biting rebukes and would grow ever more cutting as the interview progressed, and finally he would stand up and look out of the window silently for some little time and then say without turning round, 'Thank you, Mr Brown', which was the signal for the shattered Mr Brown to creep away, a most unhappy man. If a white rage was caused by a person outside Granada, perhaps a journalist or a politician, Sidney would set about drafting a letter. Never adroit with the written word, when he was in a white rage his grasp of grammar and syntax would desert him. Draft after draft flew around the sixth floor, and even when one was knocked into reasonable shape and returned to its author he might foul it up yet again by inserting, in his fury, some outrageous or improper observations and the drafting would start all over again.

One of Sidney's most memorable white rages was caused in the early Manchester days by an article by Benedict Nightingale in the *Manchester Guardian* alleging that whereas there had been a lot of fine talk about Granada's assistance to the arts in the North there had been precious little action. Amidst paeans of praise from the press generally, and the adulation of the local papers, this was the first piece critical of Granada that Sidney had ever seen and his fury was terrible to behold. He issued a writ, which was only withdrawn when he had extracted, after an interminable correspondence, a fulsome apology from the then editor, Alastair Hetherington. Not content with this, he sent a team of researchers to work to produce a small booklet refuting at length every allegation that Benedict Nightingale had made. When, after many drafts, this was completed it was circulated to every member of Granada's staff. For a long time to come any reference to the offending article (or to Mr Farthingale himself, as Sidney called him) would tend to put him into a mood of retrospective choler that could seriously interrupt whatever business might be in hand.

Sidney was litigious by nature and was prone to call in the law when he felt that he was in the right, regardless of the law itself or of legal advice. Sometimes he had a remarkable success, as when he sued the *Observer* for insinuating that he had used his private trusts to manipulate Granada shares. Against all expectations he won damages of some £35,000. On other occasions he was not so fortunate. When an enterprising small company equipped with a light aeroplane and a camera took photographs of his country home, Coppings, and then offered them to him for sale, he immediately took legal action against them for violating the private air space above his property. He lost.

Again, he mobilised the full corps of Granada's legal advisers to sue the Ford Motor Company when it had the temerity to announce that one of its new models would be called the Granada. Despite negative advice from every lawyer involved, despite the disapproval of our Group Board, Sidney persisted. 'But Sidney,' we would say, 'you pinched the title from a city in Spain in the first place.' 'True,' he would reply, 'but we have added value to the name because of the great reputation we have gained for it. And suppose,' he would add, 'this car is not a success?' The case dragged on for months, then years. The car was a success. The Group Board became restive – the non-executive members who had the most influence reasoned with him privately. At last the action was withdrawn on the grounds, as Sidney told us, that he had submitted a Ford Granada to a thorough examination, that he had taken a drive in it and that he sought the opinion of leading authorities in the motor trade. It was his opinion that even if it was not fully worthy of its title, at least it would not bring the word Granada into disrepute.

Sidney's relations with cars were not happy. Again in the early Manchester days, he decided it was time he learnt to drive. Somehow he appeared to have gained a full driving licence without going through the usual procedure of taking professional instruction and a driving test, and a Rover car was garaged beside our flat in Parkfield Road, Didsbury. After nightfall Sidney would take me as his companion on a series of experimental drives. Sometimes we would return with the car unscathed, but this was rare. Devoid of any mechanical sense, he proceeded in a series of leaps and jerks, driving very slowly and with intense concentration. We would most commonly strike lamp-posts, bollards and other road furniture, only once a moving vehicle. He had a habit of putting the car into reverse when travelling quite fast in a forward direction, and three times hit the back wall of the garage with a considerable impact by treading on the accelerator instead of the brake. At the end of each week the car was taken away for repair and a fresh one supplied for the next round of bumping and boring. Fortunately Sidney himself realised that his future as a road user was uncertain, and since no one except myself and an anonymous garage man knew of his lack of success he took the public stand that he preferred to be driven rather than to drive himself. So he ceased to drive in Manchester or London, but still occasionally subjected his guests at Coppings to the hazards of a drive to or from the station.

Cars could be driven by others, but television sets, hearing aids and telephones had to be personally operated. The story of the howl-round lunch has already been recounted, and Sidney had similar operational problems with the bank of telephones, perhaps four or five in number, which nestled unseen in capacious pigeon-holes behind his desk. Since he was totally insensitive to pitch or tone, when one of these sounded off he would seize the instrument nearest to him, which would almost invariably be the wrong one. He would then progress to the next and the next, until, by sod's law, he reached the last receiver, by which time the caller's patience had often given out. During this frantic exercise he often failed to replace correctly the receiver of a failed telephone, which would clatter to the floor and emit plaintive bleeps until it was replaced. But this was not always an easy matter, because the lead to the receiver had become entangled with the leads of others, and for some minutes Sidney would be seen struggling with a bird's nest of wires, and the base of one or two telephones would become dislodged and with a despairing little tinkle thump heavily to the floor. In extreme cases a secretary would be called in to restore the back side of his desk to good order.

But of all mechanical devices it was the television sets in the flat in Manchester that were most resistant to his attempts to master them. The sets were controlled by an internal distribution system which could take a feed off air, from the studios, telecine, etc. This, though it was not complicated, did call for a shade more mechanical understanding than the simple act of switching a set on and off. I learned from our housekeeper, Miss Thorne, that when alone and unaided Sidney would fiddle with the buttons ineffectively. He wanted to see the rehearsal of a play in Studio 6, but instead he was confronted with Hughie Green in *Double Your Money*. At first he would call in Miss Thorne to find the right button, but when she had several times explained to him the due processes of using the switches it became embarrassing for him to admit that he was quite unable to put her instructions into effect, or even to remember them. So then he would ring up for an engineer, saying the set was not working properly. The engineer would immediately press the right buttons and disappear, but it reached Sidney's ears that this was becoming a bit of a joke. Thus he was driven to ringing up fellow inmates of the flat and on some pretext asking one of us to drop into the living room, when he would say, 'By the way the IDS system doesn't seem to be working too well – see if you can get Studio 6 for me.'

I felt for Sidney in this dilemma and found a tolerably effective solution. We put two sets in the living room, and when Sidney was on his own it was Miss Thorne's duty to leave one of them turned to the drama studio, one to the BBC, while the set in his bedroom was permanently tuned to ITV. In those days there were only the two off-air signals available and Sidney never wanted to see any internal feed except drama. Thus, by moving himself, and with no need to fumble

313

with any switches, Sidney could, without any loss of dignity, see the channel he desired.

Sidney's mechanical incompetence was balanced by his determined efficiency in other fields of activity. When he was a young man he wanted to acquire some knowledge of painting and went about this in a practical manner by pinning a print of an old master, or post-Impressionist or whoever, to the back of his lavatory door. This he changed three times a week, thereby committing to memory some 150 paintings a year. Similarly, when dissatisfied with his scrawny handwriting he decided to adopt a style of copperplate, and like a Victorian schoolgirl he would spend fifteen minutes every morning practising pot-hooks until he had acquired a well-nigh perfect hand.

In the first flush of friendship with Sidney I took his love for the arts at face value. But as I grew more familiar with his genius for projecting an ideal image of himself some doubts crept in. To the outside world he was at the same time a tycoon, a lover of the arts, a socialist, a friend of liberal causes and a 'character', and this picture seemed to be so carefully conceived and so artfully projected that one could not but wonder which came first, the image or the reality. Might it be that this image of himself was created partly to camouflage another side of his nature, the driving desire to make money? To what degree was it real?

There is no doubt that Sidney delighted in good theatre, good writing, good films and a good show of any kind. His judgement was discerning and his critical faculties quite exceptional. Beyond that his traffic with the arts was limited. He had no feeling for music, and in the visual arts it always seemed that his eye was guided by outside advice rather than by any spontaneous reaction. Even in the matter of architecture, where he so loved to dabble, his interest lay in the practical rather than the aesthetic. When in a foreign city, he would admire modern buildings for their new and adventurous construction rather than old ones for their beauty. Yet Sidney's projected image was not in any way humbug. It was rooted in real elements of his character, and long ago he had begun to believe in an ideal Sidney in which these elements were embodied to the point of perfection. He had thought himself into the character he had created as an actor will think himself into the role of Lear or Hamlet; only in his case his performance became a reality.

Nothing aroused Sidney's anger more than an imputation that his image was in any respect phoney, as Benedict Nightingale had found out. Indeed anyone who threatened Sidney's image or his dignity would be consigned to the lowest ranks of *personae non Granada*.

Sometimes, if he had suffered some degree of exposure, or some minor defeat, his anger would set in train a vendetta, perhaps against a person, perhaps against an institution. Several examples of personal vendettas have been mentioned in these pages, but Sidney's wrath against the impersonal could be just as lasting and just as strong.

Soon after Granada was established in Manchester he dearly wished to own and to develop the huge block of buildings then owned by British Rail in Deansgate. Negotiations went on for over a year, and at last in a telephone conversation with a top British Rail property person Sidney believed he had made a deal. The next day he received a curt message to say that the Board had considered the matter and decided the Manchester property was not for sale. Sidney's rage was terrible to behold, but there was nothing he could do.

After the flurry of legal consultation and the drafting of letters, none of which was sent, he embarked on a bitter campaign against British Rail which was to last for many years. The railway bridges in Manchester were ugly and unpainted. We should do a programme about that. Many acres of prime land in the centre of Manchester were taken up by shunting yards now out of use. This was a public scandal. British Rail owned several miles of canals which had fallen into decay and were a danger to public safety and public health. The standard of cleanliness on the trains was disgracefully low, especially in second-class toilets. The waiters in the restaurant car had dirty fingernails. From week to week he would ruthlessly press the unfortunate head of our local programmes to include yet another item revealing the iniquities of British Rail management. This pressure was more difficult to resist by Granada producers than by the editors of the national papers who, to Sidney's chagrin, failed to publish a single one of the stream of letters they received about the shortcomings of British Rail.

The mean streak in Sidney's nature would come out in several ways and always in encountering any person who was a careless spender of money. Good housekeeping was the first article of faith in his management creed, and in a thousand little ways he spread the doctrine. In the early days no expenditure whatsoever was permitted without sanction from on high. Pencils were cut in half, notepaper used on both sides, telephone calls were logged, 'leaking taps', lights left on in empty rooms, unnecessary use of the lifts, plugs for wash-basins leading to a prodigal use of hot water, all were anathema.

The passion for economy, shared equally by Joe and Cecil, was at first applied with equal stringency to programmes. They feared nothing so much as a big budget. This would set precedents and Granada might slide into evil and extravagant ways, as had the other companies. For this reason the use of film was taboo until many years after film had been in common use in the rest of television. Tim Hewat broke the celluloid barrier. A project that might turn out to be expensive was killed at birth, or if this were not possible, watched closely until an opportunity cropped up to put it quietly away. Such a fate befell a series I was working on with Ivor Montague, *Seven Steps to the Moon*, seven programmes projecting a trip to the moon on the basis of the best scientific knowledge then available and long before a man landing was thought possible. We did some tests in shooting weightlessness, which turned out to be sensationally good, scripts were completed and excitement ran high in anticipation of what we thought must be a real breakthrough. From the first Sidney and Cecil had shown signs of budgetary terror, but the omens were so good and our enthusiasm so great they dared not speak out.

Unfortunately I had to make a visit to Japan and whilst in Tokyo I had a tip-off from Manchester that Sidney was about to cancel *Seven Steps*. Despite desperate telexes and telephone calls, when I returned the deed had been done, the team dispersed and the show erased from the list of forward projects in the Blue Book. In vain did Ivor make a compilation of all Sidney's public statements about expenditure on programmes being a first call on our profits, in vain did I tell Sidney that he was actually throwing money away in that the series was going to be a great commercial success. The budget was beyond the limit of Bernstein tolerance, such a risk was against nature, better to be mean than sorry. So it was that I set out to work steadily towards an annual budget within which I had discretion, and thereby free myself from the Bernstein inhibitions.

At least half of Sidney's time when he was working directly at the coalface on the Granada's plays was spent in cutting costs. A script would only pass muster if it could be made on a modest budget. The plays were cast well but economically. Only once or twice did the budget rise to engaging a star. The sets too were low-cost and Sidney would spend many hours with the designer simplifying his drawings and eliminating those parts of the construction that would not earn their keep in the finished show. He would then have every set-up in the finished tape photographed, and go over each one with the designer to show how much of his set was seen and how much was not. In all creative matters these were two voices speaking to Sidney's subconscious, one saying 'Do it! Do it!', the other 'Don't do it. Save the money!' Depending on his mood one voice would speak louder than the other. On a good day he could be carried away by his enthusiasm into realms of high expenditure, but when there were thunder-clouds around his mean streak could strike unexpectedly at expenditure which he himself had sanctioned only the day before.

Perhaps one of the greatest contradictions in Sidney's character lay in the contrast between his public meanness and his private generosity. Those very few who knew of it were aware that the latter was quite out of the ordinary. If a long-serving cinema manager died, his widow would immediately receive a personal cheque to cover the early difficult days. On one occasion when a young manager had died on duty of a heart attack, Sidney not only sent a cheque but paid for the education of his two young children. Once, when a senior colleague in Television was suddenly let down over the purchase of a house, I went to Sidney to ask if he thought it would be proper to sanction a company loan. Without saying a word he pulled out a chequebook and signed a personal cheque. Even I did not know the extent of his gifts to Israel and to Jewish charities, but I gathered from those who did that they were on a grand scale. And even more remarkable than the extent of his generosity was the fact that, unlike every other real or imagined good quality in his character, he made no capital out of it. When smarting under a budget cut or the withdrawal of funds from some pet project I would suddenly remember the warmth and grace of his secret and personal ways of giving, and marvel that such contrary strands could co-exist in one human being.

It was often hard to remember that Sidney had been brought up in the orthodox Jewish faith. When as a young man he began to move into the mainstream of Western culture he set out to emancipate himself from his Jewish background. In this he was only partially successful. Whilst he could joke with his café society friends about the absurdity of Jewish dietary laws, whilst he would become a socialist and an atheist, he could never quite shake off the influence of his early childhood. He was immensely proud of being a Jew and was always ready to extol the virtues of individual Jews and the achievements of the race in general.

As we have seen, he gave generously to Jewish causes and during the Six Day War became so intensely involved that he sat at home with television set, radio and telephone to help to keep him abreast of events. From time to time he would phone from Wilton Crescent to check matters with Cecil, who was similarly ensconced about one mile away in his flat in Grosvenor Square. As one of the first witnesses to see Belsen and Buchenwald after the war he had been shocked into a bitter recognition of what being a Jew could mean. And yet he would treat every Jewish holiday as a working day (but stay at home so that he might not offend his family), he would never enter a syna-gogue except for a family wedding or funeral, would run a mile to avoid a rabbi and would poke gentle fun at Cecil for his orthodox habits. This ambivalence showed up clearly at the time we were redecorating the house we shared in Didsbury. I pointed to the mezuzah on the right-hand doorpost of each door. 'Shall we take them down?' I said to Sidney. 'Sure,' he replied, so down they came, leaving only a faint reminder of their presence showing through the new paintwork. But not for long. A month or so later I was surprised to see all the mezuzahs had been put up again. I said nothing to Sidney, and he said nothing to me.

As I saw him becoming more and more isolated in his old age from his colleagues, companions and friends, I found myself asking whose friendship had meant most to him. He had loved Sandra in the early days of marriage when they had shared the fun of party-going and party-giving, but his absorption in Granada had driven her to find a separate life for herself, and so although there was never any apparent breach they had gone their separate ways. I have written earlier of his friendship with three men whom he admired and perhaps loved in a certain fashion, also with one or two younger men who gave him the easy and amusing companionship he enjoyed, for Sidney like many men was not an out-and-out heterosexual. Although he was without ambivalence primarily attracted to women, his sexual chemistry was such that there could be a romantic quality in his relationship with his closest men friends. He was interested in homosexuality as a phenomenon and was always ready to talk about the behaviour of such overt practitioners as Tom Driberg and Sergei Einsenstein.

But Sidney's closest ties were with his family. He had adored his own children when they were young, supported and worried over them as they grew up, and although perhaps at times he was an obses-sive father their mutual affection was strong and lasting. On the other hand, among his own eight brothers and sisters his affections were selective. His elder brother Selim had been killed in World War I when Sidney was only sixteen, and he had little time for any of the rest except for two of his sisters, Beryl Stone and Rae Taffler, with whom he kept in touch as long as he was able. And then, of course, there was Cecil. The brothers were essential to each other, not only in the matter of conducting a successful business but in managing life itself. From Cecil, Sidney would seek sometimes reassurance, some-times comfort, often good counsel. From Sidney, Cecil would gain courage. Often he would need an infusion of Sidney's life force to enable him the more confidently to look the world in the eye. There were times, I know, when the telephone call between the two became a confessional: each would admit to the other – as to no one else in the world – their public setbacks and personal failures. At the time of the Masons affair, Sidney had said to me, 'I love my brother,' using a word I had never heard him apply to any other person. On 18 June 1981, Cecil, returning from a trip abroad, collapsed on the pavement outside his flat in Grosvenor Square. He died in the ambulance on the way to hospital, and when he died a part of Sidney died with him.

Still he came to Group Board meetings, but without Joe and Cecil by his side he was diminished. The search for the right papers became ever less purposeful, the eyelids drooped more frequently, the sudden flashes of understanding became more occasional, and there came a day when Sidney was no longer present. When he had become President there had been speeches, gifts and a special lunch, but now he slipped away without notice, without remark and without a good-bye, and I wonder today if any board member could recall the date and occasion of his final exit.

Once he had given up attending meetings of the Group Board, Sidney's grasp on life slackened visibly. In every waking hour for nearly seventy years Granada and its affairs had filled his mind. Now there was a void. Other interests – art, theatre, cinema – once avidly pursued, had lost much of their charm, and without the Granada connection had lost their direct relevance. No longer could he purchase a painting or negotiate for a play on behalf of Granada. In the 30s he had been one of the foremost supporters of modern art, but the art of the 80s, indeed the whole art world of his nephew, Alex, and his partner Leslie Waddington, had left him far behind. He no longer liked what was new. The theatre had ceased to put on the sort of plays he admired, and films, except for *Crocodile Dundee*, were not what they used to be. Many of his friends were dead, and within Granada he was without his two main props, Cecil and Joe. He shunned any discussion of Granada business with Alex and myself, partly because he disapproved of what we were doing, partly because it was being done by us, not him. We wished he had gone more gracefully and had kept up a more friendly relationship. He wished he had been allowed a role as elder statesman. He and Sandra had drifted apart; the family had dispersed, Charlotte to Toronto, Jane to New York, and David had not yet fully recovered from the effects of a serious car accident. Sidney did not want to write his memoirs because to a great extent Caroline Moorehead had already done that for him. Since he had few inner resources there was nothing to fill the great void left by the removal from his life of his interest in the company, the creation of which had been his life's work.

Now, as he was losing touch with his own private world, the world of Granada, he saw a strange Television Board in Manchester, made up mainly of my closest colleagues – David Plowright, Mike Scott, Joyce Wooller, Peter Rennie and Bill Dickson, to whom Sidney was no more than a memory from the past. Great events took place in the Group: the unsuccessful bid by Rank to take over Granada, the decision to go in for satellite broadcasting, the decision to sell off the Social (bingo) Clubs, fresh attempts at diversification by a new Chief Executive, Derek Lewis. Sidney was aware of all these but no longer had the energy, or even perhaps the desire, to intervene.

Until late in the 80s he would still visit his office several days a week. One day we met in the corridor and he pulled a letter out of his pocket and asked me to read it. It was from a local ex-employee who suggested that since things were going wrong all over the Group Sidney should return and take over the helm and restore Granada to its former glory. I will never forget the look of mixed hope and fear in his eyes when I looked up at him. But secretly he knew he was deluding himself.

Much of his time was spent organising the minutiae of his own life – his spectacles, his shoes, his hearing aids, his ailments, of which an arthritic knee was the most painful and the most real. He was for the first time in his life unemployed and lived a bachelor life, occasionally visiting the House of Lords and spending a good deal of time dozing over newspapers and chatting with fellow clubmen at the Garrick Club. Indeed it was the Garrick which gave his mind the stimulus he needed. When by chance we met there we would chat as would two travellers from the same distant country. Once he said to me, 'You know, Denis, I belong to the most extraordinary club. They are giving a dinner for me and all the other over-eighties', and I was struck by his childish joy in being so honoured, and reflected that this was the sort of thing which he would once have dismissed with a snort of disdain. He no longer had the devotion of servants. Margaret, the much-loved housekeeper, had died many years ago; Miss Thorne, long since retired, was battling with old age in Manchester; and perhaps the two most important relationships remaining outside the family, and always excluding Bernard Levin, were the indomitable Miss Haselwood and Josephine Weston, both of whom had served him with devotion for over thirty years and looked after his interests with undiminished care and affection.

And so Sidney slipped quietly into senility and the world closed in around him. Soon came the wheelchair, and even the journey to the Garrick became too great an endeavour. By 1988 he was confined to the spacious first-floor sitting room of his flat in St James's, his lovely Modigliani at his back and before him a glorious view across Green Park. Here he sat in his wheelchair day after day, thinking, of what nobody could tell.

In January 1989 Sandra arranged a ninetieth birthday party for him. In addition to members of his family there were eighteen guests, amongst them Julian Amyes, Paul Bevan, Alex Bernstein, Muriel Haselwood, Josephine Weston, Derek Granger, Jeremy Isaacs, Caroline Moorehead, Peggy Ashcroft, Joe Warton, Mark Littman, Bernard Levin, and myself.

Sidney, almost insensible but still aware that he was part of an event and still able to recognise his guests, sat surrounded by those who had known him best, all bent on making it a jolly occasion. I remember feeling that I was at a wake rather than a party, for the central figure was no longer the Sidney I knew but a silver-grey husk which preserved the likeness of the real Sidney, just as an Egyptian mummy preserved the likeness of the once living king lying within it. Indeed, with his carefully brushed hair, smoothly shaved cheeks, combed eyebrows and lips softened with salve, there was something about his appearance that made it seem that the embalmer was already at work.

Then came the final plateau of complete insensibility. Or almost complete, for once after spending twenty minutes with him during which he gave no flicker of recognition, I subsequently heard from his nurses that after I left he had smiled and said, 'Denis'. Perhaps they were being kind to me, but I was moved by the story and still hope it was true.

Back in Golden Square, Gerry Robinson had arrived to transform Granada into a different and even more successful company. In Manchester, David Plowright came to the parting of the ways with the new regime, and as the last vestiges of Sidney's Granada disappeared he lingered on in St James's Place looking our sightlessly on to Green Park. Three things survived: his will to live, his will to have his own way, and his appetite. He ate, even when he had to be assisted to do so, with the gusto of a young man. When the nurses wanted him to do one thing – to move from his bed to his chair – and he wanted to do another, he would put up a fierce physical resistance. But the nurses – four of them, two shifts of two – put up with him cheerfully, as nurses do, reporting the trivial news of each day to his visitors ('We had two cups of tea this morning, didn't we?') and carrying out their thankless task with that front of impervious good humour that never ceases to amaze lesser mortals such as myself.

But Sidney – Sidney had gone long before he died. Each time I mustered enough resolution to visit him I asked myself why I was doing it. Towards the end there was no question of his recognising anyone; indeed his eyes did not focus on the visitor's face but followed the nurses around or looked blankly out of the window, and this was disconcerting, as was his sagging jaw and his aimlessly twitching hands. There could be no benefit to him from such visits and for me they brought nothing but pain. I could only explain my presence in his sickroom as due to some residual Scottish sense of duty – compulsion to make some symbolic gesture. But perhaps it was for a deeper reason. Somehow in the course of the last two decades our friendship, once so bright, had lost its magic and our trust in each other had been clouded. Now these silent pilgrimages were a way of atoning for whatever my part may have been in failing to keep our relationship in better repair.

On 5 February 1993 I heard that Sidney had died. I felt no emotion – that had all been spent long before. I read the obituaries, voluminous, laudatory and predictable, as if they were notices for one of Granada's greatest shows but one in which I had no personal involvement. I read Bernard Levin's impassioned manifesto on his friendship with Sidney and wondered what he would have written had he, like me, been as well as his friend his employee.

Many years before, Sidney had told me that he did not want there to be any form of memorial service after his death, to which I replied that when he was alive he could still give orders but after he was dead it would be for others to decide whether and in what way his life should be celebrated. I had visions of the Granada Tooting filled to the brim, the mighty Wurlitzer going full blast, our greatest actors and actresses declaiming from the stage, all combining to make a great show business event that would be worthy of all the Barnum in Sidney. But now, even though I had adjusted my thoughts to a more modest occasion, as I talked to his nearest and dearest, I found there was no desire for any kind of celebration of Sidney's memory. Perhaps from a respect for his wishes, perhaps because he had already been dead in all but the medical sense for so long, the reaction was muted. And so the last echoes of the obituaries died away and the mark he made on life faded from the public mind, leaving only personal memories, such as this memoir, of one of the most extraordinary men of our generation.

INDEX